*Introspection*
*in*
*Biography*

# Introspection in Biography

## The Biographer's Quest for Self-Awareness

*Edited by*

SAMUEL H. BARON and CARL PLETSCH
The University of North Carolina

 THE ANALYTIC PRESS
1985

Distributed by
LAWRENCE ERLBAUM ASSOCIATES, PUBLISHERS
Hillsdale, New Jersey                    London

The Analytic Press

Distributed solely by

Lawrence Erlbaum Associates, Inc., Publishers
365 Broadway
Hillsdale, New Jersey 07642


**Library of Congress Cataloging in Publication Data**
Main entry under title:

Introspection in biography.

   Bibliography: p.
   Includes index.
   1. Biography (as a literary form)—Addresses, essays,
lectures.   2. Introspection—Addresses, essays, lectures.
I. Baron, Samuel H.   II. Pletsch, Carl.
CT21.I57   1985        920'.001'9        85-4085
ISBN 0-88163-035-7


Printed in the United States of America
10   9   8   7   6   5   4   3   2   1

# Contents

**Other Introspections on the Biographical Process**

**Afterword**

# Contributors

**Samuel H. Baron,** Alumni Distinguished Professor of History at the University of North Carolina, is the author of *Plekhanov: The Father of Russian Marxism* and *Muscovite Russia: Collected Essays,* and is coeditor of *Windows on the Russian Past: Essays on Soviet Historiography since Stalin.*

**Richard Lebeaux,** Associate Professor of American Thought and Language at Michigan State University, is the author of *Young Man Thoreau* and *Thoreau's Seasons.*

**Joseph D. Lichtenberg,** member of the Washington Psychoanalytic Institute, is the Editor-in-Chief of *Psychoanalytic Inquiry,* and is the author of *Psychoanalysis and Infant Research* and *"The Talking Cure": A Descriptive Guide to Psychoanalysis.*

**John E. Mack,** Professor of Psychiatry at the Harvard Medical School, is the author of *A Prince of Our Disorder: The Life of T. E. Lawrence; Vivienne: The Life and Suicide of an Adolescent Girl;* and "Nationalism and the Self," in *The Psychohistory Review* (1983).

**Steven Marcus,** Professor of English at Columbia University, is the author of *Dickens: From Pickwick to Dombey; Engels, Manchester, and the Working Class;* and *The Other Victorians: A Study of Sexuality and Pornography in Mid-Nineteenth Century England.*

**George Moraitis,** member of the Chicago Institute for Psychoanalysis and faculty member of the Northwestern University Medical School, has published articles in *The Annual of Psychoanalysis,* Vols. VII and IX, and *Psychoanalytic Inquiry,* Vol. 1.

**Carl Pletsch,** Assistant Professor of History at the University of North Carolina, has written articles on Freud and psychoanalysis, and *A Psychoanalytic Study of Friedrich Nietzsche.*

**Arnold A. Rogow,** Graduate Professor of Political Science at the City University of New York, is the author of *James Forrestal: A Study of Politics, Personality, and Policy* and *The Dying of the Light.*

**Mark R. Schwehn,** Assistant Professor of History at Valparaiso University, is writing a book on Henry Adams and the advent of modernism in the United States.

**Robert C. Tucker,** Professor of Politics and IBM Professor of International Studies at Princeton University, is the author of *Stalin as Revolutionary: A Study in History and Personality; Philosophy and Myth in Karl Marx;* and *Politics as Leadership.*

**Joseph F. Wall,** Rosenfield Professor of History at Grinnell College, is the author of *Henry Watterson: Reconstructed Rebel; Andrew Carnegie;* and *Iowa: A Bicentennial History.*

**Richard S. Westfall,** Distinguished Professor of History and Philosophy of Science at Indiana University, is the author of *Never at Rest: A Biography of Isaac Newton; Force in Newton's Physics: The Science of Dynamics in the Seventeenth Century;* and *The Construction of Modern Science: Mechanisms and Mechanics.*

**Richard Wortman,** Professor of History at Princeton University, is the author of *The Crisis of Russian Populism* and *The Development of a Russian Legal Consciousness.*

# *Preface*

Most of the essays offered here are revised versions of papers first prepared for an invitational conference on "The Psychology of Biography," held in Chapel Hill, November 12–14, 1981. The conference, which was funded by the National Endowment for the Humanities, brought together twelve biographers—including historians, literary scholars, political scientists, and psychoanalysts—each of whom had composed an introspective essay describing his experience of the biographical process. Each participant was invited to proceed in whatever manner seemed appropriate to him, but all were encouraged as well to address a number of questions that we regard as central to this inquiry: Why did I decide to write a biography, and how did I select a subject? How did I achieve insight into the internal life of my protagonist? In what ways did I put my personal stamp on the portrait I produced? As a result of protracted involvement with the subject, did the latter influence my life, and, if so, how? The contributors have responded to these questions in varying degrees, but they provide evidence enough to permit, for the first time, some systematic treatment of these and subsidiary questions. On the other hand, each paper is marked by an individual approach and style. Taken as a whole, these uncommonly intimate and self-revealing essays illuminate many aspects of the biographical enterprise.

The collaborative character of the symposium deserves emphasis. It began with the request that the contributors-to-be all address a number of specific questions. It continued with the cooperation of a majority of the contributors with a psychoanalyst or clinical psychologist, as an aspect of the preparation of their papers. (More on this in a moment.) It went a step further at the conference itself, which served as a forum for an exchange of views so stimulating that it prompted the participants to undertake to revise their papers. Moreover, the conferees were so impressed by the frequent flashes of illumination, most often touched off by Dr. George Moraitis, that they asked him to compose an additional essay (an afterword) for this volume, to bring to a wider public the workings, pitfalls, and potentialities of the collaborative method.

This book, then, introduces and emphasizes the promise of the collaborative method in interdisciplinary research. The method—originated by two of the participants, Dr. George Moraitis and Professor Carl Pletsch—was resorted to, as a means of facilitating introspection, by a majority of the contributors. Others, mostly individuals who had already had analytic training or been analyzed, wrote their papers without further assistance from a psychoanalyst. The method involves a series of encounters designed to explore the unconscious relationship of biographer to subject and to gain access to hitherto unperceived psychological ties between the biographer and his protagonist. Those participants who engaged in such a collaboration attained new levels of self-awareness and new dimensions of understanding of their subjects. It is our hope that others will attempt to replicate the method and assist in its further development.

We deeply regret that two female biographers who had agreed to participate in the conference were compelled for personal reasons to withdraw, leaving us with an all-male group. One of the dozen conference participants declined to revise his paper and, accordingly, is not represented here. For Dr. Joseph Lichtenberg's conference paper, we have substituted an absorbing earlier essay of his on biography before and since Freud. Two persons who were interested in the conference but could not participate have since contributed essays. Professor Steven Marcus's piece was prepared specifically for inclusion in this volume. Dr. John E. Mack is represented by an abridged version of an article concerning his work on T. E. Lawrence, first published in 1977. We are also reprinting a valuable paper by Dr. Moraitis on the first experiment with the method, his collaboration with Carl Pletsch.

We wish to express our warm appreciation to the National Endowment for the Humanities for its support of the conference and preparation of the manuscript. We are grateful to John Mack for permission to publish an abridged version of his article, and to the editors of *The Annual of Psychoanalysis* for permission to reprint Joseph Lichtenberg's article and George Moraitis's paper "A Psychoanalyst's Journey into a Historian's World."

—*Samuel H. Baron and Carl Pletsch*

*Introspection*
*in*
*Biography*

# Introduction

# 1

# *Psychological Dimensions of the Biographical Process*

## Samuel H. Baron

---

BIOGRAPHY IS PROBABLY the most popular genre of nonfiction, but just how a biography is produced—the biographical process—is only dimly understood. To be sure, biographers and students of biography have provided us with abundant material on biography in general, but many questions remain completely or partially unanswered.[1] Among the most important and least understood aspects are the psychological dimensions of the biographical process. The author of a recent work on biography, in contemplating "the years of patient research" that bring "author and subject together into a relationship of unparalleled intimacy," asks: "is it possible, under such circumstances that . . . as he assembles his material and looks at what amounts to a marriage with his subject [the author can be] unaffected by the closeness of the relationship?"[2] This volume, and the symposium on which it is based, may be thought of as a response to what the just-quoted author posed as a rhetorical question, as well as to certain related questions. Here, for the first time, a group of biographers reflect on their experiences as biographers, exploring the relationships between themselves and those whose lives they have studied.

In an initial foray into virtually uncharted territory, it would be foolhardy to attempt a comprehensive survey. Instead, we have chosen to focus on a few of the most salient questions: Why does one decide to undertake a biography, and how does one choose a subject? How does one gain insight into the subject's inner life? In what manner does the portraitist put his personal stamp on the portrait he produces? How is the biographer, given his protracted and intense involvement with his subject, influenced by that subject? Of course, many another matter is touched on by one or more of the contributors, but these are the problems we address in this introductory effort.

When a dozen writers reflect on a set of questions, albeit to varying degrees, their accounts constitute a unique body of source material. It then becomes possible to make comparisons and contrasts, to delineate commonalities and a range of diversity, to formulate and test hypotheses, to draw at least tentative generalizations—in short, to engage in systematic study. Moreover, such study throws into relief matters that call for further investigation or new inquiry. On the other hand, our contributors are nothing if not individualistic in their approaches and styles. If taken collectively their essays provide the basis for systematic study, the unusually personal and candid character of a large majority make them arresting human documents.

Several of our contributors regard themselves as psychobiographers, but a good three-fourths do not. Accordingly, although some of the concerns addressed here overlap with those of the psychobiographer—such as the attention given to the ways and means whereby the biographer may gain insight into his subject—in the main they are different. Our primary focus is on the reciprocal relationships between biographer and subject that result from the long, intensive engagement that the writing of a biography necessarily involves.

## CHOOSING A SUBJECT

Why do people decide to write biographies? And how do they choose their subjects? These two questions seem perfectly reasonable and straightforward. But on the evidence of the papers in this collection—and we take the authors to be representative in this regard—their separation distorts reality. For most biographers, they figure as a single question. A rare bird indeed is the writer who first decides to produce a biography and then begins to look for a suitable subject. It is much more common for a biographer to decide at one and the same time to do a biography and to focus on a particular person. Yet further consideration reveals that this representation, too, is flawed. Frequently, there *is* a sequence of two stages—but in the reverse order of the way the questions are posed above. That is, generally, a writer, for one or another reason, takes an interest in a particular person and then decides to make that person the subject of a biography. This point brings into sharper focus the real question: How and why do biographers choose their subjects?

Judging by the papers before us, the answer to this apparently simple question is complex. One would suppose, *a priori*, that a biographer will select a subject whom he admires and identifies with. Although that is not always the case, as we shall presently see, most often it is. Steven Marcus gives a multidimensional account of the reasons for his selection, in what looks like an instance of overdetermination. Some of the reasons were external: he greatly admired Charles Dickens, considering him second only to William Shakespeare as a writer in the English language; he considered the existing critical literature on Dickens "fairly primitive"; he chose Dickens for polemical purposes—to show that the New Criticism, with which he was out of sympathy, was an inadequate vehicle for dealing with writers like Dickens—and he was supported in his inclination by his teacher and "surrogate father," Lionel Trilling. But Marcus also observes that he had chosen Dickens long before he was conscious that he had. In the course of psychoanalysis, he discovered that the experience of reading—and being very frightened and deeply impressed by—a condensed version of *Oliver Twist* when he was a child had established a powerful inner connection between himself and Dickens. Marcus's long and passionate engagement in the study of Dickens answered, he conjectures, to "certain of the most primordial resonances" in his own life. (In contrast, a study he later made of Friedrich Engels had no such profound resonances but was written as a response to student radicalism in the late '60s and early '70s.)

None of our other contributors traces so early a link to his subject, but Richard Lebeaux detects a predisposition on his part toward Henry David Thoreau in his early love of nature. At college, the relationship was reinforced by Lebeaux's conviction that Thoreau's ideas and conduct legitimized his own anti-war and countercultural bent. There were other resonances, too; and after Lebeaux had studied with Erik Erikson—a "father-figure and identity model"—and become familiar with the lineaments of Thoreau's life history, he recognized the possibilities of an Eriksonian-type biography of a man whose life seemed richly intertwined with his own. Especially noteworthy was his excitement at the possibility that "in coming to terms with Thoreau," he "would have a chance to work through" his feelings about himself, his life, and American society. "Working on Thoreau might be good therapy."

Carl Pletsch reports that he adopted Friedrich Nietzsche as the most important influence in his education, broadly understood, for several years. The iconoclastic aesthetic and philosophical revolutionary exercised a powerful attraction on a young man who was developing along similar lines, and he idealized Nietzsche extravagantly. In the next stage of his development, Pletsch the anti-Vietnam war activist became disillusioned in his erstwhile hero, who seemed at odds with his own evolving political and social convictions. The subterranean attachment remained strong, however, and after ultimately deciding on intellectual history as a vocation, Pletsch returned to Nietzsche, singling him out as a fit subject for a doctoral dissertation.

It is noteworthy that all three of these contributors derived psychological support for major and difficult career decisions from their subjects-to-be. The decisions were crucial in that they involved self-definition and difficult in that they entailed conflict with parents. Pletsch relied on the self-assertive Nietzsche to justify his abandonment of plans for a career in science or engineering, formed in conjunction with parental advice and example, and his election of philosophy as his next area of concentration. Lebeaux thinks it possible that Thoreau helped give him "permission" to change majors at college, to be uncommitted for a time without excessive anxiety, and especially to stand by his resolve not to study law—a career his parents thought he should consider. Marcus's decision to study literature flew into the face of his father's determination that he go to medical school. The clash precipitated a "great early crisis," and the son thenceforth had to go it alone. Marcus reports that it was partly Dickens (and partly Sigmund Freud) who gave him the "inner permission" to tackle unorthodox literary problems that a correct and ambitious graduate student would not then have normally undertaken. Whether Dickens earlier stiffened his resolve to study literature rather than science is not clear.

The duration, depth, and intensity of the relationship between these biographers and the subjects they chose are striking, but not fully representative. At the other pole is Joseph Wall, the author of two biographies, with a third forthcoming. All three of his subjects (Henry Watterson, Andrew Carnegie, and Alfred I. duPont) were offered to him rather than chosen by him, a fact that precluded his having close ties with any of them before he undertook their study. Contrariwise, his mentor Allan Nevins had dissuaded him from working on Harry Hopkins, a figure with whom Wall did have affinities, whose political and social views were "entirely in harmony" with his own. Wall admits retrospectively that he had been free to decline Nevins's proposal that he do his second book on Carnegie. He intimates that he did not, at least in part, out of a desire not to offend his "professional hero," who, like Trilling to Marcus and Erikson to Lebeaux, was evidently a surrogate father. Nevertheless, as he worked on each of his subjects, Wall relates, he took a proprietary interest in them, as if they were not only subjects of his own choosing but his own creations.

Marcus asserts—and most biographers would be apt to concur—that a writer necessarily identifies, both consciously and unconsciously, with the figure whose life he studies. In Robert Tucker, however, we have a biographer who professes to "loathe" his subject, Joseph Stalin. A moment's reflection suggests that Tucker cannot be unique in this regard, for we have no dearth of biographies of Attila the Hun, Genghis Khan, Adolf Hitler, and Stalin, to name a few of history's loathsome villains. Whether it is possible for a biographer to do justice to a subject whom he loathes is a matter to which we shall later return. Here we are concerned with how and why Tucker, a political scientist whose interests lay in different directions, became a biographer of Stalin, as he says, *malgré lui*.

Tucker's essay is principally devoted to this very question, but we might here note a few salient points. He first became interested in Stalin in the course of a nine-year period of service (from 1944 to 1953) in the American embassy in Moscow. There he developed a hypothesis envisaging Stalin as a particular type of neurotic personality, which appeared to be confirmed by events in the wake of the dictator's death. His later efforts to incorporate the personality factor into the then-prevalent conceptions of totalitarianism were generally resisted by the specialists. He realized that an effective demonstration would require him to become a historian of the Stalin era. In the process of investigating such matters as the role of the leader in the Bolshevik party and why the Bolshevik regime was transformed under Stalin into an autocracy, it dawned on him that biography was the appropriate vehicle for dealing with his concerns. Tucker's fascinating story primarily emphasizes the external circumstances that aroused and sustained his interest in Stalin. But it also includes another theme, discloses a personal side to the story. He had married a Russian woman in Moscow, but Stalin's government prohibited Soviet women who had married foreigners from leaving the country. He was therefore compelled to extend his stay in the USSR indefinitely or, even worse, abandon his wife to the whim of fate. Here was a situation well calculated to inspire extreme anxiety, and it surely explains in good measure the extraordinary elation Tucker reports having felt on learning of Stalin's death. Might not Tucker's deep emotional engagement have sustained his protracted interest in Stalin and, at least partially, underpin his loathing?

Almost all the other biographers represented here appear to belong to a different category from those considered thus far. They neither had a deep prior attachment to the subjects they chose—and, unlike Wall, they *did* choose their subjects—nor did they despise them. They explain their choices matter-of-factly, in what we may broadly call professional terms. As we shall see, however, sooner or later most of them became aware of inner, unconscious reasons for their choices.

As a graduate student in intellectual history, Mark Schwehn undertook to study the emergence of modernism in the United States. Having identified Henry Adams and William James as key figures in this development, he set out to deal with their works and ideas, and the cultural context in which these were created. Of necessity, he had to consider Adams's life history as well. Subsequent introspection was to reveal Schwehn's profound physical and emotional identification with Adams, but it is not clear whether it existed before he embarked on his study or developed only later. The psychiatrist George Moraitis, who worked with Schwehn to facilitate the latter's introspection, himself turned to Adams at a later date. He did so, he states, while looking for an appropriate subject for a paper to present to a major conference. Only after his study of *The Education of Henry Adams* was under way did it come to him in a flash that despite his surface indifference or disdain for Adams during his work with Schwehn, Adams had in reality touched him deeply, poignantly reinforcing his pessimistic feelings about the modern world and his skepticism about the omnipotence of science.

Samuel Baron, after completing an M.A. in Russian history, was obliged to select a subject for a doctoral dissertation. In the course of his search, he discovered that a large body of sources had been published since 1917 on "the father of Russian Marxism," G. V.

Plekhanov, and that no satisfactory study of him existed. He there-upon resolved to produce a dissertation on a certain phase of Plekhanov's career. The idea of a full-scale biography came later, when he recognized that the dissertation was too narrow in scope to publish as a book. Self-examination long after the book was completed prompts Baron to suppose that his choice was not determined by fortuitous circumstances and pragmatic considerations alone. He was drawn to Plekhanov, it seems, because he sensed a resonance between Plekhanov's life history and the life plan he envisaged for himself at the time he made the choice.

Richard Westfall explains his selection of Isaac Newton as a "log-ical progression of intellectual interests." As a result of his study of science and religion in seventeenth-century England, his interest shifted from English history to the history of science. Of course, Newton loomed large in that context. Somewhat like Baron, Westfall recognized that an up-to-date biography was needed, and he took on the task of filling the gap. No allusions to inner motives appear in Westfall's account, but he notes, as a result of having been exposed to the introspection of others, that there are undoubtedly reasons he does not comprehend for his having produced a Newton biography.

By way of contrast, the psychiatrist John Mack readily concedes that his ultimate motive for choosing T. E. Lawrence is rooted in his past. He prefers not to search for those roots, however, offering in-stead a set of external motives for his selection. The film *Lawrence of Arabia* triggered his interest, although—or perhaps partly because—the portrayal of the central character did not ring true for him. The discordance he sensed evidently challenged him to learn what really made Lawrence tick. He was egged on by a concern with the problem of heroism, on the one hand, and, on the other, by the realization that excellent sources were available in Lawrence's extraordinarily self-searching letters and memoirs, and the presence among the living of many who had been close to Lawrence. Despite his reticence, Mack gives a clue to his own inner motives when he notes: "It was Law-rence's suffering which originally affected me deeply and with which I could most readily identify. . . . My strongest interest has always been in how Lawrence dealt with his pain and conflict, in how he tried to surmount or transform the personal struggle in his actions, or through his writings."

Arnold Rogow adduces a variety of reasons, stemming from his concerns as a political scientist, for his interest in James Forrestal: the

origins and conduct of the cold war, the operations of the U.S. Department of Defense, the pressures of public life on high-ranking
officials and the possible consequences for policy. In certain respects,
he was to discover, he also identified with Forrestal. But most intriguing is Rogow's speculation that he was drawn to Forrestal, and more
recently to Thomas Hobbes, because each unconsciously reminded
him of a dear lost friend whom he wanted to bring back to life, so to
speak, by doing a biography of another like him.

Finally there is Richard Wortman, who implicitly rejects Ralph
Waldo Emerson's dictum: "There is properly no history; only biography." This writer sees biography and history as distinct entities, and
he is especially interested in the interface between the two. Wortman
has avoided in-depth biography of a single person, believing it does
not serve the interests of a historian concerned, as he is, with the
intersection of personal lives with political or institutional issues.
Rather like Barbara Tuchman, who has used biography as a "vehicle
for exhibiting an age," so Wortman has engaged in psychological
analysis as a means of getting at "the subjective reality of the period."[3] After working on the Russian populists, whose members
dreamed of an agrarian utopia, he turned to Leo Tolstoi, an enigmatic
figure who invites inquiry. Of course, Wortman has been interested
in probing the psyche of the great Russian novelist and man of religious and philosophical ideas. But unlike most students of Tolstoi,
he envisages the latter's ideas not as "the independent discoveries of
a lone genius," but as "inseparable from the ideological heritage of
his era." This is undoubtedly a legitimate and fruitful approach, although it may not differ greatly from what many writers of full-scale
biographies do, among other things.

We may now draw some tentative conclusions on how and why
biographers choose their subjects. As Bernard Meyer has aptly observed: "poems, like babies, are conceived for a variety of motives."[4]
So are biographies. Our survey reveals that a number of the contributors to this volume had close conscious ties (and apparently unconscious ones as well) to those whose biographies they set out to write.
They exemplify another proposition by Meyer: that the choice of a
biographical subject is "rooted" in "the author's [more or less] remote past."[5] Nevertheless, that this dictum applies to most of our
contributors seems problematic. As we have seen, they adduced a
wide variety of reasons for undertaking biographies of their respective subjects: to achieve insight into some larger question, such as the

emergence of modernism in the United States, the role of personality in totalitarianism systems, the problem of heroism, or the Russian populist movement. To fill a perceived gap in a scholarly field, to shape one's work into publishable form, and, implicitly, to advance a career. To capitalize on a rich body of source material, to serve a polemical purpose, to keep the favor of a professional hero. To help resolve personal problems. If we had a larger sample, the list could surely be extended.

Still, all conceded in principle, and almost all became convinced as a result of personal introspection, that other, unconscious reasons figured in the selection of their subjects. Are we to infer, then, that the external motives the biographers expressed were only the ostensible ones, a kind of superstructure reared on the psychic economy that masks the real motives, the hidden relationship between biographer and subject? Are the unconscious, inner processes the bedrock of motivation, and the rest merely a disguise? Our answer is emphatically negative. We insist on the genuineness of both the external and internal motives, and their interdependence. It is perfectly possible to write a biography with the external and professional objectives operating at the conscious level, while much of the energy for carrying out the task stems from unconscious motives. The two function in tandem, and they may do so more effectively if the writer is aware of the unconscious motives at an early stage of the work.

We shall have more to say about the internal and external. For just as both kinds of motive figure in a writer's choice of subject, so, ideally, the biographer ought to seek both the external and internal motives of his subject's behavior.

## GAINING INSIGHT

In the context of psychology and biography, our contributors are a diverse lot. Among them are several professional psychiatrists (Joseph Lichtenberg, John Mack, George Moraitis); an individual who recently completed psychoanalytic training as an adjunct to a long career as a political scientist (Arnold Rogow); a literary scholar who took an early interest in Freud, underwent analysis many years ago, and is currently writing a book on the founder of psychoanalysis (Steven Marcus); two who have studied psychology as an aid to their work in other fields (Robert Tucker, Richard Lebeaux); three more who have done some work at a psychoanalytic institute (Carl Pletsch, Mark Schwehn, Richard Wortman); and three who are relatively un-tutored in psychological theory (Samuel Baron, Joseph Wall, Richard Westfall). This group is undoubtedly not representative of biog-raphers at large, who are less apt to have had much psychological education and training. For most of our contributors who are psycho-logically knowledgeable, Freud has been the primary influence, al-though Tucker is especially indebted to Karen Horney and Lebeaux embraced the Eriksonian outlook with "born-again zeal."

As one would expect, the contributors' diversity is reflected in their biographical writings as well as in the papers presented here. The psychiatrists engage in psychological analysis as if by second nature. Those at the other end of the spectrum, all of whom have published well-received biographies, freely acknowledge that they made little or no effort to reconnoiter the internal landscape of their subjects. That they succeeded, notwithstanding, is perhaps a tribute to what Lichtenberg dubs "the traditional biographer's gift of empathy for his subject and intuition in selecting his materials." In a letter to us ex-pressing his hesitation about participating in the symposium, West-fall wrote: "I am not engaged in psychohistory and do not foresee that I will be. . . . It goes without saying that I have been interested in Newton's complex character, but I have not attempted to apply psy-chological categories, Freudian or otherwise, to interpret it."[6] Wall notes in his essay that he had "long been appalled by most psycho-history," and, accordingly, had passed up opportunities to indulge in such exercises vis-à-vis Carnegie. Baron both denied and rationalized his not having sufficiently engaged the issue of Plekhanov's person-ality with a remarkably inventive range of arguments, which, he is now inclined to admit, are not entirely convincing.

More surprisingly, several of those who were better equipped to take a psychological approach to their subjects were reluctant or sim-ply declined to do so up to a certain point in their work. As a graduate student, despite some psychological background, Wortman tells us, he harbored "skepticism about, if not outright hostility toward, psy-chology and psychoanalysis." His efforts to understand the Russian populists proved unavailing, however, so long as he confined himself to social and economic analysis; when he went beyond, seeking to learn what populism meant to his protagonists in personal terms, in relation to their psychological makeup, he scored a breakthrough. Subsequently, he studied psychological literature more systematically, entered into collaboration with Moraitis, and effectively used what he absorbed in a later work on Tolstoi.

Schwehn reports that he sought in his doctoral dissertation "to conceal or supress all of [his] rather elaborate psychological hypotheses about Adams" and to interpret the latter's work purely in intellectual terms. He justified this conduct to himself by reference to his beliefs that psychological explanations are "inherently reductionistic," that any such interpretation would inevitably diminish Adams's stature, and that he lacked sufficient evidence for such a portrait, as well as with still other formal, rhetorical, and methodological reasons, as he calls them. After completing his dissertation, in his collaboration with Moraitis, Schwehn overcame his distaste for psychologizing. Becoming aware of his identification and protective stance with respect to his subject, Schwehn discovered hitherto hidden aspects of Adams's makeup—his sense of personal impotence, his envy of masculinity, and his identification with the feminine—and correspondingly new layers of meaning in Adams's *History of the United States.*

Schwehn's initial reticence should be seen as a reaction to the blundering and insensitive forays some have made into the field of psychobiography. One cardinal sin is to reduce a whole life to a single psychological formula. Another involves an almost exclusive focus on the weaknesses and failings of the subject, with a corresponding deflation of the subject. For example, the Freud-Bullitt study of Woodrow Wilson, as Meyer has pointed out, is so concerned with disclosing the subject's emotional difficulties and moral weaknesses that it scarcely notices the impressive figure he cut as president and world leader.[7] This kind of muckraking (Meyer's term) is to be shunned as much as its opposite, myth-making (which Lichtenberg discusses)—the two constituting the biographer's Scylla and Charybdis.

Wortman, Westfall, and Pletsch (all three, significantly, are intellectual historians) articulate a further reason for their resistance to psychological explanation, involving another of the different ways whereby it may foster an objectionable reductionism. Wortman claims he "resisted attempts to understand [political and social] doctrines in terms of rationalization, compensation, and other diagnoses of pathology" because such interpretations "overlook the positive functions of thought for the individual and the society." Westfall echoes this idea: he was "not prepared to trace [Newton's] scientific achievements" to his "tortured psyche," opting instead for the "au-

tonomy of the individual and the autonomy of the intellectual realm."
Similarly, Pletsch found "repugnant" the suggestion that "social concern might be taken *prima facie* as evidence of pathology," discerning
in this a mode of thinking that gave psychoanalysis an unfortunate
reputation. (Here the reader will recognize once again the tension
between internal and external sources of behavior.)

Pletsch had by then written a "psychoanalytically oriented intellectual biography of Nietzsche" as his doctoral dissertation, let it be
noted, and the protest just quoted occurred in the course of a collaboration with George Moraitis designed to test Pletsch's "empathic
hypotheses" about Nietzsche. Apparently, even those who recognize
the value of psychological interpretation may simultaneously have
serious reservations—may, in a word, be ambivalent. Be that as it
may, through his work with Moraitis, Pletsch became aware that his
earlier disillusionment with Nietzsche had so markedly colored the
portrait he had drawn that it obscured Nietzsche's indubitable
achievements and insights. He would have to rewrite his thesis,
Pletsch determined, in order to bring things into proper balance.

Immensely aided by their collaboration with Moraitis, Pletsch, Schwehn, and Wortman all more or less transcended their objections to
psychological interpretation, and in the process deepened and enriched the quality of their work. Each is presumably prepared to do
further work along these lines, while seemingly having erected safeguards against reductionism and other hazards to which the psychologically oriented biographer may fall prey. Even the most experienced or most highly trained are not immune to flagrant error—
witness Freud's involvement in the notorious study of Wilson. John
Mack, evidently commenting on his own experience, conveys an
important message to the biographer who would apply psychological
insights to the study of his subject: "He must be a historian or a
biographer first, with psychology as a *part* of his equipment," employed "to deepen and broaden his view of the relationship between
an individual and certain historically significant events in which he
took part."[8]

In this context, attention should be called to Moraitis's remarkably
self-revealing account of his engagement with Henry Adams. His first
reading of *The Education,* he relates, produced negative reactions. He
was "appalled" by what he took to be Adams's lack of psychological
sophistication, puzzled by his omission of twenty "crucial and dramatic years of his life" and by his seeming disinterest in pulling

things together. As a matter of course, the psychoanalyst sought to explain in psychological terms the peculiarities he discerned in Adams's book. Only a few years later, when he reread *The Education*, did Moraitis realize that the first time he had been "so busy reading between the lines" that he had not paid "sufficient attention to the lines as written." In probing for the psychological roots of the text before him, he had ignored the intellectual content that now struck him forcefully. With becoming candor, Moraitis confesses he then recognized as never before that psychological analysis by itself is inadequate to the understanding of man in all his complexity. Having helped his younger colleagues Pletsch, Schwehn, and Wortman to overcome or at least mitigate their distrust of psychological analysis, he in turn was obliged to acknowledge the legitimacy of their reservations. Similarly, Lichtenberg regards the tendency of psychoanalytically based biographies to underrate, or their inability to deal with, intellectual issues or struggles as a serious shortcoming.

But what of the biographers of Plekhanov, Carnegie, and Newton, who, as we have seen, had no pretensions whatsoever to psychological expertise and, accordingly, refrained from other than unsystematic, commonsensical, and intuitive psychological explanation in their works? The fact that all three agreed to participate in the symposium bespeaks recognition on their part that the psychological dimension of their work may have been underdeveloped, and their willingness to entertain the possibility that something of value might result. All three—Baron well before the conference was conceived, and Wall and Westfall after having been invited—agreed to attempt a replication of the collaborative method that Moraitis and Pletsch pioneered. Each was fortunate in finding a psychologically trained colleague who appreciated the potentialities of the method (Baron, in Alan Stern; Wall, in George Litchford; Westfall, in Charles Langley), and was willing to give it a try. The attempted replications were successful in that each biographer achieved new understanding of his subject, himself, and the relations between the two. Westfall's declaration that the exploration with his collaborator of the various ways in which he, Westfall, had inserted himself into his biographical work was for him "a voyage of self-discovery" applies in varying degrees to each of the others as well.

As a consequence of our personal involvement in the collaborative method, and the evidence provided by others who have experienced it, we put a high value on its effectiveness and potential. Of course, we make no claim that it is the only way to attain important insights into a biographical subject, and a number of our contributors have in fact based their essays on their own personal introspection. Perhaps Tucker's is the most striking example of the fruitfulness of that approach. It involved the sudden perception during his stay in Moscow of a possible connection between two matters that he had until then considered entirely distinct from each other—Karen Horney's psychological theory (in which he had an academic interest) and the virtual deification of the living Stalin in the USSR (the focus of a job-related interest). The revelation took the form of a hypothesis that the public cult of Stalin emanated from the dictator himself, that it was the expression and "institutionalization of a neurotically idealized self" (a type Horney had described in *Neurosis and Human Growth*). A few years later, in 1956, Nikita Khrushchev's secret speech to the Twentieth Party Congress portrayed Stalin in terms congruent with this depiction, appearing to confirm the hypothesis that later became a key conception in Tucker's biography of Stalin.

Exemplifying still another approach, Marcus, in the course of his personal psychoanalysis, made a somewhat analogous "break-through," which provided the basis for the important appendix to his work on Dickens. The analysis, he says, not only led "to a second and new reading of [*Oliver Twist*], but it helped me to understand a part of my own life in a way that I had never understood it before." This result sounds very like statements made concerning the collaborative method by those who experienced it. Schwehn, for example, declares that his collaboration with Moraitis "enabled me to learn more about myself in the course of learning more about my subject and to learn more about my subject in the course of learning more about myself." Each case was an exercise in triangulation, with the third party facilitating the biographer's acquisition of new perceptions.

A "second reading" of a text figures prominently in Marcus's breakthrough, but by no means there alone. It is in fact a feature common to many of our contributors' accounts of how they gained fresh insight into their subjects. Schwehn, for instance, achieved a new appreciation of Adams after he reexamined him in the light of psychological considerations that he had formerly eschewed. Reference has already been made to the results of Moraitis's second reading of *The Education of Henry Adams*. Rogow remarks that if he had had psychoanalytic training before he wrote his book on Forrestal, and consequently had understood the latter's inner life better, he would have been "less inclined to view certain problems as situational." Wortman's second reading of Tolstoi's *Childhood* disclosed affective notes that had eluded him in the first reading, many years before, and enabled him to attain a more profound apprehension of the novelist's life and work. Baron, sensitized by his collaboration with Alan Stern, was better able to see how Plekhanov's personality affected his career and the fate of his ideological system.

Why have second readings so often proved fruitful? It is apparent from the foregoing that they have frequently occurred after a period of change and growth in the biographer, allowing him to discern things formerly hidden. In the nature of the craft, a serious biographer is certain to be involved in researching and writing his study over a considerable stretch of time. Inevitably he changes and, correspondingly, so do his perceptions of his subject. Writes Marcus: "Dickens changes as the observer changes." (Upon rereading all of Dickens's works some years after his study had appeared, Marcus saw the novels in a new light and felt that he could write a different and deeper book.) Lebeaux makes the same point, joining to it another important perception: "the 'truth' of the subject's life and personality is not fixed but rather given to change in significant respects with the unfolding of the life cycle, and with the shifting events and circumstances of the subject's life and culture." In this conception—and who can doubt its validity?—both the biographer and his subject change, have multiple lives, so to speak. Accordingly, the interrelations between the two are almost infinitely kaleidoscopic, impossible to capture fully, and yet susceptible to and deserving of investigation.

By way of concluding this section, let us look at two examples of such change. In the early stages of his work, despite a degree of identification, Rogow regarded Forrestal with suspicion and anticipated increasing dislike. His own liberal views conflicted with his subject's conservative ones, especially on such issues as the cold war and the establishment of the state of Israel. However, as he got to know Forrestal better, as unsuspected facets of the latter's personality and activity came into focus, Rogow reports becoming more sympathetic, even feeling a "grudging affection" for his subject. Lebeaux's identification with and dependence on Thoreau appears to be stronger than any of our other contributors admit in relation to their subjects. Still, his attitude toward Thoreau varied over time. In a summer of discontent marked by loneliness and self-doubt, Lebeaux idealized Thoreau beyond measure, spent a great deal of time in the woods, and desperately looked for similarities between his hero and himself. At a later stage, when he became a social activist, he found himself at odds with Thoreau, whose extreme individualism and hostility to reform he considered wrong-headed. The biographer dealt with such discordance by putting distance between himself and Thoreau, on the one hand, and by developing an increasingly differentiated conception of his subject, on the other.

The ways of gaining insight into a biographical subject are numerous, and we have not attempted to compile an exhaustive inventory. We have instead examined the testimony of our contributors in an effort to determine how they achieved such insight. It is safe to assume that sensitive reading enabled each and all to accomplish much by way of intuition. But over and above that, the record shows that they scored breakthroughs in the course of their own psychoanalyses, by way of introspection, through second readings, and, not least, by resort to a Moraitis-style collaboration.

## SUBJECTIVITY AND THE PERSONAL STAMP

The maxim "all biography is autobiography" is no more credible than the contrary proposition that biography is strictly objective. The quoted saying contains a kernel of truth, of course, but closer to the mark is Wall's qualified query: "To what degree is all biography autobiography?" Mark Pachter, the editor of a recent volume on biography, offers one answer: "The biographer is *there* in his work . . . in a certain way that is difficult to define."[9] Our colleague Westfall gives a rather more trenchant response: After the "voyage of self-discovery" he made in the company of Langley, he concluded: "It is impossible to portray another human being without displaying oneself."[10] Lebeaux provides a somewhat different slant: "A mysterious alchemy takes place between the biographer and his or her subject: the resulting biography is a product of that complex, elusive interaction, and cannot avoid being, in this very real sense, 'subjective.'" Related to this problem of subjectivity in biographical writing is the question of how the author puts his personal stamp on his work. This can be only a reconnaissance into an obscure realm, for, as Schwehn observes: "Biographers are necessarily involved in their subjects in ways they do not comprehend."

Let us begin by noting that at least two of our contributors had persuaded themselves that in writing their biographical studies they had largely managed to avoid subjectivity. Baron bridled against interrogation about whether he liked or disliked Plekhanov, believing that this was irrelevant, that his biography in the making was "a truthful and rather exact representation." Westfall's ready acknowledgment of the subjective factor, he says, "was always conditioned by the silent proviso that subjectivity applied more to others than to [him]," that through careful and thorough work he would succeed in confining it to the narrowest of limits.   Baron and Westfall both subsequently changed their minds, in effect endorsing Clarence Tracy's characterization of the scholarly biographer's desire to eliminate all traces of subjectivity from his work as "well-intentioned but ultimately vain."[11]

Tracy goes a step farther, seeing positive value in subjectivity, and a number of our contributors agree. Notes Wall: Though such works as Thomas Macaulay's *History of England,* Alexis de Tocqueville's *Democracy in America,* and Lytton Strachey's *Eminent Victorians* distinctly reflect their authors' own personalities and prejudices, they remain classics long after supposedly scientific monographs have been forgotten. Of his own experience, Pletsch reflects, "I realized that my insights [when trying to put Nietzsche behind him] were less vibrant than they had been when my interest so thoroughly involved my conception of myself." There was little doubt in Lebeaux's mind, he tells us, that parallels he perceived between Thoreau and himself "enabled [him] to see certain aspects of [Thoreau's] life and personality that other scholars . . . could not see or had overlooked." These remarks imply that subjectivity may promote the kind of empathy that yields special insight, as well as vivacious writing. They focus on the sensitivity and abilities of the biographer who, as Tracy observes, sifts the facts, assigns values to them, and forms in his imagination a conception of the personality to be portrayed.[12] Of course, the "shaping temperament" of the biographer can be more or less effective; the "particular eyes" through which the subject is seen, more or less discerning.[13]

Many are the uses of subjectivity, but if not kept within proper bounds it may easily produce distortion. A writer may become so completely identified with his subject that he is rendered incapable of seeing him whole. Such was the case with Schwehn, so long as he avoided psychological interpretation of Adams because of a desire to protect a figure with whom he strongly identified. On the other end, Pletsch concedes that his personal disillusionment with Nietzsche led him to produce an idiosyncratic portrayal in his dissertation. In yet another variant, Moraitis reveals that, because of his preestablished mindset, he had been determined "to read in *The Education of Henry Adams* a story the author, with equal determination, did not write." Lebeaux pinpoints an important hazard of another sort: because he identified with Thoreau in many respects, he was concerned that he "might be reading too much Lebeaux into Thoreau." All four implicitly certify the cogency of Samuel Johnson's warning about "the treachery of the human heart"; which Johnson's biographer translates as "our almost infinite capacity to delude ourselves about our own motives."[14]

Some psychologically oriented biographers have addressed this issue. Because the elimination of subjectivity is neither possible nor desirable—this is their premise—the biographer should somehow try to monitor it, to keep it from getting out of hand. This is what Erik Erikson presumably means by "disciplined subjectivity."[15] Mack suggests a way of achieving it when he writes: "The most important preparation that the biographer interested in using psychological insights could undertake might well be a study of himself or herself, to the extent of even undergoing psychoanalysis." Only through the achievement of self-knowledge, can the biographer "appropriately handle exaggerated idealization, devaluation, or other distortions of the subject's personality, psychology, and life."[16] The same end may be reached through the kind of collaboration between a biographer and a psychoanalyst or clinical psychologist that many of our contributors went through. As Moraitis has put it in his essay "A Psychoanalyst's Journey into a Historian's World," a basic objective of this method is to make the biographer "more aware of the influence of his own personality on his ideas in general and his basic thesis in particular." As a monitoring device, this method is superior to personal introspection alone, he asserts, because the latter lacks the safeguard of an external control.

Several illustrations and hints have already been given as to how our biographers put their personal stamp on their work. Some of the contributors—for instance, Mack, Rogow, Tucker, and Wortman— offer little or nothing explicitly on this score. Others indicate specific ways in which their own personal qualities and predilections affected how they represented some particular aspect of their subjects.

Marcus, for instance, finds it significant that he chose to deal biographically with two writers (Dickens and Engels) who made a great splash early in their careers. A recurrent theme in his writing has been the "arc of development" of young writers up to the point at which they achieved their first triumph and, with it, "self-definition in action." This interest, Marcus supposes, is a refraction of a major episode in his own life: his decision to pursue a career in literature against his father's wishes. We take this to mean that he had an enormous stake in proving himself, a situation that necessarily involved his early development to the point where *he* achieved his first literary triumph.

Baron allows that he chose not to concern himself more than cursorily with conflicts in which Plekhanov became involved between the Russian revolution of 1905 and the outbreak of the World War. He convinced himself that these conflicts, though full of sound and fury, had little net effect, and therefore were not worth greater attention. This is a debatable point, but other considerations surely underlay his decision, he later came to believe. For one thing, the interminable squabbles among the Russian revolutionists appeared squalid to him, prompting him to back away. More important, perhaps, these acrimonious affairs showed Plekhanov in a most unfavorable light. Baron suggests that he may have wished to divert his attention from his subject's "repellent qualities in order to promote continuing empathy" as he worked through the long process of completing the biography.

A more extensive interface between biographer and subject is revealed in Lebeaux's and Pletsch's essays, which are similar in important respects. Each had a relationship of long duration with the subject before embarking on a biography. Each idealized and identified strongly with his subject at an early stage of his development. In Lebeaux's case, this period appears to have lasted much longer, with many of his experiences and evolving values seeming to resonate with Thoreau's. With further growth, both Pletsch and Lebeaux found themselves in psychic conflict with their subjects. For Pletsch, this meant disillusionment and the assumption of a negative stance toward Nietzsche. Lebeaux had more of an investment in Thoreau and so, while recognizing his "imperfections," could continue to value him as an old, reliable friend. Lebeaux incorporated his new perceptions into a more differentiated image of Thoreau, which reflected successive encounters and changing relationships between the two.

By another route—his collaboration with Moraitis—Pletsch arrived at a rather similar destination. He became aware of his unconscious feelings about Nietzsche in consecutive stages of their relationship and recognized the possibility of integrating contradictory assessments of his subject into a multidimensional portrait.

The renditions of their subjects by Lebeaux and Pletsch are the result of a complex process of accretion, reflection, and integration through reorganization, the last two carried out in the process of writing a dissertation and preparing it for publication. By contrast, with Wall and Westfall, each presents an analysis of how he is "*there in his work,*" based on introspection after the completion of his book. In his biography Wall portrays Carnegie as a figure who desperately sought to reconcile his poverty-ridden and radical family background with his life as a plutocrat. The resolution, embodied in Carnegie's tract *The Gospel of Wealth,* required that very rich men return their wealth to the society from which it had been drawn. This interpretation, neither lionizing nor debunking, was Wall's very own. Ten years after the book's publication, its author discerns a new dimension in what he wrought. Himself a person of conservative background, Wall became a progressive who, accordingly, was likely to experience discomfort in the role of a tycoon's biographer. His interpretation, he now believes, was as essential to him as to his protagonist. It not only reconciled the radical with the plutocrat, but it also enabled Wall to empathize with someone whose biography he had been asked to write, and who was antithetical to him in so many ways. "Quite unconsciously," he observes, "I was attempting through this process of reconciling the inner tensions in both of us to find a reflection of Carnegie in me and of me in Carnegie."

In his collaboration with Langley, Westfall learned of a number of ways in which he had projected himself into his biography of Newton (although he insists he never confused himself with Newton). Most important was his explanation of why Newton performed such prodigious labor in a "ceaseless search for truth," at a time when Cambridge University, with which he was associated, was in disastrous decline, and "lack of performance was the standard pattern of the age." Newton also served assiduously at the Royal Mint; and, as president of the Royal Society, he "reinvigorated a dying organization." Westfall acknowledges that in important respects Newton was rather like a cloistered monk, yet he portrayed Newton as if he were a

Puritan scholar who dutifully fulfilled his calling, while others frittered away their resources in revelry. Westfall had long been a Presbyterian elder, but it had not occurred to him that "the Puritan ethic was also furnishing the set of categories [he] used in constructing [his] picture of Newton"; more specifically, the extent to which he "had interpreted [the] material in terms of the Puritan model of the faithful steward." Unwittingly, he concludes, he had portrayed his "ideal self."

Reference has been made to the psychic conflicts that existed or developed between Lebeaux, Pletsch, Rogow, and Wall and their subjects, and how the biographers handled it. Such conflicts are probably inevitable, Moraitis thinks, for it is most unlikely that biographer and subject will always be on the same wavelength. If so, then one might anticipate psychic conflict of stupendous proportions in certain cases, for example, between Stalin's biographer and his subject. If as Tucker confesses, he loathes Stalin, can he possibly do justice to him? Tucker himself provides some thoughts on the matter. When he reconstructs the events of Stalin's life in the 1930s, he admits, he is impelled to urge some of Stalin's associates and victims-to-be to stab him or bash in his brains. On the other hand, Tucker has steeped himself in Staliniana for so long that he believes he is able to think as Stalin did and, in that sense, "to *be* Stalin." Likening himself to a detective, he contends that his abhorrence of Stalin's crimes does not disqualify him from projecting himself into the criminal's mind and divining the latter's thoughts. Nor, he believes, does his loathing necessarily prevent him from giving Stalin due credit for his achievements. Because he is aware of his loathing, presumably he is able to keep it from overrunning and distorting his account of Stalin—something he could not do had he, like some other Stalin biographers, been a victim of the dictator's persecution. We cannot judge whether everyone will be fully convinced by Tucker's case. In any event, it is a type of problem that merits further investigation.


## RECIPROCAL INFLUENCES


Although the specifics have rarely been addressed, few readers will be surprised by the general proposition that biographers put their personal stamp on their works. Less familiar, and still less examined, is the impress made by the biographical subjects upon those who write their lives. Yet why should it be supposed that the psychological transactions between biographer and subject are a one-way affair?

As a point of departure for inquiry into this problem, let us consider the moving lines with which Lebeaux concludes his essay. The essay is the story of his long association with Thoreau, its inspirations and consolations, its separations and reconciliations. As he enters a new stage of his own life, Lebeaux is exploring his subject's mid-life in a sequel to his *Young Man Thoreau*. He hopes, he tells us, "to maintain and nurture an enduring I-Thou relationship with Thoreau, who "will continue to be [he expects] an old and cherished companion—human, fallible, admired, loved, a part of me."

Perhaps few biographers have had so long, so close, and, especially, so affectionate a relationship with their subjects as Lebeaux. Yet the difference between him and most other biographers is surely one of degree rather than kind. Though others may relate to their subjects less warmly and benignly (often ambivalently), few would deny, we suppose, that their protagonists have become a part of them. How could it be otherwise, when the biographer is so intimately and intensely involved with his subject over a protracted period? At a minimum, all biographers evidently develop a proprietary interest in their subjects. Recall Wall's assertion that he experienced this sentiment as strongly as if the persons he studied were not only subjects of his own choosing but his own creations. His own creations: that is, extensions of himself. But since he could not really have created his subjects, he must somehow have incorporated them psychologically into himself. Pletsch confirms this idea in speaking of the biographical subject becoming "part of the historian's conception of self."

Empathy is another avenue to the dissolution of the boundaries between biographer and subject. In the quest for understanding, the biographer projects himself into situations in which the subject lived and moved, and endeavors to capture his thoughts and feelings. (Recall Tucker's contention that he is able to think as Stalin did, and, in that sense, "to *be* Stalin.") In such endeavors, the subject's personal writings are of course very important; as Wortman says, they often reveal, with "peculiar intensity," "a psychological reality beneath his actions and ideals," making it possible "to enter into an author's personality and to gain a sense of how he felt about the world." As to the affect, "at such moments I have felt captivated by my subject," Wortman writes, "I sense a bond with someone living at another time and in another culture." The feelings he eloquently expresses have been experienced by every sensitive biographer.

We are reminded once again of Lebeaux's reflection: "A mysterious alchemy takes place between the biographer and his or her subject: the resulting biography is a product of that complex, elusive interaction." It is beyond our powers to project ourselves into the world of the alchemist—even Westfall, a historian of science, allows he cannot manage that. But the testimony of a number of our contributors conveys something of the powerful and vital relationship established between biographer and subject. A review of the language they use leads us confidently to assert that this cannot possibly be a one-way relationship. To be "captivated" is to be taken possession of; the subject who becomes part of the biographer or part of his conception of himself must make his presence felt in tangible ways. The biographer who lives for long periods in the intellectual and emotional world of another—particularly a person of extraordinary qualities, as a biographical subject is likely to be—cannot avoid, in some measure, seeing, thinking, and feeling—in a word, becoming— like that other.

Some of our contributors offer direct testimony on this issue. Recall that Lebeaux, Pletsch, and Marcus all feel that they received psychological support from their subjects-to-be for major and difficult career decisions they made as young men. This is a compelling indication of the effect a biographical subject may have on the life of a biographer, and we strongly suspect that analogous transactions occur with considerable frequency.

On another tack, in studying Alfred duPont, Wall observes, he frequently finds himself comparing this figure with Carnegie. The remark has broad implications, for it can hardly be doubted that the figure the biographer comes to know so well—Wall says he knew Carnegie "better than [Carnegie] knew himself"—functions long after as a reference point in the biographer's thinking. If, as is bound to be the case, the subject's life was rich in action and/or thought, the extent of his influence on the biographer's thinking must be very considerable indeed.

A striking illustration occurs in one of our papers. By the time he had completed his biographical work, Baron relates, he was fed up with Plekhanov, Russian Marxism, the Social Democratic movement, even intellectual history, and anxious to move on. In the next fifteen years, he focused his attention on such diverse and seemingly far-removed subjects as travel accounts—with special reference to the "Westernization" of Russia, merchants and commerce in sixteenth- to seventeenth-century Muscovy, and Soviet historiography. Recently, however, in reflecting upon his research in these years, he made a surprising discovery. Contrary to what he supposed, he had by no means gotten Plekhanov out of his system; for each and every one of the subjects he had explored since completing his biography was somehow related to Plekhanov. This could be no mere coincidence. His thinking had been affected so deeply by his long association with Plekhanov, Baron recognizes, that it had largely determined the range of his interests. Plekhanov seems to have taken possession of Baron, whose work on commerce and the merchants was directed toward solving a problem that had been one of Plekhanov's major preoccupations.

Similar in one major respect, although very different in others, is the experience of Pletsch. His close involvement in diverse ways with Nietzsche over a period of years had made the German philosopher a part of his conception of himself. After he had reoriented his own interests and values, Pletsch rebelled against Nietzsche's continuing hold on him. He then hit upon the idea of a psychological study of Nietzsche as a means of "disposing of him and his claim upon me" (and to get at his vulnerable underside?). Through his dissertation and his subsequent collaboration with Moraitis, he learned a great deal about himself and his complicated relationship with Nietzsche. But these enterprises failed to rid him of Nietzsche. On the contrary, Pletsch's work with Moraitis has prompted him to return once again to his subject. He plans a study in which Nietzsche figures as the last great exponent of "the ideology of genius," as well as its first great critic. This conception, Pletsch believes, will make his biographical analysis of Nietzsche relevant to a host of other prominent cultural figures of the nineteenth century.

In our opinion, the material cited here constitutes persuasive evidence for the impact of the biographical subject on the biographer. Unfortunately, most of our contributors do not address this issue, so the evidence is limited. Further exploration of this aspect of the psychology of biography will show, we are convinced, that the impact is even more far-reaching than the contents of this volume indicate.

## THE COLLABORATIVE METHOD

In the preceding pages, reference has frequently been made to the collaborative method in which a majority of our contributors engaged as a part of the process of preparing their papers. By way of a conclusion to this introduction, let us look at some aspects of contemporary thinking about psychological biography, to demonstrate just how timely the advent of this method is.

Psychoanalysis has greatly expanded knowledge of mental life, the psychoanalyst Joseph Lichtenberg remarks, but, paradoxically, this advance has not resulted in the production of superior biographies by either psychoanalysts or self-declared psychobiographers (with a few exceptions). In a recent survey of the state of the psychohistorical art, the historian Richard Schoenwald comes to a similar conclusion. Noting that the literary gifts of Freud and his followers made psychological analysis accessible and "convinced some historians that here indeed was a psychology about human beings that was waiting to be tapped by the historian," he adds, "the main orientations of psychoanalysis operated to hamstring historians."[17] Here both the psychoanalyst and the historian agree that expectations of a great harvest to be reaped through the cross-fertilization of psychological analysis and biography or history have not been fulfilled. Where Schoenwald points to the hamstringing effect of the main orientations of psychoanalysis as the difficulty, Lichtenberg indicates that "the traditional approach of the biographer and the methods of the psychoanalyst do not complement one another in any simple fashion." At issue, then, is the problem of finding ways and means effectively to join the skills and methods of the biographer with those of the psychoanalyst. Must the biographer become a psychoanalyst in order to produce good work? Must the psychoanalyst who would do a biographical study become a historian? Is there some operational middle ground?

One answer is afforded by the example of a contributor to this volume, the psychoanalyst John Mack. Schoenwald, who ruefully notes that the best psychohistorical work has been produced by non-historians, proclaims Mack's study of T. E. Lawrence "a masterpiece of psychohistorical biography."[18] It would be natural to jump to the conclusion that the psychoanalyst is uniquely equipped to produce superlative biography. But a number of counterreflections suggest the need for caution. How many psychoanalyst-biographers have

matched Mack's achievement? Then, consider Lichtenberg's assertion—spelled out in the next chapter—that Plutarch, St. Augustine,
Benvenuto Cellini, and James Boswell all "wrote biographies that
were rich in psychological understanding long before psychoanalysis
contributed its special insights to our age." Most telling of all is
Mack's own testimony, which deserves to be repeated: The biographer who would apply psychological insights to the study of his
subjects "must be a historian or a biographer first, with psychology as
a *part* of his equipment," employed "to deepen and broaden his view
of the relationship between an individual and certain historically significant events in which he took part."[19]

Psychoanalytic expertise is indubitably an asset for the biographer,
enabling him to probe the inner life of his subject. But such expertise
in and of itself is unequal to the task of producing excellent biography, which of course must give ample attention to the milieu in
which the subject moved. Gaining knowledge and insight about the
social and cultural worlds of the past is the métier of the historian
(and anyone who undertakes to do a biography cannot avoid in some
measure becoming a historian). Must, then, the historian, who by
definition possesses one of the key qualifications, become a psychoanalyst in order to equip himself to do quality biographical work? The
history of biography before Freud, and the example of our three
contributors who have produced respectable work despite their admittedly modest level of psychological know-how, would seem to
justify a negative reply. But these three, after having introspected
about their biographical work in collaboration with a psychologically
qualified partner, agreed that had they been equipped to use psychological analysis more systematically, their work would have benefited. In effect they admitted, with varying degrees of conviction, the
validity of Lichtenberg's contention that "psychoanalysis presents
the biographer with a challenge that cannot be resisted." This means,
we assume, that in our time the biographer who disregards the advantages to be derived from psychoanalysis, although he may still do
respectable work, nevertheless falls short of the highest standards.

What has been said so far is relevant, though not fully responsive,
to the question: Must the historian become a psychoanalyst to do
excellent biographical work? Schoenwald furnishes a reply that we
are inclined to endorse. Were the historian to become a psychoanalyst, and consequently employ the conceptions and methods of
that calling, he would cease to be a historian, whose conceptions and

methods are of quite a different sort. On the other hand, should he wish to pursue the historian's craft, devoting immense amounts of time to gathering and reflecting upon information about the past germane to his biographical work, he will find it physically impossible to master the psychoanalyst's craft. "The historian will have to admit," says Schoenwald, "that 'some' [psychological know-how] is better than 'all,' because 'all' is just not possible."[20] Remarkably, Schoenwald, taking off from the historian's perspective, reaches the same conclusion as Mack does from the psychoanalytical perspective. The biographer must be first a biographer and historian, "with psychology," in Mack's words, "as a *part* of his equipment."

Although this consensus is noteworthy, it leaves unanswered questions about just how large a part of the equipment of the biographer psychology should constitute, which particular aspects are most worth acquiring, and how one ought to go about acquiring them. Without attempting to deal with the first two questions here, let us begin to address the third, in conjunction with a fourth, which is most crucial for our purposes: How are the skills of the biographer-historian to be melded with those of the psychoanalyst? Lichtenberg lucidly discusses the many-faceted "problem of integration" that psychoanalysis presents to the biographer. His prescriptions, however, are couched in general terms, which, though unobjectionable, provide little guidance to the practitioner. Yet in his discussion of Boswell's *Life of Johnson* in the same article, Lichtenberg brilliantly demonstrates a technique that effectively addresses our problem. (Parenthetically, it should be emphasized that Lichtenberg thoroughly appreciates the high importance of apprehending the external world of the figures studied.)

Central for Lichtenberg—it is of course our primary concern as well—is the relationship between the biographer and his subject. As he sees it, the Boswell-Johnson relationship was one of interdependence, with Boswell acting as "the mirroring responder" to Johnson's idealized sense of himself, while the biographer gained psychic rewards from his association with the great man and his circle. Boswell presented the surface aspects of Johnson's life in "richness unrivaled," but he avoided dwelling upon Johnson's many unattractive qualities and, even more so, the inner struggles that underlay them. Boswell shunned psychologizing, Lichtenberg intimates, not because he was psychologically undiscerning but for the opposite reason. Understanding very well his friend's psychic need for support and affirmation, he met that need with exquisite delicacy, both in his relations with Johnson so long as he lived and in writing about him after he died. Lichtenberg's analysis is a model of triangulation, wherein he observes the subject, the biographer, and their interrelations, in the process throwing fresh light on all three.

If Lichtenberg's demonstration involving a long-deceased biographer and his subject seems notably fruitful, a similar process of triangulation involving a living biographer and a trained psychologist would appear to be promising. One of Schoenwald's ideas, arrived at independently, points in the same direction. To psychohistorians who, in the interest of producing more satisfactory work, might be willing to experiment, he suggests that the historian might temporarily abandon the time-honored practice of working alone and "devise some way of calling on several people to monitor a single historian's tendency to nudge and squeeze his data consciously and semiconsciously into certain favored patterns."[21] Were one to substitute for Schoenwald's "several people" the words "a person trained in psychological analysis," one would have a definition of the collaborative method many of us have used.

A number of the following essays describe their authors' experiences in such a collaboration—some scantily, others more amply, the two on the Pletsch-Moraitis encounters most fully. The afterword by Moraitis presents a many-sided discussion of the method. Here, one should point out that in such a collaboration the psychologist does not become a historian or vice versa. It is rather a question of finding a ground on which the expertise and experience of the two can be joined in a mutually beneficial engagement; or, as Pletsch puts it, "adapting the psychoanalytic *method* to the conditions of historical study." As Moraitis defines it: "The basic objective is to facilitate the [biographer's] capacity to master the complexities of the issues [he studies] and make him more aware of the influence of his own personality on his ideas in general and his basic thesis in particular."

It would be pointless to make exaggerated claims, to assert, for example, that this method provides a master key to the psychology of biography. The method in fact relates only to certain aspects of that larger field; besides, its objectives may in principle be attained by other means. Recall Mack's admonition that the would-be biographer strive to gain self-knowledge, even to the extent of undergoing psychoanalysis, as a safeguard against inadvertent distortion of the subject's personality, psychology, and life. This good advice is somewhat vitiated by the fact that it entails an investment of time and money that many a writer cannot afford. One of the attractions of the Moraitis method, by contrast, is that it requires a relatively few encounters, thus justifying Pletsch's claim that it is "an efficient method of cooperation." Moreover, although the biographer who has been sensitized by psychoanalysis is more likely than another who has not to avoid egregious errors when introspecting about his subject, his introspection may still give rise to faulty perceptions. Perfection is not of this world, needless to say: the point is that the collaborative method provides a monitoring device for correcting faults that unassisted introspection lacks.

After concluding the first experiment in collaboration, Moraitis acknowledged that before the method's effectiveness could be certified it would have to be repeated. It has now been repeated a number of times, and those who participated unanimously testify to its efficacy. Schwehn may speak for all when he asserts that his collaboration with Moraitis "provided one disciplined way to reflect upon" the extent to which his work was "shaped by unconscious or unexamined psychological processes." He cautiously adds: "I cannot predict with any certainty that [such a collaboration] will make a bad biographer a good one or a good biographer a better one." In our judgment, Schwehn's formulation is excessively diffident. We know of no way to make a bad biographer a good one, nor do we maintain that the collaborative method will make a good biographer a superb one. However, there is evidence enough in the following essays to warrant a claim that the collaborative method can help make a good biographer a better one. On that score, it deserves the consideration of biographers and would-be biographers alike.

## NOTES

[1]On biography in general, the following works are notable: André Maurois, *Aspects of Biography* (New York: Appleton, 1929); Harold Nicolson, *The Development of English Biography* (London: Hogarth Press, 1947); Leon Edel, *Literary Biography* (London: Hart-Davis, 1957); James L. Clifford, ed., *Biography as an Art* (New York: Oxford University Press, 1962); R. D. Altick, *Lives and Letters* (New York: Knopf, 1969); Alan Shelston, *Biography* (London: Methuen, 1977); Donald Capps, "Psychohistory and Historical Genres," in

*Childhood and Selfhood: Essays on Tradition, Religion, and Modernity,* ed. Peter Homans (Lewisburg, Pa.: Bucknell University Pres, 1978); Helmut Scheuer, *Biographie: Studien zur Funktion und zum Wandel einer literarischen Gattung vom 18. Jahrhundert bis zur Gegenwart* (Stuttgart, 1979); J. D. Browning, ed., *Biography in the Eighteenth Century* (New York: Garland, 1980). Also noteworthy is the journal *Biography,* published at the University of Hawaii since 1978.

2On the relation of biographer to subject, a theme little treated in the literature, see Edel, *Literary Biography;* James L. Clifford, *From Puzzles to Portraits* (Chapel Hill: University of North Carolina Press, 1970); Marc Pachter, ed., *Telling Lives: The Biographer's Art* (Washington, D.C.: National Portrait Gallery/New Republic Books, 1979).

3Barbara W. Tuchman, "Biography as a Prism of History," in Pachter, *Telling Lives,* p. 132.

4Bernard C. Meyer, "Some Reflections on the Contribution of Psychoanalysis to Biography," in *Psychoanalysis and Contemporary Science,* vol. 1, ed. Robert R. Holt and Emanuel Peterfreund (New York: Macmillan, 1972), p. 389.

5Ibid., p. 375.

6Richard Westfall to Samuel Baron, February 2, 1980.

7Meyer, "Reflections," p. 373.

8John E. Mack, "T. E. Lawrence and the Uses of Psychology in the Biography of Historical Figures," in *Psychological Dimensions of Near Eastern Studies,* ed. L. Carl Brown and N. Itzkowitz (Princeton: Darwin Press, 1977), p. 30. The quotation is from a part of the article that does not appear in the abridged version printed here under a different title.

9Pachter, *Telling Lives,* p. 8.

10It is no belittlement of Westfall's observation to note that Thomas Carlyle in 1827 made a similar remark: "In every man's writings, the character of the writer must be recorded."

11Clarence Tracy, "Introduction," in Browning, *Biography in Eighteenth Century,* p. 6.

12Ibid., p. 7.

13The "shaping temperament" is Pachter's phrase (*Telling Lives,* p. 7). The importance of "particular eyes" is stressed by Leon Edel in "The Figure under the Carpet" (ibid., p. 19).

14W. Jackson Bate, *Samuel Johnson* (New York: Harcourt Brace Jovanovich, 1975), p. 298.

15Erik H. Erikson, "On the Nature of Psycho-Historical Evidence: In Search of Gandhi," *Daedalus* 97, no. 3 (Summer 1968): 698.

16Mack, "Lawrence," p. 32. Again, this quotation does not appear in the abridged version.

17Richard L. Schoenwald, "The Psychological Study of History," in *International Handbook of Historical Studies: Contemporary Research and Theory,* Georg

G. Iggers and Harold T. Parker, ed. (Westport, Conn.: Greenwood, 1979), p. 72.

[18]Ibid., p. 71.

[19]Mack, "Lawrence," p. 30.

[20]Schoenwald, "Psychological Study," p. 75.

[21]Ibid., p. 77.

# 2

# Psychoanalysis and Biography

## Joseph D. Lichtenberg

I.

THE MORE ONE EXAMINES the relationship between psychoanalysis and biography, the greater the complexities appear. A premise with which to start an examination is that before Sigmund Freud, biographies were written without the benefit (or burden) of the discoveries of psychoanalysis, but that after these discoveries biographers' views of their subjects have been enriched (or contaminated) by explicit information (or misinformation) about the realm of "unconscious" motivation. As I hope to show, even this "obvious" premise requires considerable qualification—although I believe it to be more true than false.

Since I take a historical perspective in this examination,[1] I have selected biographies and autobiographies from different epochs. From the Greco-Roman period, I have chosen *Plutarch's Lives;* from the period ushering in the domination of Christian religious thought, *The Confessions of St. Augustine;* from the Renaissance, *The Life of Benvenuto/The Son of Giovanni Cellini;* and from the "Age of Reason," James Boswell's *Life of Samuel Johnson.*[2] Using the Augustine autobiography, Charles Kligerman has made an excellent psychobiographic study, which invites comparisons between the virtues of the original and the added depth of insight of the psychoanalyst.[3] Out of the wealth of biographical works of the present, I shall principally refer to material concerning Eugene O'Neill—an autobiography in play form (*Long Day's Journey into Night*), two major biographies, and three psychoanalytic studies.[4]

Reprinted by permission from *The Annual of Psychoanalysis,* ed. Chicago Institute for Psychoanalysis, Vol. 6 (New York: International Universities Press, 1978), pp. 397–427.

Boswell reasoned that to study the accomplishments and failings of a man of genius is both instructive and amusing. He invited the reader to take a leisurely contemplative stance and share with him the pleasure of listening to pearls of wisdom and brilliant conversational gambits. His hero was a massive accumulator of erudite and esoteric knowledge, the famed author of a dictionary. On the other hand, Plutarch is in the great tradition of biographers of illustrious men of *action*, whom the biographer sets before us as a standard and an inspiration. Writing of Pericles, Plutarch states: "We ought to apply our intellectual vision to those models which can inspire it to attain its own proper virtue . . . We find these examples in the actions of good men." Plutarch's "lives" are grouped to compare the moral character of the actions of numerous Greek and Roman leaders. His heroes are life-size; they struggle with the vices in their characters. Viewing their virtue implants "an eager rivalry and a keen desire to imitate them." Plutarch believes the reader of his examples will not "form his character by mere imitation, but, by promoting the understanding of virtuous deeds, it provides him with a dominating purpose."[5]

The comparison of Boswell with Plutarch naturally reveals the different sensibilities of two different periods 1,600 years apart. But both biographers aim to tell the story of men who will delight the curious and inspire the admirer of virtues. Neither distances himself greatly from his subject. Both are in the tradition of a democratic view of man. Thus both are outside another tradition in biography—the mythic—in which Jesus, Buddha, and Mohammed, by their lives, inspire whole dogmas of devotion and dedication. Augustine in his form—not as autobiographical, conflicted worshipper, but as "Saint" — is in the latter tradition.

Thus the story of a life—biographical or fictional—approaches the mythic either when it attempts to portray an individual as an idealized, moral guidance figure—a George Washington, Father of his country, saying, "I cannot tell a lie"—or, alternately, when it attempts to portray a person as symbolizing or dramatizing a drive satisfaction carried over from infantile life—a Casanova who seduces all the beautiful ladies under the noses of their husbands or fathers. In either case, the "mythic" biography, however instructive to the superego or titillating to the id, is a contrived and deficient portrayal of a human life. Likewise, a poor psychoanalytic study can be as superficial as the "mythic" biography when it merely catalogues a list of instinctual urges, asserts the presence of an Oedipus complex, or reduces a whole life to a single formula such as the subject's need for punishment.

The analogy between the biographical portrayal and the psychic structures can be completed by saying that an "ego" biography of the adventures of the hero and how he copes and adapts to various external conflicts comes closer to the total human being but still misses a dimension that the great autobiographies possess. The great biographies (and autobiographies) portray an empathic (and/or introspective) understanding of the full range of conflicts that developmentally mold and conceptually characterize that person as "himself." They tell a balanced story—what goes on "inside" *and* "outside"—with the adult coming alive as a recognizable person, plus at least intimations of remembrances of things past.

Cellini's autobiography can be approached with these thoughts in mind. Immediately, we become aware of one distinction between autobiography and biography. In autobiography we evaluate the same individual as author and subject; in biography we are dealing with the "psychology" of the creative artist, the biographer, and of his subject, each of whose messages may be very different. Both Cellini as biographer and Cellini as subject have been criticized for being too narcissistic. What does this mean in terms of the worth of the biography? Does it mean it fails at being "instructive" because the narcissistic person is lacking in a proper set of values? If we perceive him to love only himself, to be indifferent to others, using and exploiting them without guilt or shame, then he sets a bad rather than a good example. His life story could be read only for vicarious enjoyment through the fulfillment of infantile pleasures. Cellini would become, then, the mythic creature Narcissus reveling in eternal self-delight as the central figure in the solipsistic world of infancy. The autobiographer Cellini certainly holds before himself and us a mirror to reflect the subject Cellini because he believed himself to epitomize the highest ideals of the creative artist of the Renaissance. Had he stopped there, we would read him more as we read Vasari, to find inspirational facts about creative artists whose works we admire. But Cellini went on to tell us about a fully dimensional human being, albeit a "narcissistic" one. We meet a multitalented young man struggling between his own choice to be a goldsmith and sculptor, and his father's choice for him to be a musician. We later meet an aggressive, pugnacious man, torn between soldiering and feuding, and pursuing his craft and his creativity. At the same time we see him twisting and turning in the ambiguous position he, along with other Renaissance artists, occupied with princely patrons and hired helpers. He reacts, and all too often overreacts, to disappointments and slights with rage, destructiveness, and murder. We can in no way score him high on a scale of love for his fellow man, although he is frequently generous in material ways and attempts to be fair within his concept of justice.

But as Heinz Kohut has noted, love of self is not the evil opposite of love of others.[6] Love of self exists not only in infantile archaic forms—as exemplified by the paralyzed egoism of the mythic Narcissus—but also in adult forms of self-esteem and creative expression. The beautifully and lovingly crafted works of a Cellini exist psychologically in a transitional realm—partly as an "object" or "thing" and partly as an extension of his self. When he values himself "maturely," or when he values his golden salt cellar or his Perseus, it is one and the same.

Thus to apply the standard: "Does the Cellini autobiography 'instruct' consciously and unconsciously?" we cannot dismiss it by calling the subject narcissistic. Rather, we must ask: "infantile narcissistic or mature narcissistic"? By what scale of values did Cellini measure himself and the extension of himself in his work? The scale is, I believe, a most worthy example of the highest "ego ideals" of the Renaissance. He found the best craftsman there was—whether in coin making, goldsmithing, or sculpturing (for the latter art, Michelangelo is his ideal)—and aimed to equal and better him. Cellini wanted his design to be an aesthetic achievement, and his crafting to be scientifically innovative and functionally "perfect." He took it as a given in his standard of things that he would work and work and work. Despite Cellini's disturbed relationship with people,[7] his autobiography qualifies as one that tells a balanced story of a recognizable multidimensional human being. He is not a human being who exemplifies for the reader how to love others; but he is a man who exemplifies how one struggling individual tried to master himself in order to maintain his love of himself through his creativity. A culmination of his story came when, having an opportunity to add to his many murders by killing a rival artist who had caused him extreme anguish and disappointment, he restrained himself: "Having got free of my diabolical rage my spirits rose and I said to myself: 'If God gives me the grace to finish my work I hope by that means to vanquish all my perfidious enemies, and in that way I shall have a greater and more glorious revenge than I would have had merely on one.'"[8] Then follows the

mounting excitement of his casting of the great bronze statue of Perseus with the head of Medusa and his triumphant success despite
many obstacles. It's a love story and an adventure story, but the love is
a love of self expressed through an adventure into creativity.


II.


In this section I shall discuss the autobiography of Augustine and
the psychoanalytic biographical study by Charles Kligerman. Out of
the many similar studies by psychoanalysts, I have chosen Kligerman's work because he has done his study on a figure that leaped out
at me in my effort to take a historical perspective. In addition, I
consider his study to be a contribution by an empathic, scholarly
psychoanalyst to an understanding of the psychic world of biographer and subject.[9]

A reader need go no farther than the first chapter in the *Confessions*
to be aware of the passion of Augustine's paeans to God and of the
acuity of his power of self-exploration. Kligerman describes the *Confessions* as an exhaustive study of the self, and, using his clinical
training, observes that the text has the spontaneous quality of free
association. He approaches the subject as one would a psychiatric
history and offers two main formulations—first, the story of Aeneas
and Dido served as an unconscious motif for major events in Augustine's life; and second, Augustine's final conversion was the result
of a resolution of years of struggle with his oedipal urges by an
identification with his mother and a passive feminine longing for his
father, displaced to God.

Kligerman is alerted to a possibly significant theme when Augustine
mentions "in passing" one story of the many he studied—that of
Aeneas and Dido—and then adds he was moved by it. Kligerman
observes that Augustine's next association is to fornication, suspecting
a hidden sexual theme in the story. He reviews the details of the
legend—Aeneas's sneaking away from the possessive, widowed Dido
in Carthage to go to Rome, and then reviews the details of Augustine's
life and movements—his escape from his mother at Carthage, his
lying to her, and sailing off to Rome. Kligerman concludes: "The
parallelism is too striking to be coincidental: it was the compulsive
repetition of his boyhood fantasy."[10] Thus Kligerman reaffirms that a
story will fire the imagination of a child when it expresses the wish
fulfillment of his specific nuclear conflict. Its personal inner meaning

will often live on in the unconscious realm of his mind, playing a decisive role in decisions he believes he makes for conscious reasons.

Kligerman then rounds out his assessment of the cause of Augustine's lifelong inner turmoil. He focuses on the vivid description Augustine gives of his mother, Monica, and draws on clinical experience to postulate her influence on Augustine's development. Kligerman concludes that as a little boy Augustine felt pulled between his mother's seductive luring of him and her hypermoral aversion to sexuality. "Monica demanded that Augustine relinquish sexuality in favor of the Church, which meant, at an unconscious level, that he should belong to her forever."[11] Augustine writes his *Confessions* from the standpoint that his mother was all righteousness and goodness, and his father either wrong or unimportant. Augustine needed to maintain this biased view of his parents, Kligerman believes, to defend himself against following his father as a virile, heterosexual, "pagan" male. But, as Kligerman emphasizes, Augustine had an immense investment in his masculinity. In spite of the weeping and nagging of his mother, he maintained a mistress for sixteen years and had a son by her. Finally his mother prevailed. His mistress was sent away and, after a great deal of inner turmoil, Augustine, in a famous scene, heard a voice from heaven. He was ordered to read, and the passage was: "Make not provision for the flesh in concupiscence." A light of serenity infused his heart; "All the darkness of doubt vanished away." Kligerman interprets the voice as Augustine's own, projected and perceived in hallucinatory fashion. It derived from the injunctions of harsh school authorities to "take up and read." Augustine had introjected these fearsome words into his superego at a time when he prayed not to be beaten at school. Augustine now became so close to his dying mother that they shared a mystical, ecstatic experience, which Kligerman interprets as a passive, feminine, erotized love of God the Father. Kligerman adds that Augustine buttressed his celibacy by identifying with the church leader Ambrose. Yet this struggle against direct sexual gratification "necessitated constant vigilance on the part of Augustine to reaffirm his faith. This provided the motivation for a lifelong series of powerful polemics, supposedly to convince others, but also to still his own doubts."[12]

I believe that Kligerman's full account (which I have presented only schematically) gives a coherent and believable explanation of Augustine's struggle with sexuality and its outcome. The shortcoming I see, one which is not uncommon in psychoanalytic studies, is that Kligerman does not deal with the other struggle about which Augustine writes. This struggle is presented by Augustine as one involving faith and intellectual conception. Augustine could not believe in what he could not conceptualize as coherent and logical, and he could not respond to that which has "substance, body or flesh" as worthy of faith. Thus he needed a conceptual breakthrough. He needed to create a system that was both coherent in logic and inspiring in its lofty insubstantiality—its infinite qualities.

These issues, of course, belong to the realm of religion, philosophy, and metaphysics; as such, they represent a limitation of psychoanalytic studies that psychoanalysts have readily acknowledged. But, because of a broadening knowledge of the development of the individual's sense of "self" since Kligerman wrote his paper in 1957, I think Augustine's conceptual struggles can be approached again.

In the beginning of his study Kligerman describes the *Confessions* as "Avowedly written to show how a poor sinner found his way to God," and at the end of his study, Kligerman states that Augustine's answer for his sexual tensions was "sublimating them to a spiritual plane."[13] I suggest we leave out the word "avowedly" and state that the *Confessions* are a dramatic explanation of how a poor sinner found his way to God by himself creating a spiritual plane he could accept. We can then ask why he needed to do so. We already have one answer—to resolve his sexual conflicts. However, I think this explanation is incomplete and misses the specificity of the epic struggle that makes Augustine's autobiography the spiritual message it is. I believe we should add this explanation: Augustine needed an authority to help him resolve his grandiose sense of superiority. He was persistently seeking an authority whose idealized virtues were such that he could devote his enormous energies to establishing and affirming them as universal guiding principles. The reconstruction I offer is that the young Augustine was highly valued by both his mother and his father, but that his passionate nature—the fervor and intensity of his expanding sense of self—resonated much more closely with his mother than with his more "ordinary" father. The father, easier and less intrusive with the boy, failed him as a fully effective superego or ego ideal figure; he could not drive a wedge into the energized, dramatic world of moral superiority and preoccupation with sin that mother and child shared.

The dual nature of Augustine's struggle, a sexual conflict and a conflict with grandiosity, can be seen in the two meanings of "sin" for Augustine that are exemplified by his stealing a pear at age sixteen. The pear, in one meaning, is a sexual symbol, and the guilt about it arose from tasting the forbidden. But Augustine three times repeats the meaning he ascribed: "Nor cared I to enjoy what I stole, but joyed in the theft and sin itself"; "Not seeking aught through the shame, but the shame itself"; and "For if aught of those pears came within my mouth, what sweetened it was the sin." Augustine then asks what in that theft delighted him and hints at the answer: "For so doth pride imitate exaltedness."[14] The sin he delights in was a manifestation of his expansive self-assertiveness—of his pride in his clever mind and sensual-loving body. In his joy in sin, he could both defy his mother's authority and share in her monomaniac preoccupations.

In other passages, especially those in which he describes his easily attained skills at learning and practicing rhetoric, he hints that these talents gave him a sense of confidence approaching grandiosity, but left him with a deflated sense of being without an inner-directed purposefulness. He could feed his narcissistic expansiveness by refuting others, but the victory rang hollow because it left him with no idealized parental figure under whom he could feel secure in constructive subservience. Lacking such a figure, he invented one. Using his intellect and the education his father had encouraged, combined with the religious fervor derived from his mother's passion, Augustine fused neo-Platonism with eroticized faith.

He centered his conscious philosophical struggle on the issue of "substance" because this issue stood symbolically as an unconscious nodal point for his conflicts with sexuality and with grandiosity. The substantiality of his flesh meant for him his guilt-laden sexual urges. In addition, he regarded his expansive self-pride, the finite breadth of his knowledge, and his penetrating questioning as being as substantive as a physical body competing for space and position. In this way, the substantiality of his expansive pride in himself meant for him the dwarfing or obliteration of an idealized image of a father, one worthy of an exchange of love and respect. He needed to accomplish a childhood task—that is, to have more of his infantile self-love be experienced as love of a father seen with both self and separate qualities—an idealized selfobject father and finally God the Father.

The God Augustine had conceptualized from his childhood teachings did not have the idealized qualities Augustine felt were necessary to separate the deity from himself and exalt His position. "I was constrained to confess Thee bounded . . . by the form of a human body"; and Jesus born of the Virgin Mary was "mingled with the flesh"—as was Augustine himself. Then, in a series of moving passages, Augustine describes how he entered into his "inward self." "And I said, 'Is Truth therefore nothing because it is not diffused through space finite or infinite?' And Thou criedst to me from the afar: 'Yet verily, I AM that I AM.'" "I ceased somewhat of my former self . . . and I awoke in Thee, and saw Thee infinite." "I had found the unchangeable and true Eternity of Truth above my changeable mind. And thus by degrees I passed from bodies to the soul. . . . And thus with the flash of one trembling glance it [his doubting, changeable reasoning faculty] arrived at that Which Is."[15] Then, as Kligerman notes, Augustine would not give up his desire for direct male sexual gratification even for his idealized God the Infinite until the final hallucination from the feared teacher disciplinarians of his childhood—"Take up and read!" But I suggest the real struggle was already over. The hallucination was only the denouement.

I call on Augustine's opening lines in his *Confession* as an indication that the major struggle was one of pride, of reducing his self-expansive grandiosity, and of establishing a stable idealization of a parental figure: "Great Art Thou, O Lord, and greatly to be praised; great is Thy power, and Thy wisdom infinite. And Thee would man praise; man, but a particle of Thy creation; man, that bears about him his mortality, the witness of his sin, the witness that Thou resisteth the proud; yet would man praise Thee; he, but a particle of Thy creation."[16] I would only add that this God conceived of in this way was the product of Augustine's mature struggle with his infantile grandiosity. Through his wisdom, he achieved a profound creating of his "Creator" in an idealized form, which has been available since then to millions of others.

III.

My discussion of psychoanalysis and biography began with the statement that, before Freud, biographies were written without the benefit or burden of the discoveries of psychoanalysis. The great biographies, Plutarch's *Lives*, the autobiographies of Augustine and Cellini, and Boswell's biography of Samuel Johnson, share with Freud's psychoanalytic discoveries a hallmark of genius: an uncommon insight into man's conflicts and his motivations. How the insight is presented depends on the view of man prevalent during the epoch for which each writer remains an outstanding spokesman. Augustine's conflicts centered on religion and his relationship with Father the God and Mother the Saint, as well as with father the pagan and mother the temptress. What marks the "modernity"—in reality, the timelessness—of Augustine's story is the continuity of the struggle from its infantile origins through the sequences of periods of development that psychoanalysis has subsequently illuminated. All of the issues that psychoanalysis has formulated using the twentieth-century mode of scientific categorization—the play of forces, the struggle against sexual and aggressive urges, the oedipal rivalry, the pressure of ambition, the force of conscience and of idealization, and the consistent adaptation to the inner world and to the outer world—are easily identified in Augustine's narrative. The same holds true for Cellini's story—differing in that the religious struggle was now reduced to moral rituals and formulas, whereas the burning issues that dominated during the High Renaissance were those of artistic creativity and the relation of the artist to his rivals and to his patrons. The trick is, in reading the great biographies and autobiographies of the past, to identify, if we choose, the specific form of the oedipal struggle, the vicissitudes of grandiosity, the kind of ego functions, the severity and lacunae of superego, etc.; because (1) through psychoanalytic means, we now have a method of doing so, and (2) the intuitive genius of the biographer, through his empathy with his subject, chooses the kind of material that allows us to use the method effectively.

Let us examine the Plutarch and Boswell works for evidence of a similar intuitive selectivity. Plutarch's goal was "a portrait which reveals a man's character and inner qualities." In creating his portrait in words, he purposely deviated from an established tradition of historical accuracy to seek instead what we might call psychological accuracy. He defiantly tells his reader that if a story (myth) is in keeping with his view of the subject's character, "I cannot agree that it should be rejected because of the so-called rules of chronology."[17] Plutarch's explicit purpose was to analyze the motives or states of mind of his characters, and because he saw events in terms of people, and the "moral" decisions they made, he wrote memorable "lives," but an unbalanced, anthropocentric history.

Plutarch's approach was to use the formal outline of the conventional biography of his time—birth, family, education, character, career, posterity, and influence—to convey not only a linear set of "facts," but a sequence of development. The individual develops his character out of a set of choices influenced by his congenital proclivities. Plutarch pictures the legendary Theseus as beginning life with a keen intelligence, great physical strength, and a semidivine parentage. Having been "fired up" as a child by stories of Hercules' renown, "his desire to emulate the hero seized hold of him." He "felt that it would be an intolerable humiliation" to run away from any trial of courage that would make him inferior in value to his heroic model. Of another leader, the son of a self-serving father, Plutarch says, "Nature seems to have bred avarice in the son as if it were a congenital disease." Plutarch thus indicates endowment and identification to be two major sources of character formation. However, although these sources generally mold the individual's course in life, by an "innate excellence" a man like Cimon can overcome his early liabilities. The adolescent Cimon "earned a bad name for disorderly behavior, heavy drinking, and in general taking after his grandfather, Cimon, who was said to have been so stupid that he was nicknamed . . . The Booby." In time, though, the young Cimon revealed himself to be brave, intelligent, generous, and possessed of a fine sense of justice.[18]

In Plutarch's portrayals, lives are not static; man lives in conflict and must constantly make ethical choices. Thus, like the psychoanalytic view, Plutarch's view conceives of character as dynamic, but he narrows the dynamism to a single issue—the movement between virtue and vice. Unlike the psychoanalytic emphasis on unconscious conflicting motivations, Plutarch's emphasis is on the conscious selection of models. Where the psychoanalytic focus can delineate unconscious struggles that affect the intrapsychic life of an individual man, Plutarch, because he limits the factors in decision making to "nature" and the conscious, rational mental faculties, is forced into the restrictive device of ascribing alternative choices to men of contrasting character. For example, he wishes to introduce doubt about the effectiveness of the idealism expressed by Solon in making his laws. Rather than representing Solon as torn between his own realism and his higher idealistic hopes, Plutarch invents an exchange between Solon and a house guest who "laughed at Solon for supposing his countryman's injustice and greed could be kept within bounds by means of written laws." Themistocles and Aristides are prime examples of Plutarch's characterizations by contrast: "these two, even when they were children and pupils together, invariably opposed each other in their words and actions, not only in serious matters but even in play, and . . . this rivalry quickly revealed their respective natures. Themistocles' being resourceful, daring, unscrupulous, and ready to dash impetuously into any undertaking, while Aristides' was founded upon a steadfast character, which was intent on justice and incapable of any falsehood, vulgarity, or trickery even in jest."[19]

Even though "a man's conscious intellect is something he may bring to bear or avert as he chooses," the "power of reasoning," can be upset. Plutarch discusses the possibility of being deranged by "fraud and compulsion, pleasure and pain" and by severe physical suffering. For Plutarch, ambition is "the most powerful of all human passions" and it is best controlled by the observation of "virtue in action." The passion of ambition can be "subordinated to the country's welfare" as when Aristides "for the sake of Athens . . . helped his bitterest enemy to become the most famous of men." Envy and hatred are demeaning feelings a man might give way to when allowed "to follow his natural instincts." "It is a sign of an undisciplined nature and a lack of training never to be able to control one's temper; on the other hand to do so on all occasions is difficult and for some people impossible." Since Plutarch places ambition first in the list of passions, it is only to be expected that he believes the main source of "endless troubles and fears" arises from failure to forearm "with reason against every kind of misfortune."[20]

Placed in a modern context, Plutarch's psychology is one of consciousness and of narcissistic conflicts. "Intolerable humiliation" is the emotion most dreaded. Sexual conflicts hardly exist in his biographies. Cimon and his sister commit incest. Its adverse effect is only on his reputation. Homosexual attractions in adolescence may lead to lifelong allegiances or to the bitterest of rivalries, but this is neither a moral issue nor an indication of a pathological "passion." "Every man's soul has implanted within it the desire to love, and it is as much its nature to love as it is to feel, to understand, and to remember." A man should have intercourse with his wife "at least three times a month" as the mark of honor and affection he owes her. These precepts are noted in passing, but none of Plutarch's heroes has problems of a sexual nature that color his "reason."[21]

Reason, of course, does not always triumph. The place of the irrational is recognized, not as we would conceive it in emotional illness, symptoms, slips, etc., but at times when "the people, as so often happens at moments of crisis, were ready to find salvation in the miraculous rather than in a rational course of action." Trances are "inspired" to furnish prophecies, and these foretellings as well as the subject's own dreams furnish extremely intricate, clever rationalizations for action choices. Plutarch decries morbid, superstitious fear of natural phenomena "to the point of madness" and would replace it "with a piety which rests on a sure foundation supported by rational hopes." In this view, however, there is "nothing to prevent both the scientist and the prophet from being right." The scientist diagnoses the cause; he observes "why something happens and how it becomes what it is." The soothsayer discerns its meaning and foretells "the purpose of an event and its significance."[22]

What a contemporary reader can find in one of Plutarch's biographies is extremely limited in comparison to a modern conception. In none of the biographies do we find a balanced presentation of the dynamic interplay of inner and outer conflictual forces. Nonetheless, the biographies as a group brilliantly portray the moral and inspirational qualities of leadership during the Greco-Roman epoch. In spite of the tilted emphasis he places on conscious moral reasoning, Plutarch often makes his subjects come alive for us in a cohesive image. Plutarch is a great biographer because he was able to balance his time-bound moral psychology with his belief that "the knowledge of man's characters and passions . . . [is] the strings and stops of the soul [requiring] a most skillfull and delicate touch."[23]

IV.

James Boswell's *Life of Samuel Johnson* is the closest in time to the discoveries of Freud, yet it seems the least "Freudian." In it, the principals—Johnson, the giant of his age; Boswell, the disciple and chronicler; Oliver Goldsmith, playwright, novelist, and frustrated rival for center stage; David Garrick, the actor and caricaturist of the great man's pomposity—and a host of other supporting figures ask endless questions and offer an equally endless series of opinions. The astounding fact is that none of these inquiring minds ever asks any of the significant questions of depth psychology.[24] Moral questions are the main subject, and Johnson vigorously endorses a religious view. However, the deep, soul-searching introspection of an Augustine is reduced to an honest annual toting up of transgressions by Johnson. Writing, painting (Sir Joshua Reynolds), or acting occupies the life of most of the principals, and aesthetic criticism is possibly Johnson's greatest expression of his genius. But what emerges is not a profound revelation about creativity but rather flashes of wit, the skewering of the opponent on the point of an epigram. The grand design of the Renaissance artist to achieve the monumental and the tearing apart of himself to accomplish his vision, a design depicted by Cellini, is absent. All of Johnson's major creative efforts—*The Dictionary of the English Language,* the poem "The Vanity of Human Wishes," the novel *Raselas,* and the critical biographical studies *Lives of the Poets*— are treated as mere displays of his prodigious knowledge and intellect. We learn nothing of the inner workings of his mind as he struggled with his subject. In this sense Johnson, the creative artist, is as mythic as Hercules, who, because he had great strength, performed his heroic deeds. Only Johnson, Boswell tells us, performed his prodigies not for heroism but for money. Without the prodding of necessity, the indolence and depression of his "nature" would have prevailed—as it often did. Even the concept of an urge for artistic self-expression lies outside Boswell's understanding of Johnson or himself. Johnson the conversationalist was Boswell's preferred form of the artist.

But if the inner Johnson seems to be absent, the "surface" Johnson exists in a richness unrivaled:

> . . . his apartment and furniture, and morning dress were sufficiently uncouth. His brown suit of clothes looked very rusty, he had a little old shrivelled unpowdered wig, which was too small for his head; his shirt neck and knees of his britches were loose; his black worsted stockings ill drawn up; and he had a pair of unbuckled shoes by way of slippers. But all these slovenly particularities were forgotten the moment he began to talk.

> That the most minute singularities which belonged to him, and made very observable parts of his appearance and manner, may not be omitted, it is requisite to mention, that while talking or even musing as he sat in his chair, he commonly held his head to one side towards his right shoulder and shook it in a tremulous manner, moving in his body backwards and forwards, and rubbing his left knee in the same direction, with the palm of his hand.[25]

Boswell states, "I profess to write, not his panegyric, which must be all praise, but his Life . . . in every picture there should be shade as well as light." "I want to show him in a new light. Grave Sam, and great Sam, and learned Sam—all these he has appeared over and over. Now I want to entwine a wreath of the graces across his brow; I want to show him as gay Sam, agreeable Sam, pleasant Sam."[26]

Grave Sam, great Sam, and learned Sam do indeed appear over and over—as Boswell expounds on the rationality of belief in God, on the conflict between pleasure and virtue, on the need for subordination in all human relationships, and on every literary work and creative thinker of his time. "Sir, I do not think Gray a first-rate poet. He has not a bold imagination, nor much command of words. The obscurity in which he has involved himself will not persuade us that he is sublime. His *Elegy in a Churchyard* has a happy selection of images, but I don't like what are called his great things." And "Rousseau, Sir, is a very bad man. I would sooner sign a sentence for his transportation than that of any felon who has gone from Old Bailey these many years. Yes, I should like to have him work in the plantations." Gay Sam can poke fun at himself: "Lexicographer, a writer of dictionaries, a harmless drudge." Agreeable Sam and pleasant Sam appear as the humorous hearty drinker and man of enormous appetite, the kind befriender of the young Boswell, and the man of much generosity to his friends: "A man, Sir, should keep his friendship *in constant repair*."[27]

As seen through the keyhole by young Garrick, there is also bawdy Sam in "his tumultuous and awkward fondness" for "Tetty," his wife. As a little boy, Johnson learned about Heaven and Hell while lingering in bed with his mother. As a scrofulous, awkward youth of twenty-seven, he married Elizabeth Porter, a widow, more than twice his age "very fat, with a bosom of more than ordinary protuberance, with swelled cheeks of a florid red, produced by thick painting, and increased by the liberal use of cordials, flaring and fantastic in her dress, and affected both in her speech and her general behavior."[28]

But what emerges more forcibly to the psychoanalytic reader is the Johnson who makes a heroic struggle against chronic episodes of depression, hypochondria, and anergy. One senses his struggle to pull himself together in order to launch another fray into the world as its intellectual giant. He needed his audience to create the sense of inestimable, incontestable esteem he required to dispel his fragmented spirits; and he compulsively sought out the company of men and women at all hours. The biography is thus the story of Johnson and his audiences—or, more properly, of the driven exhibitor of greatness and the great mirroring responder, Boswell. I call Boswell a great mirroring responder because of the fidelity of his registry and the sensitivity with which he reflected back his response. Like the fabled mirror of Snow White's wicked witch, he saw the defects, but unlike that "honest" reflector, he never gave an answer that would incite to narcissistic rage and vengeance. Boswell can tell the reader what he recognized about Johnson: "his opinion of Gray's poetry was widely different from mine, and I believe from that of most men of taste"; but I doubt that Boswell ever pressed the point with the great man other than as a device to stimulate him to expound. Yet the exquisiteness of Boswell's sensitivity as responder goes beyond avoiding contention; it extends to never, never asking, "What does it mean: Is there a hidden motive?" Instead, he refutes the suggestion that Johnson's defaming of Gray "had been actuated by envy": "Alas! ye little short-sighted critics, could Johnson be envious of the talents of any of his contemporaries?"[29]

Any sensitive biographer of today would answer Yes, Yes, Yes—not only that Johnson could be envious and that Boswell *knew* he was, but that Boswell had the intuition to sense it was a psychological "fact" best for him and for Johnson not to know. Boswell tells us quite directly all the evidences of Johnson's constant envy of all other pretenders for the literary crown or even for a small moment of conversational victory. He describes Johnson's conversational devices to gain and maintain the upper hand, his infinitely skilled depreciating and caricaturing of any rival, large or small, and above all his devastating contemptuous sarcasm. On the same page Boswell contrasts for the reader two possible responses to Johnson's assaultive domination: the first—"During this argument, Goldsmith sat in restless agitation, from a wish to get in and *shine*. Finding himself excluded, he had taken his hat to go away, but remained for some time with it in his hand, like a gamester, who at the close of a long night, lingers for a little while, to see if he can have a favorable opening to finish with success." The second—"Dr. Mayo's calm temper and steady perseverance rendered him an admirable subject for the exercise of Johnson's powerful abilities. He never flinched, but after reiterated blows, remained seemingly unmoved as at the first. The scintillations of Johnson's genius flashed every time he was struck, without his receiving any injury. Hence he obtained the epithet of THE LITERARY ANVIL."[30]

In the character of Dr. Mayo we recognize not only Boswell, but also a description of a long-familiar figure, albeit one only recently

understood psychologically—the accepting, complementary responder for the scintillating sparks of the creative genius, the "other"
without whom the artist feels incomplete. By the "other," I mean
more than the audience at large, the general world of appreciators for
whom the artist creates. Many artists require an actual alliance with
another person whom they often perceive realistically, but sometimes
largely in fantasy as a soul mate to their deepest insights.[31]

The psychological set for the two men was established soon after
the celebrity-hunting, twenty-two-year-old Scottish provincial Boswell had cornered his quarry, the fifty-four-year-old literary lion.
"Finding him in a placid humor, and wishing to avail myself of the
opportunity which I fortunately had of consulting a sage . . . I
opened to him ingenuously, and gave him a little sketch of my life, to
which he was pleased to listen with great attention . . . he called to
me with warmth, 'Give me your hand, I have taken a liking to
you.'"[32]

Boswell's delight is easily understandable, and so is his frame of
mind. He asked how was it that he felt at ease with Johnson and yet
was depressed by his father. Johnson's answer, "There must always
be a struggle between a father and son, while one aims at power and
the other at independence." Johnson thereby gave both a psychologically sound precept and a prescription for their mutually supportive
interdependence. And Boswell could always sense that the form of
the support was to be one in which he was never to acknowledge that
it was the worshipping son who was providing the support for the
great man. They met. They saw each other frequently. Johnson advised him to keep a journal (thus assuring himself of an amanuensis
for posterity), and then went with him on a long, uncomfortable trip
right to the boat to see him off for his grand tour of the Continent.
"My revered friend walked down with me to the beach, where we
embraced and parted with tenderness. . . . I said, 'I hope, Sir, you
will not forget me in my absence.' Johnson: 'Nay, Sir, it is more likely
you should forget me, than that I should forget you.'" Boswell, the
celebrity hunter, had become the pursued mirror for the great man to
look into and see his best self reflected back.[33]

Years later, with Johnson dead, Boswell tells us "all," and yet still
clings to the same psychological set as at the first meetings. He is the
fortunate son who received the sage advice of "a majestic teacher of
moral and religious wisdom." He tells us that when they met Johnson
had recently suffered a severe and prolonged depression.[34] His last

living relative, his mother, had died when he was fifty. In a sudden spurt of creativity, he wrote *Rasselas,* ostensibly to pay his mother's funeral expenses, after which he went into a painful period of declining output and general depression. He was lively enough during the period of Boswell's initial attendance on him. But not long after Boswell's departure for the Continent, he again fell into "a deplorable state, sighing, groaning, talking to himself, and restlessly walking from room to room."[35] Boswell never draws any conclusions from these facts. To see himself as needed would have altered the balance between the two, and I suggest Boswell empathically knew it.

Relating the facts of Johnson's childhood experiences, Boswell depicts a sensitive, precociously brilliant boy, left, as we would see him now, extremely vulnerable to loneliness. His parents were elderly, and his father was subject to depressions. Johnson early demonstrated an ability to read and a prodigious memory, and his mother "knew her son's value." It was probably she who provided him with a target for his exuberances and childish excitements in the way that Tetty and other women did later. But Johnson was also a temperamental child who struggled with dependency in the same willful, spite-filled way he later demonstrated with patrons. From his father he received the formal framework for his ideals: High Church and Royalist, but I suspect he got little else of what he needed. We can conjecture that his childhood experiences, like those of most creatively gifted geniuses, were marked by heightened sensitivities to impressions of the world around him. Thus, confronted by an increased perceptiveness, he likely made an early intellectual effort to organize and cope with his sensitivity. At the same time, he probably experienced a desperate need to sense others as sharing in and responding to his extraordinary powers. As he sensed himself as perceiving and conceptualizing experiences in ways that marked him as unusual, he had two possible reactions. He could either accept this distinction, adding intensely to his grandiosity; or he could deny it and build up a false self-image of "normalcy" as a defense against the danger of isolation. Boswell describes Johnson as always having been aware of his "superiority over his fellows," of gaining such deference for his "liberal assistance" in their lessons "that three of the boys . . . used to come in the morning as his humble attendants and carry him to school." In fact, many of his experiences were bound to have left him with painful feelings of deflation and isolation. He was an awkwardly oversized boy, badly scarred by scrofula, and with eye-sight so defective he was prevented "from enjoying the common sports."[36]

Thus Johnson was left to cope with a personal sense of often being an isolated outsider in the world of children and, I suggest, with little sense that his melancholic, unsuccessful father had qualities of un-derstanding and accomplishment that the son could take pride in. Denied the opportunity to idealize his father, the young genius would have less chance to gain a perspective on his unquestionably high ability and uniqueness. He would be subjected to a marked tendency toward an unchecked egocentricity and to an extreme con-flict with guilt, arising from his domination of his father, both in the sexual sphere with his mother and in the intellectual sphere from the accolades he won. Johnson was to struggle with this kind of guilt over his successes all his life. He could not resist exerting his dominance, nor could he gain a perspective on the costs. Boswell knew this weak-ness of Johnson's above all others and never, never added to John-son's guilt and humiliation. Boswell describes a touching interchange when Johnson was seventy-four, a year before his death. Johnson, through his habitual boorish insensitivity had just worn out his wel-come in the home in which he lived as honored guest and had just called one of his oldest friends a vain liar. He mused, "I wonder how I should have any enemies, for I do harm to nobody?" Boswell jocularly answered, "In the first place, Sir, you will be pleased to recollect, that you set out with attacking the Scotch; so you got a whole nation for your enemies." Even this good-natured repetition of a familiar riposte was too much for Boswell. He added a footnote to give his real answer: Johnson's "reflection was very natural in a man of a good heart, who was not conscious of any ill-will to mankind, though the sharp sayings which were sometimes produced by his discriminations and vivacity . . . were, I am afraid, too often remem-bered with resentment."[37]

When he told Boswell to keep a journal, Johnson had uncon-sciously made him the recorder of his *inner* self. The marvel is that this biography, which was intended to tell all on the surface about one man, really tells in depth about two men: the one a genius whose intellectual brilliance dominated his age; the second a master biog-rapher-companion whose empathic sensitivity gave him entree into sharing the most significant secret about the other. This secret, which

Boswell conveys to his reader, was that, in spite of boorishness and pomposity, exhibitionism and sarcasm, a depressive illness and all manners of neurotic peculiarities, Johnson was a man of such vitality and fortitude of spirit that "the more his character is considered, the more he will be regarded . . . with admiration and reverence."[38]

## V.

I believe I have supported the view that Plutarch, Augustine, Cellini, and Boswell wrote biographies that were rich in psychological understanding long before psychoanalysis contributed its special insights to our age. Eugene O'Neill expressed a similar opinion. In an indignant response to a critic's accusation that he patterned a play too closely on psychoanalytic concepts, O'Neill noted that authors were psychologists, and profound ones, before psychology was invented. Nonetheless, the discoveries of psychoanalysis have increased our knowledge of vast realms of human mental life. It might be assumed, then, that a linear progression in the quality of biography would result from the advent of psychoanalysis. If the unsystematic application of the traditional biographer's gift of empathy for his subject and intuition in selecting his materials could be augmented by the systematic insights and methods of investigation of the psychoanalyst, the results would be a more complete, true, and pleasing biographical portrayal. Regrettably, this optimistic expectation has not been fulfilled. The traditional approach of the biographer and the methods of the psychoanalyst do not complement one another in any simple fashion.

Following Freud's frequently used metaphor comparing the psychoanalyst to the archaeologist, it could be said that the psychoanalyst is like a visitor describing what he has learned during a lengthy stay in Greece by writing all about the Mycenaeans and Minoans and nothing about the contemporary people. But the "archaeological" fascination of psychoanalysis with the "forgotten past" of the individual and with the influence on mental life of the "deepest strata" of the unconscious is not the principal barrier to the augmentation of traditional biography by its new insights. In fact, with the progression of time, psychoanalysts have steadily broadened their research into all areas of life that would interest the biographer and his reader.

A difficulty in integrating psychoanalytic insights and the empathic-intuitive biographical tradition lies in the fact that the origins of psychoanalysis lie in the scientific ethos of the nineteenth and twentieth centuries. The divergence between biography and psychoanalysis is, I suggest, not best described by the archaeological metaphor: the approaches differ not in "depth," but in their differing uses of information. The scientific archaeologist measures and classifies the "strata" and usually invents a whole technical vocabulary for describing his findings. In the long run he will attempt to re-create a "humanistic" view of the civilization he is studying, but in the age of science he might feel the same sense of restraint of his "romanticism" that Freud vividly described. Freud wrote apologetically that his case histories and his psychoanalytic study of Leonardo read like novels that might stimulate the "private delectation" of the curious or salacious. His concern was not limited to his high regard for the confidentiality of his patients' private communications or the esteem for his subject. It extended, I believe, to a fear that he might be exceeding the bounds of "science" and the scientific method.

Freud recognized that, within the humanistic tradition that ran parallel to the growing scientific ethos, conceptions similar to his were made by speculative iconoclastic geniuses, such as Arthur Schopenhauer and Friedrich Nietzsche; and for a long time, he avoided reading them to keep his "mind unembarrassed."

The technical language of psychoanalysis served the explicit purpose of defining and delineating Freud's novel discoveries, but borrowed as it was from the vocabulary of the physical sciences, "psychoanalese" gave a feeling of being securely wedded to the method of observation, data collecting, and theory formation at differing levels of abstraction. Consequently, a reader of the voluminous literature of psychoanalysis can easily form the impression that a description of a human characteristic under investigation is not complete until a scientifically "impressive" label has been applied. Carried over into biography, such a misapprehension could lead a biographer or a reader to believe that such labeling is required in a "modern" biography. In Freud's own writing, a dichotomy exists between his case histories with their beautifully clear "telling of a life," albeit circumscribed and specific in purpose, and his theoretical writings with their more technical language. It might be assumed that a modern biography was to be an expanded "case history"—giving all the data of the "neurosis"—a form satirically appropriated for *Portnoy's Complaint*. Or it could be reasoned that the language of psychoanalytic theory carries a special value outside its own technical area and, sprinkled through a biography, adds "depth" of understanding.

The writings about and by Eugene O'Neill can be used to describe the divergent currents that prevent a smooth confluence between biography and psychoanalysis. On one side there is an intrusion into traditional biography of science's insistence on "facts"; this is of course not a new issue in biography, as Plutarch noted in his argument about the "so-called rules of chronology." In its present form, this influence leads to the journalistic style of presentation used by Arthur and Barbara Gelb in their biography *O'Neill*. It is highly readable, breezy, and extremely informative. The Gelbs painstakingly conducted interviews, dug up old newspaper clippings, knew thoroughly all of O'Neill's extensive writings, and researched the source of the characters in his plays with the skill of reporter-detectives. The Gelbs, of course, are familiar with psychoanalysis and undoubtedly were guided by its precepts in their search for details about O'Neill's early life experiences. For the most part, however, for the Gelbs, "fascinating and valid as is the psychiatric insight," what a psychoanalyst has to say about O'Neill is just one more fact to be reported.[39] They neither avail themselves of the insights of current depth psychology to contribute a point of view to their biography, nor entrap themselves in a confusing misuse of its vocabulary or a misapplication of the precepts. However, such an eschewing of the psychologically probing inquiry carries the danger in biography of superficiality of presentation, no matter how interesting the facts or how well written the text. Thus a biography must be more than journalism in depth. It must express a point of view. If the portrait is to come alive, the biographer must express a creatively unique awareness of an aspect of his subject.

The Gelbs shine when they talk about the theater—they know the worth of their man in relation to his life work, and they depict it in a way that carries authority. They employ O'Neill's own psychological vocabulary in a straightforward way to convey their meaning . Speaking of *Desire under the Elms*, they state: "The play was a tremendous advance over his previous full-length works—far surpassing the power of either *Beyond the Horizon* or *Anna Christie*, to which it was linked by its naturalistic style. It combined all the elements most typical of O'Neill at his creative best: the crude, elemental passions of people who harbor the seeds of their own destruction; the brilliant psychological insight into the love-hate relationship of father and son, husband and wife, brother and brother; the cosmic loneliness of man; the hardness of God; and the final acceptance of an inescapable fate."[40]

A reader of these lines and the Gelbs' biography may find it strange that I say the Gelbs do not avail themselves of the insights of depth psychology to give a coherence or order to their "Life of O'Neill." Every page abounds, in fact, with references to motivation, conscious and unconscious; to emotions; to complicated relationships; and to mental illness. This is the result not of the integration of psycho-analytic insights into biography, but of the popularization of a diluted version of its tenets. Throughout the twentieth century, ideas about motivations have become as much the property of every man as the idea of gravity after Newton. A report of a life today is of necessity a report of motivation; it can't be otherwise since that is how the literate society of today thinks. O'Neill contributed much to this situation. He took his own tendency toward persistent, excoriating introspection, applied to that painful skill the tool of "self-analysis" borrowed from the Freudian intellectual movement, and, through his genius, exter-nalized the products into drama after drama, thus adding to the world's repertoire of "psychologizing." In *Strange Interludes,* O'Neill has the biological father of an eleven-year-old boy, raised as the son of another man, say to the child's mother (sardonically): "Perhaps he realizes subconsciously that I am his father, his rival in your love, but I'm not his father ostensibly, there are no taboos, so he can come right out and hate me to his heart's content."[41]

O'Neill repeatedly stated that his reading of Freud was very lim-ited (and he preferred C. G. Jung—his masks and archetypes). He claimed that whatever Freudianisms appeared in his plays "must have walked right in through my subconscious."[42] What O'Neill was referring to by his denial that he appropriated Freud's ideas, was that as a keen, empathic, introspective observer he wrote about people, especially himself, as he saw them. What must be added is that he could not possibly observe and portray those people, and especially himself, without thinking "psychoanalytically." But O'Neill could claim that he depicted his characters with an originality of insight completely independent of any "formulation," that he used his own powers of discerning hidden human motives to create dramas from each period of his life and finally to write his "authentic" autobiogra-phy in play form (*Long Day's Journey into Night*). In the writings of the autobiographical dramatist O'Neill and in the biography of the Gelbs, the "surface" has been transformed by psychoanalysis, acting as a dominant ethos of our time, just as in the other biographies the mode of presenting the person's character and mental state was determined by a dominant ethos of that time.

With a few exceptions, the professional psychoanalyst has confined his biographical efforts to a special genre—the "psychoanalytic biographical study," part biography in the traditional sense and part exploratory scientific endeavor. The psychoanalytic biographical study takes up facts about the subject and his field of endeavor and uses the information—not only to add to knowledge about the subject's life, as in biography, but to broaden the understanding of a psychological riddle, such as the interplay between intrapsychic conflict and creativity. The author of such a study has an advantage over the traditional biographer in that he can focus on one or another aspect of his subject—his goal is to explore a selected limited question fully. This specificity of aim becomes clear in three studies on O'Neill. In *O'Neill's Conscious and Unconscious Autobiographical Dramas*, Philip Weissman states that he will study the "specific features of O'Neill's oedipal conflict as reflected in his life, his choice of profession, and his writings." Weissman's technique is to compare two of O'Neill's plays, *Desire under the Elms* and *Long Day's Journey into Night*. *Desire under the Elms*, "an unconscious biography," grew out of a "healthy and creative era." *Long Day's Journey*, O'Neill's conscious autobiography, was the result of a period in which O'Neill was "neurotically disturbed in the sphere of the sublimated exhibitionistic and libidinal aims of communication to the world."[43]

Albert Rothenberg's "The Iceman Changeth: Toward an Empirical Approach to Creativity" proposes "to present some methodological problems involved in the study of creativity and suggest an empirical approach." Rothenberg selects O'Neill's *The Iceman Cometh* as a vehicle to test his experimental design. "The actual study of the creative process will focus on the development of the symbol of the iceman, which is a central creation of the play." He uses as a special methodology for studying the development of the symbol, a careful examination of revisions in O'Neill's successive manuscripts, regarding the revisions "as minute creations and potential indicators of unconscious struggle."[44]

Joseph and Charlotte Lichtenberg, in "Eugene O'Neill and Falling in Love," attempt to relate the phase of falling in love of late adolescence and early adulthood to O'Neill's creativity. "A major premise of this study is that while O'Neill could and did experience a strong sense of being in love heterosexually and while he could convey the urge for this affective state with dramatic effectiveness in his plays, personal conflicts which he could not overcome barred his way to the fulfillment of falling in love; that is, to the development of a mature stable relationship with a love object."[45] To illustrate this thesis, they select three plays: *Mourning Becomes Electra*, a major tragic depiction of all the "conflicts that can inhibit and destroy the most ardent urge to love and be loved"; *Ah, Wilderness!*, a whimsical, convincing portrayal of the adolescent love state; and *Days without End*, a semi-religious play that completely fails to convey problems arising from a mature object relationship—a state outside O'Neill's personal experience and his empathic range.

Infidelity, a major issue in O'Neill's life and a consistent theme in his plays, is treated differently in each of the studies. Weissman describes the intricate pattern of shifting fidelity and betrayal as a manifestation of O'Neill's "positive" strivings for his mother and of his "negative" oedipal, passive homosexual strivings for his father. He connects the pattern in O'Neill's life—especially that of O'Neill's "forgetting" his brief first marriage to the defensive forgetting depicted for both mother and son in *Long Day's Journey*. Rothenberg traces the complex relation of the iceman symbol and infidelity. Frequency of revisions of the manuscript center on these two concepts. Rothenberg suggests that O'Neill's personal preoccupation with infidelity at the time of writing the *Iceman* led to multiple small interferences with his aesthetic capacity. He suggests that O'Neill, like Hickey the main character, wanted his wife to be unfaithful to relieve him of guilt for an actual or fantasied infidelity. He adds the possibility of the intrusion of an unconscious desire on O'Neill's part of vicarious homosexual gratification through the wife's infidelity.

The Lichtenbergs detail the psychological meaning of O'Neill's first marriage. They connect O'Neill's guilt over his abandonment of his first wife and child to the pattern of his guilt over childhood conflicts, to his inability to do more than fantasy the fulfillment of love and marriage, and to his need to find self-realization as a creative artist. They take up the specific theme of infidelity as it appears in *Days without End*, where the entire interaction between husband and wife turns on a single act of unfaithfulness on the husband's part. They suggest that the aesthetic failure of the play arises from the involvement of the characters in passions too far removed from people interacting—they are too self-involved. They postulate that the central place occupied in the play by religion and by the passion over a single sexual act suggests the conflicts sensitive adolescents with strict Catholic backgrounds often develop over masturbation—the adolescent O'Neill may have believed that the inability to control his sexual urges (that is, his infidelity to his early religious tenets) was the cause of tragedies to himself and others.

This brief sketch of three psychoanalytic biographical studies indicates two main features. First, they are very different from conventional biographies, in that biographical data occupy the background while a specific psychological purpose or premise is brought forward. Second, the studies differ among themselves. In Weissman's, the focus is on oedipal conflicts, and the later life experiences are connected to the love, rivalry, identifications, anxiety, and guilt of the childhood period. In Rothenberg's, the focus shifts to a more scientific level of abstraction. The creative process itself is being studied. The knowledge gained from O'Neill's life and works, from psychoanalytic formulation, and from the application of a special technique for screening manuscripts makes up the conceptual input for a broad experimental design. The Lichtenbergs focus on a specific line of development, the forward thrust of those urges related to falling in love in late adolescence and early adulthood.

Comparing Weissman's emphasis on childhood oedipal conflicts and that of the Lichtenbergs on adolescence, we can see another problem affecting the coming together of biography and psychoanalysis: the focus of the psychoanalyst keeps changing with the relatively rapid shifts in the main field of psychoanalytic inquiry. The central hypotheses in psychoanalysis began with an emphasis on external trauma, then shifted to conflicts based on fantasies arising from instinctual drives. Psychoanalytic theory at one time centered on delineating conscious and unconscious systems, later on assessing the interplay of functional groupings (id, ego, superego), and more recently on object relations theories. As the emphasis shifted so did the position of the psychoanalyst, oscillating between that of an "outside" observer of behavior to an empathic senser of inner feelings. The specific experiences most under observation at different times have been the adult neurotic, the oedipal child, latency, the adolescent, the preoedipal child, the preverbal infant, the late adolescent, the early adult, and the adult in the later-life crises. All of this kaleidoscopic movement must have a dizzying effect on the non-psychoanalyst biographer, however responsive. And yet the studies that have been made by psychoanalysts in each of these shifting phases have fascinated readers—professional and nonprofessional—and will continue to do so. The readers of Freud's study of Leonardo, Princess Marie Bonaparte's book on Poe, Richard and Editha Sterba's work on Beethoven, Phyllis Greenacre's study of Swift and Carroll, Erik Erikson on Luther, Kurt Eissler on Goethe, Bernard Meyer on Conrad, and John Mack on T. E. Lawrence will find some differences in the approach each has taken but a capacity for explanation that is astounding.[46] How can this be? Is it like a magic trick in which things seem to fit together although the "fit" is really an illusion? I think not. Human experience is so complex and so overdetermined that multiple explanations are not only possible but necessary; and the "instrument" of psychoanalysis, the empathic-intuitive blending together of facts from the biographical data in the background, a specific play or dream or fantasy in the foreground, with the knowledge gained from psychoanalytic therapy of how humans experience crises, is so powerful a method that it has furnished analytic biographers with the means to penetrate deeply into the mysteries of the mind.

But of course every explanation is not of equal value. In my review of Kligerman's article, I noted that Augustine offered his own reasoning, Kligerman his, and I mine. It is as though when one looked at any creation of the human mind, one saw within it a series of "structures," each calling for an explanation and an interconnecting, one with the other. One regards a play, and one sees within it the portrayal of "people" and observes that the compositional structure, the plot, has a complex matrix, a major psychodynamic pattern that gives the play its power. Then one regards the creator of the work, the playwright, and sees in his life a complex sequence of experiences and, within that life, a major psychodynamic pattern that gives it a sense of continuity. Then one recognizes that between the pattern of the writer's life and the pattern of his play a complex interrelation exists that explains the particulars of his actualizing his creative urge. The psychoanalytic biographer may then identify an ascendant intrapsychic conflict that existed at the time of writing that explains why this play by this man at this time. The way a contemporary observer conceptualizes a "structure" of this complexity is subject to faulty explanation, of course. The limitations call forth no amazement; our relative success does. But even the attempt is possible only because

Freud opened the way to "sense out" both the pattern of the whole life and the moment in the life and the mental activity of that moment, the dream, the slip, the falling in love, the hating, the symptom, or, in the instance of the creative act, the brilliant idea and its mode of execution; to sense out by a mix of empathic feel and intuitively used knowledge. We then test one idea against another. Sometimes it is to prove one wrong and the other right, but more often it is to prove one more apt than the other.

An example, from Louis Shaeffer's two-volume biography of O'Neill will illustrate the problem of the relative "fit" of competing explanations. Skillfully utilizing his background as a newspaperman and a theatrical publicist, Shaeffer has written a biography that is a well-documented, beautifully organized, chronological detailing of O'Neill's life and artistry. More than the Gelbs, Shaeffer attempts to explain in psychological terms the major inner conflicts that colored O'Neill's personal experience and propelled the thematic lines of his plays. Taking his stand against the view offered by O'Neill in his "authentic" autobiography, Long Day's Journey—that his principal psychological motivations were for him to be at war with his cheapskate father and to be worried, protective, and guilty about his mother—Shaeffer believes that "the bulk of evidence indicates that, basically, he loved his father and was hostile toward his mother."[47] In support, Shaeffer offers much the same evidence as would a professional psychoanalyst. But the best use of psychoanalytic knowledge requires the practitioner to be not only well informed but to maintain the psychoanalytic perspective of empathic, concerned, nonjudgmental objectivity. Although he achieved an open, unprejudiced view of O'Neill's relation to his parents, Shaeffer faltered badly when he became so outraged at O'Neill's egregious behavior toward his second wife and children that he could not view O'Neill's feelings and actions empathically.

For example, at one critical point in his life O'Neill wanted Agnes, his second wife, to accompany him on an anxiety-provoking trip. For practical reasons, she chose to remain in Bermuda with their two children. Shaeffer reports, "after a single day in New York, O'Neill, who had looked forward to a change of scene, felt utterly depressed." O'Neill writes to Agnes, "and I tell you again, you have made a mistake. It is when I'm sick in the bargain." In the background was O'Neill's to-be third wife, Carlotta, whose idealization of him was a source of irresistible temptation. O'Neill developed an impulse to scream, extreme nervousness, and an overall feeling of fatigue and depletion, as well as a suspicion that Agnes was having an affair. His letters became more importuning and full of warnings. To Shaeffer, O'Neill sounds a "spurious note, as though he was flagging himself to express his grievance with the utmost vehemence." Shaeffer explains O'Neill's distress as an example of his self-flagellating, his defensive grudge holding and rationalizing. Shaeffer could not comprehend that O'Neill could really *feel* abandoned. Shaeffer could only see a wife who objectively had not *really* deserted him. But Shaeffer could not understand that O'Neill regarded Agnes as a preoedipal, narcissistically perceived selfobject—part of himself who was failing to fulfill her function to protect her vulnerable husband from fragmentation of his cohesive sense of self. Unable to empathize with O'Neill's inner state of vulnerability of loss of self-cohesion, Shaeffer sees O'Neill's whole response to this major crisis in his life as that of a self-dramatizing, masochistic child.[48]

## VI.

To return to my main theme: the relation between biography and psychoanalysis is complex. The biographer of today needs the insights of depth psychology to present a balance between the externals of the subject's life and his inner experience. The psychoanalyst does not make this easy for the biographer; his link to science pulls against the roots they share in a humanistic approach; his specialized language makes him difficult to understand; his focus on differing levels of abstraction invites a faulty application of his insights and the changes in the weight given to his modes of explanation as his theories change and enlarge are at least temporarily confusing to even the most erudite biographer. As an example of his problem, I have repeatedly applied concepts about the "narcissistic" line of development to both biographers and psychoanalytic studies written before the recent insights into this aspect of mental development. These have, I believe, proved especially applicable to the areas under consideration here—the creatively talented people who write biographies and autobiographies and the creatively talented people they generally choose to write about. The developments that center on feelings of self-worth, self-esteem, and self-realization, as well as the idealized qualities of others with whom they are in intimate contact, are important for all humans. For the creatively endowed, these developments are crucial.

I hope I have demonstrated that the intuitive knowledge of these and other singular "discoveries" made by psychoanalysis was present in biographies before their formal recognition. But the exposition by psychoanalysis of the complexity of mental life, of human feelings conscious and unconscious, and of the ever-present influence of the child's "solutions" to the adult's adaptations presents the field of biography with a problem of integration and a challenge that cannot be resisted. The biographies written by psychoanalysts present valuable contributions by the clinically trained specialist to the ancient tradition of the writing of "lives." Alternatively, Leon Edel's comprehensive biography of Henry James demonstrates the literary biographer's thorough knowledge of his subject's life and work and the respect for the biographer's craft, synthesized with a deep appreciation for dynamic conflict.[49]

Though I believe the paths of biography and psychoanalysis intersect, they do not and should not converge. The great biographers of the past created their masterworks from a unity of knowledge, which they then shared with the reader. The psychoanalyst is, however, basically not one who knows, but one who asks. His greatest contributions derive from his origins in the scientific tradition. He explores from the known into the fringe areas where discoveries can be made. In each instance, with his patients, his biographical subject, and his theorizing, he conducts an inquiry. Supported by his prior knowledge, he attempts to reduce the realm of the incomprehensible bit by bit. The informed biographer profits by the psychoanalyst's penetrating insights. But the old concept expressed in a term little used today—"the mysteries of the soul"—remains the core of what the great biography *conveys* and what the great psychoanalytic study *asks* about. To the extent that a profound enigma of man was penetrable, the great biographers "knew": the virtues of political leadership that inspire; the mystic quality of religion that leads to and follows from a conversion; the inspiration and push of creative artistry; and the awesome force of enormous learning and penetrating, moralizing wit. Gradually, these secrets of man probably will become subject to a level of explanation by the powerful research potential of the psychoanalytic method. But so many "mysteries of the soul" remain that psychoanalysts must persist in their plodding questioning for a long time to come. The biographer, I feel, is well advised to appreciate that his own great humanistic heritage is based on a knowledge of mankind integrated with the ethos of his time and that, with the advent of psychoanalysis, the new insights into man's psychological development have changed that ethos. The bridge or point of interaction lies in the sharing of a conscious and unconscious empathic-introspective-intuitive approach. Psychoanalysis and biography have much to share and much to respect in the uniquely creative contribution of each other.

## NOTES

[1]For a thorough review of contemporary studies of psychoanalysis and biography see Leon Edel, "The Biography and Psychoanalysis," *International Journal of Psycho-Analysis* 42 (1957): 458–466; Heinz Kohut, "Beyond the Bounds of the Basic Rule," *Journal of the American Psychoanalytic Association* 8 (1960): 567–586; John Mack, "Psychoanalysis and Historical Biography," *Journal of the American Psychoanalytic Association* 19 (1971): 143–179; and John E. Gedo, "The Methodology of Psychoanalytic Biography," *Journal of the American Psychoanalytic Association* 21 (1972): 638–649.

[2]Plutarch, *The Rise and Fall of Athens*, trans. I. Scott-Kilvert (Baltimore: Penguin Books, 1973); Augustine, *The Confessions of Saint Augustine*, trans. E. B. Pusey (New York: Collier Books, 1972); Benvenuto Cellini, *The Life of Benvenuto/The Son of Giovanni Cellini*, trans. G. Bull (Baltimore: Penguin Books, 1973); James Boswell, *The Life of Samuel Johnson*, ed. and abr. with an intro. by F. Brady (New York: New American Library, 1968).

[3]Charles Kligerman, "A Psychoanalytic Study of the 'Confessions' of St. Augustine," *Journal of the American Psychoanalytic Association* 5 (1957): 469–484.

[4]Eugene O'Neill, "A Strange Interlude," in *The Plays of Eugene O'Neill* (New York: Random House, 1928); Arthur Gelb and Barbara Gelb, *O'Neill* (New York: Harper, 1960); Philip Weissman, *O'Neill's Conscious and Unconscious Autobiographical Dramas* (New York: Basic Books, 1957); Albert Rothenberg, "The Iceman Changeth: Toward an Empirical Approach to Creativity," *Journal of the American Psychoanalytic Association* 17 (1969): 549–607; Joseph Lichtenberg and Charlotte Lichtenberg, "Eugene O'Neill and Falling in Love," *Psychoanalytic Quarterly* 41 (1971): 63–89; and Louis Shaeffer, *O'Neill: Son and Playwright* (Boston: Little, Brown, 1968) and *O'Neill: Son and Artist* (Boston: Little, Brown, 1975).

[5]Plutarch, *Athens*, pp. 165–166.

[6]Kohut, "Basic Rule."

[7]Kligerman, "St. Augustine."

[8]Cellini, *Life*, p. 332.

[9]Kligerman, "St. Augustine." For a few examples, see Sigmund Freud,

"Leonardo da Vinci and a Memory of His Childhood," in *Standard Edition of the Complete Psychological Works*, ed. and trans. James Strachey, vol. 11 (London: Hogarth Press, 1957), pp. 59–138; Marie Bonaparte, *The Life and Works of Edgar Allan Poe: A Psychoanalytic Interpretation* (London: Imago, 1949); David Beres, "A Dream, a Vision, and a Poem," *International Journal of Psycho-Analysis* 32 (1951): 97–116; Phyllis Greenacre, *Swift and Carroll: A Psychoanalytic Study of Two Lives* (New York: International Universities Press, 1955); Erik Erikson, *Young Man Luther* (New York: Norton, 1958); and Bernard Meyer, *Joseph Conrad: A Psychoanalytic Biography* (Princeton: Princeton University Press, 1967).

[10]Kligerman, "St. Augustine," p. 478.

[11]Ibid., p. 475.

[12]Ibid., p. 483.

[13]Ibid., pp. 469, 483–484.

[14]Augustine, *Confessions*, pp. 30–32.

[15]Ibid., pp. 75, 106–110.

[16]Ibid., p. 11.

[17]Plutarch, *Athens*, pp. 143, 10.

[18]Ibid., pp. 17–18, 189, 149.

[19]Ibid., pp. 47, 111.

[20]Ibid., pp. 165, 64, 118, 79, 63, 49.

[21]Ibid., pp. 48, 62.

[22]Ibid., pp. 91, 170.

[23]Ibid., p. 183.

[24]The absence of psychological kinds of inquiry can at first glance be explained by the emphasis of the Age of Reason on a strict separation between the rational: virtue, wisdom, and morality; and the irrational: aberrations of nature not to be further considered. However, Boswell was fully acquainted with another movement represented by David Hume, John Locke, and Laurence Sterne; in their writings, associations and links to sexuality and the "irrational" had been forged. So Boswell's approach was a matter of choice, and, as I will show, a choice he was required to make in order to be the man he was to Johnson, and a choice Johnson made himself in order to preserve his fragile sense of self-cohesion against the constant danger of fragmentation.

[25]Boswell, *Samuel Johnson*, pp. 131, 172–173.

[26]Ibid., p. 9.

[27]Ibid., pp. 135, 181, 111.

[28]Ibid., p. 59.

[29]Ibid., p. 136.

[30]Ibid., p. 279.

[31]See Bernard Meyer, "Some Reflections on the Contribution of Psycho-analysis to Biography," in *Psychoanalysis and Contemporary Science*, vol. 1, ed. Robert R. Holt and Emanuel Peterfreund (New York: Macmillan, 1972) pp. 373–391. In writing about Joseph Conrad's relations with Ford Mattox Hueffer, he has used Conrad's title to describe this special alliance as "The Secret Sharer." Meyer cites not only Conrad and Hueffer, but Nathaniel Hawthorne and Herman Melville, Samuel Coleridge and William Words-worth (see Beres, "Dream, Vision, Poem"), Gustave Flaubert and Guy de Maupassant. Of Maupassant, Meyer writes that, thirty years younger, he provided the unmarried and childless Flaubert with a protégé and a disciple, filling a void at a time when Flaubert was suffering keenly over a succession of deaths.

[32]Boswell, *Samuel Johnson*, p. 136.

[33]Ibid., pp. 147, 169.

[34]Ibid., p. 85. Johnson had suffered his first serious depression at age twenty at a time when his father had had serious financial reverses and the young Sam had few good prospects. His father died when he was twenty-two. His only sibling, his younger brother, died at age twenty-five, and his wife Tetty died when he was forty-three.

[35]Ibid., p. 172. It is interesting to note that, after Johnson's death, Boswell himself was spurred to an immediate creative effort: his *Journal of a Tour to the Hebrides*. During the writing of Johnson's life, however, he bogged down in depression and dissipation until prodded on by the supportive assistance of a secret sharer of his own, the Shakespearean scholar Edmond Malone.

[36]Ibid., pp. 35–40.

[37]Ibid., p. 573.

[38]Ibid., p. 663. These are the closing lines of the biography.

[39]Gelb and Gelb, *O'Neill*, p. 539.

[40]Ibid., p. 538.

[41]O'Neill, "Strange Interlude," p. 143.

[42]Gelb and Gelb, *O'Neill*, p. 577.

[43]Weissman, "O'Neill's Dramas," p. 113.

[44]Rothenberg, "Iceman Changeth," pp. 549, 554, 563.

[45]Lichtenberg and Lichtenberg, "O'Neill and Love," pp. 63–65.

[46]In addition to the works by Freud, Bonaparte, Greenacre, Erikson, Meyer, and Mack (all cited earlier), see Richard Sterba and Editha Sterba, *Beethoven and His Nephew* (New York: Pantheon, 1960); and Kurt Eissler, *Goethe: A Psychoanalytic Study* (Detroit: Wayne State University Press, 1963).

[47]Shaeffer, *O'Neill: Son and Artist*, p. 134.

[48]Ibid., pp. 258, 263.

[49]Edel, "Biography and Psychoanalysis."

Collaborative
Explorations of
the Biographical
Process with
George Moraitis

3

# A Psychoanalyst's Journey
# into a Historian's World:
# An Experiment in Collaboration

George Moraitis

I.

DURING THE LAST FEW YEARS I have had the privilege of working with
several historians who have offered me the opportunity to see their
laboratory and to examine the product of their work long before it is
ready for publication.[1] The discussions that these collaborative efforts
generate go well beyond a simple exchange of ideas between a psychoanalyst and a historian. They seem to produce an intense affective
response, the presence of which indicates the strength of the psychological forces operating behind the ideas exchanged. This experience
has directed my attention to the process of historical investigations,
and I have attempted to study it in a more systematic way and to
integrate it with the basic method and principles of psychoanalysis.
The historian's work is long and laborious. It involves extensive study
of many years' duration. He develops his ideas gradually and formu-
lates his findings many times before he produces his final product.
This involved process generates powerful psychological reactions
that grossly affect his life in general and change his perception of
himself and the world he lives in. When finally the historian presents
his findings to us, he exposes not simply an opinion, but a good deal

Reprinted by permission from *The Annual of Psychoanalysis,* ed. Chicago Institute for
Psychoanalysis, ed. Chicago Institute for Psychoanalysis, Vol. 7 (New York: International Universities Press, 1979), pp. 287–320.

of his personal and professional sense of self. Although we very seldom have reasons to doubt his honesty, as psychoanalysts we should know better than to take the story presented to us at face value. Looking at the historian as the instrument of the historical investigation, it is reasonable to assume that the effectiveness of the instrument will grossly influence the quality of the work.

In entering into a collaboration with the historian, I attempt to study the development of his creativity, being well aware that my presence will not only allow me to observe this process, but will also affect it. On the one hand, I pay attention to the historian's line of thinking and study some of the material that has been the basis on which the ideas have developed, whereas, on the other, I observe the collaborative process itself and the emotional responses of both participants within it. The basic objective is to facilitate the historian's capacity to master the complexities of the issues involved and make him more aware of the influence of his own personality on his ideas in general and his basic thesis in particular. Furthermore, I attempt to facilitate his capacity to define the boundaries of his investigation more clearly and bring his work to a successful conclusion.

I am reporting here on the first example of such a collaboration and hope that other reports will follow before too long. The structure and the procedure followed in these collaborations are flexible, but my basic aim is the study of creativity by directly observing the unfolding creative process. This process should facilitate the historian's capacity to master the complexities of the issues involved and make him more aware of the influence of his own personality on his ideas in general and the basic thesis in particular. All historical investigations are subject to such influences which have been generated as a result of the investigator's intense involvement with his subject and his deep concern about the response of his readers. Psychological reactions of this kind operate for the most part below the level of the investigator's conscious awareness and, according to our hypothesis, could within limits be explored through a collaborative process that involves the participation of the psychoanalyst within the boundaries of a specific role.

In testing this hypothesis we proceed with the understanding that the historian and I have entered into a collaboration in which each one is an expert in his own field only. We meet on a more or less regular basis for a two- to three-hour session, in a setting that is natural and unpretentious, but has several elements of the psycho-analytic session in the sense that anecdotal comments and personal reactions are invited. It is different from it, however, because there is an agenda to be discussed, and specific questions are to be raised. During the interview, my task is to penetrate the thought process of the investigator and to observe closely the emotional responses of both participants. Although I am aware that to an extent all these responses could be under the influence of personality conflicts, I carefully avoid any interpretive role along these lines, so that the whole project will not derail from its basic goal.

I consider associations—not only what my collaborator tells me, but the reading material he assigns to me as well. To facilitate the free nature of these associations I do not accept reading lists. The time limitation that this restriction involves puts some pressure on my collaborator to establish priorities and make selections between what is more urgent to discuss and what is less so. Such a choice is deter-mined by conscious and unconscious motives which will be gradually revealed as the process unfolds. In working with the historian I con-sider myself a guest, and him a host, and I invite him to introduce me to the area of his study in whatever way he considers most feasible. At the beginning of the project I asked the historian to express ideas freely and to convey his feelings about his subject with as little editing as possible. This directive had the quality of a modified version of the free-association rule and is in contrast to the rules of a well-disci-plined academic exchange. It is quite essential for any historian par-ticipating in such a project to be sufficiently involved with his subject matter to experience a sense of professional and emotional commit-ment. In order to achieve that, he must have spent the necessary time studying his subject and be well acquainted with the major publica-tions in the field. Most likely, he would also be either working toward or about to complete an original piece of work.

Such a scholar has probably assumed a certain thesis which he feels the need to test. The more committed the historian is to his thesis, the more strongly he feels the need to defend and protect it. Our collaboration here will be grossly enhanced not only by the histo-rian's capacity for commitment, but also by his capacity to be flexible in the presence of new observations. There are significant differences of attitude among historians depending on the degree of commitment to their theses and the nature of this commitment. When the historian is entrenched in his position because of personal and professional investments, the work of the psychoanalyst—collaborator can become extremely complicated. It can be equally difficult if the historian very quickly abandons his thesis for another as the process unfolds.

Deeper understanding of the historian's thesis will clarify the nature of the investigator's commitment and identify to whom this commitment has been made. This understanding will make clearer the motivation behind the historical inquiry and the particular audience the historian wants to address. It is important to keep in mind that the historian works not only for himself; he works primarily to inform others. Although he is not always conscious of the degree to which the anticipated reader has affected his work, a careful examination of the writing process consistently reveals the presence of a continuous "dialogue" between author and reader. Consciously, the author may perceive the reader as an anonymous group which escapes definition, but on a deeper and less conscious level the reader is represented by the selected few whose opinions and responses, real or imagined, will decisively influence the outcome of the investigation and the conclusions that will be reached.

In this experiment I am making every effort to remain a real person in the eyes of the historian and to avoid analyzing and interpreting personal conflicts. Inevitably, however, transference reactions will develop which will affect the particular way the investigator views the collaborating psychoanalyst. These reactions differ basically from the ones encountered in the therapeutic situation in that the regression involved is minimal. Their presence, however, facilitates the understanding of the investigator's psychological reaction to his subject and the nature of his expectations and concerns about his readers.

The analyst's attitude toward the material under study needs consideration too. He may be so attracted to what he reads that his attention could be directed away from the historian and the historian's professional function. If the proposed methodological approach is to succeed, it is important for the psychoanalyst not to become a historian himself. The presence of two historians with two sets of ideas competing and debating with each other could easily derail the whole collaborative effort. It may be important for the psychoanalyst to observe certain safeguards, so that these undesirable developments can be prevented. He should maintain a certain neutrality and distance from the subject of the historian's investigation. Before entering into the collaborative work with the historian, the analyst should carefully examine his own personal involvement with the subject to be studied. As an educated man, he probably has some degree of familiarity with the person under scrutiny and the subject's productive work. If, however, he considers himself an expert in the field or has developed an unusually strong interest in the subject involving publications with a thesis of his own, then this analyst is not a suitable person to work with the historian within the guidelines of this methodological approach.

In this paper I will discuss my first attempt to test the effectiveness of the new method. The narrative of the experiment provided here is detailed enough to give the reader the opportunity to formulate his or her own opinions about the process. I hope, too, that it will provide sufficient support to the author's point of view. To add every possible safeguard against bias and distortion, a third person was added to the team, as an observer-consultant. His function was to observe the process from the proper distance, so that he could bring to the attention of the other two participants responses and reactions that they may not have been aware of, as well as possible areas of difficulty. The observer was kept informed of the deliberations between the analyst and the historian, and about the material assigned for study.

The introspective science of psychoanalysis requires all its practioners to undergo analysis themselves before they can analyze others. Personal analysis combined with individual supervision represents a form of scrutiny designed to reinforce the basic psychoanalytic principle that there can be no psychoanalytic investigation or therapy without introspection and self-knowledge.

In the field of psychohistory, the personal analysis of an investigator, as desirable as it may be, is not sufficient to prevent the misuse of psychoanalysis and its clinical concepts. The absence of a patient and his responses, combined with possible anticipated personal satisfaction, creates a situation lacking any external controls. The proposed method is designed to provide certain safeguards which should reinforce the investigator's self-analyzing capabilities in a way that is directly relevant to his work.

If the psychological exploration of history is to become a scholarly activity, the researcher must feel accountable not only for data but also for his own psychological reactions. A psychoanalytic collaborator could facilitate and reinforce whatever level of self-knowledge the investigator has achieved through other means and help him or her to apply it directly to the investigation.

## II.

The historian and I started our work very enthusiastically because we were both eager to experiment with the new method and to test its effectiveness. Since I knew that the historian's area of endeavor has primarily been the study of Friedrich Nietzsche's life, I had assumed that our focus would be on Nietzsche. To my surprise, I discovered that my collaborator was genuinely convinced that Nietzsche would not be a suitable subject for investigation. Instead, he proposed that we focus on German history of the nineteenth century, and on Otto von Bismarck in particular. He stated that his interest in Nietzsche was declining, and he probably would not pursue the subject after his dissertation was finished. The shift in focus disappointed me, and at the first opportunity I reminded the historian of the need to work on a subject to which he has already developed a significant commitment. Although I was prepared to discuss Bismarck, had the historian insisted that we do so (as a matter of fact I did some reading of Bismarck's biography in preparation for this), I was not going to proceed in that direction without some effort to convey to the historian that I thought he was advocating a mistake in focus.

During the second meeting, the historian produced a more psychological explanation for the objections he had expressed so far about studying Nietzsche. He said that working on Nietzsche all these years had given him the impression of a highly private and personal relationship which would be very difficult to share with a third person without the strong feeling of having been intruded upon. His statement made me identify his response as resistance, and it became even more evident to me that we should indeed focus on Nietzsche, if the methodological approach were to be tested. It may be easy, and at first glance convincing, to assume that the historian's reluctance to engage in discussion about Nietzsche was nothing but an intellectual issue. Yet if one considers the alternative suggestion he made, that of discussing Bismarck and the German nationalist movement, one may come to a better and more accurate view. The historian suggested that we study what Nietzsche strongly condemned, and especially a man for whom Nietzsche had contempt. I found it more reasonable to conclude that my collaborator's reluctance was motivated by resistance generated by his involvement with Nietzsche, and by the feeling he had transferred onto him.

The first structured interview with the historian further supported this notion. The reading assignment for that interview was Nietzsche's last piece of intellectual work, *Ecce Homo*—"Behold the Man"—which represents a form of autobiography written shortly before his collapse in 1890.[2] I found reading this book to be particularly exciting, despite the provocative and somewhat obnoxious tone of Nietzsche's writing. This book, as well as *Thus Spake Zarathustra*,[3] which we read somewhat later, produced a very powerful and positive emotional response in me toward Nietzsche's psychological sophistication. As I entered the interview full of excitement about the reading assignments, I was shocked to hear that the historian's first concern was about Nietzsche's honesty and his impression that Nietzsche had actually made himself ridiculous in that book. His concern about honesty was in direct contrast to what I experienced while reading the material and indicated a strong negative emotional response to Nietzsche as a person. The biographer elaborated on Nietzsche's position and his alleged "dishonesty." He felt that Nietzsche attempted to create a "fantastic" picture of himself which was opposite to his real personality. Nietzsche was described as an extremely polite, proper, and ingratiating man. Thus, his vitriolic literary attacks contrasted strikingly with his public self. According to the historian, Nietzsche pretended interest in the minute affairs of everyday life, making it appear that he had mapped out a life superior to everyone else's. Yet, in reality, he lived a miserable existence. He assumed he was above other philosophers, when in fact he identified with them. He denounced German culture and Germany, but was a German in every sense of the word.

I was puzzled by the historian's intensity. At first, I attributed it to discomfort associated with the beginning of our work. I attempted to temper his negative feelings by introducing the word "ambivalence" instead of "dishonesty" and by directing his attention to the first part of the book where Nietzsche mentioned the death of his father, and to the effects the death had upon him. Reading these passages, it is hard not to empathize with Nietzsche and the grief he expressed so beautifully. The historian was, of course, well aware of Nietzsche's identification with his father, but he was more influenced by Nietzsche's sense of grandiosity than by his grief. He saw Zarathustra as a poorly disguised image of Nietzsche and more specifically an image of Nietzsche's grandiosity and sense of immortality. He postulated a

psychological formulation along the lines of oedipal victory following
father's death, emphasizing the competitive element in the relationship.

The negative tone in the biographer's voice, his choice of words,
and the intensity of his feelings made me realize that what he was
expressing had deeper roots. His emotional response resembled a
negative transference and might have been connected with his reluctance to accept Nietzsche as the subject of our investigation. I brought
my observation about his affect to his attention. First, he explained
his reaction in intellectual terms and provided many quotations and
passages from Nietzsche's books to support the notion that Nietzsche's ideas, full of aggression and a desire to destroy, offer no alternatives. He believed that Nietzsche was ignored by his contemporaries because of his anger; even up to the present time, he pointed
out, teachers in philosophy find it difficult to use some of Nietzsche's
books, such as *Zarathustra* and *Ecce Homo.* He thought of *Ecce Homo* as
an elaboration of Nietzsche's grandiose fantasy about himself, first
revealed in *Thus Spake Zarathustra.* He expressed the conviction that
Nietzsche deluded himself and attempted to delude others. In the
early books, he did not use the first person at all. In *Ecce Homo,* "I" is
used throughout. The biographer was particularly distressed about
Nietzsche's lack of "action." He postulated that Nietzsche was not
systematic and that he lacked self-knowledge. In parts of *Ecce Homo,*
he even comes across as irrational. The biographer attributed this
to Nietzsche's deteriorating mental condition preceding his collapse.

My collaborator presented his arguments eloquently but emotionally. At first his presentation was a monologue, but as I tried to
explain my response to the material, we entered into a dialogue.
Before long, however, I felt pushed into the position of defending
Nietzsche. The biographer was the first to remark that the dialogue
had taken the form of a debate and wondered how to reach a consensus. Although reaching a consensus was not, of course, my primary
concern, his question focused our attention on the process and increased our observational capacity.

The historian expressed concern about his bias in selecting reading
material, but I encouraged him to feel free to suggest any books he
wanted, even if he thought, or maybe especially if he thought, he
suggested them because of bias. It was this very bias that we wanted
to understand. His response was enlightening. He gave a brief histo-

ry of his feelings about Nietzsche, as he perceived them from his first exposure to Nietzsche's philosophical ideas up to the present time. He discussed his first enthusiastic response, the disappointment and anger that followed, and how he reached his present relatively "neutral" position. He promised to send me a few pages he had written some time ago about the stages of his development as far as his interest in Nietzsche was concerned. *Ecce Homo* disappointed the historian the most, because here Nietzsche revealed a lack of awareness of his own personal feelings. The biographer recognized in my enthusiasm his own early feelings about Nietzsche, and indicated that I, too, would become disappointed eventually.

It had become apparent to me that the historian was reacting to material that pointed out real or apparent contradictions between the subject's life and his philosophical ideas. The historian's disappointment and anger revealed a sense of personal frustration, the nature of which could not be understood by intellectual means alone. It was obvious that *Ecce Homo* had a different meaning to me than it did to him. However, my objective was not to establish the correct meaning. My immediate goal was to explore the historian's reaction and avoid premature closures or assumptions. The fact that my collaborator had already begun this introspection and was willing to share the results with me was a promising and welcome sign.

I indicated to the historian my own anxiety in reading Nietzsche, and I tried to communicate how the analyst deals with apparent contradictions and distortions. I emphasized the need to search for connecting links which would make the book intellectually more consistent and aesthetically more pleasing.

Gradually, the discussion had taken the form of a dialogue with neither of us trying to take the position of debater. The historian indicated that he understood how likable Nietzsche could be, especially if one disliked what he disliked. Nietzsche dared to say what others did not say and what they did not even dare to think. The historian saw psychological reasons for an initial positive response, especially for intellectuals who wanted to believe Nietzsche possessed self-knowledge. Nietzsche's extremism about the Germans and Richard Wagner, however, showed that his anger had deeper personal manifestations which were probably related to his relationship with his father. According to the biographer, Nietzsche had difficulty constructing a memory of his father, and the anger was displaced onto the philosophers, Germany, and eventually Wagner.

The historian discussed Nietzsche's family background. In addition to a younger sister, Nietzsche had a younger brother who died shortly after his father's death. Nietzsche wrote an autobiographical statement at the age of fourteen in which he reported a dream he had had shortly before his brother's death. In the dream he heard the bells of a church ringing. The grave of his father opened up; the father came out of the grave and walked into the church as the organ was playing. The father was holding a child in his arms and went back to the grave with it. Nietzsche believed this dream predicted his brother's death. The biographer pointed out fear of his father's revenge in the dream. (He made no comment about the possibility that Nietzsche may have wanted to join his father in the grave.)

The session ended after we made arrangements for the next interview. The assignment was the second chapter of *On the Genealogy of Morals*—the chapter on "Guilt and Bad Conscience."[4] The biographer also promised to send me the pages he wrote on his personal feelings about Nietzsche.

The first session provided immediate support to the methodological hypothesis I have outlined. It made clear that powerful conflicting feelings had been transferred onto the subject of the historian's study. These feelings had precipitated a wide shift in the historian's affective response from strongly positive to strongly negative. Although the investigator claimed that at the time of the interviews he had reached a neutral point, my observations indicated that this was not actually the case. There was ample evidence of a strong negative reaction toward Nietzsche's theoretical position and personal life which closely resembled the negative transference experienced in an analytic situation. The historian's evaluation of his subject's creative work seemed to have been affected by his transference reaction. The most disturbing effect of the negative transference was the fact that it had interfered with a deepening involvement in his subject, to the point where the investigator was about to abandon further exploration beyond what was absolutely essential to complete the dissertation.

If this had been a therapeutic situation, the approach and direction to take would have been obvious. The discussion about Nietzsche would have been just an opening for entering into an exploration of the historian's early personal experiences, with particular emphasis on his relationship with his father. The transference manifestations in the therapeutic situation would have eventually provided the ground to make the proper interpretations and bring to his attention the underlying neurotic conflict. When this was resolved, the historian should then have been able to view Nietzsche without the bias of the negative transference.

This of course was not the direction I took. My primary interest was not the historian's humanity but his creativity. My approach was not to explore the historian's personal life but to focus on the subject of his investigation. Personal vignettes were introduced, but these were just openings for an exploration of Nietzsche's life and creativity.

Personality elements and conflicts are present in all manifestations of an individual's mental life. They can be identified along the whole spectrum which begins with the most primitive mental functions and ends with the most refined ones. The collaboration is not aiming to eliminate the influence of the investigator's personality on his research—this is neither possible nor feasible. The aim is to identify these influences in the specific area that pertains to the historian's investigation in the hope that this awareness will enable him to understand the nature of the stimulus that produced them.

Our basic objective was to understand Nietzsche's personality, not the investigator's. I saw my function as helping the historian in applying certain limited aspects of self-knowledge within the boundaries of his field of investigation. We were both careful to maintain these boundaries and not to let the process become an open-ended exploration of the investigator's life.

In preparation for the second interview, I read the second chapter of *On the Genealogy of Morals*. According to the historian's written account, this book and *Beyond Good and Evil* had profoundly impressed the historian when he first read Nietzsche. (He corrected his memory later during the collaboration.) In contrast to *Ecce Homo* which disappointed him, I was now to read what appealed to him in Nietzsche.

In view of the continuous evidence of negative transference and the desire to focus on the historian's feelings, during the second session we decided to concentrate not on *Genealogy* but on the autobiographical statement the investigator had sent me prior to the interview. The historian discussed several important memories from his early involvement with Nietzsche, and he remembered distinctly "not wanting to be like Nietzsche" as a person and having difficulty completing the reading of Nietzsche's books. At that time, he deliber-

ately avoided learning much about Nietzsche's personal life, and he
experienced the wish to become a "teacher-proof" student, which
was taken to mean that he wanted to avoid idealizing his teachers. He
thought that focusing on Nietzsche's philosophical ideas would help
him maintain the autonomy of his intellectual function and did not
become concerned about the social implications of Nietzsche's theories until some years later. With the gradual increase of the historian's
commitment to social issues, his feelings toward Nietzsche became
negative, yet he didn't want to "throw the baby out with the bath
water." Gradually he became more selective in what he accepted
from Nietzsche's intellectual work.

I wondered what prompted him to resume his historical investigation of Nietzsche, after he had already gotten what he thought he
wanted from it. He pointed out his "proprietary interests" in Nietzsche and his competitive feelings with other historians who thought
they "owned" Nietzsche because they studied him in depth. During
this second interview, he reaffirmed his wish to "forget" about Nietzsche after he finished his dissertation. He expressed the conviction
that he could not build upon Nietzsche the way the psychoanalyst
builds upon Freud. He saw no movement, school of thought, or
cohesiveness in Nietzsche's philosophical position. He offered several theoretical psychoanalytic propositions to explain Nietzsche's effect on readers, mostly along the lines of oedipal rivalry and the wish
to destroy the paternal image.

I was particularly impressed with the historian's openness, intellectual honesty, and candor in revealing his intense feelings about the
subject of his investigation. He expressed his thoughts with clarity
and a sense of conviction. Although eloquent, his associations could
be described as "free" in the sense that he seemed to be doing little
editing or attempting to conceal the content of his thinking consciously. Powerful feelings were evident, yet there was no indication
of antagonism or intent to debate. We were both experiencing the
same strong wish to test the new methodological approach in the best
possible way and had formed a working alliance without which our
work would have been enormously complicated. However, my appreciation of this alliance did not stop me from trying to understand
the nature and the objectives of the historian's motivation for our
collaboration on a deeper level. I thought that the first two interviews
provided important clues. I sensed the strong identification between
the historian and his subject and assumed that his criticism of Nietz-

sche was an expression of his desire to reduce the intensity of the bond between himself and his subject.

The biographical study of a historical personality can be conceptualized as an attempt to differentiate between the "I" and the "him" and thus draw a distinction between external and internal. This is particularly relevant when the study is undertaken by an individual who has been intensely involved with the historical personality's creative work and has experienced a strong identification with his subject. The writing of the biography could represent, in a sense, an effort to disrupt the intrusion and achieve a sense of freedom and autonomy. The differentiation between the "I" and the "him" that I refer to pertains to the historian's intellectual function and scholarly work. It is important that the reader keep in mind that I am not discussing a defect in personality but a stage in the development of my collaborator's creativity. My effort to identify the nature of the historian's struggle with himself to develop his creative function does not constitute a reference to his personality as a whole, and my formulations do not relate to psychopathology.

The fact that my collaborator had handed me part of his dissertation prior to the third interview had raised several important questions about how to proceed. At that point I had the benefit of an extensive discussion with the consultant, who wondered if the biographer was planning to submit his dissertation in the near future. If so, he thought it might be better to avoid an extensive discussion of the thesis for a while. After I understood that the submission of the thesis was not imminent, I decided to share with the historian my concern about the effect of such discussions on his work.

The historian's thesis is an attempt to analyze, Nietzsche's relationships with the principal people in his life—family, friends, Arthur Schopenhauer, Richard Wagner, and key women like Lou Salomé—in terms of narcissistic and oedipal pathology. His thesis could be debated in terms of methodology and in reference to his basic assumption about the nature of Nietzsche's pathology. However, this was not my intention. I opened the discussion by pointing out some of my concerns about discussing the thesis at that time because of possible interference with its completion and submission in the near future. Although the historian indicated his readiness to discuss the chapter, we referred to the thesis only indirectly. We focused on the advantages, and, more important, in my opinion, the disadvantages of discussing Nietzsche's psychopathology rather than his creativity. By focusing on creativity, we had bypassed the narrow focus of psychopathology. Without entering into the details of our exchange, I would like to point out how impressed I was with the historian's change of position as far as further involvement with his subject was concerned. He announced his intent to write two theses: one for the thesis committee for the purpose of graduation and later a second for the purpose of publication. I understood his announcement as a clear indication of a reawakening interest in his subject and an indication of a change in his affective response. His statement also revealed a sense of readiness to face a wider audience than his thesis committee. The historian's use of psychological concepts and his emphasis on psychopathology indicated an intent to address a psychologically sophisticated audience. His background and knowledge were consistent with this assumption. Consequently, the historian's area of interest led to the paradoxical position of his being more interested in psychopathology whereas I seemed to be defending "straight history."

For the fourth session we were to return to our discussion of the *Genealogy of Morls,* with emphasis on the first essay. However, the assignment became a point of departure for a more lengthy discussion on the issue of how Nietzsche affected his readers. Upon the historian's request, I shared with him both the excitement and the discomfort that the readings had given me, as well as my impression that Nietzsche's writing style had some similarity to "free associations." The historian emphasized Nietzsche's deliberate attempt to upset his readers and his success in this regard. He referred to the work as "philosophy with the hammer," and he pointed out Nietzsche's relentless attack on commonly accepted values and morals. He gave Nietzsche some credit for self-analytic functions in his work but was critical of the lack of modesty and humility displayed in *Ecce Homo.*

There was a marked change in the historian's affective response toward his subject during the interview. Most noticeable was the softening of his negative position. As his anger was subsiding, there was evidence that he was experiencing embarrassment on behalf of Nietzsche—a sign indicating both continuing identification with Nietzsche as well as an effort to break this identification and achieve a sense of separateness and autonomy. As long as the biographer was angry, his words were directed against Nietzsche and Nietzsche's philosophical position. However, his attitude and approach were as consistently strong as were those of Nietzsche. The historian had "psychologized with the hammer" as Nietzsche had philosophized with it. I thought my collaborator's lack of awareness of his readers was a milder version of Nietzsche's insensitive attack against them.

At some point the biographer visualized my analyzing Nietzsche and "laughing my head off" because of Nietzsche's exhibitionistically defensive positions. With this comment the historian gave the first clear indication of his emerging awareness of me as his reader. On the one side he was probably identifying with Nietzsche on the "couch," whereas on the other he was developing an identification with the collaborating analyst and his function.

The fifth interview took place two weeks after the fourth. The historian had asked me to read Nietzsche's *Thus Spake Zarathustra*, and by the time I met with him I had read part of it. Reading *Thus Spake Zarathustra* is an emotional experience and an intellectual challenge. It consists of four parts, and by the fourth interview meeting I had carefully read the first and part of the second. During my reading, I remembered the book from my years in Greece. I had read Zarathustra's meeting with the Saint during my adolescent years, and I remembered my strong reaction to his assertion that God was dead. In the first part of the book, Zarathustra is described as carrying the body of the tightrope walker and eventually burying it in the trunk of a tree. This brought to mind Nietzsche's dream from his early childhood in which his father carries the body of his brother to the grave. I associated it with J. W. von Goethe's poem "Erlkoenig," in which a father rides through the night with his gravely ill child in his arms in an effort to reach the doctor but does not reach him in time. Being grossly absorbed by the imagery of the book, I found it easy to direct my attention away from the historian and his feelings and focus it on Nietzsche's book and my own reactions.

It is hard to summarize this two-and-a-half-hour session and do it justice. We explored the resemblance between Zarathustra and Jesus as well as the differences between the two. We identified some references from the New Testament and a Darwinian element in Nietzsche's philosophy. We emphasized the ambivalence in Zarathustra and his relative lack of "human qualities." We compared Zarathustra to a prophet and discussed the distinction between overman and God. Since the historian had the German edition and I had an English version, we made comparisons and discussed the use of certain words and their various meanings. We explored Nietzsche's ideas about animals, women, and children. Animals seemed to be on the same level with men, children were idealized, whereas women were grossly devalued. We found of particular importance Zarathustra's continuous transformations and the New Testament style used to present different incidents involving Zarathustra and his students. The biographer reported a strong urge to confront Nietzsche's hero and challenge him. He believed that Nietzsche never attempted to test Zarathustra. Instead, he condemned Zarathustra's opponents to a position of silence or ridicule. We wondered about Zarathustra as a personification of Nietzsche's ideal for the period of transition between man and overman. The historian described Zarathustra as a projection of Nietzsche's own image, but I expressed preference for the word "creation" instead of "projection." We talked about the creation of an ideal, how it is pieced together, and what makes it cohesive and effective. My collaborator saw the Zarathustra image as brittle and inviting challenge. He expressed his fascination for the way Nietzsche put the image together and its effect on readers. He expressed the opinion that by creating Zarathustra, Nietzsche temporarily liberated himself from his concern about his readers. He created a spokesman who had no need for endorsement or support of others. As a matter of fact, he contemptuously rejected any approval.

I raised the question: What did Zarathustra do for the historian? The historian answered by pointing out that Zarathustra liberated him from certain illusions and greatly affected his sense of values. In a way, he felt that Nietzsche wrote the book in such a way that it could have a liberating effect on practically anybody, depending on what one wanted to be liberated from.

The last part of the interview focused on discussing *Thus Spake Zarathustra* as a literary work. Nietzsche's capacity to communicate on an affective level made his point more effective, but it created complications if one wanted to use an intellectual approach.

Toward the end of our discussion, we commented on analytic studies of novelists and the effect these studies have on the reader. The historian said that many studies tended to make the author look like "just another guy." I agreed and added that analyzing the author seemed to have the effect of discrediting him.

After the end of the structured interview, as we were chatting over a glass of wine, the historian shared his concern about my enthusiasm for Zarathustra. He did not want me to become a Zarathustra expert and direct my attention away from him. I agreed and jokingly added that maybe I should be reading less.

In order to facilitate our capacity to observe the collaborative process, the sessions with the historian were taped. These tapes (despite their poor quality) were useful in preparing the summaries of the sessions which I was sending to the observer-consultant. They were also valuable in preparing for the next session by increasing my awareness of overall continuity. The historian seemed indifferent to the tapes until the end of the fifth interview. At this time, after a casual discussion, he decided to listen to all the previous tapes. I welcomed this opportunity, because I wanted him to direct more attention to the process and share his observations with me.

The historian's opening remarks during the sixth session referred to his having listened to the tapes and more specifically to the degree of my participation in the discussions. He thought I was not aggressive enough and seemed at times reluctant to comment. He wished I had "cross-examined him" instead of being a "nice guy." He had come to realize that he saw me as the trained reader whose comments and responses would help him to prepare himself for the ultimate reader—the public. He asked me to put across my responses and ideas more aggressively and to avoid hedging or withholding.

The historian had accurately observed some reluctance on my part to do much "thinking out loud" and a sense of uncertainty about my proper "stance" within the limits of the experimental situation. More important, though, he was addressing the fundamental question of what he would like to have from the psychoanalyst and whether or not I was providing it. His desire to be "cross-examined" reminded me of his earlier urge to confront Zarathustra and "put Nietzsche's hero to a test."

I responded to his request for more feedback by explaining my efforts to maintain an empathic understanding of both him and his subject. Instead of "taking sides" by trying either to debate the issue with the historian or to join forces with him in criticizing his subject, I adopted the position I thought would help clarify not only the historian's intellectual understanding of his subject, but his feelings as well.

The collaborator did not object to my comments, and he pointed out that he studied Nietzsche psychologically because of his awareness that his own reaction was a psychological one. He wrote down his ideas in an effort to rid himself of his own negative feelings about his subject. He put them on paper to prove how angry he was and also to relieve himself of discomfort. After doing so, he was better able to appreciate both his own psychological reaction and Nietzsche's psychology.

Later in the interview, the historian wondered how I would compare Nietzsche to my analysands. I told him I could not compare the two. Analyst and analysand are two people working together and earning something from each other. I learned a good deal from Nietzsche, whereas Nietzsche obviously learned nothing from me. If I had to compare my experience of reading Nietzsche with the analytic situation, it might be more appropriate to see Nietzsche as the analyst and the reader as the analysand. Whereas the reader provided the associations, Nietzsche provided the interpretations. My curiosity to know more about him seemed to be related to the fact that he made many effective interpretations. There may be good reasons why as his "analysands" we should be on guard about our curiosity in psychopathology, which could stem from our desire to discredit Nietzsche and his disagreeable interpretations.

The sixth interview ended with the historian commenting on the fact that we had not directly discussed theoretical issues. Originally, he had the notion that our work would focus on theoretical psychoanalytic concepts, and he was concerned by the fact that this had not occurred.

The historian opened the seventh interview by indicating that he had had a very positive impression of the previous session. He proceeded to tell me how he attempted to apply what he learned from his experience with me in working with a friend who was writing the biography of a historian-politician. In the example he gave me, he had assumed my role. He was amazed at how effective the short interaction was and expressed a good deal of enthusiasm about it. He proceeded to tell me that, as a result of our work, he had entered another stage of interest in Nietzsche. He felt that the principal change had been his increased awareness of his readers, which was precipitated by his identifying in me the reader he wanted to address. Up to that time, my collaborator had not expressed any concern or revealed anxiety about the potential reader. Until the collaborative work began having its effect, it appeared that his highly developed self-critical ability was his main source of feedback. It is not unusual for authors to be cautious about the choice of people to whom they show the unfinished version of their work. Being vulnerable to criticism and in doubt about their product, it is understandable that they want limited feedback and from selected people. The historian had selected the members of his thesis committee, who represented his readers. Occasionally, he talked about them but indicated no desire to discuss his work with them before it was finished. As far as I know, I was the first person the historian accepted to discuss his work with, and my acceptance initiated important changes in his attitude toward his subject and his writing.

The historian discussed the different versions of his thesis. He considered the last version "not a bad job" because it took into account the complexities involved in understanding Nietzsche. His first attempt was focused on statistical studies designed to measure the waves of interest in Nietzsche during different chronological periods in both Europe and the United States. Although the American data were not statistically significant, the European data showed increases in interest in Nietzsche before World War I and II and during the 1960s and 1970s. He now believed that the statistical approach was impossible to complete satisfactorily and that different approaches must be used to study Nietzsche's effect on his readers. Lately, he had focused on the personalities with whom Nietzsche interacted, and more specifically on Lou Salomé. A recently published biography about her, written by another psychohistorian, was of particular interest to him. He was anxious to compare that author's hypothesis with his own and to extract conclusions. When he wrote his chapter about Nietzsche versus Wagner, he could find no psychobiography on Wagner with which to compare his ideas.

We talked about the wide range of Nietzsche's contemporaries and questioned how much we could learn about Nietzsche by studying those personalities. I emphasized the need to avoid directing our attention away from the subject of the investigation. Although I saw the historian's approach as reasonable and potentially effective, I sensed an eagerness to involve himself with Nietzsche's contemporaries, possibly at the expense of his investment in the main subject. As a result of my comments, we discussed the issue of choosing and maintaining in a historical inquiry the proper focus consistent with the goal of the investigation. We identified the difficulties in deciding what was worth researching, which arose when the investigator was not clear in his own mind about the boundaries of his research. The historian reflected on the development of his own interest in Nietzsche, which he believed started with the realization that Thomas Mann was one of Nietzsche's admirers. He saw in Nietzsche the ideal of the rebellious defiance he wanted for himself and believed that he could achieve a sense of independence by studying him.

I indicated that the historian's notions of his own psychological development might have influenced his thinking about the psychological forces that affected Nietzsche's development. Often he referred to Nietzsche's oedipal victory in his formulations. I had some difficulty recognizing that from what I had read. Nietzsche's philosophy strongly reflected his struggle with issues concerning values. Furthermore, he wanted to make sure that these values were strictly identified with him, so that he would be clearly associated as an individual apart from others. Autonomy, separateness, and values seemed to be his main concerns.

My comments were directed toward increasing the historian's awareness of the boundaries between "me" and "him." It was evident that the historian had made important steps toward establishing such psychological boundaries, but I thought that there were still areas of confusion that significantly affected his work.

The issue of boundaries of the investigation was further discussed during the eighth interview. A comparison was drawn between the work of the psychoanalyst and the work of the historian. The historian assumed that the boundaries are freer in history, because the historian is not bound by the same commitments as the psychoanalyst. He indicated that in the field of history there is no codified research method or approach, whereas a psychoanalyst operates under methodological rules.

I thought that if, during a historical investigation, the historian elects to extend the boundaries of his investigation, one must raise the psychological question as to the motivations behind his decision. If the biographical study of "A" leads to the study of "B" with whom "A" was involved, it is important to establish the reasons for this shift. Is the change in focus to understand "A" better? Or, does it represent a detour to avoid further exploration of "A"? My comments were intended to alert the historian to the possibility that his interest in Nietzsche's contemporaries could represent "resistance" against involving himself further or deepening his understanding of Nietzsche. Without using technical terms, I attempted to introduce an important aspect of the psychoanalytic method which could be applicable to history. More specifically, I wanted to impress him with the need to establish boundaries which would clearly indicate not only what is to be investigated, but also what is not. These boundaries are essential if the historian is to keep the psychological forces that influence his work in check.

The primary focus of the ninth interview was a further discussion of *Thus Spake Zarathustra*. We both were prepared, although I wonder if anyone can ever be well-enough prepared to discuss such a book. I was immediately impressed with my collaborator's enthusiasm and capacity to elaborate on Nietzsche's ideas. Zarathustra was no longer "brittle" as he had appeared to him before. On the contrary, he was impressed with Zarathustra's "self-affirmation." In the beginning of the book, Nietzsche's identification with his hero is more evident, with the overman representing the "ideal being" Zarathustra wishes for. However, at the end of the book, the overman is not mentioned, and instead "eternity" seems to take his place. The historian elaborated on Nietzsche's concept of eternal recurrence, and for a while the historian came across as an effective lecturer of philosophy. He was particularly effective in explaining how Nietzsche struggled to arrive at his affirmative position on eternal recurrence and why this position was affirmative.

My collaborator never presented himself as a philosopher. However, he was fully cognizant of the need to appreciate his subject's creative work in order to accomplish his own biographical goal. I thought that, by presenting Nietzsche's ideas to me, he was demonstrating both his capacity for appreciation and his arrival at a more affirmative position on Nietzsche and his work.

As we focused on Zarathustra's transformations, we talked about Nietzsche's struggle to accept loss and change. Nietzsche seemed to have spent his life in a state of continuous mourning which he would or could not complete. We compared the philosophical concept of external recurrence, as presented by Nietzsche, to the psychological concept of the oceanic feeling and found both important differences and similarities. Both concepts are timeless, but Nietzsche perceived no peace, tranquillity, or sameness. His "eternal recurrence" involved continuous struggle, change, and pain with few moments of real triumph to make the recurrence worth reexperiencing. To be consistent with his philosophy, *Thus Spake Zarathustra* has no real ending and hardly a beginning.

While reading this book, the reader has a wide choice of topics on which to focus. Nietzsche's unorthodox thinking offers powerful stimuli in many areas, and the reader has the difficult task of integrating them. We both noticed periods of "lagging" interest during the reading of the book. We attributed it to the overstimulation and anxiety associated with the difficulty of integrating so many ideas.

Gradually the discussion changed focus. We seemed to have moved from Zarathustra to theoretical concepts in psychoanalysis, and before long we were talking about Nietzsche's psychopathology. The shift was so gradual and smooth that I hadn't fully realized how it occurred until I later listened to the tape. The historian once more attempted to support the "diagnosis" of narcissistic character. I tried to dispute it by indicating that I saw Nietzsche as a man apart, a man who was fully aware of the world around him. He introspected and observed with amazing accuracy and seemed to be aware of his separateness from the people to whom he related.

After reflecting on the ninth interview, I realized my own need to "analyze" Nietzsche, despite my intellectual objections to it. I understood this need as a reaction to the frustration I experienced in reading *Thus Spake Zarathustra* and the realization of my limitations in mastering his philosophical concepts. By analyzing him, I attempted to compensate for the narcissistic injury suffered. My reaction, however, helped me to empathize better with my collaborator and to understand the effect of Nietzsche's writings on him.

The reading assignment for the tenth interview was the three chapters of Rudolph Binion's biography of Lou Salomé that dealt with her relationship with Nietzsche.[5] The chapters we read referred to Nietzsche's breif but intense personal relationship with a young, attractive admirer who openly treated him as her teacher and subtly tried to seduce him. Nietzsche's brief fascination with Lou Salomé ended with an abrupt cancellation of his plans to live with her and his (current) friend Rée in Paris. Soon after Nietzsche changed his mind, Lou and Nietzsche became hostile to one another. The end of their relationship also precipitated a break with Nietzsche's mother and sister. All these traumatic events seemed to relate both chronologically and psychologically to Nietzsche's resignation from his position in Basel as professor of philosophy and the writing of his masterpiece

*Thus Spake Zarathustra.* This important and dramatic period in Nietzsche's life seemed to represent an agonizing struggle between two choices. On the one side was a solitude that fostered creative intellectual work which satisfied Nietzche's sense of mission. On the other side were family attachments, romantic involvements, and a deep sense of loyalty to selected friends and admirers. When he made his choice, Nietzsche became a man apart, deeply wounded, grieved, and with a sense of betrayal. At the same time, however, Nietzsche's decision gave him a sense of freedom that enabled him to express all the ideas he had concealed or suppressed up to that time.

The discussion generated by Binion's scholarly presentation was not limited to the wealth of information provided in it. We speculated on the author's emotional response toward Lou Salomé and Nietzsche in order to compare his reaction to that of my collaborator. More specifically, we assumed that the psychohistorian of Lou Salomé "favored" Nietzsche and was critical of his subject. In contrast my collaborator, the psychohistorian of Nietzsche, seemed to "favor" Lou Salomé at the expense of Nietzsche. I thought this juxtaposition raised interesting questions about the psychohistorian and his subject. It seemed that in psychohistory the investigator appears more as an adversary than a defender, which is the more standard position in conventional biographies.

It was a month later when I met the historian for the eleventh interview. He had taken a trip to Germany and Italy and appeared in high spirits. He had a strong interest in our work, and he had completed a new section of work on his thesis. Before he left, he had given me a book containing Nietzsche's correspondence, which I had read carefully.[6] (I thought his assigning this book at that time was not unrelated to the investigator's trip.) A good deal could be extracted from the letters: material about Nietzsche's personality as well as specific information about his activities, interests, and the quality of his relationships. His capacity for affection, his sensitive perception of other people, and his bouts of depression and anger came through with amazing clarity. I was particularly impressed with Nietzsche's capacity for written expression early in life and the agony he suffered shortly before his collapse.

In the beginning of the session, we talked about the possibility of involving another historian in a similar project. My collaborator thought this would be a good idea and compared himself to other professionals, wondering about their readiness for such an involvement. Our discussion revealed some anxiety, probably related to his awareness that our collaboration could be concluded in the near future. My inquiries about his thesis may have given him the impression that I was putting pressure on him, but I made no intended connection between the completion of his thesis and the completion of our work.

It was hard to concentrate on the letters, because the historian had not reread them recently. Instead, he proceeded to describe recent personal experiences in Germany which had revealed his fascination with the nineteenth-century intellectual atmosphere in Europe and his capacity to recreate that atmosphere in his own mind. Under the influence of his Romantic fascination, the historian's evaluation of Nietzsche's behavior was colored by his emotions. It seems that Nietzsche's attitudes and philosophical position represent a kind of cacophony which upset the melodious and soothing quality of the nineteenth-century Romantic era as the historian perceived it. He was no longer willing to identify Nietzsche's stubbornness as neurotic, however, as he had done in the past. Instead, he realized that Nietzsche's sense of mission dictated a disregard of external influences.

The historian's "defense" of Nietzsche against theories of neurotic behavior contrasted to his earlier attitude. When I brought this to his attention, it appeared momentarily as if we were "back to the first day." Taking my comment as criticism, he "turned the tables" and wondered why I was now less protective of Nietzsche, pointing out my new willingness to view information about Nietzsche more critically. In a somewhat defiant tone he stated, "I can say exactly the same things I said the first day." Expressing the conviction that his intellectual analysis had not changed, he emphasized his increased capacity to appreciate the positive and his conviction that I had previously expressed an unrealistically positive attitude toward the material. He thought that as a result of our discussion, positive and negative were leveling off and we were in a process of reconciling our views.

His statement reminded me a little of the beginning of our collaboration. He expressed himself forcefully, and although we both recognized the change in his intellectual and emotional response, I did not think it described our work accurately, because he had presented a painful and long internal struggle in external terms.

Thus, the main focus of the eleventh interview became an assessment of our work. In a psychoanalyst's clinical work, such an assessment could represent "termination material." The historian's vacation, our discussion about working with another historian, and, more important, the progress made brought the issue of termination into focus. The reappearance of our "first day" might also have been connected with this issue.

Some important questions involving the conclusion of this type of collaboration had to be taken into consideration. Since there was no precedent to follow, I had to use my clinical knowledge as the basis for my approach. It dictated that I pay careful attention to my collaborator's implicit and explicit communications in this regard.

At the end of the eleventh interview, I felt a dichotomy between the progress made and the possibility of termination. I believed both that we had barely scratched the surface of the subject and that sufficient progress had been made to bring the collaboration to a close in the not-too-distant future. Whereas these two notions appeared mutually exclusive, in actuality they were not. They represented an appreciation of the two basic realities every investigator must come to terms with: (1) The historical inquiry is a long and, in a sense, interminable process which can never be brought to a satisfactory conclusion in a short period of time. (2) As the investigative process unfolds, there is a periodic need to pause and share with the readers what has been learned so far. These "pauses" represent the end of a cycle of creativity without which further progress would be difficult.

I assumed that for the historian the "pause" represented the completion of his thesis, with possible reinvolvement with Nietzsche at some later time. In addition, we both wanted to pause to share the results of our experiment with others. The two most important clues indicating the historian's desire to "pause" were his increasing capacity to write the unfinished part of his thesis and his decreasing interest in giving me additional reading assignments. We both experienced a sense of loss associated with the approaching end of our work, the awareness of which alerted us to the danger of procrastinating and unnecessarily delaying the writing in which we were engaged.

A timely call from our observer-consultant to assess the status of our experiment facilitated further awareness of the direction to be taken. During the meeting and in response to the consultant's request, the historian promised to share the completed part of his thesis with us, part of which had been written a long time before the experiment began, and part of which had been completed during the period of our collaboration.

During the last two sessions of our collaboration, the historian and I discussed his thesis in some detail. I will not attempt to summarize the discussion. In its original form the thesis represented a serious effort to analyze an enormous amount of historical information on Nietzsche along the lines of familiar psychoanalytic clinical theory. In his formulations the author utilized Freud's concepts of oedipal rivalry and Heinz Kohut's descriptions of the narcissistic transference in an effort to explain Neitzsche's relationship with the important figures in his life and some of the effects these had upon his relationships with others. The completed part of his thesis consisted of seven chapters. Half of this was completed before the collaboration began and is characterized by a high degree of conviction about Nietzsche's pathology and personality.

As a result of our work, the historian became more aware about his deep disappointment in Nietzsche and his anger toward him, and he realized that these feelings were reflected in some of the psychopathological formulations he had offered. In the part of the dissertation written during the collaboratoin or after its termination, the author's effort to avoid the pathographic character of the previous chapters is evident. Emphasis was now placed on examining the quality and nature of Nietzsche's relationships in a much broader sense. As a result of this effort, Nietzsche emerges from the pages as an extremely complex personality who defies a simplistic diagnostic formulation. Furthermore, the scope of the historical investigation was widened and enriched, with the author showing increased awareness of the complexities of the methodological and theoretical issues involved.

The following vignette reflects some of the changes that occurred as a result of our collaboration. In the final draft of his thesis, the author had included his own autobiographical notes (the ones we had discussed during the second interview) pretaining to his evolving interest in Nietzsche's philosophy. After reading the draft, I noticed a change from the original that the historian had not noted.

The final draft read: "The books of Nietzsche that most interested me in these (early) years were his most personal and individualistic ones, especially *Zarathustra* and his early aesthetic writings such as

*Birth of Tragedy* and *The Use and Abuse of History*." In the original manuscript this paragraph read, "The books of Nietzsche which most interested me in these years were the generally iconoclastic ones— *Beyond Good and Evil* and *On the Genealogy of Morals*. These went well with my general mood of rebelliousness and my desire to survey the whole spectrum of intellectual activity in search of something to which I could dedicate myself."

It seemed that the change represented the correction of a distortion and the recovery of a memory. Having successfully dealt with his negative feelings toward his subject, the historian could acknowledge his early appreciation for Nietzsche's aesthetic writings. This realization led him to rewrite his "personal" history so as to reflect the nature of his experience more accurately. Nietzsche's influence on him had had a much deeper and more positive effect than he had originally thought.

### III.

A narrative such as the account of this experiment presented in the previous section constitutes a "historical" document. It is a record of a recent event experienced by the author, who attempts to present a comprehensive summary of the facts involved in a certain cause-and-effect sequence. The author or chronicler is a psychoanalyst who both observed and participated in the process and makes a conscious effort to give an objective account of it with the least possible bias. From a psychoanalytic viewpoint, I know better than to claim actual objectivity. The psychoanalyst, too, is under the influence of psychological forces, and his account is bound to be colored by them. The whole process of editing the notes and summaries provides ample opportunities for these forces to interfere, causing distortions that could lead to erroneous impressions and assumptions. I entertained the idea of giving the reader the transcripts of tapes in their entirety instead of the condensed narrative. Though such a method would have been impractical, to offer a verbatim account without the editing and commentary would have been an effort to present history and leave the participants out of it. It would have put the burden on the reader to become the historian by filling the gaps.

I present the narrative with the understanding that it is a subjective account and only one of several possible ways to understand the process. It represents an educated guess about the nature of the psychological forces that influenced the historian's investigative work. At this point it is important to add what I as a psychoanalyst observed in myself and how I understood it. It is only through this understanding that I could empathize with the historian's internal struggle and grasp his attempt to resolve it.

At the beginning of this experiment, I thought it essential to maintain a position of neutrality toward the subject matter of the investigation. I assumed that doing so would be a relatively easy task. I had never studied philosophy systematically, and I did not anticipate a strong emotional response to the reading of Nietzsche's work. I found out very quickly that my assumption had been in error. I had a very strong positive response to *Ecce Homo, Thus Spake Zarathustra*, and to the second chapter of *On the Genealogy of Morals*, and a negative response to the first chapter of that book. The intensity of my feelings made me wonder whether I could actually maintain the neutral stance called for by our experimental design, and I felt the need to do some introspection in this regard. Both dreams and conscious thoughts led me to the realization that the material I was reading had personal meaning for me.

My introspective efforts added something to the knowledge I had of myself; more significantly, they seemed to generate interesting ideas about the subject under study. For example, my insight about the connection between Nietzsche's dream at the age of five and Goethe's poem "Erlkoenig" emerged from imagery in one of my dreams, the day residue for which was *Zarathustra*. My initial personal reaction to the material was as positive as the one my collaborator reported from the beginning of his involvement with Nietzsche, but with one basic difference. I was particularly impressed with Nietzsche's attachment to his memory of his father and the affection he had for the latter, whereas my collaborator remembered his initial positive reaction in reference to Nietzsche's rebelliousness and declaration of separateness from the parental image and the ideal associated with it. These differences are probably related to two distinct transference reactions toward the material, consistent with the specific personality configuration of each investigator. Each reaction seems to set into motion a screening process that sharply illuminates the probable significance of certain pieces of information while it leaves others relatively unprocessed. Accordingly, I saw Nietzsche as a loving son struggling to complete the mourning associated with his father's death; my collaborator identified his rebelliousness, oedipal rivalry, and wish to destroy. Both views seem to represent partial insights about Nietzsche that complement each other rather than being antithetical. In this sense, the varied transference reactions of a number of investigators might contribute to the overall understanding of one life history, in spite of their seeming lack of congruence with each other.

Reflecting on my reactions to Nietzsche's philosophy, I can identify an area of "blindness" that puzzled me. Although I admired Nietzsche for his awareness of intrapsychic processes and saw him as the immediate forerunner of Freud, I was not bothered at all by the fact that he seems contemptuously to disregard the issue of the individual's adaptation to the environment as well as the areas of mental life pertaining to what psychoanalysis refers to as ego psychology or object relations. Perhaps this reservation would imply overly high expectations from Nietzsche, although I don't really think so; but to have such reservations is definitely not too much to expect from an analyst of our time who studies the work of this psychoanalytic forerunner. Although I have no direct explanation for this observation, it raises several questions about how we dealt with Nietzsche's intellectual work in the experiment: my collaborator, who had a superior grasp of it, tended to bypass it, whereas I wanted to give it more attention, although I had read very little of it. The historian seemed to operate with the basic premise that the understanding of Nietzsche's work would be enhanced by an understanding of his personality, whereas I seemed to experience this premise as a form of resistance to the appreciation of Nietzsche's intellectual work and possibly even as an effort to demean him. To put it in more technical terms, I saw the historian's premise as a possible rationalization; I also assumed that the expression of my enthusiasm over Nietzsche's work might bring the historian's isolated affect into focus. Of course, this assumption on my part could have been a rationalization too.

In the experiment we dealt primarily with Nietzsche as a living person, but we also focused to a degree on the products he created, especially when we discussed *Zarathustra*. As a matter of fact, we could refer to the person as "Nietzsche" and to his product as "Zarathustra."

An individual's creative work is not actually extraneous to his personality or his sense of self; on the contrary, it forms an essential part of him, one that begins at a very early age in the matrix of his self-organization. Nonetheless, in certain contexts it is more fruitful to make the distinction between a person's creativity and the other part of his personality. In certain individuals, particularly those with the greatest talent, creativity may not be in the service of optimal adaptation and may therefore give rise to intrapsychic conflicts. Instead of internal harmony, many persons with great gifts experience severe problems and internal pain as by-products of their creative activities. Such activities may also bring about difficulties in the interpersonal realm.

The transference reaction observed in my collaborator seemed to have been generated by the philosopher's work; it is Zarathustra that skewed his view of Nietzsche as a human being. There seemed to be very little influence in the opposite direction. It was Nietzsche's work that aroused the historian's interest in the first place; the study of his personality had been necessitated by this interest. As a matter of fact, the historian did not know anything about Nietzsche's personal life until he had become quite knowledgeable about the philosopher's writings. With me, the opposite seems to have been true. I reacted to Nietzsche's biographical material before I had a chance to familiarize myself with his philosophy. My reaction was triggered by the person, and it determined my reception of his work. My strong emotional response to *Ecce Homo* in contrast to the historian's reaction illustrates this duality.

Transference reactions associated with reading biographical materials are bound to be relatively common. They occur when we read novels, view films and plays, etc., and they may be intense. In contrast to the transference reactions of the professional biographer, however, they are generally transient and lack depth. The stimulus seems to act like the day residue of a dream in precipitating the emergence of a memory and in evoking a wish. It triggers an affective release in the form of sadness, fear, or nostalgia which has pleasurable components even when painful. The reader can often make some connection between the stimulating material and the experiences in his own past with which it reverberates. The whole process is partly preconscious, but in part it may have much deeper roots.

In-depth study of an author's creative work, however, creates transference reactions of a different nature. This is particularly true with authors who have made contributions of great originality. There is nothing more anxiety-provoking than the realization that someone else's perception of the universe is grossly different from one's own.

I developed such reactions by the time I read *Zarathustra*. *Zarathustra* was not simply a mirror reflecting some of my personal memories, wishes, and ideas. Reading this book brought me under the influence of Nietzsche's intellect and the power of his ideas. Through *Zarathustra*, Nietzsche became a real object for me, one who was giving me a lot to think about, exciting me, confusing me, and angering me. I first noticed what I agreed with and underlined all these passages in an effort to illuminate them. I thought of Nietzsche as a forerunner of psychoanalysis, if not the first psychoanalyst. In the process of admiring his work, I obscured some of the fundamental differences between Nietzsche's philosophy and psychoanalysis, and I slurred over those of his ideas that are unrelated to it. I took some of his vulgar attacks against women, Jews, Germans, and so many others as some sign of eccentricity or as humor in order to deflect my anger and repulsion. I must have wanted very much to see Nietzsche as a person like myself. Hence I had a need to struggle hard against making the distinction between my ideas and ideals and his. My awareness of this struggle evolved gradually, and it was greatly enhanced by what my collaborator communicated to me verbally and in his writings about his own attempts to resolve the same issue, which he had experienced with considerably greater intensity.

Reading Nietzsche is not merely an exposure to new ideas. His writings constitute an intrusion deliberately designed to challenge the reader's values and sense of self. The reader who does not put the book aside may survey the entire text but comprehend selectively in order to reduce the intensity of the shock. Nietzsche as an author has done everything possible to make it difficult for his readers to master the disturbing effects of his writings in a gradual manner. Instead, he creates a sense of urgency which threatens his readers' internal psychological balance and cohesion. If this balance is to be restored, Nietzsche must be "understood"; if his philosophy is beyond reach, at least his personal life must become meaningful to the reader. This "understanding of his personality" will bring author and reader closer together and bridge the gap created by the intrusion of philosophical position.

I attempted to cope with the anxiety by directing my attention to that aspect of Nietzsche's work which appeared like the writings of a psychoanalyst, identifying Nietzsche as "one of us" in this manner. Apparently my collaborator chose another approach. When repelled by some aspects of Nietzsche's writings, he directed his attention to the biographical material so that he could "understand" and "empathize" with Nietzsche by identifying oedipal or narcissistic elements in the latter's personality. Both approaches represent transference phenomena in the sense that they are partial and selective observations of Nietzsche's personal life and work. These choices are in the service of alleviating the reader's anxiety and inner tensions. I am not questioning the accuracy of our observations about Nietzsche; on the contrary, I believe such conclusions can be amazingly precise on a limited, microscopic level. However, they could cause serious distortions of understanding if taken out of context and used on a macroscopic level to extract global hypotheses about the creative work or personal life of a historical figure.

In the narrative of this experiment, I have occasionally alluded to Nietzsche as the analyst and to his readers as analysands. These allusions were designed to draw a parallel between the readers' transference reactions and those evoked by the psychoanalytic situation. In the latter, the analyst's stance and his interpretations help to remind the analysand about the difference between the actualities in the present and those aspects of figures or transactions from the past which he might confuse with them. This awareness is quite disturbing and precipitates anxiety, which the analysand attempts to master by experiencing the analyst as if he were indeed like people from his past: this is the process called "transference resistance." By repeating the past in this manner, the analysand attempts to defend himself against the input of disturbing novelty.

These well-known phenomena of the analytic situation have their counterparts in other circumstances as well. Relevant for our purposes is the power of literary works and other artistic products to provide stimuli comparable to those of analytic interpretations in their radical differences from routinely experienced stimuli as well as in their focus on matters, for the most part unconscious, which are invested with intense concern. Nietzsche provides many such "interpretations" and very little help to his readers in working through their responses. The stimulus thus produced threatens the reader's internal balance and cohesion and generates intense anxiety.

Kohut has pointed out that man's knowledge of himself can only be achieved by acts of courage that are related to discarding the illusions that have protected him from anxiety.[7] Some authors' writing styles and ideas demand more courage than others; some take the reader's anxiety into account whereas others completely disregard it.

The study of an original idea or a work of art represents an act of courage. It requires the individual's capacity to tolerate the tension such an input creates and the ability to integrate it into his own perceptual system of the universe. If the material is too threatening, this input may be blocked. If impossible to block, it may be neutralized by focusing on partial, nonthreatening aspects of it. True integration of a new input, however, requires the capacity to produce an output through the utilization of the reader's own creative functions. The creativity of one individual can only be mastered through the creativity of another.

In this case the biographer of Nietzsche utilized his own creativity in order to integrate the creativity of his subject, and I had to become an author myself in order to integrate the input the collaboration produced.

The intense relief and excitement that the finishing of a piece of intellectual work creates are associated with the completion of the cycle of creativity and the restoration of the internal balance that such completion involves. This cycle consists of input, integration, and output. Sometimes completion takes a long time because of the investigator's inability to integrate the input. Other investigators may produce a quick discharge simply to prevent further involvement.

It seems that, before producing their final work, most investigators need a protective, friendly, and nonintrusive reader who will become their confidant and function as a buffer between them and the audience-at-large they will eventually face. Thus the first reader is uniquely different from the others. He has been assigned a specific function, that of fulfilling a fantasy on the part of the investigator that is at least in part unconscious.

The consultant of this experiment became my first reader. When I first invited him to participate in the experiment, I had not formulated an understanding of the specific functions he was to perform. My primary concern at the time was with my own intense involvement in a new field and my readiness to make a very substantial commitment in time and effort without the prospect of immediate or apparent reward. I felt seduced by a new idea, and as I was about to embark on the journey, I had a need to establish sources of restraint and support against the siren song of the humanities. I wanted a personally selected audience for my initial excursions into the application of psychoanalysis in this area. I needed a person who would maintain the proper distance in order not to interfere with the unfolding process, but one who could nonetheless provide sufficient closeness for me to receive continual feedback from a representative of my own field.

There were at least two specific occasions when the consultant intervened. The first had to do with the issue of focusing our discussion on Nietzsche as opposed to accepting the historian's counterproposal to study Bismarck and nineteenth-century Germany. The second occurred in reference to the question of discussing the historian's thesis and the problems connected with it. On both occasions he warned us of possible complications. The consultant's main contribution, however, was his role as reader, which facilitated my capacity to integrate the input of the collaboration and eventually produced the present discussion.

The cultural shock I experienced in reading Nietzsche's philosophy was not the only one during this experiment. My intense interaction with the historian was another source of such reactions, as I have already indicated in the narrative. Every psychoanalyst has long experience with two basic forms of professional collaboration. One is the clinical setting of therapeutic psychoanalysis, and the other that of supervision. Neither of the psychoanalytic models involved in these settings is really descriptive of the role designed for me in this experiment. In this collaboration there was no therapeutic intent, and the hierarchical structure of supervision had no place in the interaction of professionals who are recognized experts only within their own discipline. In my dealings with the historian, I had to adopt a stance which had some elements of both basic forms of psychoanalytic collaboration but was identical with neither. I started from what I had learned and am familiar with and hoped to develop a new model consistent with the demands and objectives of the new situation.

The psychoanalyst is attached to his method and experiences anxiety when he has to depart from it. I came to recognize this anxiety as the collaboration proceeded. It took the form of a conscious and consistent dilemma, which was perceived and identified by my collaborator: how much to say and when. Being determined to avoid any "psychotherapeutic" interventions as well as the hierarchical structure of the supervisory model, I was listening analytically to the verbal and written communications but was cautious and uncertain about how to respond. As a result, I did a lot more observing than participating, and my approach had a strong "clinical" element that was evident not only in the interviewing situation but in the way I reported it as well. I don't see how it could have been otherwise. As an analyst, I brought my tools with me, of course, without being sure which of them I would find useful. Not only did I observe the interaction with the tools available to me; I also reported them in the language and style I know.

The narrative of the first interview may lend us support to the notion that initially I did perceive the interaction along the lines of a supervisory process. I identified the historian's negative (counter-) transference toward Nietzsche, as well as his anxiety about the latter's philosophy. I responded to the defensive and introspective material presented so as to facilitate the historian's awareness of the psychological forces that influenced his judgment and position. Furthermore, I attempted to deal with the anger expressed against Nietzsche by presenting my collaborator with my understanding of his "patient's" communication, hoping that by doing so I would increase his empathy and reduce his anger. Despite the more conscious effort to avoid it and the procedural steps instituted to depart from the supervisory model, it seems that my responses were consistent with the role of a supervisor. Being quite aware that the historian could not be my supervisee, as Nietzsche could not be his patient, I experienced considerable anxiety as I came to see the nature and quality of our interaction.

In retrospect, I realize that my concern was excessive. Given the nature of our task and the different kinds of knowledge and experience we brought to it, it would have been quite reasonable to predict that a supervisor-supervisee relationship could not be maintained for very long. In clinical supervision the insights gained from the collaborative work are tested in the arena of the therapeutic process. In a sense, the patient represents a aboratory where all the hunches, hypotheses, and theories will be tried; his responses will determine their validity. The historian does not have such a laboratory. Where and when will he test a new idea? He may elect to do more research or rethink his conclusions about the data he has, but this approach is slow and may not be very effective. In our experiment, the analytic collaborator can serve as the testing ground, so that his function will undergo a major change. In the interviewing situation this change could take several forms. In this instance, it became evident to me when I stopped experiencing the demand to produce ideas and became the historian's reader—as he put it, the ideal reader. This change was noted by the historian in the sixth interview, and it was expressed with his demand that I respond to his writings.

More specifically, by seeing me as his reader, the historian tried to differentiate between his ideas and those of others, to differentiate between Nietzsche and himself. Through most of the experiment, I was in the position of defending Nietzsche's philosophical views or objecting to the diagnostic formulations postulated by the historian. My position was so consistent that it could not have occurred by accident. In some measure, I must have been placed into it by the historian's needs: he wanted to see me as Nietzsche and to test his insights on me. In this situation, the reader position was actually a Nietzsche position, which impelled the historian to identify me as the ideal reader. There can be no more ideal reader for the author of Nietzsche's biography than Nietzsche himself.

It is hard to evaluate the effect of this displacement upon me objectively. It probably intensified my anxiety about Nietzsche's philosophy and contributed to the defensive position of seeing Nietzsche as the first psychoanalyst. By doing so, I could effectively protect myself not only from the full impact of Nietzsche's philosophy but from my collaborator's transference expectations as well.

I am cognizant of the fact that these findings do not represent proof of the effectiveness of the proposed method. Before we can claim to have conclusive evidence, it will be necessary to repeat the experiment with projects of various kinds and to await the publication of the scholarly work that results. Because this process is bound to be time-consuming, this preliminary report has been prepared with a psychoanalytic readership primarily in mind. Aspects of this account may leave historians in some perplexity. Psychoanalytic collaborations probably must be experienced before their actual qualities can be appreciated or accepted; descriptions or theoretical explication may never suffice.

Yet I present our preliminary findings with the hope that they may interest professionals from both fields in experimenting with the proposed method. In order to do so, the historian must take a bolder step than the psychoanalytic collaborator is called upon to do. For the psychoanalyst, such an experiment represents a variation of his accustomed work, in a research situation outside any practitioner-client relationship. For the historian, the experiment must represent a lot more. The highly personal demands placed upon him can only be shouldered by individuals with a deep sense of conviction and trust.

The first experiment with this method provided many indications that the advantages of its use extend beyond the benefits the historian can receive in terms of new ideas on a specific subject. It offers a unique opportunity to study in close proximity the unfolding creative function.

So far the study of creativity has been approached either theoretically and in combination with historical biographical material or clinically and in reference to cases where therapeutic psychoanalysis was applied. The new methodology offers the hope that the creative process can be directly observed. To those who accept this view, as well as to the skeptics, I can only offer the promise of further research to validate or to refute this hypothesis.

## NOTES

[1]Cf. Carl Pletsch, "A Psychoanalytic Study of Friedrich Nietzsche" (Ph.D. diss., University of Chicago, 1977).

I am deeply indebted to my two collaborators, Professor Carl Pletsch and Dr. John Gedo, for their enthusiastic participation and advice, which made this experiment a true learning experience for me. I am also very grateful to them, as well as to Dr. Joseph Lichtenberg, for their contributions in the preparation and organization of this paper. To Dr. George Pollock, who helped me understand some of the more personal responses this experience produced in me, I express my deepest appreciation.

[2]Friedrich Nietzsche, *On the Genealogy of Morals/Ecce Homo,* ed. and trans. Walter Kaufmann (New York: Random House, 1967).

[3]Friedrich Nietzsche, *Thus Spake Zarathustra,* trans. Walter Kaufmann (New York: Viking, 1975).

[4]Nietzsche, *Genealogy.*

[5]Rudolph Binion, *Frau Lou, Nietzsche's Wayward Disciple* (Princeton: Princeton University Press, 1968), pp. 35–111.

[6]Christopher Middleton, ed. and trans., *Selected Letters of Friedrich Nietzsche* (Chicago: University of Chicago Press, 1969).

[7]Heinz Kohut, "Creativeness, Charisma, Group Psychology: Reflections on the Self-Analysis of Freud," in *Freud: The Fusion of Science and Humanism,* ed. John E. Gedo and George H. Pollock (New York: International Universities Press, 1976), pp. 424–425.

# 4

# *Returning to Nietzsche*

## Carl Pletsch

I WAS AN UNDERGRADUATE in the early 1960s when I first encountered *Zarathustra* and Friedrich Nietzsche's radical individualism. Apolitical and still uninvolved in the protest movement, I had just decided to abandon the study of physical science. My interest in science and commitment to a career in engineering had been formed in the wake of Sputnik with the encouragement of my father, an inventor. Throughout high school I assumed that I would become a scientist or an engineer (although I wrote poetry and had many other interests too). So far as I can remember, no other type of career crossed my mind. But after one year of college science in the atmosphere of a large university, I realized that I was bored and alienated.

The decision to quit science was difficult, but once it was made the alternatives seemed limitless and I felt capable of success in any of them. My first impulse was to take up art and writing and establish my "creativity" in opposition to science; but I was also attracted to philosophy, a discipline that seems to have held out the promise of putting all other intellectual activities, including the sciences, into rigorous perspective. Nietzsche spoke to both needs that I felt so keenly after separating myself from the commitment to science—the need to experience creativity and the need to subordinate science in some larger frame of intellectual order. In Nietzsche I recognized a welcome model of both artist and philosopher. But more than a model of alternative selves, he was an iconoclast, an aesthetic and philosophical revolutionary. This so appealed to me that I adopted Nietzsche as the most salient influence in my education for several years; I idealized him in a way that I can compare only to Nietzsche's own early idealization of Schopenhauer. In retrospect, it seems that I used Nietzsche both to legitimate my rejection of the career plans I had formed under the conjoined influences of parental advice and example and the cold war against Russian science, and to integrate my new conception of myself as a radical intellectual person.

My new sense of myself was one of liberation and satisfaction at having "overcome" the values that I had formerly held and the restrictions that had formerly bound me. The books of Nietzsche that most interested me in those several years were his most personal and individualistic ones, especially *Zarathustra* and his early aesthetic writings such as *The Birth of Tragedy* and *The Use and Abuse of History*. These writings went well with my mood of criticism and my desire to survey the entire spectrum of intellectual pursuits in search of something worthy of my dedication. But in spite of the depth of my involvement with Nietzsche and the seriousness of my attitude, this initial encounter with Nietzsche was with a personal abstraction. I had no idea of the sources or context of his thought or of the possible consequences of his nihilism. It was in a posture of adolescent idealization, therefore, that I took a course in German intellectual history and began to remedy my naiveté. I learned about German Idealism and Historicism and how Nietzsche was reacting against these modes of thought, and about the Second Empire as the context of Nietzsche's work, but none of that surprised me. More interesting was the professor, who seemed to squirm in his attempt to portray Nietzsche as a "good European," a Nietzschean phrase with which he meant to exonerate Nietzsche from the suspicion of having been a proto-Nazi. That Nietzsche might be seen as a proto-Nazi had never occurred to me until then. This alarmed me, but I found the professor's attempt to assimilate Nietzsche's radical individualism to his own liberalism à la John Stuart Mill downright ridiculous. My reading of *The Genealogy of Morals* dispelled any thought that Nietzsche was a liberal and suggested that he was hardly at his best as a social theorist.

At the same time that I began to have these second thoughts about Nietzsche (for reasons that were anything but academic), I became politically conscious. The war in Vietnam, the death of one of my friends there, the threat of being drafted myself, and of course the similar concerns of my contemporaries, all induced me to become involved in the movement of protest against American involvement in Vietnam and domestic racial injustice. These new concerns quite naturally helped reshape my intellectual interests. They certainly conditioned the resolution of my new-found doubts about Nietzsche, for he came to seem irrelevant, if not positively in conflict with my growing social and political convictions.

Turning away from Nietzsche for social and political reasons involved more than a rejection of the reactionary strain in his thought, however. I also rejected Nietzsche's systematic nihilism and relativism in favor of a (then) vaguely Marxist humanism. I can now see that this gave me both the satisfaction of renewed defiance of generally established values and an affirmative orientation to social questions (by comparison with Nietzsche's nihilism). This step, like my abandonment of the natural sciences, has never seemed regrettable; it still seems to have been logical and, on balance, quite positive to have dissolved my idealization of Nietzsche in this fashion. For at the same time that I expanded my intellectual orientation from things personal to things social, I got beyond my first Nietzschean relativism to an admittedly vague set of general principles. But having idealized Nietzsche in such a comprehensive and personal way, my turn away from Nietzsche entailed disillusion and resentment of him. He had disappointed me. This, however, was a dimension of my relationship to him that I became aware of only much later.

My rejection of Nietzsche was hardly complete, however. When I graduated from college, I was still interested in Nietzsche as the author of certain discrete ideas which I perceived to have been particularly valuable solutions to outstanding problems in the history of Western thought. I felt that I could salvage these from my former discipleship to Nietzsche. One of these was the idea of eternal recurrence, on which I wrote my senior honors essay.[1] (It fascinates me now to see that while I took the idea of eternal recurrence as a discrete idea that I could manipulate on a purely intellectual plane, dissociated from Nietzsche's comprehensive meaning for me, this idea was the point of entry for my repeated return to Nietzsche as an object of study, in spite of my apparent turning away from him as a model.)

The books that interested me then were *The Gay Science* and, to a more limited extent, *Zarathustra*—books in which Nietzsche set out the fragmentary affirmative side of his philosophy, and in which it is most apparent that his gifts were not those of a system builder. With some effort on my part, these writings permitted a superficially impersonal interest in certain of his ideas and an only suppressed (and hostile) interest in his personality.

At the same time I made another decision which can be understood in the context of my interest in Nietzsche. I decided to study history instead of philosophy in graduate school, for what seemed to me to be fundamentally social and ethical reasons: I became convinced that philosophical personalities pursued truth abstractly and without careful reference to society—in a way that often vitiated ethics. I made this decision with several professors of philosophy in mind rather than Nietzsche, but one of them was also a Nietzsche enthusiast and I knew these professors personally only because of our common interest in Nietzsche. Of course I was perfectly happy about the prospect of studying philosophers like Nietzsche in their historical context—something that now seems suspiciously analogous to how my initial interest in philosophy was stimulated by the prospect of putting the natural sciences in another kind of context after my interests had turned away from them. I have naturally had reason to revise my judgment of philosophy and philosophers, but I now understand that this judgment was informed by my rejection of Nietzsche as a personal model.

One of the courses I took during my first year in graduate school was a seminar on "political irrationalism" in *fin de siècle* Vienna and modernism more generally. The professor guiding the seminar was under no illusions about Nietzsche's anti-liberal ideas, but he was more interested in the aesthetic reaction against liberalism and Nietzsche's influence on the creators of aesthetic-reactionary politics.[2] As this general phenomenon could hardly be understood unpsychologically (my paper was on Nietzsche and the young Hugo von Hofmannsthal), it occurred to me to take another look at Nietzsche as a whole, to see if his ideas might not be systematic after all, if understood as a psychological rather than a philosophical system. This became my dissertation topic: a psychoanalytically oriented intellectual biography of Nietzsche.

My dissertation was only part of what resulted from this return to Nietzsche. The psychological dimension of my own interest in Nietzsche finally began to dawn on me, and it became an agenda in its own right. Although it was personally satisfying to discover that I had psychologically identified with Nietzsche, it was a mixed blessing so far as my ability to intellectualize about Nietzsche was concerned. On the one hand, I grew confident that I had come to a fairly mature understanding of my subject. I could see how certain common interpretations of him were partial to the degree that they were psychologically determined (as my own had been). I was sure that my interpretation of Nietzsche was going to be more comprehensive than most, inasmuch as it comprehended several psychological reactions to him. Unquestionably, I felt that the psychological approach to

Nietzsche was proving intellectually useful. On the other hand, doing something to Nietzsche that resembled psychoanalyzing, I was trying to put Nietzsche on the shelf in my mind, much as I did the sciences and philosophy at earlier stages. I was trying to put Nietzsche behind me by writing a dissertation on him. I realized that my insights were less vibrant than they had been when my interest so thoroughly involved my conception of myself, and I was not nearly so anxious to pronounce about Nietzsche in public as I had been earlier. I felt positively apathetic about publishing my not quite finished dissertation.

Then, in 1976, I began an experiment in methodology with Dr. George Moraitis, a psychoanalyst. In 1975 I had already written a didactic review of several biographies by psychoanalysts, in which I concluded that the future of psychohistory lay in adapting the psychoanalytic *method* to the conditions of historical study, rather than in applying diagnostic categories and psychoanalytic theory to historical personalities or relationships.[3] But I had not settled on an adequate means of incorporating my conclusions about how psychohistory should *not* be done into a method of testing my actual empathic hypotheses about Nietzsche. It was not until I met George Moraitis at the Center for Psychosocial Studies in Chicago that I found an opportunity to do anything specific in that direction.

Dr. Moraitis had arrived at remarkably similar conclusions about the necessity of adapting the psychoanalytic method, and he was anxious to collaborate with a historian in a psychohistorical investigation. We decided that we wanted to cooperate in a substantive research project, involving historical materials and psychological methods; we also wanted to avoid the drastic and lengthy alternatives of either reeducating the psychoanalyst (Moraitis) to be a historical specialist, or retraining the historian (me) to be a psychoanalyst. In other words, we were both looking for an efficient means of cooperation which would productively exploit our different kinds of expertise without diverting either of us from our professional goals and responsibilities. These preliminary considerations suggested a strategy for selecting a subject upon which to base our experiment in method. Rather than pick a subject at random or on the basis of intrinsic psychological interest, we decided that it should be one in which I had already invested enough work to admit of emotional commitments, and at the same time one in which Dr. Moraitis would not be significantly invested—in order that he be relatively free to respond to my already developed emotional reactions to the subject. From this point of agreement, our work consisted of a series of conversations, free associations, and responses, all of which we taped, and periodic reviews and evaluations of these conversations, which we made with the help of a third collaborator, Dr. John Gedo, also a psychoanalyst.

Our experiment began almost before we had decided to do it, at least so it seems in retrospect. My reluctance to invest so much time talking about my thesis on Nietzsche—a project which then seemed virtually complete—was a prominent dimension in our discussion of whether to collaborate, how to proceed, and what to choose as our subject matter. From Dr. Moraitis's point of view, it seemed advantageous to take a topic in which I was *very* deeply involved, namely my thesis on Nietzsche. I, on the other hand, suggested we start by experimenting with possible topics for my next project in the general field I knew best: Germany in the late nineteenth and early twentieth centuries; I was apathetic about Nietzsche and anxious to move on to a new project. I was also fairly confident about the theoretical consistency and coherence of my analysis of Nietzsche, and felt that I might not get much out of collaborating with Dr. Moraitis on anything concerning Nietzsche, except perhaps confirmation or refinement of my hypothesis. Moreover, there was the danger that I might change my mind about Nietzsche altogether, and thus find myself without any confidence in my almost, but not quite, finished dissertation. Although that concern did not preoccupy me consciously, it must have been one of my unconscious motives for resisting the idea of collaborating with Dr. Moraitis on the basis of my work on Nietzsche.

The problem was not that Dr. Moraitis envisioned an unequal apportionment of the work—in which I had done and would do the research, and he the analysis. We agreed from the first that that would be an uninteresting basis for collaboration. He merely wanted a subject in which I would have a deep emotional investment. I thought I would have some emotional allegiance, no matter which aspect of my major field we chose to discuss. He acceded to my wish, but after a rather dull session on Otto von Bismarck's memoirs I realized how different the emotions I felt toward him and the characters relevant to a study of him were from those I felt about Nietzsche. It was clear that it would take a long time to develop sufficiently elaborate emotional reactions to make conversations about Bismarck worthwhile.[4]

Perhaps even more important, Dr. Moraitis provoked me with his speculation that scholars generally resist talking about subjects in which they are invested. This seemed plausible enough, but I did not think it was my case. Yet there was the question of why I was so reluctant to make Nietzsche the subject of our investigation. Was it really only the practical and professional necessity of moving on to another project? The introduction to my thesis offered a convenient jumping-off point for reflecting on this question, since I had already detailed the stages of my interest in Nietzsche there (these are the opening pages of the present paper). I had tried to explain to myself my periodic attempts to deal with him intellectually, concluding where I finally hit upon the idea of a psychoanalytic study of Nietzsche as a way of disposing of him and his claim on me. From there it was only a short step to the realization that I did not want to be as deeply invested in Nietzsche as I still had to be in order to finish my thesis, and certainly not so deeply as to want to begin a new project on him. This desire to be rid of Nietzsche after all this time was clearly an emotional reaction of a different order from any I might have had to the other familiar figures of Wilhelmian Germany. And that was incentive enough to make me anxious to open the issue again.

This interesting development had several consequences which gave impetus to the experiment. First, it seemed not only to confirm the importance of a strong emotional attachment to the subject on the part of a historian or biographer, but even to suggest that the time to think about collaboration is after the research project itself is well under way and has become part of the historian's conception of self. More concretely, I realized that certain negative feelings toward Nietzsche, which had stood behind my initial decision to write psychologically about him, now had a role in my desire to get on to a new project—and this realization infused me with new interest in the thesis itself. As far as the experiment was concerned, I was elated by the prospect of testing my more concrete responses. If Nietzsche was to be the subject of our investigation, obviously Dr. Moraitis and I would have to discuss the stages of my interest in him in greater detail. My long-term interest in Nietzsche was a kind of evidence that would not even have existed for a subject with whom I had not already been profoundly involved. So we put that on our calendar. But before beginning to analyze my reactions to Nietzsche, it seemed necessary for Dr. Moraitis to know something about Nietzsche's personality. I was naturally thinking of Nietzsche as the analysand and of Dr. Moraitis and myself as his analysts. So I suggested that Dr.

Moraitis read *Ecce Homo*, both for the autobiographical information it contains, and for its value as evidence of how Nietzsche thought of himself and his writing near the end of 1888. *Ecce Homo* seemed the closest thing possible to the kind of evidence with which psychoanalysts are usually confronted, and I wanted to see how Dr. Moraitis would react to it.[5]

I was surprised to find that Dr. Moraitis reacted favorably and enthusiastically to *Ecce Homo*. At that time it seemed to me a greatly exaggerated if not deluded self-description, indicative of Nietzsche's gradual loss of inhibition about expressing his grandiosity. Dr. Moraitis balked at this for the good reason that it suggested a diagnosis of Nietzsche, and he was even more opposed to making psychohistorical diagnoses than I was. He wanted to consider the possibility that Nietzsche's self-evaluation was realistic; furthermore, he was fascinated with the idea that Nietzsche's autobiographical writings constituted a species of free association, or even self-analysis. Nietzsche's discussion of his sickness and the role of his father's death in his creativity seemed to suggest impressive self-knowledge. I was struck by this enthusiasm, but could not help discounting much of what Dr. Moraitis said as superficial first impressions made without an appreciation of the contrast between Nietzsche's conception of himself and his actual life.

I argued the case for Nietzsche's having deceived himself, tracing the evolution of his idealizing exaggeration, first of Arthur Schopenhauer's and of Richard Wagner's qualities, then of Zarathustra, and finally of himself in *Ecce Homo*. I pointed to his messianic pretentions and suggested that his claim (in *Ecce Homo*) to have been the first philosopher to have lived in harmony with his body was a flagrant contradiction of the actual facts. I made as good a case as possible in the brief span of our interview for my contention that Nietzsche had failed to live up to the claims he made for himself in *Ecce Homo;* that *Ecce Homo*, with its subtitle "How One Becomes What One Is," is a description of the person he would like to have been but had not become. To Dr. Moraitis, this seemed an indictment of Nietzsche, and he wondered why I was so hostile toward him. I countered with the question of why he was so enthused about him.

This was not so much an impasse as the first of many opportunities to confront the problem of what to do when two collaborators have conflicting emotional responses to the autobiographical writings of their subject which lead them into different intellectual interpretations of his work. I had more information about Nietzsche at my command than Dr. Moraitis, and could have tried to overwhelm him with illustrations supporting my hypothesis. He, on the other hand, could have shifted the ground to question the unconscious sources of my hostility to Nietzsche and vitiated my interpretation in that way. But either of these strategies would have involved an abdication of our one precondition: either I would be making the psychoanalyst into a historical specialist, or he would be undertaking therapy. Instead, we turned to consider the contexts in which we had derived our insights. Obviously, Nietzsche provoked anxiety in both of us, and we had reacted in ways appropriate to our interest in him. Dr. Moraitis looked at Nietzsche as the subject of our experiment and the author of exciting material relevant to his professional training—an introspective genius and predecessor of Sigmund Freud, an analysis of whom might be favorably received among his colleagues. I, on the other hand, had originally taken Nietzsche as a personal ideal and had then been disappointed in his every discernible weakness. In contrast to the interest Dr. Moraitis might expect to awaken in his psychoanalytic colleagues, my dissertation on Nietzsche had begun to seem something of a liability in the social-scientific context important to me.[6] In the light of these different situations, it was clear that our intellectual communities guided our responses by forming important parts of our self-conceptions. Therefore, it could hardly be our strategy to use our respective kinds of expertise to find out which of us was nearer to the truth. We would have to use our divergent responses as poles of reference in a process of triangulation in order to arrive at a more differentiated and adequate picture of Nietzsche.

It became apparent that there were three of us involved in this experiment—Dr. Moraitis, myself, and Nietzsche. Both Dr. Moraitis and I would have to divide our empathy. He would have to empathize with both Nietzsche and myself, and frequently be faced with differences between Nietzsche's and my interpretations of Nietzsche's life and personality. If he could do this and express his sense of the disjunction—and his psychoanalytic experience prepared him to do just that—I would have an opportunity to test my empathic reactions to Nietzsche continuously. I would have to compare Dr. Moraitis's response to Nietzsche with my own and reflect upon the difference as introspectively as possible, however, if I were to take advantage of the opportunity. Conceiving of our collaboration in this way, I began to think of Dr. Moraitis as a first reader of my work. But unlike first readers who help authors test their data or substantive arguments, his psychoanalytic training enabled him to help me test the emotional dimension of my ideas about Nietzsche. As for Nietzsche, he began to seem more like the analyst than the analysand! He was teaching us both about ourselves.

Our next tack was to discuss those pages of the introduction to my thesis in which I had described the stages of my interest in Nietzsche. Speculative lines of discussion led us to important ideas in spite of my inability to remember additional facts. In regard to the first stage of my interest in Nietzsche, in which I idealized him freely, it became clear that for years I had been able to ignore important aspects of Nietzsche, which would eventually play an important role in my disillusionment with him. In spite of easy access to information about Nietzsche's anti-democratic ideas and his impoverished emotional life, I had remained oblivious to the many indictments leveled against him. In spite of my enthusiasm for Nietzsche, I had obviously not read everything about him that I could get my hands on. This, in conjunction with the other obvious fact that I had used Nietzsche for unconscious purposes of my own, suggested that only a part or particular aspects of Nietzsche's personality and thought were useful to me at that time—his oedipal rebelliousness and his intellectual and aesthetic individuality. Thus, I had held a somewhat idiosyncratic view of Nietzsche which incorporated what was psychologically useful to me and excluded whatever might have disturbed my idealization of him (which must be an extremely common phenomenon among biographers). This one-sidedness produced a certain tension between my view and that of my professors and Nietzsche's translators, editors, and commentators. I could see what was wrong with my professors' views because of my intense empathy for Nietzsche, and I could see through the proprietary attitudes of those who had translated and interpreted Nietzsche; but I was apparently unaware of my own unconscious and proprietary interests in him. I began to suspect that something like this would be the case in the early stages of any psychohistorical or biographical investigation (as well as other investigations). Such partiality can of course seriously skew a research project, but it can also be an immense advantage to an investigator attuned to the idiosyncratic source of his and other investigators' interests in various subjects, since here again one has the opportunity to triangulate among different empathic points of view.

Another fruitful disagreement emerged in regard to my subsequent period of disillusion in Nietzsche. My avowed reason for turning against Nietzsche was a social and intellectual one—that he was incompatible with my growing interest in social questions. Dr. Moraitis suggested, however, that Nietzsche may simply not have provided what I was seeking, either because he was not the personality I had thought he was, or because I was unable to integrate his example into my own personality. And, he asked, why was I so interested in things social? Why could I not just relax and enjoy a great thinker like Nietzsche? Could it be that I empathized excessively with the victims of the war in Vietnam, or that I felt guilty about my privileged position in not having to go to Vietnam while my friends were dying there? I wanted to take these possibilities seriously, but I found it so repugnant that social concern might be taken *prima facie* as evidence of pathology, that I posed the issue anew by asking Dr. Moraitis whether introspection and self-knowledge are good in themselves, or if the full realization of human potential does not imply going on to social action based on self-knowledge. I found myself indicting psychoanalysis and wanting to convince Dr. Moraitis that he was posing a false dilemma—*either* social action as the expression of unanalyzed conflicts *or* a satisfying personal life for the individual as a result of analysis, as if healthy individuals were *ipso facto* perfect egotists unconcerned about social problems. I thought that sort of thinking was what gave American psychoanalysis the reputation of merely reconciling patients to the unfortunate circumstances of their lives.

The emotional tone of our discussion of these issues was such that we were able to draw some conclusions directly. First, it was clear from my impassioned defense of social concern and action that I had indeed looked for some additional values at the time of my disillusionment with Nietzsche and that I had found them in my Marxist orientation to social questions. Second, it seemed that Dr. Moraitis wanted me not to have become disenchanted with Nietzsche, and I speculated that this might be due to his allegiance to the psychoanalytic method and the similarity he perceived between it and Nietzsche's autobiographical reflections (in *Ecce Homo*). And third, Dr. Moraitis pointed out that whatever the precise fate of my original idealization of Nietzsche, my disenchantment with him and my turn to social concern had not involved a complete repudiation of my experience, for I had returned to him in my thesis. These points yielded subjects for several subsequent interviews.

We next discussed *The Genealogy of Morals*.[7] I hoped that this would allow us to explore further the possibility that each of us had an emotional allegiance to our professional methods and the sorts of materials to which they are appropriate. The book also seemed to represent a point in Nietzsche's thought where readers separate into those who idealize and those who reject him. But our discussions were productive in ways I had not expected. Although reading Nietzsche inveighing against social movements in the First Essay convinced Dr. Moraitis of the unsympathetic side of Nietzsche's character and set us talking about how Nietzsche provokes his readers and makes it difficult for them to accept his propositions, we came no closer to resolving what I came to think of as the ideological differences that separate some social scientists from psychoanalysts. In retrospect it seems foolish for me to have hoped that we would resolve them, for these differences were just what made the process of empathic triangulation possible. Each point of view—the psychoanalyst's appreciation of introspective capacity and self-knowledge and the social scientist's esteem for social consciousness—consists of diffuse but deeply internalized values connected with the choice of profession, the process of training, and all sorts of ambitions and aspirations. Breaking down these differences would probably have been impossible and certainly undesirable—both personally and for the sake of the experiment.

These thoughts led me to a more specific conception of how thinking of Dr. Moraitis as a first reader could expand my empathic horizon. I would not have to suppress my social values to avoid alienating readers whose admiration of Nietzsche was based on the revolutionary introspective nature of his thought. I would merely have to find a way of enabling such readers to accept my critique of the antisocial and unsympathetic side of Nietzsche's personality and philosophy without depreciating his introspective achievement (which I myself had exclusively valued when I first encountered Nietzsche). From this point on I was less interested in registering the difference between our perceptions of Nietzsche and deciding whether the differences invalidated my hypotheses than in finding ways of integrating the differences into a single characterization of Nietzsche. Instead of striving for agreement, I found myself wanting Dr. Moraitis to be more contrary and give me more feedback.[8]

Our next tack was to discuss my chapter on Nietzsche's relationship to Richard Wagner. The gist of my argument was that Nietzsche had idealized Wagner, using him as an extension of his own grandiosity, an argument based substantially on my reading of Heinz Kohut. Drs. Moraitis and Gedo both found my argument consistent and plausible with regard to theory and diagnosis, and that was gratifying, but they were both relatively uninterested in discussing it, as if they were slightly embarrassed by the diagnostic categories themselves. Dr. Moraitis was timid about saying what he really thought about the chapter because he did not want to disturb my work on the rest of the then still unfinished thesis. Moreover, he hesitated lest his comments on my emotional posture in the chapter constitute something like therapeutic intervention. Only after I had complained several times that he was not joining the issue did he tell me that he thought I was extremely critical of Nietzsche between the lines of this chapter. He could see that I was disappointed in Nietzsche and was not sure how aware of this I was.

Of course, I had already written in my introduction (before we began our experiment) that my return to Nietzsche in my thesis was a way of disposing of him and a sort of therapy in itself. But oddly enough, it had not occurred to me how the evidence of my disaffection that had crept into the text might strike a reader who admired Nietzsche. I was being severe with Nietzsche for my own benefit, trying to slough off the inordinate influence he had had on me as an undergraduate. But this might easily wound a reader's admiration, or, more likely, discredit me and my interpretation in the reader's mind.[9]

There seemed no reason to burden my readers with my resentment of the fact that Nietzsche needed Wagner so thoroughly. I realized I had other, more significant reservations about Nietzsche's personality and philosophy, which I did not need to obscure with petulance about his need for an ideal. Although my reaction may have been useful in working through my very similar attachment to Nietzsche himself, I concluded that it would be more politic to put my awareness of this straightforwardly into an appendix than to couch it between the lines of a whole chapter. Thus, I came to regard the entire thesis as a private draft and an experiment—with the subject chosen because of my earlier idealization of and disillusionment with Nietzsche, and the writing serving as a partial resolution of my conception of myself as an intellectual. Whereas this stance might be of interest to other historians and social scientists engaged in similar enterprises, it would certainly distract readers interested primarily in Nietzsche himself, especially if it came to pervade the text of the published version. Consequently, I decided to revise the text with the psychological exigencies of the reader foremost in my mind. This was perhaps the most immediate result of my conversations with Dr. Moraitis.

In the same breath I should add that I have wondered if this was not a trivial conclusion. Would not a gifted biographer have instinctively understood the exigencies of his audience and their relationship to his personality? But I am not *naturally* a biographer. If I were, I probably would not have gone to graduate school; I would simply have begun to write biographies. Thus, the value of my simple conclusion seems twofold: first, it enabled me to turn what was partly a personal and partly an academic exercise into an essay for the general reader; second, to the benefit of other scholars, it helped to delineate the functions psychobiography may serve and suggest a method of resolving them. Scholars seldom create works of genius; we more often produce knowledge rather methodically. My thesis and collaboration with Dr. Moraitis became an experiment in a method of psychobiography that may be repeated, in some respects at least, by other scholars.[10]

This conclusion was not the endpoint, however. We then proceeded to discuss *Thus Spake Zarathustra,* the book Nietzsche felt to be the keystone of his philosophy.[11] After having made so much progress on the general issues of collaboration and having turned our conversations to good use on one of my chapters, I thought it was time to look back to Nietzsche himself and do again what we had done at the outset—compare our responses to an important text. By this time our differences were far subtler than they had been with *Ecce Homo,* and I felt we might have many fruitful discussions about *Zarathustra.* That we did may have been due in part to the fact that I had not yet finished writing about this book and was not entrenched in a complete interpretation of it. Certainly, it was due in part to the ambiguous nature of the book. At the same time the fact that we could have come up with myriad interpretations of particular passages was disquieting in that this pointed beyond the scope of our experiment. We had thought we were moving toward a "right" or more refined interpretation, but we found ourselves multiplying interpretations.

The most generally useful part of our discussion of *Zarathustra* was our attempt to focus on the personality of the character Zarathustra and its relationship to Nietzsche's personality. I already had a theory about Zarathustra as a projected ideal, which Nietzsche had substituted for the human ideals (Schopenhauer, Wagner) he had once cherished and then grown disillusioned in. It was around this contention of mine that we had our first extended conversations about theory (with Dr. Moraitis pointing out that ideals, which have not been integrated into the personality, can hardly be projections) and psychoanalytic literature (on the subject of parent loss and uncompleted mourning). I had almost concluded that our collaboration would consist of the adaptation of method to the exclusion of theory, but these exchanges on theory and literature opened several avenues of thought I had not considered. For example, I came to consider the relationship of Zarathustra not only to Wagner, but also to Nietzsche's father, and the difficulty Nietzsche had in mourning—making himself independent of—his father.

We did not exhaust the philosophical themes in *Zarathustra*, or even the explicitly psychological themes. It would have been foolish for us to try, for this would have involved Dr. Moraitis in a massive effort to familiarize himself with nineteenth-century German philosophy and the rest of Nietzsche's book. Plus, it would have meant many more conversations. Once again, we restricted ourselves to limited collaboration: using Dr. Moraitis's expertise in testing my responses to Nietzsche's work. He was not a co-author but a consultant.

Another occasion for testing my emotional stance in my research on Nietzsche arose when we discussed my reactions to another psychobiographer's ideas about an important episode in Nietzsche's life. In his book *Frau Lou*, Rudolph Binion looks at Nietzsche's involvement with Lou Salomé in considerable detail.[12] I was irate about what I considered Binion's systematic slur of Lou and suggested that Dr. Moraitis read several of the relevant chapters, so that we could compare our reactions. This topic naturally raised a multitude of new substantive issues about Nietzsche's sexuality, his capacity for intimacy, his secrecy vis-à-vis his mother and sister, etc. These issues were even more intricate than those that had come up in our discussion of my chapter on Nietzsche's "Lou-affair." Furthermore, we now had fully five psychological points of view to consider (those of Nietzsche, Lou Salomé, Pletsch, Binion, and Moraitis). Consequently, it seems, our discussion of Binion's biography of Lou and my feelings about Binion's treatment of Lou and Nietzsche was relatively unproductive. Perhaps it is too much to expect such a collaboration to resolve the psychological focus of other biographers as well.[13]

After this, we had a number of diffuse conversations in which we went over ground already covered and discussed the implications of our conclusions. The one new theme that emerged was the meaning

of my completed thesis and of the products of psychohistorical research generally. We were both dissatisfied with the fact that almost
all published psychobiographies tend to discredit the historical actors
they treat. I have already indicated that one of the prominent features
of my own chapter on Nietzsche's relationship to Wagner was my
accusatory attitude toward Nietzsche's dependence on Wagner. My
disappointment in Nietzsche over this was something that could only
impede verification of my more significant empathic insights. In ex-
tending this conclusion I surmised that the derogatory nature of
much psychobiography undoubtedly invalidates it in the mind of the
reader. This counterproductive feature of so much psychohistorical
writing must be credited to the researcher's personal investment in
his subject, to his attempt to "work through" his attachment to the
subject. And to the extent that this process is incomplete, the result is
bound to be unconvincing to a sensitive public.

By this time I had come to see the whole collaboration as tending
toward completing the "working through" of my attachment to
Nietzsche. This shift was apparent from my increasing concern with
empathic validation and my decisions about the revisions necessary
for publication. But I was not yet clear about what the result would
be. Dr. Moraitis suggested that historical conceptions are like memories of earlier life: although coming to terms with them may not make
our picture of actual events in the past much more accurate, it certainly increases our self-understanding. Yet if this is true for the author, is it also true for his readers? I wondered if it would be too much
to expect readers to understand themselves better as a result of reading my work on Nietzsche.

When such self-knowledge does not arise, I began to think, a debunking psychobiography is little different from a naively idealizing
portrayal of a hero. Both attempt to mobilize in the audience the same
unanalyzed emotions that motivate their authors. No matter how
many details are presented, the final picture of the historical personality is no more complex than the emotional reaction of the author. It
seemed to me that a biography based on a more complete working
through of the original investment in the subject would have the
potential of leading readers to a more differentiated conception of the
subject. I hoped that my work on Nietzsche would make the clichés
about Nietzsche (like those of the culture-hero and the proto-Nazi)
untenable, or at least unsatisfying to my readers. I hoped my book

would make it difficult for them to react to Nietzsche with simple, unanalyzed emotions. This, of course, would be the very opposite of what is commonly called the "reductionism" of psychological studies. To me, it seemed that good psychobiography should not only result in greater self-understanding on the part of its authors, but develop more complex and differentiated memories of figures particularly susceptible to emotional simplification by the group. At the same time I realized that I was losing my interest in the problems of psychohistory per se and growing more interested in biography as a genre of historical writing.

In the summer of 1981, I reread what I had written in 1975 and 1977. I read with surprising interest, since the sensation was quite different from that of rereading other things I have written. In rereading these autobiographical notes I see and experience myself as an author then, whereas reading my finished thesis and published work, I find myself receding as an author and emerging as another reader. This rereading was uncanny enough for all the reasons that confrontations with oneself ever are. But the rereading also revealed our collaboration to be yet another point of return to Nietzsche, and the point of departure for yet another venture into thinking and writing about Nietzsche.

The account that I wrote of our collaboration, of the metamorphoses of my thoughts and feelings about Nietzsche, and writing my thesis on him, has become part of me. In psychological parlance, I seem to have internalized it. (By contrast, I have externalized my published work—a difference that accounts, I think, for much of the difference in sensation upon rereading.) But if the account rings true after four years, it is not the whole story, and not merely because the whole story is inaccessible to consciousness.[14] Even more significant than the incompleteness of the story is that my view of these matters has not changed in four years, except to grow richer. This may not seem remarkable to those unaccustomed to scrutinizing the changes in their views of the research projects they have pursued. Every reader of these pages will have noticed, however, that my regard for Nietzsche changed dramatically in the course of my study of him. So now to find that my memory and understanding of my collaboration with Dr. Moraitis, in which I become clearly and systematically aware of these changes for the first time, should itself have remained con-

stant over four years is an important datum. It testifies to the significance of our collaboration in fixing (in the photographic sense) the
quality of awareness that I achieved then.[15]

The practical consequence is that our collaboration has given me
leverage for building another stage onto my writing about Nietzsche.
I shall not describe what further work I am doing on Nietzsche at any
length, but I may note that as Dr. Moraitis and I began our collaboration my primary impulse was to get through with Nietzsche and on to
something else—a new and different project. Certainly our work together helped to moderate that impulse and permitted me to think
more freely of how to expand upon and extend the work I had already done on Nietzsche.

Now I am enlarging my "psychoanalytic study of Friedrich Nietzsche" into a book to be entitled *Nietzsche and the Ideology of the Genius*.
In this book, the biographical writing on Nietzsche from my thesis is
placed between an exposition and critique of the great nineteenth-
century ideology of culture that invested such significance in the
creators of ideas (the ideology of the genius), and a discussion of the
devolution of the role and self-understanding of the intellectual in the
twentieth century (approximately since Nietzsche). Nietzsche now
figures as the hinge upon which a profound change in the Occidental
conception of creativity can be seen to turn. The significance of the
changed shape of the project—for our consideration of the psychology of biography, at least—is that the revision represents the gradual
integration or resolution of the several conflicting motives and attitudes revealed in the collaboration I have described. Certainly my
capacity to integrate the terms of these conflicts, which seemed inher-
ent in the project in 1977, is based to some degree on my collaboration
with George Moraitis. Only after I became systematically aware of the
tension between my commitment to and disillusionment with Nietzsche, and my later commitment to the protest movement, Marxism,
and social science, did I begin to realize that the deeper relationship
they had for me could be transformed once more into my work.

In the manuscript of the book, Nietzsche appears ambivalently as
the last great exponent of the ideology of the genius and its first great
critic. As its critic, he appears (paradoxically) to be very much the
path-breaking genius I had originally idealized. And as its last great
exponent, he appears as the decadent—alienated from society, dis-
affected from social problems, and even callous about the culture-
hero's place in society. Thus, somewhat to my own surprise, as I

reread the report on our collaboration, I realized that my plans for the book now seemed to encompass the tension between my earlier, transferencelike idealization of Nietzsche, in which I focused primarily on his heroic individuality, and my later disillusionment. Again, making Nietzsche the hinge upon which the ideology of the genius turns is making my biographical analysis of Nietzsche relevant to understanding a host of other prominent cultural figures of the nineteenth century. This and the problem of describing the relation of the genius to society generally have become the social context for my biographical writing. Recasting my project in this way has permitted me to integrate my humanistic-psychological concerns, originally attached very particularly to Nietzsche, with the social concerns that began to grip me during the Vietnam war and impelled me in the direction of Marxism and social science.

I realized the connection between the collaboration and the gradually developing plans for my book only upon rereading my report. It was not, in other words, a plan that I consciously conceived immediately upon concluding our collaboration. A considerable period of gestation was needed, during which I wrote and published on other subjects, but only ruminated upon how I would finish my book on Nietzsche. Yet it seems to me that our collaboration was the point of departure for my thoughts on the ideology of the genius.

## NOTES

[1]A later version was published as "Friedrich Nietzsches Philosophie der Zeit und die Geschichte," *Saeculum* 24 (1973): 41–49.

[2]See William J. McGrath, *Dionysian Art and Populist Politics in Austria* (New Haven: Yale University Press, 1974).

[3]Carl Pletsch, "A Note on the Adaption of the Psychoanalytic Method to the Study of Historical Personalities," *The Psychohistory Review* 8 (1979): 46–50.

[4]In retrospect I am astonished and not a little amused that I should have chosen to try to discuss Bismarck. I can hardly imagine a less appropriate research topic for me. So it seems that while I was unconsciously trying to escape discussing Nietzsche with Dr. Moraitis, I selected an alternative that made the escape impossible—also unconsciously!

[5]Friedrich Nietzsche, *On the Genealogy of Morals/Ecce Homo*, ed. and trans. Walter Kaufmann (New York: Random House, 1967), pp. 215–335.

[6]The "social-scientific context" also inspired my interest in Bismarck. Again, in retrospect, I can see that my return to intellectual history was

facilitated by my growing awareness of the degree to which my aversion to Nietzsche as the subject of our collaboration was determined by the fashion for social history.

⁷Nietzsche, *Genealogy*, pp. 13–163.

⁸I tentatively concluded that disagreement is productive in principle; indeed, I would go so far as to suggest that collaboration without some real confrontation must be considered incomplete. More specifically, I would revise our original stipulation about choosing a subject about whom the psychoanalyst knows little to include the provision that the historian should lead the psychoanalyst immediately to introspective material with which he can feel some kinship and develop an initial positive reaction. I had done this quite by accident, thinking that *Ecce Homo* would show what a megalomaniac Nietzsche was (or seemed to me at that time), but the outcome was instructive, because the introspective side of Nietzsche appealed to Dr. Moraitis's professional values and allegiances. I should add that I expect arguing over a philosophical text like *The Genealogy of Morals* to be less conducive to particular insights about the text than to a general awareness of reactions that must be taken into account.

⁹This now seems to be the most crucial area in which the psychoanalytic partner in a collaboration of this sort can help the historian as an empathically trained reader: giving the biographer, the historian, or the scholar generally a good view of the probable emotional responses of readers to the subject—not merely by listing such possibilities, but by actually feeling and expressing them. For it is not enough that the author understand his own response and the way in which it is peculiar to his own personality. Verification of empathic insight is possible only to the degree that readers can share such insight. And whereas all investigators may derive one or another idiosyncratic satisfaction from their insights, there is no need to burden the reader or the verification with these private satisfactions, which will only arouse defenses in others.

¹⁰It is repeatable in the psychological and not the natural scientific sense, of course. On the role of case studies in psychology, see Carl Pletsch, "Freud's Case Studies," *Partisan Review* 44, no. 1 (1982): 101–118.

¹¹*The Portable Nietzsche*, ed. and trans. Walter Kaufmann (New York: Viking, 1954), pp. 112–439.

¹²Rudolph Binion, *Frau Lou, Nietzsche's Wayward Disciple* (Princeton: Princeton University Press, 1968).

¹³In spite of this, I believe that it frequently would be productive to explore a biographer's feelings for other writers on the subject of investigation. Certainly some of the investment in a subject is transferred to other investigators in the field, and rivalry with them must sharpen one's psychological insight into their unconscious motives. But it also seems probable that an investigator might project some of his own unconscious anxiety about the subject onto his rival. In either case, this strategy should not be overlooked, even though it did not yield dramatic results in our particular experiment.

[14]My reservations about examining in public every lead that has emerged from my unconscious are essentially the same as those that Freud expressed in the concluding paragraph of that chapter of *The Interpretation of Dreams* in which he analyzed his own "specimen dream" some eighty years ago. See Sigmund Freud, *Standard Edition of the Complete Psychological Works*, ed. and trans. James Strachey, vol. 4 (London: Hogarth Press, 1953), pp. 120–121.

[15]This leads me to suggest that the written report is an important part of such a collaboration, and that no one who decides to follow our procedure should neglect to write out an account of what he has done and learned.

# 5

# Henry Adams: An Intellectual Historian's Perspective Reconsidered

## Mark R. Schwehn

IN THE OPENING CHAPTER of his nine-volume *History of the United States during the Administrations of Thomas Jefferson and James Madison*, Henry Adams sketched the following imaginary scene as a kind of symbolic picture of his elaborate analysis of the state of American society and politics in 1800:

> A government capable of sketching a magnificent plan, and willing to give only a half-hearted pledge for its fulfilment; a people eager to advertise a vast undertaking beyond their present powers, which when completed would become an object of jealousy and fear—this was the impression made upon the traveller who visited Washington in 1800, and mused among the unraised columns of the Capitol upon the destiny of the United States.[1]

This passage alludes to a portion of Edward Gibbon's *Autobiography*, a text that Adams knew well. In that book Gibbon recalled the moment when the idea of writing the *Decline and Fall of the Roman Empire* first occurred to him "at Rome on the fifteenth of October 1764, as I sat musing amidst the ruins of the Capitol while the barefooted friars were singing Vespers in the temple of Jupiter."[2]

The image of Gibbon on the steps of the Church of Santa Maria di Ara Coeli, musing amidst crumbling columns about the meaning of the fall of Rome, obsessed Adams. He carefully prepared the imaginary scene in his *History* by noting, in a passage immediately preceding the one quoted above, that in 1800 congressmen and the chief executive clustered together "as near as possible to the Capitol, and there lived, *like a convent of monks.*" Their Capitol, moreover, "threatened to crumble in pieces and crush Senate and House under the ruins, long before the building was complete."[3] In the *Education of Henry Adams,* a book that Adams composed in 1905, fifteen years after he had finished his *History,* he revealed that, during the summer of 1860, he had more than once sat on the very spot where Gibbon had sat some hundred years before. Adams returned to this place, in fact or in imagination, several times during the course of his life.[4]

In the course of my own thinking and writing about Henry Adams, I have had occasion to return "more than once" to this allusive passage in his *History* and to the text of which it is a part. In re-viewing Adams's life and work again and again, I have written two different historical interpretations of his *History.* In the essay that follows I should like to recount those two interpretations and to describe the process that led me to my current reading of that text. I should like finally to suggest some of the methodological implications of my experience.

I.

I began my study of Henry Adams almost ten years ago as a part of an effort to understand the development of modernism in Western thought. In my Ph.D. thesis I sought to clarify the nature of modernism by focusing on the ideas of both Henry Adams and William James, and by construing the development of some of these ideas as strands of a larger cultural pattern. I interpreted Adams's *History* by placing it within the sequence of its author's intellectual life and by locating some of its major themes within the network of problems that Adams faced during the 1870s and 1880s. In addition, I tried to elucidate those aspects of Adams's cultural context that seemed directly pertinent to a historical understanding of his work.[5]

The substance of my interpretation emphasized the ironic structure of the *History.* The book was, I argued, the story of the improbable but triumphant growth of American democratic nationality despite the persistent failures of American leaders, despite even the initial mental deficiencies of the Americans themselves. The *History* accordingly stressed the dissonance between consciousness and purpose, on the one hand, and unconscious nature, on the other. As a result of Adams's absorption of Sir Charles Lyell's developmental geology and Herbert Spencer's evolutionary positivism, he had come to believe that American democracy had "as fixed and necessary a development as that of a tree; and almost as unconscious."[6] Since democracies progressed only by developing naturally, according to laws exactly like those that governed the physical universe, principled and idealistic political action was ineffectual at best. Indeed, American nationality emerged triumphant at the end of the period from 1800 to 1817, even though American politics, the major preoccupation of the American people during this period, tended to retard national development.[7]

The *History's* ironic interpretation of American politics served to rationalize Adams's own political failures. During the 1870s he had been active in the liberal reform movement, which sought to expose and check corruption in government, to restore political parties to a state of ideological purity, and to devise some system whereby government would rest in the control of those best equipped to deal scientifically with social and economic questions. After these efforts failed repeatedly during the 1870s, Adams abandoned politics for scholarship. That scholarship, informed as it was by the evolutionary positivism that Adams had adopted during his tenure as a Harvard history professor, fortified his will to believe that *all* political action was superfluous in a democracy. Thus, as I wrote in 1978, Adams's *History* "served to justify his own temporary occupation in writing it."[8] It proved, to his own satisfaction at least, that scholarship and not politics was the only viable pursuit for the intellectual in a democratic society.

II.

In 1978 I presented my interpretation of Adams's *History* to Dr. George Moraitis, a Chicago psychoanalyst. This presentation constituted a part of a long-term experimental collaboration between Dr. Moraitis and myself. During the course of our experiment, I selected portions of my own work on Henry Adams, such as my chapter on Adams's *History,* or portions of Adams's own writings. After Dr. Moraitis, who knew nothing about Henry Adams, read these materials, we met to discuss them. (I will not recount our procedures at greater length here, because our experiment was modeled closely on an earlier experiment that Moraitis has described.[9])

My own objectives during the experiment were clear. I sought to discover the nature and perhaps some of the roots of my own long-term involvement with the life of Henry Adams. I hoped that as I became more aware of the range and the depth of my own subjectivities, my study of Henry Adams would become more "objective"—freed from the potentially distorting effects of unexamined motives on the substance of my interpretation.

During our discussion of my Ph.D. thesis, I realized that I had strongly identified myself with Henry Adams. The sources of this identification were many and various, but it manifested itself most markedly in my initial refusal to publish any psychological or partially psychological interpretations of Adams's work. Indeed, in my Ph.D. thesis I had sought to conceal or suppress all of my rather elaborate psychological hypotheses about Adams. I believed that psychological explanation was inherently reductionistic, and I argued that any psychological interpretation of Henry Adams's life and works would invariably diminish his intellectual stature. I also invoked the historian's ultimate principle to justify my doubts about publishing my own psychological hypotheses: I denied that I had sufficient evidence to substantiate them.

I also offered other defenses of my refusal to press psychological interpretations in my projected book, objections whose logical force ought not be denied simply because some of them may have sprung from dubious motives. First, I argued that my projected book sought to emphasize the connections between Adams's works and the culture of which they were a part. Hence, psychological interpretations, however well informed, seemed irrelevant to *my* purposes. This might be called the defense of my position in formal terms. Second, I feared that, regardless of the care and restraint with which I employed psychological interpretations, my envisioned audience would seize upon *just those* aspects of my work as the crucial part of my overall argument about the development of modernism. This might be called the defense of my position in rhetorical terms. Finally, I maintained that my efforts to understand the meaning of my materials, such as Adams's *History*, entailed recovering the intentions that governed those works, not the motives that were accidentally and contingently related to them. This might be called the defense of my position in methodological terms.

I am still somewhat persuaded by my own formal and rhetorical defenses against the use of psychological interpretations in my present book, and these reservations will doubtless shape the final form of my overall argument. Nevertheless, I do believe that all of these defenses stemmed in part from my desire to protect Henry Adams. Furthermore, in seeking to protect Adams, I was, up to a point, seeking to protect myself, and I often resisted our collaborative investigations by finding excuses for postponing our sessions. As a result of this resistance, the timing of our meetings was highly irregular. Even so, my reading of the *History* has changed appreciably as a result of our experiment, and I no longer maintain my methodological objection to using psychological interpretations in my work.

III.

In 1980, after Dr. Moraitis and I had stopped meeting together to discuss Henry Adams, I wrote an article on Adams's *History* entitled "Making History: Henry Adams and the Science of Democracy."[10] It presents a multicontextual interpretation of Adams's work, and I still remain as committed as I was during the 1970s to this kind of historical explanation. Indeed, I incorporated much of my thesis chapter into this article. I added, however, a psychological dimension to my interpretation, a dimension that emerged directly from my collaboration with Dr. Moraitis and that yielded new and, I think, more incisive readings of the *History*.

Unlike the thesis chapter, the 1980 article explored the psychological relationship between Henry Adams and the leading character in his *History*, Thomas Jefferson. Once I had discovered how closely I had identified with Henry Adams, I realized how closely Adams himself had identified with Jefferson. Most Adams scholars have minimized his positive characterizations of Jefferson, and they have tended to explain negative ones by the seemingly plausible argument that Adams was settling family grievances against the man who had so soundly defeated John Adams in 1800.[11] On the basis of a wide range of historical evidence, both internal and external to the text of the *History*, I wrote in 1980 that Adams had lavished such unsparing criticism on Jefferson, "not in spite of his identification with him, but because of it."[12] This hypothesis led me to an understanding of certain features of Adams's characterization of Jefferson that otherwise seem mysterious or unimportant. Moreover,I now understand how Adams's very choice of Jefferson as his leading subject permitted him to exercise some of his own ambivalent feelings toward his distinguished ancestors in the course of writing about a man who was at once a bitter enemy and a close friend of Adams's great-grandfather.

The psychological dimension of my historical interpretation of Adams's writings also deepened my understanding of numerous passages in the *History*. As an illustration of this understanding, I should like briefly to reconsider the passage from Adams's *History* that I quoted at the beginning of the present essay. In my 1980 piece I did not discuss this particular passage, but I believe that its meanings become more accessible in the light of the psychological aspects of my 1980 interpretation of the *History* as a whole. One measure of the value of an interpretation is its capacity to illuminate portions of a text that would otherwise remain obscure.

As I have already suggested, the scene that the imaginary traveler surveys in 1800 symbolizes Adams's preceding analysis of the state of American society at the turn of the nineteenth century. "The city of Washington," Adams wrote, "rising in solitude on the banks of the Potomac, was a symbol of American nationality."[13] By virtue of its allusion to Gibbon's decision to write the *Decline and Fall of the Roman Empire*, the passage also suggests the grandiosity of Adams's design, and it connects the theme of Adams's *History* to Gibbon's theme. Gibbon, musing amidst ruins, decided to trace the history of a falling action, the decline of Rome. Adams, placing an imaginary traveler among the unraised columns of the Capitol, forecast the rising action of his work, the history of the progressive development of American democracy. As I noted in my 1980 piece, several features of Adams's *History*, such as its erudite allusions, its sly and sometimes savage ironies, and its carefully balanced phrasings, bore the stamp of Gibbon's influence. When Adams completed the narrative portion of his work, he compared his feelings on that occasion to Gibbon's feelings on the completion of the *Decline and Fall*. Adams was indeed inviting the kind of comparison that has been made by at least one critic of his work. Yvor Winters has judged Adams's *History* to be "the greatest historical work in English, with the possible exception of the *Decline and Fall*."[14]

Though the formal and thematic elements of this allusive passage seem clear enough, some of its phrasings seem obscure. For whom would the completion of the American experiment in democratic nationalism "become an object of jealousy and fear"? For the imaginary traveler? For other nations? For the narrator of the *History*? Adams certainly was jealous and fearful of American power. Indeed, as I have tried to show in my 1980 essay, the same democracy whose progress Adams explained in his *History* had vitiated his inherited world view, thwarted his political ambitions, and had thereby confirmed his feelings of impotence and despair. I have also suggested in the 1980 essay that Adams's whole life was marked by a syndrome of impotence, including his deep feelings of physical inferiority; his envy and hatred of his older brother, Charles Francis Adams, Jr., precisely because of Charles's masculine strength and military valor; his childless and tragic marriage; and his repeated failure to attain any position of political power.

Since the envy of masculinity so pervaded Adams's life, I believe that the very image he used in this passage from his *History* to symbolize American nationality provides a clue to the sources of the obscurely assigned feelings of jealousy and fear. The symbol of completely developed American democracy is, by extension so to speak, a fully erected column. Indeed, the phrase "unraised columns" seems utterly oxymoronic unless it has sexual connotations as well as architectural denotations. In any event, Adams chose to symbolize the rise of American power in indisputably masculine images. As for the central character of his *History*—the one with whom Adams had become so deeply identified, the one who was powerless to control the growth of the country that he sought to govern—"Jefferson's nature was feminine."[15]

Jefferson was not the first of Adams's "feminine" figures to be perplexed and overtaken by the uncontrollable masculine force of American democracy. Adams twice interrupted his work on the *History* to write novels, both of which featured female protagonists. The dramatic action of one of them, tellingly entitled *Democracy*, consists of the tragic romance of Madeleine Lee, a woman who sets out for Washington in order to discover the secret of American power. As early as 1871, Adams had begun to contrast impersonal, rational, and masculine forms of life with personal, emotional, and feminine ones. And long after he completed his *History*, Adams continued to contrast various forms of power—political, economic, spiritual, military, and technological—in terms of gender. The most famous chapter of his *Education,* entitled "The Dynamo and the Virgin," marks the culmination of this tendency.

By now it should be clear that the passage I have been interpreting represents a classic instance of an overdetermined verbal action. I have been arguing that, in addition to formal and thematic considerations, feelings of grandiosity and sexual inadequacy were also at work in determining the passage's composition. The *History* shows how Adams managed to transfuse these feelings, which were doubtless two parts of the same psychological syndrome, into the tensions between the impersonal, inexorable, and masculine evolution of American democracy and the "feminine" Jefferson who was "sensitive, affectionate, and, in his own eyes, heroic."[16] The passage, then, is a kind of microcosm of the *History* as a whole, for both represent cases of the transmutation of psychic stress into cultural expression disciplined by the requirements of the historian's art.

IV.

Thus far I have tried to detail how and why my interpretation of Henry Adams's *History* changed in the course of my collaboration with a psychoanalyst. Yet these new readings of the *History* have in turn encouraged me to reexamine the intellectual merits of some of my former defenses against the use of psychological interpretations in my projected book on modernism. I should like briefly to reconsider some of those objections now, before suggesting some of the methodological implications of the experimental collaboration itself for historians, especially biographers.

I now believe that what I referred to earlier as my formal objection to psychological interpretations was misguided. A historical account of the development of modernism should at least provide some understanding of how intellectual transformations occur. In terms of my own projected study, such an understanding is best rendered through an intelligible account of how and why Henry Adams and William James changed their minds over time, developing, in the course of these changes, ideas that finally contributed to a distinctively modern style of thought. Both men came from families that were exceptionally accomplished and hence formidable; moreover, families are arguably the principal agencies of the transmission of culture from one generation to the next. Any account of the intellectual development of Adams or James would therefore be incomplete without considerable attention to their family relationships and to some of the psychic strains that these relationships engendered.

When I first voiced my formal defense, I believed that I was simply reporting a choice I had made between a culturally oriented and a psychologically oriented interpretation. I now believe that, although it is possible to distinguish between the cultural and the psychological components of a historical interpretation, it is often fruitless and perhaps misconceived to make sharp distinctions or to assert causal relationships between the cultural and the psychological features of an individual's intellectual development. I say this, not on the basis of some theory of culture or psychological development, but on the basis of my efforts to make historical sense of the life and works of Henry Adams and William James. Take, for example, the masculine-feminine distinction that I emphasized in the course of my interpretation of the allusive passage from Adams's *History*. Understanding the meaning of this distinction for Adams and interpreting his use of it in the *History* entail, as I have already suggested, some attention to the psychic conflicts engendered within the context of his family. But historical understanding of the *History* also entails an appraisal of the significance of the fact that Adams's dichotomy between intuitive, emotional, and feminine qualities, on the one hand, and scientific, rational, and masculine ones, on the other, represented—as I wrote in 1978—"a widespread cultural tendency among upper class Victorian men."[17] In Adams's case at least, culturally defined gender distinctions doubtless shaped the way that he was reared, and the way that he was reared in turn shaped his own self-conception. That self-conception prompted him to develop a certain set of masculine-feminine distinctions, to cultivate a unique network of associations between those distinctions and, say, the relationship between American nationality and political idealism, and to articulate these associations as tensions within his *History*—a form of expression that was at once personal and cultural. Did culturally defined gender distinctions determine Adams's psyche, or did Adams's psyche, together with the minds of others, determine gender distinctions? Did cultural conflict cause psychic distress, or did psychic distress cause cultural conflict? These latter questions manifest, I believe, a certain kind of conceptual confusion to which historians are especially prone. Asking such questions is rather like asking whether one side of a lens is convex because the other side is concave, or whether the other side is concave because the the one side is convex.

Alas, I fear that such questions are very much like the ones that historians most commonly ask one another. The defense against psychological interpretations that I articulated in rhetorical terms stemmed from just such a fear about my envisioned audience. The most common complaint about multicontextual historical explanations is that such explanations typically fail to single out *one* context in terms of which all the others can be understood. Reviewers often seek to remedy this perceived failing by seizing upon one of the contexts a given book provides and arguing that it *really* explains or illuminates the book's subject better than all the others combined. My fear was that my audience would seize upon the psychological aspects of my interpretation as the key to the whole, and, given my identification with Henry Adams, I expressed this fear in terms of a rhetorical argument for omitting psychological interpretations altogether.

Can these anticipated objections to multicontextual interpretations be effectively countered? I believe that they can be countered in three ways. First, the readers of a multicontextual interpretation need to be reminded that contextual explanations are not disguised causal explanations. Readers who insist that historians should privilege one of their contexts are often really asking that historians should specify a principal cause of the process they seek to interpret and explain. Second, the readers of a multicontextual interpretation need to be informed that the choice of this kind of explanation is linked to a certain conception of the subject matter of history. I believe that the subjects of my history are beings whose mental processes are informed, developed, transmitted, and expressed in cultural terms. A human being's culture defines his (or her) mind and his mind defines his culture; in that sense he is like the lens I described above. A person's psychological side does not cause his cultural side any more than the cultural side causes that person's psychological side. Instead, both sides "define" the contours of the human being just as concavity and convexity "define" the shape and the powers of a particular, indeed any, lens. This view of the subject matter of history is certainly open to dispute. My only point here is that multicontextual explanation, as opposed to causal explanation, is connected, in my case at least, to this conception of my subject.

Finally, historians can counter the standard objections to multicontextual explanations by casting their interpretations in a form that best realizes their own peculiar purposes. This essay is not the place to mount a defense of narrative explanation, but I do believe that narration seems especially well suited to the purpose of articulating subjects within several relevant contexts without either losing sight of the subjects altogether or reducing them to mere illustrations of some oversimplified explanatory principle. I believe that much of what Clifford Geertz has written about anthropology applies to intellectual history: intellectual history is not a positivistic science in search of causal laws but a descriptive science in search of meanings. But intellectual history, like all history, aims to understand change over time. I therefore believe that intellectual historians are well advised to cast their "thick descriptions" in narrative form.[18]

My methodological defense against psychological interpretations was more closely related to both my formal and my rhetorical defenses than I had initially believed. It is, of course, perfectly possible and even at times useful to distinguish theoretically between motives, defined as a complex of psychological impulses that are accidentally and contingently related to an action, and intentions, defined as characterizations of the action itself.[19] I have, however, found this distinction much easier to maintain in theory than to exercise in the practice of historical interpretation. What, for example, am I to make of my own claim that Adams's *History* "served to justify his own temporary occupation in writing it"? Does this claim characterize Adams's *point* in writing the *History* (does it describe the work's intention)? Or does it posit a psychological condition antecedent to and contingently connected with the writing of the book (does it describe a motive)? I confess that I am not sure about the answer to this question, nor am I sure about the exact point of the distinction that the question raises. It seems to me that motives and intentions shade into one another in the same way, and partially for the same reasons, that psychology and culture shade into one another. In any event, I have found motives and intentions equally pertinent to a historical understanding of the text of Adams's *History*. Thus, in my brief methodological prologue to my 1980 essay, I wrote: "Interpreting Adams's classic history entails two related tasks. Adams's changing views of the nature of the historical process must be explained, and his *History* must be understood by placing it within the several different contexts which serve to clarify the motives that inspired its creation."[20]

V.

"One sees what one brings," Henry Adams wrote in his account of why he, his "idol Gibbon," his friend Augustus St. Gaudens, and his contemporary John Ruskin viewed the Gothic cathedrals of Northern France in such radically different ways.[21] During the course of my collaboration with Dr. Moraitis, I learned the extent to which I had seen what I brought to my study of Henry Adams. I had, of course, brought myself to that study, and in learning more about myself and the sources of my involvement with Adams, I also learned why I had failed or refused to see some of the material of Adams's life and work that had always been, in some sense, in front of my eyes. Or, to put matters a bit differently, as I began to modify my interpretation of Adams's work during the course of our experiment, some of the evidence in support of my emerging interpretation became, for the first time, visible as evidence.

The relationship between our experiment and my most recent views of Adams's life and work is difficult to state with confident precision. During the course of this present essay, I have suggested that my 1980 reading of Adams's *History* "emerged during the course of" or "resulted from" our experiment, but these ways of stating the connection may be too strong. I do believe that my thinking about Adams's *History* changed between 1978 and 1980, and I have tried to specify and document those changes here. But of course I can never be certain about the extent to which my interpretation would have changed without the experiment.

For this reason, and for several others, I commend such collaborative experimentation to other historians, especially biographers, on humanistic rather than scientific grounds. It would be odd indeed to suggest, for example, that my 1980 interpretation of Adams's *History* should be appraised by repeating the experiment that in some sense led to it. It should be obvious that the experiment is in no sense repeatable. Furthermore, the validity of my 1980 interpretation depends on the logical character of the arguments I have advanced on its behalf and on the sufficiency of the evidence I have marshaled in its support, not on the nature of the experimental procedures I happened to follow in arriving at it. Even if I could confidently claim that my 1980 interpretation of Adams's *History* resulted directly from my collaboration with Dr. Moraitis, I would have to add that the validity of the result was in no sense contingent upon the methods that brought it about. And, of course, it is certainly conceivable that my 1980 interpretation is less valid than the one I formulated prior to our experiment.

Still, historians do see what they bring to their research, and they have readily written a great deal about the effects of ideological, cultural, and temporal biases on their work. They have been less ready until recently, however, to reflect upon the extent to which their work is shaped by unconscious or unexamined psychological processes. My collaboration with Dr. Moraitis provided one disciplined way to reflect upon this matter, and I would defend the value of our experiment on this basis alone. It was also valuable to me, however, because it enabled me to learn more about myself in the course of learning more about my subject and to learn more about my subject in the course of learning more about myself. As a result of this experience, I now believe that biographers are necessarily involved with their subjects in ways they do not fully comprehend. If they choose to reflect upon this involvement in a disciplined manner, a collaborative experiment with a psychoanalyst might well be the best means for doing so. But though I can promise that such an experiment will yield self-knowledge, I cannot predict with any certainty that it will make a bad biographer a good one or a good biographer a better one.

## NOTES

[1]Henry Adams, *History of the United States during the Administrations of Thomas Jefferson and James Madison,* 9 vols. (New York, 1891), 1:31.

[2]Edward Gibbon, *Autobiography* (New York: Oxford University Press, 1960), p. 124.

[3]Adams, *History,* 1:30–31; my italics.

[4]Henry Adams, *The Education of Henry Adams,* ed. E. Samuels (Boston: Houghton Mifflin, 1973), p. 91.

[5]Mark Schwehn, "The Making of Modern Consciousness in America: The Works and Careers of Henry Adams and William James" (Ph.D. diss., Stanford University, 1978).

[6]Henry Adams to Francis Parkman, December 21, 1884, in Harold Cater, *Henry Adams and His Friends* (Boston: Houghton Mifflin, 1947).

[7]Schwehn, "Modern Consciousness," pp. 79–80.

[8]Ibid., p. 65.

[9]George Moraitis, "A Psychoanalyst's Journey into a Historian's World: An Experiment in Collaboration," *The Annual of Psychoanalysis* 7 (1979): 287–320. Reprinted here as Chap. 3.

[10]Mark Schwehn, "Making History: Henry Adams and the Science of Democracy" (1980). This paper is currently under consideration for publication.

[11]The most recent version of this error appears in Otto Friedrich's *Clover* (New York: Simon & Schuster, 1979), a biography of Henry Adams's wife Marian Hooper. Friedrich claims that "it was with a pretense of praising the vanished hero that Adams began his infinitely malicious portrait [of Jefferson]" (p. 284). A more subtle instance of the same error appears in Ernest Samuels, *Henry Adams: The Middle Years* (Cambridge, Mass.: Harvard University Press, 1958), pp. 388–392. Samuels observes that "Adams could not help but identify himself with Jefferson"; however, Samuels believes that this identification sprang principally from Adams's appreciation for Jefferson's wit and refinement (p. 388). Samuels then reverts to the standard thesis to explain Adams's criticisms of Jefferson. Many of them, especially those that Adams undertook in response to promptings from his brother Charles, came from "the effect of family tradition" (pp. 391–392).

[12]Schwehn, "Making History," p. 20.

[13]Adams, *History*, 1:30.

[14]Yvor Winters, *The Anatomy of Nonsense* (Norfolk, Conn.: New Directions, 1943), p. 29.

[15]Adams, *History*, 1:323.

[16]Ibid., p. 324.

[17]Schwehn, "Modern Consciousness."

[18]Clifford Geertz, "Thick Description: Toward an Interpretive Theory of Culture," in *Interpretation of Cultures* (New York: Basic Books, 1973), Chap. 1.

[19]For an elaboration of these distinctions, see Quentin Skinner, "Meaning and Understanding in the History of Ideas," *History and Theory*, 44–45.

[20]Schwehn, "Making History."

[21]Adams, *Education*, p. 387.

# 6

# A Psychoanalyst's Perspective on Henry Adams

## George Moraitis

I BECAME FAMILIAR with *The Education of Henry Adams* during the course of my collaborative work with Professor Mark Schwehn in 1978. A few years ago I described a similar collaboration with Professor Carl Pletsch, a biographer of Friedrich Nietzsche.[1] I met with Schwehn several times for two- to three-hour sessions and discussed with him selected materials that had been assigned by him. In this, as in my collaboration with Pletsch, we proceeded with the understanding that we would not attempt to become experts in each other's fields. I consider myself a visitor in the historian's laboratory and invite him to introduce me to the subject of his research in whatever way he considers feasible within the limitations of time. The objective of such a collaboration is to study the development of the historian's creativity and to identify the origins of the ideas and attitudes presented in his writings. I assume that all historical investigations are subject to influences of the historian's personality. These influences can be identified as transference reactions, in the sense that elements of the material under investigation reverberate with experiences from the investigator's past and produce emotional responses that affect his thinking about his subject.

Transference reactions associated with reading biographical materials are bound to be common. They occur when we read novels or view films and plays, and they may be intense. In contrast to the

Reprinted by permission of the Chicago Institute for Psychoanalysis from *Psychoanalysis: The Vital Issues*, Vol. 1 (New York: International Universities Press, 1984), pp. 233–253, where it appeared under the title "The Two Readings of *The Education of Henry Adams*."

transference reactions of the professional historian engaged in writing a biography, however, they are transient and superficial. The stimulus seems to act like the day residue of a dream in precipitating the emergence of a memory and in evoking a wish. It triggers an affective release in the form of sadness, fear, or nostalgia, which has pleasurable components even when painful. Readers or viewers can often make conscious connections between the stimulating material and the experiences in their own past with which it reverberates. The whole process is close to consciousness and represents a reenactment of the past.

In-depth study of an author's creative work, however, leads to transference reactions of a more complex nature. This is particularly true with authors who have made contributions of great originality. In order to clarify this difference it is important to draw a certain distinction between creative and adaptive motives within the individual's personality structure. This distinction is particularly evident in persons with great talent whose creativity interfered with adaptation and gave rise to intrapsychic and interpersonal conflict. Internal harmony is seldom, if ever, experienced by people with great gifts. Perhaps the same can be said of scholars who attempt to grasp the work of the great masters. In their attempts to come to terms with someone else's perception of the universe, basically different from their own, scholars are bound to experience tensions that involve various aspects of their personalities.

The scholar's transference reactions to reading material often appear as avoidances. What the reader fails to perceive consciously and respond to is determined by his wish to maintain a certain perception of reality that he is emotionally attached to. Sometimes the avoidance is conscious and deliberate, with the reader feeling that he can logically argue in defense of his own position. When unconscious, however, the avoidance assumes a true transference meaning. More specifically, it indicates that the reading material interferes with the reader's capacity to reenact his perception of the universe as formulated from previous knowledge. In this paper I shall attempt to discuss my own experiences with two readings of a historical document separated by three years. In describing my observations of myself and my collaborator, I hope to identify two distinctly different responses to reading material that seem to correlate with two different sectors of a reader's personality. This observation has some important implications concerning the nature of transferences as they occur during the course of a scholar's work, and concerning creativity in general.

My collaboration with Professor Schwehn began with his asking me to read selected portions of his dissertation, which pertained to the development of modern consciousness in America and included much biographical material on Henry Adams and William James. (My collaborator's thesis had already been accepted, and he was in the process of revising it for publication.) After the first exploratory session, during which we focused primarily on Henry Adams, he suggested that I read Adams's novel *Esther*, which had been published under a pseudonym so that nobody would "profane it." During the second, rather dramatic, session we discussed this novel at length. I was struck by the ineffectiveness of the characters in the story and the "play-acting" quality of their interactions. I had had a difficult time keeping my attention on the book and found myself trying to understand why the author failed to engage his reader. The main character, Esther, seems aimless and depressed, probably because her father is dying. She is not an active member of the society she lives in, and no information about her background is provided. She is never truly engaged with the other characters in the novel, but consistently maintains her polite, proper and pleasant attitude.

Our discussion about Esther led to some consideration of the women in Henry Adams's life. We talked about the death of his sister from tetanus, which he had witnessed, and the death of his wife, who committed suicide after thirteen years of marriage. Gradually we turned our attention to the male characters in the novel. Professor Schwehn emphasized Adams's idealization of his father and the importance of his distant presence for Henry. Henry Adams was secretary to his father as Esther seems to have been to hers in the novel. From Schwehn's erroneous communications, I assumed at the time that Henry Adams's father had died shortly before the novel was written, and that led me to believe that the writing of the novel represented an effort to grieve for his father's death. I concluded that he expressed his grief by identifying with a fictional woman who was also mourning her father's death. Adams's identification with Esther raised questions in my mind about his feminine identification and a possible negative Oedipus complex. Recently, however, in writing his paper, Schwehn discovered his error. Adams had not written the book *Esther* at the time of his father's death; instead, my collaborator had read Adams's work at the time of his father's death.

This revelation reinforced my initial impression concerning Schwehn's identification with Henry Adams. Henry Adams, a small, frail man, had felt ineffective, unable to compete physically with other males his age. With considerable affect, my collaborator provided information about his early identification with Henry Adams, which he connected to the fact that he, too, was unusually small until age nineteen. He had suffered a good deal as a result of this. My collaborator's father was a minister, as were many of his ancestors, and shared all the moral values of the Adams family.

My collaborator's associations confirmed the presence of an intense transference reaction barely under the surface of his consciousness. He revealed his feelings to me with candor. Had this been a therapeutic situation our direction would have been obvious. We would have explored in more detail the investigator's past, in an effort to understand more accurately the hidden meaning of these early experiences. This course, however, would not have added much to our understanding of Henry Adams and his intellectual work. In line with the objectives of our work, we took a different path. To begin with, we observed that two investigators, a historian and a psychoanalyst, with very different professional backgrounds, had reached a consensus about the meaning of a given document and developed a sense of in-depth communication with each other and the subject under study. We thought that this provided a triangulation that could add to the validity of the interpretation.

It is important to note that Professor Schwehn did not even refer to *Esther* in his dissertation, and yet he assigned this book to me to read at the very beginning of the collaboration. I understood his approach as an effort to protect his work from transference reverberations, and thus maintain the necessary objectivity and neutrality that enabled him to complete his thesis. Only in the presence of a trusted collaborator did he decide to deal directly with material that aroused transference reactions of great intensity. The investigator's regulation of the input of investigative material into his own work is directly related to the degree of stimulation the material produces. When overstimulated, he takes steps to shield his creative function temporarily from overwhelming influences and contains his activities within certain protective boundaries.

Several months passed before we resumed the collaboration. When we got back together, it was no surprise to either of us that my collaborator assigned for reading several chapters from *The Education of Henry Adams*. The preface, "Quincy," "Boston," "Twenty Years Later," and the "Dynamo and Virgin" were among the chapters assigned, but my reading extended considerably beyond this, covering most of the book. I did not reread *The Education of Henry Adams* until three years later, when I selected this topic for a paper to be given at a symposium on biography at the Institute for Psychoanalysis in Chicago.

The two readings of *The Education of Henry Adams,* spaced three years apart, were in several respects an education for me. Each reading helped me understand something about the author and his ideas. Even more educational for me, however, was the way the two different readings taught me something new about myself as a professional and the psychoanalytic view I adhere to. Having presented some information on how my study of *The Education of Henry Adams* began, and how my first intervention provided some insight for my collaborator, I shall now focus primarily on my own educational experience.

My first reaction to *The Education of Henry Adams* was negative. I was appalled by what I took as the author's lack of psychological sophistication. Given Adams's intellectual abilities, I assumed that he must have taken great pains to maintain the unpsychological nature of his work. My collaborator emphasized Adams's deliberate attempt to create a sense of discontinuity and disorientation in the reader: "if he were here," he would have been pleased with my response to his book. I wondered why Adams did not feel the need to put things in order. I noted his comfort and even pleasure in discovering ignorance in himself and in others, as well as his distaste for continuity and "unity," and probably even education as we know it.

Professor Schwehn saw in Henry Adams an old man filled with genuine grief and distress over the illusionary unity of the prevalent formulas for apprehending the world, one who alerts the reader that these formulas have nothing to do with realities or true discoveries. In contrast, I was struck by the author's difficulty in describing his feelings and his failure to provide personal information in his book. I wished to make clear to my collaborator how transference elements had biased his view of his subject. I wondered how Adams justified omitting from this account of his life twenty crucial and dramatic years, which included the death of his parents, the marriage and suicide of his wife, and several major publications. At the time I did not give sufficient credence to Adams's intent to present the story of his *education,* not his life; I did not appreciate how separate the two stories were in the author's mind.

Only during the second reading did I come to realize how determined I had been the first time to read in *The Education of Henry Adams* a story the author, with equal determination, did not write. I was so busy reading between the lines that I failed to pay sufficient attention to the lines as written. As a matter of fact, I even thought of putting all the statements Adams made about his personal life in sequence and reading them, to the exclusion of the rest of the book. My fantasy was a clear indication of how selective my reading was. My attention was riveted on the author's defensiveness in not telling us the story I wanted to hear. In the process I failed to recognize my own defensiveness in not reading what was written or dealing with the intellectual content of the book. I approached the text with certain preconceived notions that had emerged from the previous discussion with my collaborator of the novel *Esther*. I saw Henry Adams—or, more accurately, the character he created in the book—as an angry, depressed, obsessive individual whose negative view of the world served a psychologically defensive purpose. I assumed that early in his life he developed highly idealistic and largely unrealistic expectations of himself and of others, and that he went through life suffering the inevitable disappointments. Becoming president was, for him, the very least he could accomplish in his life; failure to do so probably represented an intolerable disgrace. His attacks on people in power seemed to me an expression of envy and narcissistic rage, and his admiration of women's power, an idealization of women based on identification with them. I sensed that he maintained a highly exaggerated perception of himself and his influence on others, despite his overt display of modesty and continuous claims to ignorance.

Understandably, my collaborator was deeply disturbed by my perception of Henry Adams, whom he was consistently inclined to idealize. Although willing to accept his own feelings of inferiority and envy, he refused to go along with my interpretation of Adams's ideas as the product of these feelings. Our positions were in direct contrast to those I described in my collaboration with Carl Pletsch, in which Pletsch emphasized Nietzsche's neurotic pride while I defended Nietzsche against Pletsch's negative transference. With eloquence and enthusiasm, Schwehn described Henry Adams as an individual who offers himself as a symbol to illustrate the fate of modern man. To understand Adams, one must resort to aesthetics rather than any psychological or social theory. His metaphors are comparable to those of a poet. He points to the stupendous failure of spirituality in the nineteenth century and to the grotesque, mindless force of the dynamo: "All the steam in the world would not create a cathedral." Scientific theories retreat behind the horizon of a universe that escapes human understanding. Scientific theorizing is but a parody of knowledge and sooner or later proves to be puerile.

At the end of his long effusion, my collaborator apologized for his "passionate sermon." What particularly disturbed him was my treatment of Henry Adams's ideas as an outgrowth of his personality conflicts. This approach to the text, as it later became evident, was an attempt on my part to avoid taking notice of the intellectual substance of *The Education of Henry Adams.* In retrospect, I can see that this avoidance was a reaction on my part to the author's ideas, one that skewed my capacity to maintain a more even approach in analyzing this historical document. In contrast, my collaborator's transference reactions were triggered by his knowledge of Henry Adams's personality, with whom he identified. The intensity of this identification affected his capacity to appreciate other aspects of Adams's personality and place him more accurately in historical perspective.

My first reading of *The Education of Henry Adams,* then, was highly selective in both the literal and psychological senses. I read primarily the parts my collaborator assigned and expanded only into those areas that attracted my curiosity and interest. As already noted, I approached the text with certain preconceived notions, derived from the earlier discussion with my collaborator concerning the novel *Esther.*

I returned to *The Education of Henry Adams* on my own initiative. As I was searching for an appropriate topic for a major presentation, I realized how strongly I wanted to pursue the study of this document. This time I had no difficulty involving myself with the book and read all of it systematically. In a personal sense, the most moving of the second reading occurred when I recognized the effect Henry Adams's ideas had had on my thinking and my work. In a recent paper on "The Analyst's Response to the Limitations of His Science," I described a patient who opposed my efforts to "know" and "understand" her and defended her claim to "ignorance."[2] I suggested that I should have appreciated the unique nature of my patient's experience, resisted my need to interpret, and shared with her the awareness of my own ignorance. This is precisely what Henry Adams invites the reader to do in company with the persona Adams in his book—an invitation I totally ignored during my first reading. Later in my paper I remarked on two approaches, on how some people create a perception of themselves that, in its clarity and consistency, resembles a seventeenth- or eighteenth-century painting whereas others portray themselves in terms closer to the abstractions and distortions characteristic of modernist painting. It struck me that I had borrowed this imagery from *The Education of Henry Adams*. Adams, who saw himself as the "child of the seventeenth or eighteenth century," and projected his own image into the twentieth-century intellectual world.[3]

My paper, written a few months after my first reading of *The Education of Henry Adams*, is in a sense a statement about my psychoanalytic education. In it I describe my original blind adherence to the explanatory theories of psychoanalysis, the frustration and disappointment I experienced in the application of those theories, and finally the realization that considering "the stage in development and the nature of the science of psychoanalysis . . . we do not have the instrument that would explain all aspects of the patient's behavior and, under certain circumstances, we may better serve our science by taking notice of certain clinical data without the compelling need to classify them under one or another theoretical schema."[4] The term "explanatory theories" directly relates to the concept of unity used by Adams, and the direction I propose is the movement from unity to multiplicity that constitutes the central theme of *The Education of Henry Adams*.

Even if my proposal could have originated in a number of other sources, I still must explain why I refused to deal with ideas so close to my thinking during the first reading. The second reading made it quite clear that the selectivity of my first reading was defensive in nature and not accidental. I had directed my attention to the author himself, to the exclusion of his ideas, probably because his ideas so profoundly affected me. My psychological reaction constitutes, in my mind, an example of reading on two levels, which I will attempt to analyze.

Henry Adams did not write the *Education* for his contemporaries, but for an audience a century later: it is we who are his intended readers. He accurately anticipated the collapse of our faith in a mechanical universe and the frustration of our efforts to establish "objective reality." Henry Adams's ideas are not difficult for a contemporary reader to empathize with. For the contemporary psychoanalyst, it may be even easier. Psychoanalysis today is disengaging itself from the mechanistic, energistic theories with which it was first associated by its founder and is reexamining its relationship to the physical sciences. Ths psychoanalyst constantly searches for meanings, whose multiplicity defies previous efforts to unify them under one or another schema. Given my enthusiastic support for the new direction of psychoanalysis, I doubt that my resistance, evident in my first reading of Adams's book, is connected to objections to the author's intellectual position per se. Indeed, my interest in *The Education of Henry Adams* was not restricted to my intent to help the historian with his work. It was also motivated by the fact that this historical document deals with issues of education—a subject of particular interest to me for a number of personal and professional reasons. So far psychoanalysis has produced no systematic theory of education, and it has even been argued that it does not need one. Such views discourage the psychoanalytic study of man's pursuit of knowledge, although this pursuit is obviously parallel to the pursuit of self-knowledge in therapeutic psychoanalysis.

In his preface Henry Adams declares: "The object of study is the garment, not the figure. The tailor adapts the manikin as well as the clothes to his patron's wants. The tailor's object in this volume is to fit young men, in universities or elsewhere, to be men of the world, equipped for any emergency, and the garment offered to them is meant to show the faults of the patchwork fitted on their fathers."[5] In contrast to Adams's objective, my first reading aimed to take the garments off and expose the manikin as well as the author hidden inside it. For strictly clinical purposes, perhaps this was a perfectly understandable aim, insofar as the garment represents a protective shield or a simple extension of what lies underneath. For scholarly purposes, however, this is a very inadequate procedure. The study of education, psychoanalytic or not, cannot proceed without taking into account the person who is being educated. As an educator, Adams could not study himself without examining the figure, but as an analyst, I cannot examine the figure without taking the garment seriously into account.

Understandably, such a combined approach will address motivational issues that *The Education of Henry Adams* totally bypassed. The accidental nature of the educational events the authors describes gives no evidence that the person subjected to the educational process exercised selectivity. In the book the persona Adams constitutes a mechanical receptor, simply accepting or, more frequently, rejecting the input provided. The persona Adams appears as an inanimate robot subjected to an interminable series of false teachings; only after a long and tedious odyssey does he arrive at the unshakable belief about his own ignorance and that of his masters. The degree of conviction is reflected in such statements as: "Chaos is the order of nature and Order was the dream of man."[6] As the author moves consistently from chapter to chapter, from travel to travel, and from experience to experience, to the same familiar conclusion of man's infinite ignorance, one wonders to what extent ignorance represents the Ithaca of this new Ulysses, the destination he intends to reach after great effort and long years. To want to know absolutely everything and to confess absolute ignorance may seem to represent opposite ends of a spectrum of aspirations to knowledge. In actuality, they are merely two manifestations of an aspiration to absolute clarity about the outcome of learning and education.

During my second reading of the book, I was conscious of the extent to which Adams sustained his thesis. He envisaged education largely as a negative process in the course of which one unlearns false learning. Viewed in this way, education is a systematic pursuit of ignorance, which inevitably dethrones the idealized images of the "masters who are responsible for the false learning." In *The Education of Henry Adams* there are no heroes, no truths, no gods. The lonely, disillusioned persona Adams reaches the pinnacle of his knowledge when he "realizes" that his masters are not only ignorant but impotent as well. They lack both knowledge and power.

It can be argued that the persona Adam is too much of a a caricature to do justice to the author's intellectual position. My initial eagerness to diagnose him may have been an expression of my anger at his creating a persona who inadvertently ridiculed an intellectual position with which I was basically in sympathy. Admittedly, Adams did not intend the persona in his book as a caricature but as what he called a "variation." The joke was to be on the teachers who never succeeded in taming the boy. The unintentional ridicule stems from the imagery evoked in the reader, especially the reader who is searching for the personification of an ideal. Freud said that a caricature entails "the exaggeration of traits that are not otherwise striking and it also involves the characteristics of degradation."[7] I think my reaction to the persona Henry Adams was on that level, suggesting a fallacy in my perception of reality that I was not emotionally prepared to deal with.

Only three years later was I ready to return to the book and deal consciously with the ideas it generated. In the meantime I had come to realize the pride and arrogance of modern man, myself included, hidden behind the deceptive apologies about our ignorance. In traveling through the vast unknown—the universe that surrounds us, as well as the inner depths of the individual's own psyche—the explorer is in frequent need of shelter, way stations that provide comfort and relief from the tension that encounters with novelty create. Resignation to ignorance can be as effective a shelter as the illusion of knowledge. Both provide, experientially, a sense of arrival of having reached one's destination. The traveler who thinks he knows his point of arrival, as well as the one who thinks he knows he can never arrive, both share the illusion that the destination is familiar and predictable—an illusion that interferes with the true appreciation of novelty.

Adams accurately predicted that man's concern about the limitations of his knowledge would dominate the intellectual world of the twentieth century. In science, as in all scholarly pursuits, we are reminded of the limitations of our senses and our capacity to perceive both external and internal reality accurately. Psychoanalysis has been greatly influenced by these trends. During the last several years, basic assumptions of psychoanalytic theory, such as its metapsychology and the centrality of the Oedipus complex in psychopathology, have been questioned or discarded. In the process, old heroes have been overthrown, and there seems to be reluctance to create new ones. The harder we try, the less we are sure what we really know. Education, psychoanalytic or not, can no longer be defined as a fixed point of intended arrival; it is a *process* in need of systematic psychological study. The pursuit of knowledge is an urge deeply rooted in the human psyche. Individuals and societies may triumphantly declare their convictions of knowledge, or they may give up in the face of this formidable task and confess their ignorance. Psychoanalysis cannot help the scholar establish the relative accuracy of these declarations. It can, however, approach knowledge as a problem of the human mind that can be studied through introspection, with the hope of developing a systematic method of inquiry.

The psychoanalyst who ventures into the social sciences must develop a wider motivational hypothesis to explain the scholar's pursuit of knowledge and pleasure in discovery. The psychoanalytic concepts of sublimation and the duality of primary and secondary processes do not suffice to explain man's compelling struggle to perceive the universe on an organized level. Lately much has been written in the psychoanalytic literature about the development of the sense of self and the individual's capacity to maintain it. In contrast, our capacity to perceive the other, the nonself, has not been dealt with in psychoanalysis. Some assume that the one is the simple outcome of the other; once the sense of self is developed there will be enough psychic structure available for the perception of the nonself. Others may simply postulate that such inquiry is outside the realm of psychoanalysis. It seems to me, however, that to place the perception of the self into proper perspective, the perception of the "other," of the nonself, must undergo a parallel development. To facilitate a more balanced view of ourselves, we must direct our attention to the "other person" and to the "other" that is not a person. We should not rest assured that reality-oriented thinking is an epiphenomenon, the mere outcome of a successful adaptational struggle. Logic and reason, the supreme functions of the human mind, may be present from the beginning of life; the "secondary process" may not be so secondary after all. Psychoanalysis may not need to "rest its arms" when confronted with the task of understanding creativity. If our desire to know and discover is "primary" in nature, education and the scholar's pursuit of knowledge represent an effort to satisfy a basic human need that exists along with others and does not necessarily derive from them. Such a conceptualization can open the door to an investigation of creativity without the limitations imposed by the present theoretical schema. The study of autobiographical documents like *The Education of Henry Adams* provides a good illustration of this point. Great thinkers offer information about themselves in order to facilitate the reader's understanding of their perceptions. The autobiographical writings of creative personalities are not just exercises in self-indulgence. The psychologically minded reader must appreciate this basic principle in order to achieve a useful interpretation.

Like many other authors with great gifts, Henry Adams produced an important piece of autobiographical writing toward the end of his life. Writings like *The Education of Henry Adams* represent a historian's effort to go beyond the writing of history, to reveal aspects of himself in an attempt to make history. The *Education* reveals not only the ideas of Henry Adams but also the spectacles through which he perceived the world and developed his ideas. The reader who takes possession of these spectacles can examine them as clues toward an understanding of the author's personality, or he can put on the spectacles in order to see the world approximately as Henry Adams saw it. My two readings of *The Education of Henry Adams* revealed how complementary these two approaches are. This paper represents the autobiographical account of a psychoanalyst who ventured into the world of an intellectual historian. At first I scrutinized Henry Adams's spectacles as a way to understand his personality. After a time I realized that my subject's intellect and perceptions had affected my own perceptions of the science I serve and the larger world in which it belongs.

The revelations Henry Adams offers us about his educational garment provide enough glimpses of the author's humanity to demonstrate that he was no ordinary student. He refers to himself as a "variation" and blames the scarlet fever that left him small and frail. In my first reading I took his statement as a thinly disguised sense of superiority. My second reading convinced me that he is more an exception than a variation. Throughout his life Adams showed unusual curiosity and eagerness to explore and master the complexities of the world. Such eagerness might be partly explained by the compelling need he felt to prepare for the presidency. His long odyssey was not suspended, however, when he realized he would not become president. Instead, he persisted in a journey that eventually revealed an image of the universe too formidable to master and an image of a self too small and weak for the task. The innerly driven quality of his pursuit, with its disregard for adaptive needs and self-serving considerations, is characteristic of the exceptionally gifted individual who has achieved an early awareness of external and internal realities. As John Gedo has pointed out, people with extraordinary gifts feel very special, and rightly so, because they are exceptions.[8] When the caretakers fail to recognize the extraordinary abilities of such gifted children, intrapsychic conflicts become inevitable.

It is hard to tell from the *Education* whether Henry Adams was understood and recognized by his caretakers. His mother may have been just an "atmosphere," but in all probability his father was an "influence." As his readers, however, we are now the caretakers of his creativity. In examining his work, it is important to take into account his unusual gifts and appreciate the contribution of his gifts to our own pursuit of knowledge. The psychological study of creativity is in essence a study in introspection in which the investigator reports the experiences and educated assumptions generated by his subject's creative product.

In the interdisciplinary study described here, the introspective work of both investigators was facilitated by the presence of a collaborator who provided the necessary feedback and element of control. First, I provided Professor Schwehn with information that enabled him to recognize his intense identification with his subject and the restricting effect of this identification on his scholarly work. Subsequently, Schwehn provided the feedback that eventually helped me recognize my avoidance in dealing with Henry Adams's intellectual position. During the second reading of the *Education*, I became conscious of my identification with Henry Adams's intellectual position and my refusal to accpet the persona Adams as a representative of a thesis that I had, at the time, highly idealized.

## NOTES

[1]George Moraitis, "A Psychoanalyst's Journey into a Historian's World: An Experiment in Collaboration," *The Annual of Psychoanalysis* 7 (1979): 287–320. Reprinted here as Chap. 3.

[2]George Moraitis, "The Analyst's Response to the Limitations of His Science," *Psychoanalytic Inquiry* 1 (1981): 57–79.

[3]Henry Adams, *The Education of Henry Adams*, ed. E. Samuels (Boston: Houghton Mifflin, 1973), p. 4.

[4]Moraitis, "Analyst's Response," pp. 75–76.

[5]Adams, *Education*, p. xxx.

[6]Ibid., p. 451.

[7]Sigmund Freud, "Jokes and Their Relation to the Unconscious," in *Standard Edition of the Complete Psychological Works*, ed. and trans. James Strachey, vol. 8 (London: Hogarth Press, 1960), p. 208.

[8]John E. Gedo, "The Psychology of Genius," *International Journal of Psycho-Analysis* 53 (1972): 199–203.

# 7

# *Biography and the Russian Intelligentsia*

## Richard Wortman

---

### I.

UNLIKE THE OTHER contributors to this book, I have never made an extended study of the life of a single individual. Rather, I have approached biography as a way to comprehend history, to understand movements and currents of thought by examining the lives of individuals who contributed to them. As a result, my intellectual and psychological involvement may be somewhat different from that of the typical biographer. The experience of steeping oneself in the concerns, aspirations, and feelings of a single figure over an extended period is not one that I have shared. Indeed, except for my work on Leo Tolstoi, I have avoided major figures, seeking the typical rather than the outstanding and examining dominant and widespread responses rather than the original visions of a genius.

My avoidance of involvement with a single figure can undoubtedly be explained by my own psychology. After a certain stage of my work, I admit to feelings of unease and impatience with an individual subject, as his obsessive self-involvement or dedication to specific ideas or goals becomes wearying. Casual acquaintance with historical figures suits me better than prolonged intellectual cohabitation. But my approach also has intellectual grounds. In studying the lives of individuals, I am seeking the interface between history and biography. For that purpose, the personal world of one figure can be enclosing. The experiences of the individual become historically meaningful to me only when they are set in the context of experiences of others with similar concerns. This approach also avoids the pitfall of ascrib-

ing originality to thoughts of the subject that were in fact only the
common currency of the time. Tolstoi's ideas, for example, are frequently presented as the independent discoveries of a lone genius,
even when they were in fact inseparable from the ideological heritage
of his era.

Nonetheless, I have always been attracted to psychology and psychological approaches to history. In high school and college I began
reading the classics of psychoanalysis; indeed, I had intended to become a psychoanalyst before turning to history. My initial impulse is
still to understand human behavior in psychological terms, or at least
to notice its psychodynamic aspects, though this is an impulse I do
not fully trust. When I study history, it is the *individual's* ideas and
experiences that seem to me most meaningful and informative. Biography, for me, is a historical source—the best way to capture the
subjective reality of a period. Generalizations about historical groups,
I have found, often seem meaningless or inappropriate when applied
to the lives of the individuals who compose that group. For example,
"the repentant noble" psychology ascribed to liberal or radical no-
blemen in nineteenth-century Russia is frequently applied to figures
who voice the idea of a debt to the people even if they display no
signs of guilt or repentance. On the other hand, certain values shared
by the group, such as an aversion to individual enterprise, or even
individual happiness, may have a special resonance in the life of the
individual member. I have tried to study how group ideals influenced
the individual's life and how they were in turn affected by his own
experiences. I have taken this approach first to members of the Russian intelligentsia, and later to officials in the tsarist bureaucracy. My
particular interest has been in the way personal lives intersect with
political or institutional issues. I have found that childhood experiences, marital relations, friendship, all figure in the relationship to
power and the social world, and thus demand attention.

The importance of the personal lives of thinkers became clear to me
during my initial study of intellectual history. Ideas have played an
exceptional role in Russia's history. The autocracy's monopoly of
power and the high esteem enjoyed by European culture made
thought the realm of politics and gave the thinker a powerful voice as
a leader of society. My own study of Russian history only strengh-
thened my conviction of the importance of ideas and attitudes. Again
and again, the subjective mentality of a group, rather than an objective political and social cause, proved the principal determinant of

political action. In the early twentieth century, it was members of the intelligentsia who led Russia's first political parties. They conceived of politics within the framework of their intellectual heritage. Ideas defined the range of possibilities and desirable goals; in this respect too, ideas continued to be omnipotent.

The fascination that Russian intellectual history holds for me is not something I can easily explain. In part, it stems from curiosity about a culture different from our own, one in which thought played a central role and evoked respect and even fear. In part, it may be the influence of the times when I was educated. The 1950s, a period of disillusionment with ideology and skepticism about all intellectual systems, bred curiosity about a milieu that centered on such systems. In the 1950s, social thought seemed suspect, in some respects even incomprehensible, and ideology appeared to serve personal as much as social needs. On the other hand, I have resisted attempts to understand doctrines in terms of rationalization, compensation, or other diagnoses of pathology. Such interpretations overlook the positive functions of thought for the individual and the society, and often impose current intellectual vogues on past experience. My goal has been to examine how ideas and personality interact rather than to fit varied experiences under a single rubric.

My study of Russian intellectual history has revealed how much ideas dominated the intellectual's personal life as well as his relationship to government and society. In his reading, the intellectual sought guides to the way he should live, love, and earn his livelihood. Ethical and political imperatives engulfed personal life; success or failure in one was bound to have an impact on the other. In this respect the history of ideas can tell only part of the story of the Russian intelligentsia. Russian intellectuals embraced Western doctrines but filled them with their own meanings, often transforming them as they tried to apply them to their lives. Idealism, positivism, Marxism, Nietzscheanism—all appeared in versions quite different from and on occasion contrary to the spirit of their Western originals.

The personal significance of ideas comes out clearly in my research. Reading all the writings of a figure in a period, together with his biographical materials, often reveals a psychological reality beneath his actions or ideals. This emerges at moments of peculiar intensity when personal concerns break into a discussion of general questions and illuminate them with individual meaning; biography and intellectual history then intersect and disclose the particular, per-

sonal role of ideas. Such psychological moments afford rare opportunities for empathy. They make it possible to enter into an author's
personality and to gain a sense of how he felt about the world. At
such moments I have felt captivated by my subject. I sense a bond
with someone living at another time and in another culture. His internal landscape becomes bold and compelling. The social group, the
broad historical context fade in the distance.

But though the experience is enthralling, it is also suspect. A fascination with the details of personal life seems in some respects intellectually illicit, and I have frequently backed away from such preoccupation. The plunge into subjectivity threatens critical distance. It
can make the historian his subject's captive, magnifying idiosyncrasy
and thereby distorting the historical picture. The immediacy of personal experiences takes the historian away from the public sphere,
where the individual's ideas assume their meaning. Personal experiences often seem to me as they did to R. G. Collingwood: "the blind
forces and activities in us which are part of human life as it consciously experiences itself, but are not parts of the historical process:
sensation as distinct from thought, feelings as distinct from conceptions, appetite as distinct from will."[1] I share Collingwood's solic-
itousness about the historical process just as I feel intuitively the
historical importance of the individual's personal quandary.

The research for my first book, *The Crisis of Russian Populism*, led
me directly to the consideration of the psychology of members of the
intelligentsia.[2] The book was a study of several populist writers'
search for the agrarian ideals the intelligentsia cherished during the
1870s and 1880s. Once in the countryside, these writers found to their
dismay that the peasantry displayed the spirit of acquisitiveness and
egoism they dreaded, and offered a poor ideal of social life. Their
disappointment led to intellectual bewilderment and desperate
efforts to reformulate their approaches to reality. One of them sought
to change the peasantry by teaching them to farm collectively; another struggled to discover the ideal elsewhere, even in his own
fantasy. A third constructed elaborate retionalizations of his experience to explain why the collective ideal was actually immanent in
reality. All three communicated their distress and their ways of dealing with reality to their readers in the city.

I first viewed their responses as a consequence of the social and
economic change Russia underwent after the emancipation of the
serfs in 1861. Graduate school was a stage in my life of skepticism

about, if not outright hostility toward, psychology and psycho-analysis. But the more closely I examined the materials and the social change taking place, the less sense my approach seemed to make. Relations in the countryside, it turned out, were not suddenly chang-ing. What was interesting was what these writers imagined to be there and their personal responses when it proved absent. In each case, the failure to find the ideal brought on a personal crisis. Their glimpses of the sordid sides of village life drove them to introspection and self-doubt. The ideal played a crucial role in their psychology. It created the possibility for a meaningful ethical life; its failure was disastrous. Their writings described a struggle to salvage their ideals and to reinterpret reality.

Most important in my shift of viewpoint were the moments of psychological candor that occurred in the sources. The writings of Gleb Uspenskii, one of the writers I analyzed, were particularly revealing in this respect. When I examined Uspenskii's descriptions of his experi-ence in the provinces during the later 1870s, I decided to use the original journal versions rather than the book editions of his works, which had eliminated inconsistencies, repetitions, and changes of viewpoint. Such close analysis of the individual reports dispels the artificial unity of viewpoint the writer imposes on a more polished final product and reveals more clearly the turmoil that led to key insights and conclusions.

The significant episode for me appeared in a minor work Uspenskii wrote in 1875, while he was working in a railroad office in the provin-cial town of Kaluga. He observed and was shocked by the brutal and ruthless methods of the railroad managers, who seemed to let noth-ing stand in the way of their striving for wealth. He was especially disturbed by the submissiveness of the educated men who served as office clerks, meekly assisting the managers. As one of those clerks himself, he felt his own tacit complicity in the managers' greed and inhumanity.

At this point, in the middle of the descriptions of his work in Kaluga, Uspenskii presented the image of his maternal grandfather, the family patriarch of his childhood, Gleb Sokolov. Sokolov was an important official in the town of Tula, where Uspenskii had grown up. Stern and despotic, he had dominated the lives of his children, whom he settled around him, and his terrifying figure lived on in the memory of his grandson, Uspenskii. Now, in 1875, Uspenskii re-called the mournful atmosphere in the settlement around Sokolov's home. He remembered how craven the adults and children were, in constant trepidation of Sokolov's rebuke. He described his own sense of guilt and worthlessness before Sokolov, as well as his love for him.

Uspenskii's image of the brutal, stupid figure of male authority made me acutely aware of the fragility of his psychology and the central role of the social ideal in it. His belief in social justice was not an abstraction borrowed from the works of Aleksandr Herzen and Nikolai Chernyshevskii; it was a self-justification that gave him the sense of esteem denied to him by his society and his ancestry. Without it, his grandfather's rebukes rang in his ears, and he became an accomplice in evil.

A similar process followed his disappointments during the later 1870s. The sight of individualism and greed among the peasantry, he felt, reflected upon himself. It prompted self-recrimination, self-hatred, recollections of childhood traumas. It made it clear that populism, for this *intelligent,* was far more than a scheme of political and social renovation. It was a basis of personal survival. The alternative was not simply continued political repression and injustice, but impotence and infantilism. My research on other populist writers revealed similar patterns, though with completely different responses to the problem.

The episode also suggested why it was Uspenskii who had revealed the negative aspects of peasant life to the intelligentsia. Other writers had confronted similar scenes in the countryside and yet not felt that their world view was shattered by what they saw. The structure of populist ideology was supple enough to account for contradictory phenomena, and their personal defenses were strong enough to rationalize disappointment. It took a person with the delicate psychology of Uspenskii, who personalized everything he saw, to give the unrelievedly bleak picture of the countryside that forced a rethinking of the premises of Russian radicalism. The doubts his accounts raised led some to question their populist assumptions, others to modify them to accommodate the disturbing facts. In this way, his subjective experience had a decisive intellectual impact.

My second book, *The Development of a Russian Legal Consciousness* also involved the use of extensive biographical materials in what was a group biography of leading legal officials.[3] Here, however, I was concerned mainly with the evolution of a professional ethos, and the examination of individual experience was a secondary interest. I will therefore pass on to a discussion of my later work on Tolstoi and the intelligentsia. The possibilities offered by a study of Tolstoi's religious and philosophical ideas had always intrigued me. His ideas were a strange combination of prophecy and self-justification, other-world-liness and unrelieved self-involvement. It was also at this time that I became seriously engaged in the study of psychology. During 1975 and 1976, I was associated with the Chicago Institute for Psycho-analysis and workshops at the Center for Psychosocial Studies in Chicago. Tolstoi was a good subject for close psychological analysis. Like his idol Jean Jacques Rousseau, he believed in revealing every-thing about himself and left copious personal materials.

My choice was also prompted by dissatisfaction with the existing literature on Tolstoi. Most of the studies described the evolution of his thought as an intellectual process, minimizing or misconstruing the personal factors involved. They also set him apart from his milieu, presenting him as an inspired, if eccentric prophet, dedicated to his own search for the truth. In the light of the intellectual history of the period, such a depiction seemed completely implausible.[4] When I reread many of Tolstoi's works in the late 1970s I felt that his person-ality had been significantly misrepresented.

Most important was my rereading of Tolstoi's first novel, *Child-hood*, a fictionalized autobiography written when the 21-year-old Tolstoi was serving in the Caucasus. When I had first read the novel, it had seemed to me, as to most who had written about Tolstoi, a nostalgic evocation of a happy, aristocratic childhood.[5] It presented childhood in the hues of sentimentalism, an important literary influ-ence on the young Tolstoi. Tolstoi exclaimed about the beauty of childhood; the characters he described were, like so many of his characters, larger than life and surrounded with the author's feelings of affection. The setting seemed quite attractive; the members of the family appeared to share a certain warmth, culture, mutual respect. They lived in comfort in the picturesque landscape of the nineteenth-century noble's estate. The work thus provided evidence of Tolstoi's happy childhood, the basis for a strong and confident personality.

When I returned to *Childhood*, it was as if I were reading a different novel. The aristocratic surroundings now seemed to conceal a rather frigid world in which feelings had to be invented rather than felt or expressed. The sentimentalism appeared as a veneer over a descrip-tion of the miseries of childhood. The death of the hero's mother when he is nine or ten (Tolstoi's mother died when he was two) cast a spirit of mourning over the novel. Genteel manners came to veil cool manipulativeness. The tenderness seemed to be only in the author's emotional approach to the material.

A crucial moment for me was the scene in Chapter 15 when the hero's mother teases him with the threat of her death. "You won't forget your mama if she isn't there any more, will you? You won't forget her, Nikolenka?" she says, then kisses him tenderly. After a few objections, he begins to weep "tears of love and rapture." This classic, if brutal, invocation of filial guilt, takes on pathos since it was fulfilled. The sentimental tone of the novel, it became clear to me, concealed Tolstoi's rage. Indeed, that seemed to be part of the function of sentimentalism for Tolstoi. At this point, rage became a vivid presence in the novel for me. Tolstoi regarded the bereavement, like most children, as an intentional act. Through the novel he holds back his rage, but it nonetheless dominates many scenes. It is especially striking in the somewhat playful opening chapter. The child is annoyed at his tutor Karl for awakening him in the morning. He immediately regrets his vexation with the gentle and kindly man. But Karl it seems, is only an accidental object. The boy was in fact vexed beforehand. He makes up a dream about the death of his mother to explain his tears, then begins to believe he actually had the dream. Tolstoi's loss of his mother pervades his fictionalized autobiography. The rage simmers within his hero. Other innocent victims feel its force. They then earn his sympathy. The pattern becomes more explicit in the next section of Tolstoi's trilogy, *Boyhood*.

This moment was crucial to my understanding of Tolstoi's personality. At the age of twenty-one, Tolstoi expressed the basic feelings of love and rage toward women that would recur throughout his work. Love and enchantment carried with them the threat of abandonment, the ultimate perfidy. The theme was no mere literary figment. Tolstoi, as his diaries reveal, alternated between rapture and fury. The genius of his art makes his turmoil vivid and disturbing. Again I felt captivated, taken into a world where feelings were ferocious and the smallest occurrence took on momentous significance. Affection between men and women concealed feelings that had to be tragic in their meaning and ultimate outcome.

This insight opened onto a different view of Tolstoi's work. It became impossible to regard it with my previous detached interest. My sense of the autobiographical in all, even his most artistic works, was heightened. Anna Karenina was, for Tolstoi, far more than a Russian Madame Bovary, far more than an object of moral censure.

Such insights may do little to explain or understand his literary greatness, but they do reveal the genesis of his ideas. The sexual conflict reemerged with renewed intensity in the later 1870s, when Tolstoi began to develop his ideas, and when his marriage, which had been happy during the previous decade, became troubled. The theme of woman intruded frequently into his religious and philosophical discourses, often leading to his most important insights and conclusions.

The different readings of the same novel reflect the basic changes in my own views that took place after graduate school. As a graduate student, I was hostile to psychology and entranced by Russian culture and thought, which represented something exotic and new to me. I was given, like many at the time, to a romanticism that seeks, with some justification, a kinship of the spirit with people living in different places and at different times. My second reading took place fifteen years later. I had become accustomed to Russian culture after several lengthy stays in the Soviet Union and was more aware of the common personal distress that a culture conceals. At the same time, a personal crisis I underwent during this period resulted in a rejection of my earlier romantic preconceptions and a greater ability to see people as they were rather than as what I wanted them to be. In 1975 to 1976, when I was associated with the Chicago Institute for Psychoanalysis and the Center for Psychosocial Studies, I made a more systematic study of psychoanalytic literature. I reread *Childhood* first in preparation for a course on the Russian memoir that I gave at the University of Chicago in the spring of 1976, and found it at odds with my recollections. By this time my concern for personal psychological motivation, which had developed during my work on my first book, had become a more consistent and informed view of human nature and way of approaching historical sources.

## II.

It was to deepen and refine my psychological perceptions that I entered into a collaboration with Dr. George Moraitis. We began our collaboration with *Childhood,* and some of my specific observations above come from that rereading. We have continued our discussions of Tolstoi and other Russian thinkers over a period of about five years. My departure from Chicago, I fear, set them back considerably. We

have continued our exchange through the medium of tape, with
occasional meetings when possible. Although this has worked reasonably well, it lacks the immediacy of face-to-face interaction. My attention has also been diverted by my project on the Russian autocracy,
which has become another subject of our discussions. Nonetheless,
though incomplete, our collaboration has been extremely valuable to
me, and I expect to devote myself to a work on the intelligentsia after
my present project is finished.

Our procedure has been similar to that followed by Dr. Moraitis
and Professor Carl Pletsch and Mark Schwehn in their collaborations.[6] We read texts of my choice, then discussed them at informal
and unstructured meetings. We gave our reactions to the works and
our thoughts about their significance for the general themes we have
been considering. Initially, we focused on the works of Tolstoi. Later,
we widened our discussions to include other members of the Russian
intelligentsia and general questions about the interaction between
psychology and thought.

Our collaboration, however, has differed in some fundamental respects from those with Pletsch and Schwehn. Most important, my
initial purpose differed from theirs. I was not trying to work out a
dominant hypothesis or deal with my close intellectual involvement
with a particular historical figure. Rather, I regarded the collaboration
more as an exploration in which I could share the analyst's refined
intuition and perceptivity in dealing with personality. In this way the
historian's sense of the text as a product of history can be enriched by
the analyst's complementary understanding of the text as a product
of personality. During the collaboration I have frequently had the
experience of seeing a text anew and have had to reconsider my initial
view of its historical significance.

Our collaboration, as a result, has had a more casual and desultory
character than the others, taking the form of absorbing and informative conversations about texts. We have not divided over deep
differences in interpretation; instead, I have felt engaged in a common exploration of the possibilities of the sources of Russian intellectual history. It has been more a way to raise and consider new approaches and ideas than a path to a particular truth.

To illustrate how our process of collaboration has worked, I shall
focus on our discussions of one particular work—Tolstoi's *What Then
Must We Do?*, about which I wrote an article.[7] Like *The Confession* and
many other works of the late 1870s and 1880s, *What Then Must We Do?*

is an introspective, autobiographical essay. The questions Tolstoi raises are religious and philosophical, but self-examination is his means to solve them. The artistic overlay is thin or absent. He reveals his self for the world to see, his personal quandary becoming a vivid example of the quandary of all mankind.

The problem considered in *What Then Must We Do?* is the existence of poverty. This, of course, was a question current during the 1870s and 1880s, indeed one that dominated the thought of that period. But as with the other problems he wrote about, Tolstoi discovered poverty as if no one had thought about it before. Poverty came to his attention in Moscow, where he had begun to spend the winters in the 1880s against his will, at his wife's insistence. The sight of beggars and the indigent in Moscow overwhelmed him. It convinced him of the shame of his own life. He made an effort to deal with it through charity, but this seemed futile and immoral. The tract presents his own experience interwoven with long and tortuous discourses on all aspects of current thought. It reaches the conclusion that poverty can be conquered only by living from the work of one's own hands and giving up the amenities of civilization. *When Then Must We Do?* is the most complete and elaborate statement of the notion of "simplification" that became connected with Tolstoi's name.

The personal element is particularly prominent in this work. Unlike Tolstoi's other tracts, here the element of logic seems elusive or altogether absent. Indeed, he never makes it clear why the involvement of the rich in manual labor and a return to a natural economy should eliminate poverty. The conclusions he draws from his personal experiences, moreover, seem highly arbitrary and magnified out of proportion to the apparent significance of what had happened: his responses seem comprehensible only in terms of his personal needs. Finally, the work was written fitfully, over a period of more than three years, with little of Tolstoi's usual attention to organization and form. But it is the richest in biographical data of all the tracts of the 1880s. Statements about social injustice blend with painful personal experiences in a rather chaotic, but nonetheless absorbing presentation.

Dr. Moraitis and I discussed this work at length and in considerable detail. We agreed on a great deal, and I profited enormously from his sharp psychological sensitivity and ability to penetrate to the basic workings of the author's personality. But I shall describe here only our fundamental differences in approach, since it was this dialogue that yielded the most valuable insights for my understanding of Tolstoi.

My initial approach was to see the work in terms of Tolstoi's intellectual evolution at the time. In his *Confession*, he had described the solution he had found to the problem of individual ethical self-justification in his own particular interpretation of Christianity. He had discovered in Christ a model for personal conduct that would show him the way to a pure personal life. But this prescription for individual conduct did not provide answers to the problem of social injustice. The attempts to remedy poverty through generous charity, described at the beginning of *What Then Must We Do?*, showed him how little personal goodness could do. His anguish appeared, I understood, because of the collapse of his rationale for the just life. Convinced as always of the omnipotence of ideas, he thought that it was his own error, reflecting the error of society, that was the cause of the misery of the poor. The grandiose sense of his responsibility led to a grandiose sense of shame. He again was overcome by feelings of futility and despair. His letters and diaries indicated the loss of his desire to live. His solution of returning to manual labor appeared to follow the populist pattern of shedding civilized identity and identifying with the peasantry to overcome the ethical ambiguities of privileged society.

Dr. Moraitis was less impressed by Tolstoi's conscious goals and effort to work out a doctrinal solution. He saw Tolstoi's approach to the poor as largely exploitative. Tolstoi was seeking not an answer to their needs, which he evidently had difficulty understanding, but to his own psychic needs. His efforts at generosity, as he himself became aware, veiled feelings of superiority and aggression. He sought in the poor succor for his chief distress—the sense of his own incompleteness; his fragmentary self sought wholeness in objects in the outside world. By making himself poor, he strove to merge with poor people, and thus gain a sense of unity within himself.

I found this approach a highly useful corrective to my own emphasis on the role of conscious factors. Most important, it directed my attention again to the problem of women. Dr. Moraitis stressed the maternal ideal that Tolstoi sought in the poor, especially the poor women he described. Tolstoi was horrified by their gross conduct, vituperative language and general degradation. It became clear that encounters with them served as occasions for the greatest onrushes of shame described in *What Then Must We Do?*

At this point I began a close examination of Tolstoi's letters and diaries of the early 1880s. The pattern was even more explicit in this material, which often recounted episodes that later appeared in the text. The psychological moments, when personal concerns broke into his discussion, were frequent. Described with Tolstoi's ferocious candor, these incidents left no doubt that his search for female affection in the midst of his marital strife underlay his extreme sensitivity to the suffering of the poor. His anger at his wife alternated with shame at the plight of poor women, for which he felt himself completely responsible. His prescription of a simple life of physical labor, it became clear, was in many respects an effort to identify with women. Women as mothers performed the most noble task, exploited no one, represented the embodiment of selflessness.

My article on Tolstoi sets forth my observations about the genesis of Tolstoi's answer to the problem of poverty.[8] It links Tolstoi's personal life, as described in his letters and diaries, with the writing of *What Then Must We Do?* and traces the emotional process that accompanied his thinking. During the long period of writing, he was horrified by the sight of poor women, which filled him with pity and shame and recalled early sexual encounters. He realized that to deal with poverty one first had to perceive it in all its horror, and for that one had to go through some type of shattering emotional experience like his own. To induce the rich to combat poverty, they had to be shown first how to see it and how to enter into direct empathic involvement with the lives of the poor. From this insight flowed Tolstoi's prescriptions for the simple life and his final extolling of motherhood.

My article, I believe, accurately characterizes Tolstoi's intellectual quest in these years. But it also prompts questions about the significance of such an analysis for an understanding of both Tolstoi's personality and his ideas. Both Dr. Moraitis and I have experienced these doubts. Dr. Moraitis urged me to more sweeping psychological explanations of Tolstoi's personality. I felt that these explanations were interesting but did not shed light on Tolstoi's ideas. I again felt doubts about the historical significance of such an analysis. Collingwood's distinction between the world of immediacy and sensation and the world of thought seemed particularly apt. Tolstoi's ideas on poverty and simplification, whatever their origins, were understood within the intellectual context of the time without regard to their personal psychological significance. Those who followed his prescription of the simple life did so because of its ethical appeal. Their own personal motivations were varied and probably quite different from Tolstoi's. For me, the question became: Why did the ethical and ideological appeal resonate with the particular concerns of individual members of the intelligentsia?

As a result, my interest has shifted to the general question of how culture and ideas shaped Russian intellectuals' understanding of their personal experiences. I have thus come to the same issue as Mark Schwehn, though from the opposite direction. In our collaboration Dr. Moraitis and I have turned to the problems and ideas of such figures as Nikolai Gogol, Nikolai Chernyshevskii, Maxim Gorkii, and V. I. Lenin. They, as well as lesser writers, were concerned with issues similar to those confronted by Tolstoi. It is clear that the similarity is not accidental but reflects a shared mentality or cultural disposition that gave personal feelings a distinct and particular meaning. I have been trying to define the psychological setting that as an aspect of the culture, shaped the personal lives of the intelligentsia. In this way I hope that we will be able to reach an understanding of how the personal experience of one intellectual becomes transformed into a meaningful statement of ideas for other intellectuals sharing his basic values and goals.

## NOTES

[1]R. G. Collingwood, *The Idea of History* (New York: Oxford University Press, 1956), p. 231.

[2]Richard Wortman, *The Crisis of Russian Populism* (Cambridge, Eng.: Cambridge University Press, 1967).

[3]Richard Wortman, *The Development of a Russian Legal Consciousness* (Chicago: University of Chicago Press, 1976).

[4]The literature on Tolstoi is vast. The two most prominent Western biographies present this image of Tolstoi: Ernest J. Simmons, *Leo Tolstoy*, 2 vols. (New York: Vintage Books, 1960), esp. 2: 92–94; and Henri Troyat, *Tolstoi* (Paris: Fayard, 1965), esp. pp. 423–528. A psychoanalytic work of considerable insight, which appears to have been largely ignored, is N. Ossipow, *Tolstois Kindheitserinnerungen: ein Beitrag zu Freuds Libidotheorie* (Vienna: Internationaler Psychoanalytische Verlag, 1923), which I found after my rereading of *Childhood*. A brief but perceptive discussion of Tolstoi that does place him in his context is Martin Malia, "Adult Refracted: Russia and Leo Tolstoi," *Daedalus* 105, no. 2 (Spring 1976): 169–183. Recent literature on Tolstoi has begun to revise the previous picture of his personality.

[5]Simmons, *Tolstoy*, 1: 19–21; Troyat, *Tolstoi*, pp. 453–528.

[6]See Chapter 3–6, this volume.

[7]See Richard Wortman, "Tolstoi and the Perception of Poverty," *Rossia/Russia* 4 (1980): 119–131.

[8]Ibid.

# Repeating the
# Moraitis Method

# 8

# Newton and His Biographer

## Richard S. Westfall

NOT TOO LONG AGO I sat down to compose a preface to my biography of Isaac Newton. It seemed at first a pleasant task. If I was writing a preface, the book had been completed—I was finally done with a work I had begun more than twenty years before.

Against the background of my earlier scholarly concerns, my very writing of a biography may seem strange; indeed, in the wake of reflecting on this paper, I realize there were undoubtedly reasons for it that I still do not comprehend. When I began the biography, however, it appeared to have seized my attention and commanded my energy through a logical progression of intellectual interests. When I was a graduate student in European intellectual history, work on a seminar paper had convinced me that the shift in the focus of European thought from Christianity to science—a shift in which the seventeenth century seemed decisive—was both a possible dissertation topic and a problem of major importance in itself. The dissertation, narrowed down to the religious ideas of English scientists of the late seventeenth century, aroused in me a fascination with the history of science, which has never waned. Inevitably Newton loomed large in my seventeenth-century investigation. My initial acquaintance with him in the dissertation had shown me that an up-to-date biography was needed. Why should I not fill the need? At the time I had no serious conception of the problems beyond the history of science into which working on a biography would plunge me. Nevertheless, I persevered, and now at last I was engaged in the pleasant task of writing the preface.

The more I wrote, however, the less pleasant the task became. As I wrestled with the preface, I finally confronted a truth that I had managed until then to conceal from myself—that over the years Newton had receded from me, that I knew him less well than I had at the beginning. Years ago, when as a young scholar I was only beginning to think of writing a life of Newton, I met Perry Miller, who knew a thing or two about Newton himself. Newton, he told me, was a mystery to him. Not to me, I assured him brightly! It is painful to remember how naive I was. Today, a quarter of a century later, after mastering a large body of information about Newton, I have arrived where Perry Miller then stood. Newton has become a mystery to me as well.

Recently we had a student in our department who possessed a considerable gift for satire. He composed a departmental theme song, "Galileo Is Just Great," with a verse for every member of the department. Mine was set to the music of "How Do You Solve a Problem Named Maria?"

> How do I tell the world about my Newton?
> How do I write a great biography?
> How do I grasp a mind, as bright as one can find?
> How do I hold a genius in my hand?
> How do I tell the world about my Newton?
> He is the greatest, greatest of them all.

Aside from the last line, when the flame of inspiration unfortunately burned a bit low, the student did lay my quandary bare, and I am willing to let his verse stand as the expression of my dilemma.

Consider the difficulties Newton presents. I myself chose to begin with the study of his work in optics, guided perhaps by the unconscious perception that this was the area most likely to conceal the perplexity Newton embodies and to lure me in. In optics Newton concerned himself with an experimental demonstration of a hitherto unknown property of light, its heterogeneity. To be sure, even in his optics there are concealed depths apt to confound the unsuspecting. Nevertheless, probably no one who is informed would deny that the work in optics is the most accessible of Newton's major achievements. Certainly it was for me, and I was indeed lured in.

From optics I went to mechanics and the *Principia*. There was no avoiding the Newton problem here. For one thing, I had to deal with a different mode of scientific activity—theoretical rather than experimental science. There is enough difference between the two enterprises that in the twentieth century they are handled by distinct groups; a single scientist seldom achieves prominence now as both a theoretical and an experimental scientist. Not only did Newton's mechanics involve a different form of scientific activity, but the issues to which it addressed itself were of the greatest complexity, involving both the creation of a new science (dynamics) and the revision of fundamental assumptions about the operation of natural agents held by the then-prevailing philosophy. Moreover, Newton set his achievement in dynamics forth in a work of intimidating profundity. Published nearly three hundred years ago, the *Principia* established the basic paradigm of modern science (to use Thomas Kuhn's phrase),[1] yet its difficulty is such that very few people alive today have fully probed its content. Contemporary scientists seldom deal with it because the geometric idiom it employs has passed out of style. Among historians and biographers, not many have the technical equipment to handle the *Principia*'s every demonstration.

Nor has the biographer, having coped with Newton's work on mechanics, surmounted the obstacles Newton presents. He was also a mathematician of the first order. To be sure, his mathematics was closely related to the *Principia,* but the two were by no means identical. In my own case, I had mastered the calculus with reasonable facility and expected to encounter no serious impediment in Newton's mathematics. The reality, alas, differed from the expectation. On the one hand, in its complexity and sophistication, the fluxional method (as he called his calculus) was a sterner challenge than I had anticipated. On the other hand, Newton the mathematician pursued a variety of other enterprises rich in their diversity—infinite series, advanced analytic geometry, interpolation theory, projective geometry, the porisms of classical geometry. As it happens, mathematics offers a concrete illustration of the stumbling block Newton places in the biographer's path. His mathematics has been the subject of study of D. T. Whiteside, who would be my unhesitating nominee as the outstanding scholar active in the history of science in the world today. I will not venture to say whether Whiteside has fully probed Newton's mathematics; if he has not, he has come closer to it by several stages than anyone else.[2] By making it virtually his exclusive subject of study, he has been able, in twenty years, to comprehend what Newtom, as one part of his activity, created *de novo* in about two. With scholars of lesser stature than Whiteside, the disproportion is correspondingly greater.

If optics, mechanics, and mathematics are three different enterprises, at least they are all related to the basic endeavors of modern

science. The ultimate problem of studying Newton lies in his other
activities. I was vaguely aware that he had left behind a large body of
papers on alchemy. As I was writing his biography, there was no way
to avoid what was apparently one of his significant concerns. Only
when I immersed myself in the papers did I feel their full impact. I
had entered a wholly different intellectual world, a world not of hard
evidence and demonstration but of allusion and metaphor. "Our true
sperm," wrote Eirenaeus Philalethes, a pseudonymous English alchemist of Newton's age, who was his favorite authority, "flows from
a Trinity of Substances in one essence of which two are extracted out
of the earth of their nativity by the third, and then become a pure
milky virgin-like nature drawn from the menstruum of our sordid
whore."[3] Not only did Newton read this; apparently he understood
it. He knew it by heart and repeated it at least seven different times in
his own papers. He left behind extensive laboratory notes, sober
accounts of experiments with carefully measured quantities of specific substances, but accounts interrupted by exultant exclamations in
the imagery of alchemy: "I understood the trident." "I saw sophic sal
ammoniac." "I made Jupiter fly on his eagle."[4] It is with alchemy that
Newton most eludes me. I can compose facile formulas to explain his
participation in the art; I can continue to repeat them. There is, however, no sense in which I understand, in the full meaning of the
word, how the author of the *Principia* became engaged so extensively
in an enterprise that differed so profoundly from his other scientific
work.

Nor is alchemy the final obstacle. Beyond it lies theology, from the
study of which Newton left behind a body of manuscripts more extensive than the alchemical ones. Newton's theology had served to
introduce me to the man, but over the years the problem underwent a
profound change. When I wrote my dissertation, the great bulk of
Newton's theological papers had been lost as far as most people
knew. By the time I returned to the topic for the biography, they had
surfaced in a library open to the scholarly world.[5] They embody still
another intellectual world, a world in his case (whatever theology
may be in other hands) of empirical historical research. Moreover,
because he was Newton, he bent it to a theme of some scope—to wit,
that the dominant Christian tradition, which had shaped European
civilization, was not only mistaken but was also a fraud which had
been foisted onto the church by evil men in the fourth century.

All of this—a life made up of immense achievement mixed with immense diversity, a life that was on both accounts beyond my ability fully to grasp—is what I finally confronted as I wrote my preface. What an incredible piece of effrontery to have undertaken to write the biography of such a man! The honest thing for me at that point would have been to burn the manuscript. To be brief about it, I did not. No doubt many things led me to go on and publish, but I was influenced in part by the conviction that my dilemma was a problem endemic among biographers. Among historians of science and intellectual historians in general who write biographies, I am convinced it is universal. By definition almost, we deal with figures of major importance, figures who exceed us, their biographers, in intellectual capacity. Outside of intellectual history the dilemma may not be universal, but surely it prevails in the great majority of cases. As I look over the biographical subjects discussed in this collection of essays, I see a list of people who have contributed importantly to the shaping of the modern world. Few indeed will be the biographers who attain that rank. By and large, biographers are attempting to deal with people who must in the end elude them.

This seems to me a fact from which there is no escape. Since I do not draw a counsel of despair from the general case, perhaps I was wrong to react as I did to my plight. I am utterly convinced of the irreplaceable value of historical understanding. We cannot avoid dealing with the Carnegies, the Adamses, the Nietzsches, the Stalins—and the Newtons. The biographies of persons we cannot fully seize are bound to be imperfect. They will be better, nevertheless, than none at all. They are apt to improve as we recognize our limitations.

You will note that nothing in the preceding paragraphs is meant to suggest a return to the school of biography that refused to see the "warts and all" on the faces of its subjects. In the case of Newton, the leading biography was composed by a Scottish Presbyterian, David Brewster, during the first half of Victoria's reign.[6] Though no one should make the mistake of belittling Brewster's powerful study, it has in our eyes the major defect of assuming that moral perfection had to accompany intellectual genius. Hence he obscured the unpleasant aspects of Newton's character and largely suppressed the regrettable incidents in his life. Newton attacked Robert Hooke furiously over minor trifles and treated him with open contempt.

When John Flamsteed, the Astronomer Royal, refused to bend his own career to Newton's needs Newton attempted, through his position as president of the Royal Society, to appropriate Flamsteed's observations. He deliberately and repeatedly lied about questions concerned with discovery of calculus in his protracted dispute over that issue with G. W. Leibniz, who to be sure replied in kind. One looks in vain for a full and impartial discussion of these matters in Brewster. On a question that is obvious grist for the psychohistory mill—the relations of Newton's favorite niece, Catherine Barton, with Charles Montague, Earl of Halifax—he is almost silent. The relationship was fraught with ambiguities and is difficult finally to unravel, but it manifestly cannot be reconciled with Victorian sexual mores. From the point of view of the late twentieth century, the issue is almost ludicrous for its triviality as far as Newton is concerned, and it prompts us to reflect on what deep preoccupations of our own will appear equally ludicrous a hundred years from now. Meanwhile, the gulf I perceive between myself and Newton has nothing to do with matters of this kind, and I feel in no way inhibited from portraying them frankly. They are, on the one hand, that aspect of Newton with which I can most easily identify because it is most like me. On the other hand, they form no part of what made him a figure of world-historic importance, and it is precisely his world-historic aspect that eludes my full grasp.

At least one reviewer took umbrage at the similar sentiments I expressed in the preface of the published biography, charging that they were essentially self-serving.[7] The exercise in reflection that this paper has entailed inclines me to recognize that such sentiments, when put into a preface, may indeed be self-serving. They may also embody a device learned from Newton himself. Fearful of possible criticism, I attempted to disarm it by confessing beforehand my own dissatisfaction with the product. Nevertheless, whatever my motives for inserting these sentiments in the preface, I want to insist on the reality of the problem they seek to express. Biographers only inflate their egos if they delude themselves into thinking they have overcome this problem. The danger of the warts-and-all approach is the possibility of substituting the warts for the achievement that raised a person into the class of possible biographical subjects. Warts we all have in abundance. Warts we can understand. Few of us indeed can justly claim world-shaping achievement, but exactly here, at the heart of our interest in our subjects, they most elude us.

Such considerations were running through my mind when, after receiving the invitation to participate in the symposium that underlies this book, I began a series of discussions with Charles Langley of Melbourne University. What emerged for me from those fruitful sessions seems radically at odds with the above. Although Newton had receded from me, I had nevertheless unwittingly depicted myself in writing his biography. I hesitate to announce as a revelation the trite realization of how far I had projected myself into the book I wrote. Let me only insist that there is a difference between acknowledging a general proposition and directly experiencing its truth. The direct experience of it, the exploration with Langley of the various ways in which I had inserted myself into Newton's biography, was for me a voyage of self-discovery.

Some aspects of the self-discovery seem, in retrospect, fairly obvious. In the biography I had to deal with Newton's move to London and his duties at the Royal Mint. Langley was interested in the fact that, when I discussed the Mint, I repeatedly offered disclaimers to the effect that such activities were obviously of less significance than Newton's scientific work but could not be omitted from a biography. Do I despise administrative work? Not in the least, I replied; I consider the maintenance of civil society absolutely essential for the pursuit of most human ends, including science, and I honor those who administer necessary institutions well. Why then the repeated disclaimers? As we pursued the matter, we both recognized what my ultimate values were. Let me honor administrators as I may, the pursuit of understanding is a higher activity in my eyes, and administrators have value for me only insofar as they contribute to a climate in which others can pursue understanding more effectively. It is not exactly a surprising discovery for an academic to make, and I would not have been as pleased with the whole investigation as I am had nothing deeper than that emerged. Nevertheless, I do not scorn the insight. I had written those disclaimers without much thought, as though I were stating an obvious truth. I had not realized the extent to which they were expressions of a personal outlook on life.

Langley insisted that we also consider the implications of certain turns of phrase that appeared in the chapter on the mint. I had discussed the terms under which the great recoinage was carried out and the government sinecures that many persons in that age enjoyed. It was clear that I deplored the arrangements by which the ruling class of the time assured their material well-being. On the other hand, I did not refer to the men involved, as I did to the counterfeiters it was Newton's duty to control, by the blunt term "hoodlums." Why the disparity in language? As we explored the question, I recalled an incident from my own life when I had directly confronted raw violence that I knew I could not control, and I remembered again the terror it had aroused. There was no doubt in my mind that I would have been less at ease with the coiners than with the powdered sinecurists of London society. I might deplore the latter's greed, but I could imagine sharing a bottle of wine with them. They would have had some appreciation of the things that matter most to me. The coiners represented a threat to all that I value, violence unleavened by reason. It was not entirely by accident that I had called them "hoodlums."

Before our sessions began, I had suggested that one possible avenue into our investigation might be for Langley to compare passages from Frank Manuel's Freudian *Portrait of Isaac Newton*,[8] with corresponding passages in my book. As a consequence, Manuel frequently appeared in our discussions. I was aware of some complexity in my reaction to him. I had welcomed his insistence on the neurotic tendencies in Newton, some of which I alluded to above, but I had objected to many details of his portrait and had frequently inserted footnotes in my biography to point our where we differed. As Langley and I discussed Manuel, I became conscious of even more complexity in my reaction, and I found it increasingly difficult to separate intellectual objections from personal feelings of inadequacy and envy. We introduced the images of the tortoise and the hare. I was the tortoise, at once nonplussed at the hare's quickness and speed and disapproving of his readiness to leap too quickly. The images are ultimately self-serving in a most invidious way. At first glance they appear self-deprecating. The tortoise acknowledges that he is a plodder unable to keep up with the lively hare. The final conclusion of the story was never completely out of mind, however. When I designated myself the tortoise, I knew that he does win in the end. The hare's speed is revealed as superficial brilliance. Solidity is what finally counts. I could even find Newtonian support for my position in his methodological stance against speculation in scientific discourse.[9] And since I did not see Newton as a tortoise, the Newtonian support could feed my suppressed aspiration to run with the hare after all.

The discussions about Manuel delved into my resistance to what appears to me as his excessive psychologizing. I was quite prepared to trace much of Newton's conduct—his difficulty in carrying on relations with others except on a basis of hostility or domination, for example, or his almost total lack of generosity toward intellectual peers—to his tortured psyche. I was not prepared to trace his scientific achievements to the same source. On this topic we introduced a second pair of images: darkness and light, with darkness representing irrational psychic drives and light standing for reason and intellectual achievement. In my understanding of Manuel's book, darkness wholly dominates the portrait. If there were flashes of light in Newton, they were the products of the darkness, that is, the results of something akin to Freudian sublimation. As I saw my own view in contrast, there was in Newton a realm of light that was wholly independent of the darkness, a realm assaulted by the darkness but not finally overcome by it. In my picture of Newton, as I compared it with Manuel's, light was central. Though darkness was present, it appeared largely as shadows, which in the end functioned to emphasize the light still more.

Philosophers of science make a distinction between the context of discovery and the context of justification, which does not coincide with my difference from Manuel, as I perceive it, but which may help to clarify it. The context of justification is confined to the realm of reason. It does not involve questions about how a scientist arrived at a discovery, but only its claim to be considered a valid and true conclusion worthy of the name "science." Inquiry into the psyche of a scientist can have no place in the context of justification. Such an inquiry, however, can properly belong to the context of discovery, which has to do not with the validity of a conclusion but with the process by which a scientist reaches it. My difference from Manuel, as I perceive it, locates itself entirely within the context of discovery. Though I readily concede that psychological causes must operate, for example, in determining an individual's interest in one topic instead of another, I am not ready to surrender the entire process of investigation, the context of discovery, to psychologizing. This was our figure of darkness, the dominance of irrational psychic drives. To me, the evidence on which Manuel bases his explanations of Newton's scientific work is too slender to command any degree of assent. Thus Newton's optical experimentation was allegedly an unconscious effort to have intimate visual contact with his mother, and the concept of universal gravitation, arrived at (in Manuel's mistaken account) when Newton was at home because of the plague in Cambridge, was a translation of his attraction to his mother. I cannot prove that these speculations are untrue, of course, but the evidence that they are true is so scanty that I see no point in spending energy in such activity—and all the more so when there are other factors at work that are subject to investigation. I see in the seventeenth century a tradition of rational inquiry acessible to us in books and papers, in terms of which Newton's research makes sense. In the extensive manuscript record he left behind we can trace his steps, follow his mistakes, and chart his confusion as he edged his way forward, This was our image of light, which I mentioned before.

As I began to perceive, a basic conviction stood behind my reaction to Manuel, a conviction to which I could give intellectual formulation though it clearly extended its roots beneath the intellectual into the soil of basic attitudes toward life. I wanted to believe in the autonomy of the individual and the autonomy of the intellectual realm. I chose to believe in them, and although I acknowledged that psychic forces might compromise those ideals, I resisted suggestions that psychic forces might finally subdue and negate them. Langley and I found ourselves discussing Manuel's view that Newton was tied to his mother's apron strings. Not only did I object to that view; I took offense at it. It seemed to attack my conception of Newton. Perhaps more deeply, it seemed to attack my conception of myself. If Newton could be tied to his mother's apron strings, how much more could I— to my mother's or to someone else's. Clearly we were probing matters of some emotional intensity.

Behind the separate topics of our discussions, I was beginning to recognize a common thread, a set of attitudes more consistent than I had expected to find. Let me call them the Puritan ethic, a topic we had also been exploring almost from the beginning of our sessions. Over the years I have taken a certain pleasure in announcing myself a Presbyterian elder. Usually I do this with younger colleagues who have gone our of their way to attempt to offend my sensibilities. They have proved strangely slow, for such intelligent people, to recognize that I might be playing the same game—not to mention strangely intolerant for such a liberal group. It is not really a game, however. I am a Presbyterian elder, offspring of a long line of Presbyterian elders, and as such I have long been aware of the role of the Puritan ethic in my own life. It had not seriously occurred to me that the Puritan ethic was also furnishing the set of categories I used in constructing my picture of Newton.

Let me consider several instances. I spent considerable time studying the Cambridge University scene in which Newton worked, and in
the biography I attempted to place him in that context. Two general
perceptions struck me. For one thing, the years of Newton's resi-
dence in Cambridge roughly coincided with a decline in the university which can only be called disastrous. There was a major contrac-
tion in numbers as the university dwindled to half its former size.
There was a more serious collapse of morale. The university ceased to
enforce prescribed academic exercises. Professors converted their
chairs into sinecures. Those who drew their living from the university
came to see it as an institution to be exploited for personal advantage
rather than served for the sake of the values it embodied. The second
thing that struck me was Newton's isolation within Cambridge. After
he left in 1696 for a position in London, for example, he never returned to visit the university except when it suited his purpose to
electioneer for one of its seats in the House of Commons, and he
never exchanged a single letter with any friend he had made there.

What I came to realize during the sessions with Langley was the
extent to which I had interpreted this material in terms of the Puritan
model of the faithful steward. On the one hand, Newton despised the
irresponsibility about him and withdrew from it. He adopted decid-
edly heterodox theological opinions early in his professorial career; I
am convinced that these opinions functioned initially as his way of
rejecting the banality of orthodox Cambridge. At the same time, although he took advantage of the university's laxity, he did not do so
to gratify personal desires. Like the other university professors, it is
true, he converted his chair into a sinecure from which he drew a
sizable income without performing any duties during the final fifteen
years of his tenure. In more than thirty years as a fellow of Trinity
College, he tutored a total of three students, not one of whom proceeded as far as a Bachelor's degree. His lack of performance was the
standard pattern of the age. But where others used their leisure primarily to indulge themselves at the table and the tavern, Newton
served the higher end of the university, an end that transcended the
immediate goals of degenerate Cambridge, by devoting his leisure to
the ceaseless pursuit of truth. As John North, the master of Trinity,
said of him (but of no other don), if Newton "had not wrought with
his hands in making experiments, he had killed himself with
study."[10]

Newton's position in the mint provides a second example. Langley and I discussed it at length because I saw it as a topic on which I differed with Manuel. As warden of the mint, Newton was responsible for the suppression of counterfeiting. In Manuel's interpretation, the climactic event of Newton's life had been the remarriage of his mother when he was three years old; throughout his life he took vicarious revenge on a series of surrogates for the Reverend Barnabas Smith, who had deprived him of his mother. The London coiners fit this role. In pursuing them beyond the demands of his office, Newton found a socially acceptable means of venting the inexhaustible rage, directed against his stepfather, which welled up inside him. Inevitably, I gave a different account of these affairs, one fully in keeping with ultimate Puritan ideals. I saw the social and political context in which every concerned agency of the government recognized the threat to the currency at that particular time. I treated Newton as the responsible civil servant, assiduously performing a significant task which was also his appointed duty, and, for that matter, responding with similar energy to the other duties attached to the position.

I treated his relation to the Royal Society in much the same terms. When Newton moved to London, the Royal Society was in a state of decline not many steps removed from dissolution. For a number of years it had followed the practice of electing as president prominent governmental officials, who gladly accepted the prestige but paid no heed to the society's affairs as it slid steadily toward oblivion. When Newton accepted election as president in 1703, he embraced the duties attached to the position as well. During the preceding decade, an elected president had presided at a total of one meeting. Newton in contrast presided at nearly every one. He attended all the meetings of the council. He oversaw the society's financial affairs and looked to the content of the meetings. In a word, he reinvigorated a dying organization and preserved the central institution of British scientific life.

It was of course easy to present a Puritan interpretation of an administrator of public institutions. But how was one to reconcile this with my scale of values that set intellectual achievement on a higher plane, especially when the intellectual achievement belonged to a reclusive scholar who kept his discoveries to himself? I have already indicated how I presented a Puritanical scholar who dutifully employed academic resources for an academic end while the society about him wasted similar resources in frivolous revelry. Nevertheless, there is a broader dimension to the problem. Newton, the

Cambridge scholar who made revolutionary discoveries in mathematics and physics which he locked away in his desk in disregard of his social obligations, is a figure who reminds us more of the cloistered medieval monk than of the Puritan in his calling. Hence it appears significant to me that I perceived him in terms that essentially modified this appearance. Newton did not keep his discoveries locked up forever. Though the prospect of criticism and ridicule terrified him, his sense of public obligation did finally overcome his reclusive tendencies. Seen from the perspective of the centuries, moreover, Newton fulfilled more effectively than a thousand vigorous Puritan merchants the peculiar Puritan imperative to be active in the world and to reshape it. Prominent at the time, the merchants have faded into oblivion. The secluded academic, however, changed the course of history. Interpretation here slides imperceptibly into self-justification. Though I think of it consciously in purely secular terms and would never set out explicitly to build the New Jerusalem, there can be no doubt that I feel the same imperative to justify my existence in socially useful achievement. Without meaning to suggest that I have any measurable proportion to Newton's heroic scale, I manifestly draw satisfaction from the suggestion that the scholar may in the long run have more impact on the world than the practical men of affairs who seem to run it.

Thus I emerge with a seeming paradox: I recognize an unbridgeable gulf between myself and my subject, yet in writing his biography I have nevertheless composed my own autobiography. There is an obvious partial resolution to the paradox. When I say "autobiography," I impose a special meaning on the word. There has never been a point at which I confused myself with Newton. The book I have written is not a portrait of myself. Rather, it is a portrait of my ideal self, of the self I would like to be. In one way I had always known this. I consciously chose to pursue an academic, intellectual life, and over the years I have taken my personal heroes, not from the statesmen, warriors, or industrialists of the world, but from the intellectuals and scientists. An early session with Langley brought up one of my personal fantasies, to which we returned several times: what we called my Faustian bargain—to wit, that I would readily accept all of the acute unhappiness of Newton's life in return for the privilege of writing a *Principia*. As I now realize, that bargain contains Puritan overtones I had not fully grasped. In a similar way, I now understand that the ideal self I drew in Newton was more than just a superbly achieving intellectual; he had a significant ethical dimension as well, a

Puritan ethical dimension. I presented Newton as a faithful steward, a man to whom his master had entrusted an extraordinary talent, a man determined not to bury his talent in the ground but to employ it in order that he might return more than he had received.

It is impossible to study history seriously in the second half of the twentieth century without acknowledging its subjective aspects. Like every other historian, I dutifully learned that lesson early and have never dreamed of denying something that seems obvious. My acquiescence was always conditioned by the silent proviso that subjectivity applied more to others than to me. By careful and thorough work, I would constrain such elements in my own scholarship within the narrowest of limits. In my sessions with Langley, I discovered subjective facets in my own work where I had not thought to look for them. Biography is indeed autobiography. It cannot avoid being a personal statement. It is impossible to portray another human being without displaying oneself.

There is one last point I would like to make. The discussions with Langley, the self-examination involved, had an unexpected dividend. In one session, apropos of my resistance to psychological explanations of Newton's science, Langley asked me why, then, I had chosen to engage in this inquiry at all. To gain self-knowledge, I replied. A significant increment of self-knowledge it has provided, together with what I shall call the pleasure of reaffirmation. The Puritan ethic is not exactly in great favor these days, especially in academia. To announce myself a Presbyterian elder, I am well aware, is roughly equivalent in most academic eyes to calling myself a syphilitic dinosaur. As I confronted the Puritan ethic anew with Langley, I realized the extent to which it does indeed express my deepest convictions of how life should be led. You will understand that I am speaking solely of the realm of ideals and am making no claim whatsoever about my personal success in embodying the ideal. One session moved on, as such discussion will, from the gulf I perceive separating me from Newton to the different gulf I see between myself and my society, and finally to my growing sense of alienation from a society bent on consuming the world's supply of nonrenewable resources to produce meretricious trash, bent as well on sacrificing institutions that once fostered a free life in order to pursue short-term advantages of the most superficial sort. Do I really believe that such conduct is ethically wrong—that it is, to use a theological term, sinful? Do I really believe that every gift imposes an obligation and that the obligation increases in greater proportion than the gift? Do I really believe that life itself, the life each of us must receive since we cannot give it to ourselves, is the greatest gift of all and that we are responsible for what we do with it? Damn well right I do. Does anyone want to tell me I should prefer what I see around me?

## NOTES

[1]Thomas S. Kuhn, *The Structure of Scientific Revolutions* (Chicago: University of Chicago Press, 1962).

[2]See especially D. T. Whiteside, ed., *Mathematical Papers of Isaac Newton*, 8 vols. (Cambridge, Eng.: Cambridge University Press, 1967–1981).

[3]Eirenaeus Philalethes, *Ripley Reviv'd* (London, 1678), p. 28.

[4]The notes of his alchemical experiments are found in *Add. MSS. 3973* and *3975* among the Portsmouth Papers in the Cambridge University Library. I quote from *3973*, f. 17, and *3975*, pp. 121, 149.

[5]The Yahuda Papers in the Jewish National and University Library in Jerusalem. Anyone interested in the location of Newton's papers can find a general discussion in the bibliographical essay at the end of my biography of Newton: Richard Westfall, *Never at Rest* (Cambridge, Eng.: Cambridge University Press, 1980).

[6]David Brewster, *Memoirs of the Life, Writings, and Discoveries of Sir Isaac Newton* (Edinburgh: Constable, 1855).

[7]Roger Hahn, Review, *Science* 213 (August 28, 1981).

[8]Frank Manuel, *A Protrait of Isaac Newton* (Cambridge, Mass.: Harvard University Press, 1968).

[9]The classic expressions of his position are found in his third and fourth "Rules of Reasoning in Philosophy" at the beginning of Book III and the "General Scholium" appended to the end of the *Principia*.

[10]Quoted in Roger North, *The Lives of the Norths*, ed. Augustus Jessop, 3 vols. (London: Bell, 1890), 2:284.

# 9

# *My Life with G. V. Plekhanov*

## Samuel H. Baron

WHEN MY BOOK *Plekhanov: The Father of Russian Marxism* was published in 1963,[1] I had been closely involved with G. V. Plekhanov for some fifteen years. My research for a dissertation on a phase of his life and thought began in 1948, but my involvement did not end with the completion of the dissertation four years later. Believing that what I had produced was too narrow in focus to warrant publication, except perhaps in article form, I resolved to write a full-scale biography, with scant appreciation of the implications. Because the sources were so voluminous, the subject so complex, and my free time so limited, it took eleven years to see the plan through. During these years, although I was burdened with a heavy teaching load and had a home and family to care for, Plekhanov was rarely out of mind. I spent many an evening during the teaching year, as well as weekends, holidays, and vacations, in research and writing. Over the years my research took me to New York, Cambridge, and Palo Alto; to London, Paris, and Leningrad. My sleeping as well as my waking hours were often filled with reflections and refractions of my subject. The task I had set myself seemed so interminable that sometimes I wondered out loud whether it would finish me before I finished it. Yet there could be no thought of quitting. I had too much invested, and so I continued doggedly at my Sisyphean labor. A turning point came in 1959, when, thanks to the encouragement given by a leading university press, I was able to muster the vigor and enthusiasm to complete the book in the next few years.

By the time the manuscript had been accepted, I was ready to wash my hands of Plekhanov, Russian Marxism, the Social Democratic movement, and intellectual history. In the next fifteen years, except for two articles on Plekhanov's historical ideas and their status in the

USSR (published in 1974), my research and writing centered on such seemingly far-removed subjects as travel accounts of Muscovite Russia in the sixteenth and seventeenth centuries, the Muscovite merchant elite, and certain aspects of Soviet historiography. Then, in 1978, I experienced a new surge of interest in Plekhanov. Having learned that the International Institute for Social History in Amsterdam had acquired a new collection of Plekhanov papers, I contrived in the course of a brief visit to Europe to spend a few days gaining an overview of these materials. The papers appeared to be far richer than I had anticipated, and I decided then and there to return to Amsterdam as soon as possible to study them with the care they deserved. Meanwhile I secured permission to carry away a copy of an intriguing seventeen-page letter on Plekhanov's circumstances following the Bolshevik Revolution (which he opposed), with the hope of transcribing, editing, and publishing it.

A few months later, while this enterprise still occupied my attention, I was asked to speak to a seminar at a neighboring university on a certain dimension of Plekhanov's thought and activity. As I believed that I had covered the matter in question quite adequately in my book, I brushed aside this suggestion and countered with a proposal to talk about my long association with Plekhanov. Obviously I wished to go beyond the boundaries of my earlier study, and my new engagement had kindled a particular desire to reflect on my personal relation to Plekhanov. This desire was not a bolt out of the blue. A recently aroused interest in self-examination had led me in 1975 to prepare an autobiographical address, entitled "Scholarship and Politics: The Education of an American Historian of Russia," for presentation to an organization of Russian and East European historians.[2] In composing this paper, I had been prompted to review the circumstances that shaped my outlook prior to graduate school, the experiences that determined my professional career, and the evolution of my thinking on the relations between scholarship and politics.

Now, in collecting my thoughts for the seminar talk, I made an unexpected discovery. I had assumed that with the publication of my book I had gotten Plekhanov out of my system, but I was mistaken. Immediately following its completion, I launched an investigation of the Westernization of Russia, which led me to translate and edit *The Travels of Olearius in Seventeenth Century Russia* and to write an article on the West European suburb in seventeenth-century Moscow.[3] At the time these subjects seemed far-removed from Plekhanov, but some reflection suggested otherwise. Among other things, Plekhanov was a historian who envisaged the Westernization of a society once Oriental (or semi-Oriental) as the central theme of his uncompleted, multivolume *History of Russian Social Thought*.[4] I could hardly have been unconscious of this as I dealt with Olearius, for in 1958 I had published an article called "Plekhanov's Russia: The Impact of the West upon an 'Oriental' Society."[5] Yet the connection does not seem to have been at the forefront of my mind. Nor was it the only connection. A few years ago I was astonished to encounter an unpublished letter from Plekhanov to an associate who owned a large library, asking to borrow a copy of Olearius's book. When I went back to Plekhanov's *History*, I noted what I must once have known but was almost certainly unaware of while working on the travel account— that Plekhanov cites Olearius a number of times in his characterization of seventeenth-century Russia.

In 1970 I began a series of studies on the upper-level Muscovite merchants in the sixteenth and seventeenth centuries.[6] I assumed that a careful examination of their business practices and the context in which they operated would throw some light on a problem in which I had been interested for some time—the failure of capitalism to develop in Russia when that economic system was taking shape in Western Europe. Plekhanov had little to say on the Muscovite merchants, and certainly did no primary research on them, but he had a decided interest in the pattern of Russia's historical development. In his opinion, the system of Oriental despotism with which Russia had been saddled for centuries was an institutional complex distinct from that of Western Europe, one so structured as to inhibit capitalist development. He emphasized such features as the ruler's extravagant power and the peasantry's communal organization in what was an overwhelmingly agrarian economy. He was convinced that these arrangements militated against the growth of commerce and towns, whose weak development had profound effects on Russia's history.[7] Though not fully aware of it at the time, it seems that my own research was an effort to resolve a problem that figured as one of Plekhanov's major preoccupations.

While investigating the Muscovite merchants, my attention was drawn to a related controversy in Soviet historiography—the question of the transition from feudalism to capitalism in Russia. I immersed myself in the literature, particularly the proceedings of a conference in 1965 which brought into sharp focus the conflict between different sectors of the Soviet historical guild on this matter. After publishing an article on this controversy,[8] I went on to study Soviet historiography further. Inevitably, I came up against M. N. Pokrovskii, the dean of Soviet historians from 1917 until 1932. To my great surprise, once again I encountered Plekhanov.

I found that at roughly the same time each had produced a history of Russia, and their histories were sufficiently different to warrant my speaking of two Marxist interpretations of Russian history. For political reasons, Pokrovskii's had prevailed after the revolution. In the 1920s, he mounted a campaign designed to outlaw Plekhanov's views, and his own continued to influence Soviet historiography powerfully even after he was dethroned in the 1930s. In the 1960s, de-Stalinization liberated Soviet historians somewhat, frozen positions thawed and controversy flared on many fronts. Pokrovskii was personally vindicated of the charges leveled against him in the '30s, but his overall historical conception was generally repudiated. By contrast, Plekhanov's interpretation made itself felt in the writings of a number of historians. Not the least interesting, the '60s saw a sensational revival of a Marxist concept Joseph Stalin had banned in the '30s: the "Asiatic mode of production." This is another name for the Oriental despotism or Oriental society that figured so prominently in Plekhanov's historical work. The "resurrection of Plekhanovism," a danger Pokrovskii foresaw in the '20s, seemed to be occurring.[9]

For me, the principal finding of my seminar talk was that virtually all the research I had undertaken in the fifteen years since completing my biography was somehow related to Plekhanov. As I had pursued my various projects, I experienced fleeting moments of awareness of a connection, but little sense of a definite, persistent, and comprehensive pattern. Now, trying to explain this connection, I wondered: Was it because Plekhanov's interests were so all-embracing that he had touched everything I turned to? Or had my thinking been so deeply affected by him in the course of our long association as to determine the range of my interests and my research program? There is probably some truth in both propositions, but the force of the latter was particularly striking for it revealed something I was disposed to doubt—that my protracted and intense association with Plekhanov had important, enduring effects on me. In turn, this perception helped to prepare me for an enterprise in which I was about to become involved.

A few days before my presentation to the seminar, I mentioned my topic to my colleague Carl Pletsch. He responded with extraordinary interest. He himself had done a biographical study for his recently completed doctoral dissertation; and, together with a psychiatrist, George Moraitis, had designed an experiment calculated to determine systematically his relationship to the person whose life he had examined. The experiment had proved stimulating, productive of fresh insights.[10] Pletsch urged me to have my seminar remarks taped, and soon thereafter he listened to the recording. He then showed me some material he had written on his experiment and suggested that I attempt to replicate it, to explore more fully my relations with Plekhanov in conjunction with someone who had had psychoanalytic training. After my initial misgivings had been allayed, and once a suitable collaborator had been found in Professor Alan J. Stern, I agreed to participate, on the assumption that the further work on Plekhanov I planned to do might benefit from a clearer understanding of my relations with him.[11]

As the experiment began, it occurred to me that I had never carefully and straightforwardly defined Plekhanov's personality and my attitude toward it. To be sure, I did make a sustained effort to analyze and deal critically with his intellectual evolution, the ideological system he created, and the ways he responded to changing circumstances. In the process, various facets of his personality were revealed, but I had to admit that my efforts to probe and delineate that personality were more episodic than systematic, and left a good deal to be desired. Sensing some inadequacy in this area while working on my book, I had done some reading on psychology and the writing of biography, but without much profit. Accordingly, at the time this concern made hardly a dent on my cast of mind, as the following incident illustrates.

In the later years of writing, a colleague had asked me more than once whether I liked Plekhanov. I had never really considered the question, and it struck me as somehow offensive. My personal attitude was irrelevant, I thought, and I resisted giving a direct reply. One has to empathize with one's subject in order to understand him, I observed, but one must also maintain detachment if an objective portrayal is to be made. I neither liked nor disliked Plekhanov, I told myself; I was presenting a dispassionate account. Well aware though I was of discussions of the subjective factor in historical writing, I evidently expected through conscious effort to reduce it to negligible proportions. As I wrote the book, awareness that I might be putting a personal stamp on it was dim at best. Occasional impressions to the contrary notwithstanding, I conceived of my work as a truthful and rather exact representation of what had been, as an objective biography.

In the course of the experiment I was impelled to examine more closely the belief in my neutrality and a series of important subordinate propositions. The first concerned my selection of a subject for a doctoral dissertation. When asked how I happened to choose Plekhanov, I replied along the following lines: As the completion of my work for an M.A. drew near, I was obliged to find a suitable subject to investigate in order to be admitted to the Ph.D. program. A more advanced student suggested it might be useful to look at a bibliography of sources published in Russia since the revolution. In poring over this work, I came across a number of substantial collections of material relating to Plekhanov: his collected works in twenty-four volumes; a further eight volumes billed as his literary legacy; six volumes of documents on the Emancipation of Labor Group, Russia's first Marxist revolutionary organization, which Plekhanov and a few associates founded, and which served as the vehicle of his organizational activity for the first decade or so of his Marxist career; and a two-volume collection of his correspondence with his closest collaborator, P. B. Akselrod. I also discovered a bibliography on Plekhanov and the Emancipation of Labor Group with abundant references to still other materials, both primary and secondary. Although Plekhanov was generally recognized as a major figure, almost nothing had been written on him outside the Soviet Union, and the sources available for a study of him were apparently more than ample. As I saw it, my decision to elect "Plekhanov and the Emancipation of Labor Group, 1883–1894" as my dissertation topic resulted from fortuitous circumstances on the one hand and pragmatic considerations on the other.

Like any fledgling, I had read that historians generally choose research topics related to contemporary problems and preoccupations, and which somehow articulate with their personal backgrounds and concerns. Plausible though this sounded, my case seemed to be an exception to the rule. Professor Stern and I tacitly undertook to determine whether it was in fact what it seemed to be. Under his persistent prodding, I strove to recapture my concerns and attitudes around the time I was casting about for a dissertation topic. The autobiographical paper I had written a few years before proved helpful, for it evoked the mood of my early years as a graduate student, but in a context unrelated to my quest for a dissertation subject.

As an undergraduate I had majored in botany, but following four years in the armed forces (from 1942 to 1946), I enrolled in the first class of Columbia University's newly created Russian Institute. I had decided to abandon what now seemed like an escapist pursuit for a more engaged career in the social sciences. As one who had grown up during the Great Depression and lived through World War II, I was appalled by the injustice, brutality, and irrationality that afflicted mankind. Believing in the possibility of corrective action, I hoped through work as a teacher, and perhaps as a writer, to strike a blow in favor of more rational social and international relations. I thought of myself as an anti-fascist, I harbored friendly if not uncritical feelings toward our erstwhile Soviet ally, and my aspirations found an immediate outlet in political activity of a leftish sort. While a graduate student at Columbia, I joined the American Veterans' Committee, an organization created to counter the influence of the American Legion. I worked in political campaigns of New York's American Labor Party and for Henry Wallace's candidacy for the presidency on the Progressive Party ticket. In these same years, as a consequence of the preoccupation with Soviet affairs at the Russian Institute, I had my first serious encounter with Marxism. A skeptical streak in my nature held me back from total commitment, but I found it illuminating, and it deeply influenced my outlook. Marxist ideas affected the way I thought about history, and they somehow buttressed my aspirations for progressive social change through professional and political work.

When all these circumstances were brought to the conscious level, it appeared doubtful that my choice of a dissertation topic was entirely fortuitous or determined largely by pragmatic considerations. I may well have encountered other possible subjects of investigation that I shunted aside for one that had greater appeal. Or I might have followed the example of most of my fellow students, who seemed content to take on topics suggested by our supervising professor. I knew relatively little about Plekhanov when I made my choice, but I was certainly aware that he devoted his life to study, writing, and politics, with Marxism his lodestar, in an effort to change his world for the better. It would seem that I chose Plekhanov because I sensed a resonance between his life history and my life plan.

Professor Stern persistently intimated that I had scanted attention to Plekhanov's personality, especially the emotional side. Though I recognized some truth in these intimations, I adduced a whole series of arguments to the contrary, along with justifications for what I had done along this line. For one thing, the sources set severe limits: much the largest block consisted of Plekhanov's formal writings; he had left little material of an autobiographical nature; data on his childhood and youth were extremely sparse. Nevertheless, I had done as much as possible with these materials, and the considerable volume of published correspondence, to bring my subject to life and make his behavior intelligible. My first chapter focused on the formation of his character and values. Subsequent chapters treated other aspects of his personality as they were brought to light by the circumstances of his experience—his aggressiveness in polemic, his thirst for knowledge, the pronounced rationalistic cast of his thought, his intransigence on theoretical issues and readiness to stand alone, his willingness to suffer privation for the cause he had made his own, and so on.

Moreover, I had given sustained attention throughout my book to motivation—I was concerned to record not just what Plekhanov thought and did but also the whys and wherefores. My analyses were usually—perhaps too often—couched in rational intellectual terms, but not always. Some of the most successful chapters, those on Plekhanov's struggles against Revisionism and Economism and his early relations with V. I. Lenin, so I thought, made the reader aware of irrational elements in his conduct. If I did not consistently address issues of personality, I argued, my episodic consideration of them was effective. One reviewer found the book moving, another colleague told me privately that it was the only work of history she had ever read that made her cry, and a selection from the chapter on Plekhanov's early relations with Lenin had been excerpted as an example of excellent biographical writing. I was willing to admit that I had not drawn the elements together into a fully integrated portrait, but I could point to sections throughout the book that furnished abundant material for such a portrait.

Finally, the way in which I conceived the work and my literary inclinations and values played a part too. As I had set out to write what was primarily an intellectual biography, my concentration on the development of Plekhanov's multifaceted outlook, and the interaction of ideas and historical developments, was entirely appropriate. Conceiving the book in some measure as a work of art, I strove not to be comprehensive but instead to single out the most revealing episodes, those which produced important, enduring effects. I wished to make the book dramatic, and success in this required sustained movement, without rambling digressions. These aims dovetailed with my long-standing concern for conciseness and the selection of material for inclusion according to strict standards of relevance to the main thrust of the work. I wanted desperately to avoid boring the reader, and so produced a comparatively short book where another historian might have written one twice as long.

With each passing session, I sensed increasingly that these protestations were less than fully convincing, that to some degree they were rationalizations. I was compelled to confront the notion that I might have slighted Plekhanov's personality partly because I was ill equipped to deal with it. Thanks to teaching obligations which required me to do a good deal of careful reading in primary sources of intellectual history, and to the particular attraction such figures as Erasmus, Montaigne, and Albert Camus exercised on me, my tendency to skepticism was reinforced, and I was comparatively well prepared to deal critically with Plekhanov's ideas. By contrast, I possessed too little knowledge of psychology to deal confidently and comprehensively with his personality. Having made a brief and unprofitable excursion into psychology, and lacking time to go farther, I may have persuaded myself—as a measure of self-defense—that it had little use to my enterprise anyway. As I could not in practice ignore Plekhanov's personality, I ended up treating it sporadically, intuitively, and perhaps at times superficially.

This was not the only circumstance that determined my orientation while I wrote the book. Even though the influence of Marxism on my thought diminished during those years, its emphasis on laws, objective processes, and impersonal forces in history still conditioned me to slight the role of personality. I recognized that my interpretations of Plekhanov's clashes with the so-called economists in the last years of the nineteenth century, and with Lenin in 1900, differed from those of earlier writers. I went to considerable effort to demonstrate that what they took to be struggles motivated mainly or exclusively by personal considerations were in fact primarily ideological or principled in character, with personal aspects secondary at most. For better or worse, in this I followed Plekhanov's lead, for he never admitted that clashes of personality, matters of ego, and the like were basic reasons for the endless conflicts that wracked the Russian revolutionary and the international socialist movements. In this he was surely wrong sometimes. Nevertheless, I persist in thinking that my interpretations here are correct; I find unpersuasive my collaborator's arguments for a primarily psychological explanation of the differences between Plekhanov and Lenin.

Continued pondering, stimulated by the questions and suggestions of my collaborator, has brought to light another possible reason for my underestimation of personal considerations in dealing with Plekhanov's life. His personality seems to have revealed itself most clearly in conflict situations. I believed that I had given due consideration to the most important of these up through the revolution of 1905. Perhaps mistakenly, I supposed that the clashes of personality I had dealt with had produced no significant net effects, and so I may have assumed that little or nothing was to be gained by pursuing later conflicts in depth. Now I wondered whether my personal tastes might have played a role. The interminable squabbles in which Plekhanov and the Russian revolutionists so often became entangled were replete with factional bickering, backbiting, deception, and intrigue. Perhaps because such behavior offended me, I chose to think that to examine it could not possibly be productive or important. It may be, too, that I wished to minimize attention to these acrimonious affairs because they often showed Plekhanov in a most unfavorable light—petty, arrogant, overbearing, and unscrupulous. I may have wished to divert my attention from his repellent qualities in order to promote continuing empathy as I worked through the long process of completing the biography.

As my study exposed me to various facets of Plekhanov's character, I discovered—and this clearly fostered empathy—that we shared a good many intellectual and personality traits. Notable among these were a high regard for learning and rationality, a passion for communication via the spoken and written word, and a striving for lucid, carefully constructed analysis and argument. These qualities bespeak a somewhat overintellectualized apprehension of life and history, and a tendency to underestimate the extent and power of irrational forces. Overintellectualization had a counterpart in some underdevelopment of the affective side of personality in both parties. Then, there was the will to achieve, a compulsion to use time productively, a penchant for high expectations of oneself and others, and perhaps as a consequence, a comparative lack of close friends and a tendency to be a loner.

A related characteristic—a need to find order in the world—perhaps deserves special consideration. This may have derived from an early involvement in science, with its belief in a fundamentally orderly universe and man's capacity to apprehend it by way of rational analysis. My interest in biology at school led me initially to contemplate a career in science; Plekhanov grew up at a time in Russian history when science was in vogue, and he spent two years as a student at St. Petersburg's Mining Institute. Each of us at some point was impelled by an overriding concern with social and historical problems to quit preparation for a career in science, but we apparently carried over into our new area of activity concepts and modes of analysis and understanding peculiar to science. Persons so disposed seem especially likely to find the Marxist outlook attractive, with its claim to have discovered the laws of history, to have deciphered the workings of society, and to possess predictive powers—in short, to be *the* science of society. Because of its intimate relationship to such ideas, Plekhanov understandably put a high premium on objectivity, believed in its attainability, and strove to achieve it in his studies of different phenomena of social life, both past and present. Though less consciously and consistently, I too evidently held such ideas— witness my conviction, alluded to above, that my personal circumstances and tastes were irrelevant to my choice of a dissertation topic or the manner in which I should deal with it.

These correspondences, of which I only gradually became aware, facilitated empathy and understanding. But this kind of link may also produce contrary results: if the biographer imperceptibly passes from empathy to more or less complete identification with his subject, he forfeits the detachment essential for at least relatively objective work. Even George Moraitis, the experienced psychiatrist who was involved in the earlier experiment with my colleague Carl Pletsch, reported that he "wanted very much to see Nietzsche (the subject of Pletsch's biography) as a person like myself."[12] I may in some measure have fallen victim to the same hazard; although, interestingly, except for one reviewer of the book who professed to see a "whitewash" of one aspect of Plekhanov, the two dozen or so others found no fault on this score.

I certainly recognized in Plekhanov qualities I found unattractive, as some scattered citations from the book will indicate. Though one gets occasional glimpses of warmth and tenderness, as in his relations with his wife and with his colleagues P. B. Akselrod and Vera Zasulich, he impressed many people as "severe," "cold," and "unbending." His sense of intellectual superiority at times appeared to others as "intolerable arrogance"; "His sharply polemical style, replete with pejoratives, penetrating thrusts, and merciless mockery undoubtedly made many readers recoil." "When he resolved to be disagreeable, Plekhanov had few equals." His "offensive against Economism overflowed with rancor. . . . With highly questionable taste, he published . . . private letters not addressed to him." He called some of his adversaries "political castrates," and dismissed others as "persons who had not yet emerged from their diapers when [he] was already an established revolutionary." In his dispute with A. N. Potresov in 1908, he "displayed that combination of egotism, irascibility and intolerance that had shocked some of the Russian Social Democrats in earlier intraparty conflicts."[13]

As a result of my experiment with Professor Stern, I came to realize that although I had called attention to such matters, I may not have emphasized them sufficiently or plumbed their consequences. Now I was willing to entertain the idea that these features of Plekhanov's personality may have been more than incidental, significantly affecting the course of his life and the fate of his ideological system. Thus sensitized, in May 1979 I arrived in Amsterdam to examine the fresh archival material that had recently become available. I also deemed it advisable to reread some of the secondary sources in which Plekhanov figured, and to look at other materials not available to me before publication of the book. My new openness enabled me to gain some fresh insight into the connection between Plekhanov's personality and his historical destiny.

For one thing, I gained more of an appreciation of how the military ethos shaped Plekhanov's personality. My book recorded that his father was a military man, who evidently had attempted to mold the character of his son, and that Georgii was educated at a military school. I did not pursue the matter in relation to Plekhanov's adult life, but now I perceived this as a damaging omission. A fair amount of evidence suggests that his military background strongly and permanently affected Plekhanov's mentality. He sometimes spoke of himself as a "soldier of the revolution" and referred to the duty this office imposed on him. He reproached himself for "desertion" when he failed to return to Russia during the revolution of 1905. And in 1918 he brooded over Russia's "dishonorable" abandonment of its allies to sign the Treaty of Brest-Litovsk with the Germans. As his wife noted, he was wont to say (only half-jokingly), "When the superiors command, I must obey."[14] However, the only living person he seems to have recognized as a superior was Friedrich Engels, whom significantly, he addressed in his correspondence as "My general."[15] Plekhanov seems to have assumed that hierarchy, command, and subordination were normal and necessary in social organization. As he plainly considered no one in the Russian Social Democratic movement his equal, he no doubt envisaged himself through most of his career as its commanding officer, its general.

If, in a government-constituted military organization, men are compelled to serve and to obey the commands of their superiors (no matter how disagreeable the latter may be), a movement such as Russian Social Democracy had no powers of external compulsion at its disposal; leadership could be exercised and confirmed only by winning the internal assent of those involved in or potentially sympathetic to the movement. Plekhanov enjoyed great prestige for having laid the foundations of Russian Marxism in his theoretical work and for having launched Russian Social Democracy. But because he so often was personally disagreeable—arrogant, vituperative, spiteful, and petty—he failed abysmally to win a sizable number of dedicated followers.

As the key figure in the Emancipation of Labor Group, he was undoubtedly responsible for its elitist stance. Though it was a tiny group, whose survival and success depended on the lively expansion of its numbers, Plekhanov insisted on maintaining both its exclusiveness and its unchallengeable leadership, while relegating those who sympathized with its aims to auxiliary-service roles. Repeatedly, as in 1888 and between 1896 and 1899, Plekhanov's inflexibility in the face of pressure from the younger social democrats in the emigration for a larger and more significant role in the movement led to acrimonious ruptures. In the latter case—and it was neither the first nor the last— the younger people were alienated. When in 1903 he provoked another bruising episode, even though he subsequently reversed himself, his "most respectable" followers no longer held him in esteem, according to F. Dan, another party leader.[16] Even when conflict did not erupt, Plekhanov's personality put people off. A perceptive revolutionary observed that "by nature," he was "evidently incapable of destroying that 'pathos of distance' that his fame . . . aroused in us."[17]

Plekhanov was occasionally accused of being so hypercritical that he stunted the growth of fresh literary forces in the movement. In fact he fostered the development of at least two figures who attained prominence in early Soviet philosophy—L. I. Akselrod and A. M. Deborin. Significantly, they were both extremely deferential. In correspondence, Deborin addressed Plekhanov as "Dear teacher" and closed by describing himself as "deeply respectful and loyal." He once remarked: "I am accustomed to taking seriously your every word"—and it is plain from her correspondence that Akselrod did no less.[18] The emergence of even more notable figures such as Lenin, Leon Trotsky, and Rosa Luxemburg would seem to belie the charge against Plekhanov. Yet it is important to note that, except for two brief intervals, Plekhanov's relations with Lenin were extremely stormy; in respect to Trotsky and Luxemburg, he was perpetually at daggers drawn. All three willingly accorded Plekhanov the deference due him, but at the same time they were people of unusual talent who possessed "self-assurance aggravated by youth."[19] They were not content to be mere subalterns, and Plekhanov—constitutionally incapable of sharing the limelight, and sensing in them threats to his supremacy—treated them disdainfully or worse. In a famous encounter with Lenin in 1900, Plekhanov so infuriated the younger man by his obstinate, egotistical and domineering conduct that Lenin soon after wrote: "Never, never in my life have I regarded any other man with such 'humility'. . . and never before have I been so brutally spurned."[20] Luxemburg's biographer reports that she described Plekhanov as the kind of man at whom one wanted to stick out one's tongue.[21] Isaac Deutscher relates how in 1903 Trotsky saw at Lenin's side "the haughty aggressive Plekhanov, who had snubbed him on every occasion for no apparent reason."[22] Worse was to come, for in the following year Plekhanov presented an ultimatum to his colleagues on the editorial board of *Iskra*: either Trotsky should be excluded from collaboration or he, Plekhanov, would quit.[23]

How low Plekhanov might stoop is apparent in his comments on his closest collaborators when he found himself seriously at odds with them. In 1903 or 1904, after he had joined with Lenin to oust P. Akselrod and Vera Zasulich from the editorial board of *Iskra*, in private he reportedly called Akselrod "a cripple, a man who had become completely valueless to the party."[24] Such conduct evoked a cruel cut from several erstwhile associates who were Menshevik leaders. In 1912—in response to an attack that Plekhanov made on two long-time colleagues and friends, Akselrod and Zasulich—Dan, Iu. Martov, and A. S. Martynov wrote that Plekhanov tragically combined in himself "a mind worthy of a Chernyshevsky [a highly venerated nineteenth-century revolutionary figure] and the soul of a Don Basilio [the crafty, conniving specialist in calumny of *The Barber of Seville*]."[25]

Data of this kind—and more could readily be adduced—lead to certain conclusions. Plekhanov once lamented that where there were two Russians, one was apt to find three parties. But his own conduct helped to produce the very thing he deplored. His personality and behavior promoted factionalism within Russian social democracy, causing its severely limited resources to be diverted from revolutionary struggle to fratricidal warfare. At one level, there was his inability to permit satisfaction of the modest aspirations of younger comrades, some of whom responded by setting up rival organizations and publications. One such person, Lev Iogiches, went so far as to abandon the Russian for the Polish movement, becoming one of its leaders.[26] He and his comrade-lover, Rosa Luxemburg, were so hostile to Plekhanov, and vice versa, that despite their common interests the two parties cooperated little. Something of Plekhanov's style communicated itself to Lenin and others, and may at least partly account for the endless sniping, abuse, and organizational splitting so characteristic of the Russian Social-Democratic Labor Party. At another level, it is apparent that Plekhanov was incapable of sustained collaboration with anyone who was not prepared to put up with his domineering behavior. As regards his ideological system, which began to crumble in 1905, he was too proud and self-important to admit that he might have been wrong or could learn from others. Again and again he engaged in maneuvers that led to his self-imposed isolation. Accordingly, his aspirations were frustrated, he was politically ineffective, and he ended up a general without an army.

My recent effort to explore my relationship to Plekhanov has, I believe, enhanced my understanding of him, made me more self-aware, and brought to light some of the apparently countless psychological transactions between us. Had these explorations been carried on earlier, with a qualified collaborator, I am reasonably confident that I would have produced a better book, presenting a more balanced, and perhaps more integrated, portrait of Plekhanov's personality. I might also have more effectively shown how his personal qualities affected his thought, shaped his relationships with others, and helped to determine his life history. Yet, however much this might have made for a more richly textured biography, I do not think that the main contours of the work would have been fundamentally altered. Admittedly, I may be mistaken, for this experiment has also given me some appreciation of the myriad guises in which psychological defensiveness may manifest itself.

It remains to be noted that some thirty-five years after I first made his acquaintance, my life with Plekhanov shows no sign of drawing to a close. Two new articles on him have emerged from my research in

Amsterdam a few years ago.[27] As a consequence of my collaboration with Professor Stern, these articles definitely give greater consideration to the impact of Plekhanov's personality than did my earlier study. The present essay bears witness to the opening for me of a new kind of research interest. Where it will ultimately lead I cannot say, but my short-range agenda lists, along with inquiries into seafaring, commerce, and economic thought in seventeenth- and eighteenth-century Russia, a psychological investigation of the stormy and perplexing relationship between Plekhanov and Trotsky.

## NOTES

[1]Samuel H. Baron, *Plekhanov: The Father of Russian Marxism*. (Stanford: Stanford University Press, 1963).

[2]This unpublished paper was delivered to the Conference on Slavic and East European History, meeting of the American Historical Association, Atlanta, Georgia, 1975.

[3]Samuel H. Baron, trans. and ed., *The Travels of Olearius in Seventeenth Century Russia* (Stanford: Stanford University Press, 1967); idem, "The Origins of Seventeenth Century Moscow's Nemeckaja Sloboda," *California Slavic Studies* 5 (1970).

[4]This constitutes four volumes (20–23) of Plekhanov's *Sochineniia* (Collected Works), 24 vols. (Moscow: Gosudarstvennoe izdatel'stvo, 1923–1927).

[5]Samuel H. Baron, "Plekhanov's Russia: The Impact of the West upon an 'Oriental' Society," *Journal of the History of Ideas* 19, no. 3 (June 1958).

[6]The first was entitled "The Weber Thesis and the Failure of Capitalist Development in 'Early Modern' Russia," *Jahrbücher für Geschichte Osteuropas* 18, no. 3 (September 1970). This essay and six others on related subjects are included in Samuel H. Baron, *Muscovite Russia: Collected Essays* (London: Variorum, 1980).

[7]For a summary of his ideas along these lines as set forth in his writings to 1903, see Baron, "Plekhanov's Russia." He further elaborated this conception in his *History of Russian Social Thought*.

[8]Samuel H. Baron, "The Transition from Feudalism to Capitalism in Russia: A Major Soviet Historical Controversy," *American Historical Review* 77, no. 33 (June 1972).

[9]Apropos the matters in this paragraph, see Samuel H. Baron, "Plekhanov, Trotsky, and the Development of Soviet Historiography," *Soviet Studies* 26, no. 3 (July 1974); idem, "The Resurrection of Plekhanovism in Soviet Historiography," *Russian Review* 33, no. 4 (Oct. 1974); idem, "Feudalism or the Asiatic Mode of Production," in Samuel H. Baron and Nancy W. Heer

eds., *Windows on the Russian Past: Essays on Soviet Historiography Since Stalin* (Columbus, Ohio: 1977).

[10]A brief outline of the method was presented in Carl Pletsch and George Moraitis, "A Psychoanalytic Contribution to Method in Biography," *The Psychohistory Review* 8 (1979): 72–74. See also George Moraitis, "A Psychoanalyst's Journey into a Historian's World: An Experiment in Collaboration," *The Annual of Psychoanalysis* 7 (1979): 287–320 (reprinted here as Chap. 3).

[11]I am deeply indebted to Professor Stern, a member of the Department of Political Science at the University of North Carolina, Chapel Hill, and Research Candidate in Full Clinical Training in the University of North Carolina–Duke Psychoanalytic Program, for his patience, sensitivity, and skill as collaborator in this enterprise.

[12]Moraitis, "Psychoanalyst's Journey," p. 54.

[13]Baron, *Plekhanov*, pp. 129–130, 134–135, 201, 213, 283n.

[14]Ibid., p. 276; R. M. Plekhanova, "God na rodine" (unpublished manuscript in the Plekhanov archive, International Institute for Social History, Amsterdam), pp. 30, 34.

[15]He had begun by addressing Engels "Dear Teacher." After the older man asked to be called "simply Engels," Plekhanov shifted to "Dear Citizen Engels," and after a little while to "My General" or "Dear General." See *Perepiska K. Marksa i F. Engel'sa s russkimi politicheskimi deiateliami* (Leningrad: Gosudarstvennoe izdatel'stvo politicheskoi literatury, 1947), pp. 265–267, 270, 273, 277, 279, 283, 285. The German Social Democrats often referred to Engels as "The general," and Plekhanov may simply have borrowed that usage. Nevertheless, he showed remarkable reverence and humility in his relations with the old man.

[16]Quoted in Abraham Ascher, *Pavel Axelrod and the Development of Menshevism* (Cambridge, Mass.: Harvard University Press, 1972), p. 193. The preceding items in this paragraph are treated in Baron, *Plekhanov*.

[17]P. A. Garvi, *Vospominaniia sotsial-demokrata* (New York: Fond po izdaniiu literaturnogo nasledstva P. A. Garvi, 1946), p. 418.

[18]*Filosofsko-literaturnoe nasledie G. V. Plekhanova*, 3 vols. (Moscow: "Nauka," 1973–1974), 1: 219–220; 3: 287; *Literaturnoe Nasledie G. V. Plekhanova*, 8 vols. (Moscow: Gosudarstvennoe Sotsial'no-ekonomicheskoe Izdatel'stvo, 1934–1940), 1: 292, 295, 296; 5: 309. Lenin may have exaggerated when he wrote of L. I. Akselrod's "blind worship" of Plekhanov, but not much. See V. I. Lenin, *Collected Works* (New York: International Publishers, 1927–?), 4: 27.

[19]The phrase is J. P. Nettl's in *Rosa Luxemburg*, 2 vols. (London: Oxford University Press, 1966), 1: 68. His accompanying suggestion that Plekhanov also disliked Trotsky because he was a Jew is hardly to be credited. Plekhanov's wife was a Jew.

[20]Lenin, *Collected Works*, 4: 29.

[21]Nettl, *Luxemburg*, 1: 22.

[22]Isaac Deutscher, *Trotsky: The Prophet Armed* (New York: Oxford University Press, 1954), p. 83.

[23]*Pis'ma P. B. Aksel'roda i Iu. O. Martova* (Berlin: Russkii revoliutsionyi arkhiv, 1924), p. 101.

[24]Ascher, *Axelrod*, p. 204.

[25]*Otkrytoe pis'mo P. B. Aksel'rodu i V. I. Zasulich* (Paris, 1912), p. 7.

[26]Nettl, *Luxemburg*, 1: 65–69.

[27]Samuel H. Baron, "Plekhanov in War and Revolution, 1914–1917," *International Review of Social History* 31 (1981); idem, "Plekhanov, International Socialism and the Revolution of 1905" (Paris: in press).

# 10

# A Second Look at Andrew Carnegie

## Joseph F. Wall

THE PROSPECT OF participating in a conference on "The Psychology of Biography" both interested and disturbed me. Why does a biographer pick a particular subject for a biographical study? Once having chosen a subject, how does the biographer affect the life of that subject by his or her own particular and idiosyncratic interpretation? Finally, and perhaps most important, how, during the course of long years of research and writing, does the subject affect the biographer? These basic questions had interested me throughout the thirty-five years I had been engaged in biographical study.

The first question, concerning why a particular subject is chosen, I initially believed I could dismiss rather easily. With each of the three major biographical studies in which I have been engaged,[1] the subject had been offered to me. None has been of my own choosing. In the first instance, when I enrolled in Allan Nevin's doctoral seminar at Columbia University soon after World War II and was required to choose a topic for my doctoral dissertation, I had the rather grandiose idea of selecting Harry Hopkins as my subject. Nevins, who quite correctly judged that I was hardly ready to take on so major a figure as Hopkins, quietly but determinedly lowered my sights. I was in effect "given" Henry Watterson, the former editor of the *Louisville Courier-Journal*, as my dissertation topic. Following the publication of my dissertation in 1956 and the quite favorable reviews it received, Nevins must have felt I was ready for bigger things, for it was again he who suggested that I take Andrew Carnegie as my next major project—a subject large and complex enough to keep me occupied for the next twelve years.

With the publication of the Carnegie biography in 1970, I felt I was perhaps finished with biography. Most certainly I believed I was finished with capitalists of great wealth. For the first time, I began research on a subject of my own choosing: a reevaluation of the election of 1872, which I regarded as more significant than the election of 1876 (the year that historians have traditionally emphasized as the terminal point of the Reconstruction era).

I was soon to discover, however, that it is as easy to get typecast in the history profession as in Hollywood. The reviews I was asked to write for professional journals, the articles I was asked to contribute to the *Dictionary of American Biography* and other reference works—all were related to big business in general and to Carnegie and the steel industry in particular. This typecasting seems particularly ironic in my case inasmuch as I am not an economic historian by training and business history per se has never been of great interest to me. Although of necessity I had to learn a great deal about the steel industry in writing the biography of Carnegie, it was not steel nor the business structure that Carnegie built that fascinated me; rather it was the man himself.

In 1972, having barely started on my research on the 1872 election, I received an inquiry from the trustees of the Jessie Ball duPont estate regarding my availability to undertake a new biography of Alfred I. duPont. Jessie Ball duPont, Alfred I.'s third wife, had but recently died. In her will she had left a request that a biography be written of her husband, and she had provided ample funds to cover research costs.

My initial response to the trustees' inquiry was to say no. I was finished, I said, with entrepreneurial biography and even if I weren't, I had no desire to write an authorized life to serve as a widow's memorial to her late husband. Moreover, it seemed to me that Marquis James some thirty years earlier had written a quite adequate biography of Alfred I. duPont.[2] But the trustees were persistent. They asked me to come down to Florida to discuss the proposal in more detail and to look over his voluminous papers, which were stored in an office in the First National Bank of Jacksonville, Florida. At that time I was a visiting professor at Brown University, teaching a course on (what else!) late-nineteenth-century American business history and trying to do some research on my 1872 election project. It was early March, and Providence was cold, damp, and buried in snow. An all-expenses-paid trip to Florida at that moment was not without its own peculiar attraction. I agreed to come down.

I came, I saw, I was conquered. The papers, although in disarray, were overwhelmingly voluminous and detailed, and they included much that James had not seen. The book would be my own. I could find my own publisher and collect my own royalties. The trustees simply wanted to fulfill the terms of Mrs. duPont's will as expeditiously and completely as possible. Finally, there was the irresistible lure of money—all research expenses up to what seemed to me a very generous sum would be paid by the trustees. As a result, for the last eight years I have again been deeply involved with another entrepreneurial biographical study, with time out to write two other books: a short history of Iowa for the W. W. Norton Bicentennial States and the Union series, and a centennial history of the Bankers Life Company of Des Moines.[3] Again, perhaps significantly, these books were not of my own choosing but ones I was asked to write.

All of the above is a rather lengthy preface to provide some understanding as to why I initially felt that the question of selecting a subject for biographical study had little pertinence for me. Watterson, Carnegie, and duPont, as well as the two nonbiographical books on Iowa and the Bankers Life Company, had all been given to me by others. Upon further reflection, however, I realize that this question cannot be so easily dismissed. It is true that these subjects were offered to me, but certainly I was free to reject these assignments. In each instance, moreover, I became fascinated with the subject and I came to feel a proprietary interest of discovery, as if the subject were not only a topic of my own choosing but of my own creation. I am also haunted by the fact that the only major project that I myself chose lies inchoate and abandoned. Could it be that I have remained curiously arrested in a schoolboy mindset, finding it easier to write on an assigned topic than to write on a subject of my own choosing? Yet a certain ego satisfaction is clearly involved. I was tremendously flattered that Allan Nevins, my teacher, mentor, and professional hero, should approach me to write the biography of Carnegie. To a lesser degree, I was also flattered by being asked to do the other studies mentioned above. It was I who was being selected, not the subject of my study. Obviously, the question of "choice" is not as simple or as irrelevant to me as I once thought.

The other two questions raised by the conference were also of interest to me. After living with Carnegie for more than a decade, how had I been affected by him? And perhaps more important, how had I affected him by my interpretation, an interpretation that must inevitably be influenced by my own personality, background, and previous experiences? To what degree is all biography autobiography, and by extension, all history personal history?

These are not new questions for the history profession. Indeed, one can argue that our profession, as a discipline separate from simple storytelling, began with the asking of these questions. It was Herodotus who proposed that the historian must look to himself for the evidence of what is said. The question of the historian's own involvement in his historical narrative has remained, but since the time of Leopold von Ranke, we have too often ignored it in our quest for objectivity and detachment. A few years ago Martin Duberman shocked the profession anew by denying objectivity and narrational anonymity. In his introduction to *Black Mountain: An Exploration in Community*, he wrote:

> I've felt the final responsibility of letting myself be known. Some will take exception to that as self-indulgence. Yet the issue is not, I believe, *whether* the individual historian should appear in his books, but *how* he should appear—covertly or overtly. Every historian knows that he manipulates the evidence to some extent simply because of who he is (or is not), of what he selects (or omits), of how well (or badly) he empathizes and communicates. . . . Yet the *process* by which a particular personality intersects with a particular subject matter has rarely been shown, and the intersection itself almost never regarded as containing materials of potential worth. . . .
>
> This book is an effort at such a demonstration, an effort to let the reader see who the historian is and the process by which he interacts with the data—the actual process, not the smoothed-over end result, the third person voice, or no voice at all.[4]

Duberman's book carries the overt revelation of the historian's interaction with his subject to its logical extreme. Many historians would argue that Duberman's extreme goes beyond the logical, even beyond good taste, and thus is not worthy of serious consideration. Most reviewers, in fact, did not know how to deal with *Black Mountain*, for in format it is a curious blend of an author's personal journal with the more traditional historical narrative. They were, moreover, embarrassed by Duberman's self-revelation. One of the issues that Duberman had to deal with in writing the history of Black Mountain College was the disruptive impact that the charges of homosexuality made against some of the faculty and the students had upon the community. Any historian of that institution would perforce have to deal with this issue. But Duberman used it as his personal doorway to come out of the closet and confess his own homosexuality.[5] Far from the Rankean tradition in which most of us have been schooled, this kind of public exposure seems self-confessional in the Rousseauean manner we have long abjured. Even Lee Benson's more moderate pronouncement—that, as a historian, it is one's duty to bring one's own moral values and judgment explicitly into one's historical interpretations—created a not unexpected storm of controversy at a meeting of the Organization of American Historians.

The implications of Duberman's and Benson's philosophical positions have long fascinated as well as troubled me. When we read Thomas Macaulay's *History of England*, Alexis de Tocqueville's *Democracy in America*, Lytton Strachey's *Eminent Victorians*, Matthew Josephson's *Robber Barons*, or even George Bancroft's *History of the United States* (of which it is said that every page votes the straight Jacksonian Democratic ticket), we know we are not reading objective, value-free history. We are seeing history warped in a mirror fashioned by the individual historian's own personality and prejudices, for these historians make explicit their own interaction with the material they are treating. They have all written bad history according to the social-scientific standards of our profession. Yet their works remain classics of our literature long after the scientific monographs of the objective quantifiers have been forgotten.

Biography, as a particular form of history, must be especially affected by the issues Duberman and Benson raise, for it is a one-on-one exercise. The social, demographic, and institutional historians can hope to lose themselves in the broad panoramic landscape they are delineating. Robert Fogel and Stanley Engerman can try (not very successfully to be sure) to conceal their biases and idiosyncratic interpretations behind a mass of quantitative data.[7] But the biographer is the portrait painter, not the photographer, of the profession. Here the interaction between author and subject is most exposed. Just as the viewer of *Arrangement in Grey and Black* knows he is seeing James Whistler as well as Whistler's mother, so the reader of biography must, if only subliminally, accept the fact that he is getting Allan Nevins as well as Grover Cleveland, Samuel Eliot Morison along with Christopher Columbus.

Having lived with Andrew Carnegie as long as I did, and now with Alfred I. duPont for what promises to be nearly as long, I have, of course, sensed this interaction and been concerned about it. I knew when I finished my many years of research on Carnegie that I had more factual information about the man than any living person. I had seen papers that no other historian has been allowed to see and visited every place in which he had lived, quite literally following him from the weaver's cottage in Dunfermline, Scotland, where he was born, to the grave site in Sleepy Hollow cemetery, North Tarrytown, New York, where he now lies buried. In some respects, I knew Carnegie better than he knew himself, for I had unearthed old documents that he had quickly forgotten he had ever written, read his associates' evaluations of him that he was never privileged to hear. But lengthy as my biography is, I still had to make selections from the mass of data collected, to provide interpretations that were my own evaluations. My Andrew Carnegie is not Burton Hendrick's, John Winkler's, or Harold Livesay's Carnegie.[8] How much of this personal interaction between Carnegie and myself was, and indeed, should have been explicit in my biography? It was because such questions have remained with me some ten years after the book was published and because I must face these questions anew in writing Alfred I. duPont's biography that I welcomed the invitation to participate in a symposium on the psychology of biography.

I must admit reluctance in facing what I considered the ordeal of a series of sessions with a psychoanalyst or clinical psychologist as the basis for writing my paper. For one who had never before consulted either a psychologist or psychiatrist, who indeed is such an antique as to have gone to high school and college at a time before there were even career counselors, not to mention drug and sex therapists, this consultation promised to be a new and not very welcome experience.

I was not even sure that this particular exercise was necessary for me to go through in order to become a more effective participant in the project. I was well aware of the lasting effect Carnegie has had on me, of how I continue to compare Carnegie with all other biographical subjects, most notably Alfred I. duPont, with whom I have become involved. I had experienced no such lasting attachment with my first biographical subject, Henry Watterson, possibly because I had not spent as long a time with Watterson as Carnegie, or possibly because the Watterson biography had been a doctoral dissertation and my personal involvement with him seemed to terminate with the granting of the degree. But I rather imagine it is more complex than that. With Carnegie, there was a curious love-hate relationship, an identification with and at the same time an alienation from the man, which has continued for a decade after the publication of the book. I still hold a proprietary interest in him—the irrational feeling that somehow Carnegie belongs to me alone, is my child, and that no one else can claim paternity. Recently, for example, I was visiting the Cooper-Hewitt Museum of Decorative Arts and Design, which is now housed in Carnegie's old mansion on 91st Street in New York. I found myself, first of all, distressed by the alterations in the rooms that the Smithsonian has had to make in order to transform the house into a functional museum. It was almost as if my own home had been desecrated without my permission. And this distress turned to anger when I overheard one of the curator's assistants giving another visitor some quite erroneous information about Carnegie and how he happened to build this home. It was almost more than I could do to remain silent, not to rush over and shout, "It's my Carnegie you are talking about, and what you are saying is not right. Let me give you the true story." Quite obviously, Carnegie will remain with me for the rest of my life.

I also was fully cognizant of the fact that as biographer, I had quite purposefully imposed a central theme upon Carnegie's long and variform life. It seemed to me that the one thing above all else that gave Carnegie's life an inner tension and made him the interestingly complex and often contradictory figure he was was the continuing necessity he felt to reconcile the radical egalitarianism of his grandparents, his parents, and his own childhood with his insatiable desire for material acquisition. He expressed this tension many times in many ways—in the private memorandum he wrote to himself in 1868, telling himself that he must abandon business within three years or he would be corrupted beyond redemption; in the writing of his best-known book, *Triumphant Democracy*; in his articles on the rights of labor; in his founding of a chain of radical newspapers in Great Britain advocating the abolition of the monarchy, the House of Lords, and the established church—all done at the same time that he continued to run faster and faster to acquire more and more wealth. How could he reconcile his pronouncement for the rights of labor—"Thou shalt not take thy neighbor's job"—with his allowing Henry Frick to hire scabs and Pinkertons that led to the horrors of Homestead? How could he oppose the landed aristocracy of Britain while creating a plutocratic aristocracy in America? Carnegie finally found the answer that resolved these tensions in his "Gospel of Wealth." In listing all the reasons why men of great wealth should give all their wealth back to the society from which it was drawn, he added, almost as an aside, a most revealing reason: that in so doing, the very rich can "perhaps also find refuge from self-questioning."[9] Here at last Carnegie had found a way to reconcile his radical past with his plutocratic present; here was his refuge from tension.

Although it seemed patently clear to me at the time I was writing the biography that this was indeed the basic theme of Carnegie's life, I nevertheless realized it was a theme I had selected and imposed upon Carnegie. It was one none of his other biographers had chosen. In this very central way I had made myself the organizer of Carnegie's life, and had found my own solution to my self-questioning about Carnegie's contradictory actions. He was no longer the base hypocrite portrayed by Winkler, nor the kindly, beneficient patron of Hendrick's imagining. Rather, he was a protagonist in the classical mode, torn by his own inner doubts and tensions—a tormented hero of my designing.

To select and develop this central theme was, of course, a deliberate act on my part. I felt it essential in giving rational meaning to Carnegie's life. What I did not realize at the time, however, was that this theme was as essential to me as it was to Carnegie. Only now, with hindsight and with the experience of preparing this paper, do I realize that I needed this theme to reconcile myself to Carnegie, to find my own "refuge from self-questioning" about why I should choose to write upon and live comfortably—even empathize with—a man who was in many ways so antithetical to my own personality, ambitions, and achievements. Only by offering a thesis that reconciled Carnegie the radical with Carnegie the plutocrat could I reconcile me, the liberal, with the me who was the biographer of Carnegie, the steel king. Quite unconsciously, I was attempting, through this process of reconciling the inner tensions in both of us, to find a reflection of Carnegie in me and of me in Carnegie.

There were other psychological problems with Carnegie that I had to deal with in my own way, such as his abnormal attachment to his mother. At an early age he had made a vow to his mother, apparently not solicited but certainly welcomed by her, that he would never marry as long as she lived. When at the age of forty-five he at last became seriously attracted to a young woman twenty-two years his junior, his mother did everything she could to discourage the romance. Carnegie and Louise Whitfield became engaged, but it was a troubled courtship, one that is well documented in a collection of letters between Louise and Carnegie (which Carnegie's daughter allowed me to read), and one that Louise terminated when she finally realized that Carnegie would never marry as long as his mother lived. Immediately upon his mother's death in 1886, however, he once again proposed to Louise, they were quickly married, and for years after, he never mentioned his mother's name.

Obviously here was rich material for a psychohistorian, but not for me. I have long been appalled by most psychohistory, which I regard as being both bad psychology and bad history. With proper Barzunian skepticism for "Clio's doctors," I allowed myself only one brief moment of speculation about Carnegie's mother fixation:

> There must have been, of course, basic psychological reasons for his inability to defy his mother. All of the psychological explanations so dear to the amateur Freudian could be brought forth in way of explanation: a weak, ineffectual father who had been unable to provide for his sons; a domineering, ambitious mother who *had* provided; an unduly prolonged childhood innocence of sexual knowledge; a sense of competition with a younger brother for his mother's affection; a personal vanity so strong as to indicate latent narcissism. There is evidence in Carnegie's background for all of these diagnostic evaluations. But the historian [and by that I really meant *this* historian] lacks the competence to probe so deeply into Carnegie's psyche as to offer an explanation for Carnegie's attitude toward his mother and marriage.[10]

This one brief paragraph of explanation—or, rather, of refusal to explain—did not satisfy all my readers as much as it satisfied me. In particular, John Brooks, in his lead review for the *New York Times Book Review,* found my "reticence odd and disappointing":

> Through hundreds of pages about his youth and young manhood we hear not a word of his relations with women except for one reference to a girl of whom he said, after having lost her to another man, "If anybody else in the world could win her, I don't want her!" His courtship of his wife, Louise, began when he was forty-five, and continued for six years; marriage was apparently out of the question for him until the death of his septuagenarian mother, whom Louise Carnegie later described as the most unpleasant person she had ever known. These tantalizing few facts—suggesting domestic slapstick or gothic horror, one isn't sure which—are left almost entirely unelaborated;

> Mr. Wall segregates Carnegie's courtship and marriage into a
> rather short, non-committal chapter. For the most part, he sticks
> all too strictly to Carnegie's business affairs and ideology.[11]

Mr. Brooks seemed to be suggesting that I needed psychological help
as much as did Carnegie.

Perhaps I did. I decided to play the game along the lines suggested
by the conveners of the conference. I made this first encounter as easy
for myself as possible, however, by enlisting the cooperation of a
colleague at the State University of New York at Albany, the clinical
psychologist George Litchford.

We were able to work in six sessions in the spring of 1980, before
my departure from Albany to Grinnell. Fortunately, the sessions
were taped and in preparation for the writing of this paper, I have
replayed the tapes. Upon hearing the first session repeated on cas-
sette this summer, I found it even more confused than I had remembered it. Dr. Litchford had not had time as yet to do more than barely
sample a few pages of my massive biography of Carnegie. I, in turn,
did not know exactly what was expected of me in such a session and,
as a result, played out a kind of parody of couch revelations. After
speaking briefly of Carnegie's childhood, his poverty, his relations
with his mother, his father and brother, I found myself, to my own
surprise, babbling away about my childhood and my relations to my
father and mother. Litchford, whose approach was largely nondirec-
tive, patiently endured this rambling.

What finally emerged out of this initial rambling, however, was an
important idea—the mirror-image thesis: Carnegie, born into radicalism, broke with the faith of his father by becoming a conservative
Republican capitalist; I, born into standpat Midwestern conservatism,
broke with the faith of my father by becoming increasingly radical in
my political and social views. Perhaps my choice of subjects for biography, Carnegie and duPont, had not been as nonvolitional as I had
thought—*Andrew Carnegie* may have been my version of *Triumphant
Democracy*, my attempt to reconcile my past with my present.

The mirror-image thesis poses some interesting insights into both
our characters and to our relationship with each other: radicalism
converted into conservatism versus conservatism converted into liberalism; geographic, social, and economic mobility versus remarkable
stability in these same three areas; the mother as heroine versus the
father as hero. The mirror image was there all right and might well
have been a reason for my attraction to Carnegie. But one can carry

this thesis only so far, and I was obviously trying too hard in this first session to find myself reflected in Carnegie and he in me.

After this painful first encounter with psychological counseling, things went much better. I found myself looking forward to our weekly discussions. I discovered in Litchford "the ideal reader" of whom George Moraitis has written.[12] Litchford's perceptive reading of *Andrew Carnegie,* the questions he raised, and the details his training in psychology enabled him to see, helped me gain new insights. To illustrate: Litchford picked up the point that Carnegie's only sister had died when he was just six years old. I had merely recorded the fact, together with the brief statement on the economic depression that hit the weavers of Dunfermline in 1841: "the number of deaths in the city totaled 513, the largest number ever recorded in the burgh for one year. Among those who died was Andrew's young sister Ann. Her short life seems to have made no impression upon the boy, for he was never to mention her name in his later writings about his family or his childhood."[13]

It seems to have made no impression upon me either, for I made no further mention of what must have been a traumatic experience for a young boy of six. But Litchford saw its possible significance. Here was the effect of widespread poverty and disease brought home to a child in its most dramatic form. It could well have been the most significant event of his childhood in Scotland, an event too painful for Carnegie to wish ever to recall, but for both him and his mother a major determinant of future behavior. It was shortly after the death of Ann that Margaret Carnegie took control of the family. It was she who brought in what little income the family had by her skill at mending shoes—a skill more in demand in depressed Dunfermline than the hand-weaving skill of her husband. It was she who later decided the family must move to America, and it was she who taught her older son, an eager pupil, that the acquistion of wealth was more important than the radical idealistic dreams of his father. Carnegie would later utter pious sentiments about the "advantages of poverty," but the only true value of poverty he saw was that it served as a spur to those sensitive enough and fast enough to run all the harder for the prize awaiting the winner.[14] For those who refused to run hard to escape the cruel prod of poverty, the only prize was death.

From this consideration of the significance of Ann's death, our discussion led us into a more general consideration of Carnegie's almost pathological fear of death. This theme, although implicit throughout Carnegie's life, was one I had failed to emphasize. An agnostic like his mother, Carnegie had no hope of heaven, no belief in an afterlife to soften the blow of death. This life was all that there was, and death was total annihilation. Consequently, "death" was a word he never used in any of his writings. When anyone close to him died, even someone as close as his mother, she or he became a nonperson, someone not to be mentioned again, whose every evidence of having existed must be removed from his sight. His personal aversion to any form of physical violence (his crusade against football as a college sport, for example), his extreme pacificism and abhorrence of war were other indications of his dread of death. His refusal to start school until he was eight, even though the starting age for Scottish children was four; his postponement of marriage until he was fifty-one; his delay in begetting a child until he was sixty-two—all could be seen as manifestations of his desire to prolong youth and to slow down the normal aging process. For many years, he gave a false year for the date of his birth, and when called to account by the press for this inaccuracy, he professed innocence of deception through ignorance. "Sorry to lose those few years" was his revealing comment. His philanthropy was perhaps his most obvious attempt to avoid total extinction. Carnegie could never be accused of wanting to take his wealth with him because for him death was no exit to anywhere. But if he could not believe in the immortality of the soul, he did believe in the immortality of wealth. His libraries, museums, foundations, and scientific institutions would endure, ensuring that death could never turn him into a nonperson. This particular discussion with George Litchford gave to me a whole new dimension for the interpretation of Carnegie's life.

Our last two sessions were largely devoted to a comparison of the task of the clinical psychologist with that of the biographer. I hope that Litchford enjoyed these sessions as much as I did. We each emerged from these sessions, I believe, with a new appreciation for the other's profession, with some understanding of how each could be of some assistance to the other, and with each satisfied to be in the particular profession that he had chosen. That at least was my reaction. I might have to spend years in researching a single person's life, but at least I didn't have to try to cure Carnegie of his mother fixation. I had only to try to understand it.

What are the potentials for this kind of cooperation between psychologist and historian? For some, undoubtedly, it could be—and profitably so—full collaboration. Traditionally, of course, historians, much like novelists and poets, have tended to work alone, reluctant even to discuss their work in progress with anyone except their spouses. This is becoming less true, I think, as history is pushed by quantification more into the mainstream of the hard social sciences. But I belong to the old tradition; for me personally, full collaboration would be impossible. This experience, however, has shown me the value of consultation.

The most opportune time for this consultation, it seems to me, is after the research has been completed and a first rough draft prepared. Only then would the field be prepared for the engagement. So convinced am I now of the value of such consultation that, at the conclusion of the Chapel Hill conference, I made arrangements with Dr. George Moraitis to discuss with him my biography of Alfred I. duPont when I complete the first draft of the manuscript. The story of Alfred I. duPont presents even more difficult psychological problems than that of Carnegie. Fortunately, unlike Carnegie's personal life, his is much more thoroughly documented in the hundreds and hundreds of letters to and from his three wives, his four children, and his brother and sister. The lode is rich, but I welcome the miner's cap that Moraitis can provide to light the way into the interior.

Some years ago, Theodor Reik wrote a popular book on psychiatry entitled *Listening with a Third Ear,* in which he stated the necessity for the psychoanalyst to listen for what was not being said as well as for what was being said, to listen with a third ear.[15] I now see the value for the biographer, with his data all collected and with manuscript in hand, of "reading with the third and fourth eye," of seeing his subject—and himself, for that matter—through the additional eyes of a consultant skilled in the analysis of human personality and behavior.

## NOTES

[1]Joseph Frazier Wall, *Henry Watterson, Reconstructed Rebel* (New York: Oxford University Press, 1956); idem, *Andrew Carnegie* (New York: Oxford University Press, 1970); idem, *Alfred I. duPont, the Man and His Family* (New York: Oxford University Press, under contract).

[2]Marquis James, *Alfred I. duPont: The Family Rebel* (Indianapolis: Bobbs-Merrill, 1941).

[3]Joseph Frazier Wall, *Iowa, a History* (New York: Norton, 1978); idem, *Policies and People* (Englewood Cliffs, N.J.: Prentice-Hall, 1979).

[4]Martin Duberman, *Black Mountain: An Exploration in Community* (Garden City, N.Y.: Doubleday, 1973), pp. xiii–xiv.

[5]Ibid., p. 270.

[6]Lee Benson, "Doing History as Moral Philosophy and Public Advocacy," presented to meeting of Organization of American Historians, Detroit, April 1981.

[7]Robert W. Fogel and Stanely L. Engerman, *Time in the Cross* (Boston: Little, Brown, 1974).

[8]Burton J. Hendrick, *The Life of Andrew Carnegie* (New York: Doubleday, Doran, 1932); John Winkler, *Incredible Carnegie* (New York: Vanguard Press, 1931); Harold Livesay, *Andrew Carnegie and the Rise of Big Business* (Boston: Little, Brown, 1975).

[9]Andrew Carnegie, *The Gospel of Wealth and Other Timely Essays*, ed. Edward C. Kirkland (Cambridge, Mass.: Harvard University Press, 1962), p. 67.

[10]Wall, *Carnegie*, pp. 416–417.

[11]John Brooks, "Andrew Carnegie," *New York Times Book Review*, sec. 7 (October 11, 1970), p. 1.

[12]George Moraitis, "A Psychoanalyst's Journey into a Historian's World: An Experiment in Collaboration," *The Annual of Psychoanalysis* 7 (1979): 313. Reprinted here as Chap. 3.

[13]Wall, *Carnegie*, p. 58.

[14]See Andrew Carnegie, "The Advantages of Poverty," in *Gospel of Wealth*, pp. 57–70.

[15]Theodor Reik, *Listening with a Third Ear* (New York: Farrar, Straus, 1952).

# Other
# Introspections on
# the Biographical
# Process

# 11

# *Thoreau's Lives, Lebeaux's Lives*

### Richard Lebeaux

---

IN BERNARD MALAMUD'S *Dubin's Lives*, William Dubin, an award-winning biographer of Henry David Thoreau, is engaged in writing a biography of D. H. Lawrence. Reflecting on his experience with biography in general and with Lawrence in particular, Dubin observes:

> No one, certainly no biographer, has the final word. Knowing, as they say, is itself a mystery that weaves itself as one unweaves it. And though the evidence pertains to Lawrence, the miner's son, how can it escape the taint, subjectivity, the existence of Willie Dubin, Charlie-the-waiter's son, via the contaminated language he chooses to put down as he eases his boy ever so gently into an imagined life? My life joining his with reservations. But the joining—the marriage?—has to be, or you can't stay on the vicarious track of his past, or whatever "truth" you think you're tracking. The past exudes legend: one can't make pure clay of time's mud. There is no life that can be recaptured wholly; as it was. Which is to say that all biography is ultimately fiction. What does that tell you about the nature of life, and does one really want to know?[1]

As one who has himself been a biographer of the young man Thoreau and who is now working on a psychobiography of Thoreau's later years, I can identify strongly with Dubin. Yes, biography for me has been a "joining with reservations," a "marriage" of my life with Thoreau's; the relationship has lasted—not without some stormy arguments, separations, and passionate reconciliations. And yes, I am aware that biography—certainly psychobiography—is like a marriage in that it is more than the sum of the individuals involved. A mysterious alchemy takes place between the biographer and his or her subject: the resulting biography is a product of that complex,

225

elusive interaction and cannot avoid being, in this very real sense, "subjective," even as it strives to get closer to the "truth." To complicate matters further, the "truth" of the subject's life and personality is not fixed but rather given to change in significant respects with the unfolding of the life cycle, and with the shifting events and circumstances of the subject's life and culture. The biographer whose life is joined to the biographical subject can also change in important ways as life proceeds and he or she is influenced by personal and suprapersonal events and circumstances. Indeed, one profound influence on the biographer may be the person chosen for study and the work of the biography itself. In the "conclusion" to *Walden*, Thoreau explains, "I left the woods for as good a reason as I went there. Perhaps it seemed to me that I had several more lives to live, and could not spare any more time for that one."[2] For me, it has been crucial to recognize that Thoreau lived "several lives" and that I, too, have led "several lives" in the course of my relationship with Thoreau, that my responses to Thoreau over the years have been informed by my own personality and "passages," and that in fact the subject has himself exerted an influence on the developing life and perspectives of his biographer.

Acknowledging these realities of the biographical process, one must conclude, as Dubin does, that a psychobiography or psychohistory is in some way ultimately fiction. However, this very recognition of subjectivity may, I believe, bring us substantially closer to the truth. Erik Erikson writes, "The only methodological certainty that I could claim for my specialty, the psychotherapeutic encounter, was 'disciplined subjectivity.' "[3] Such a methodological stance, as applied to psychobiography or psychohistory, would encourage, as Carl Pletsch indicates, a "more complete working through" of the biographer's "investment in the subject," which holds out the "possibility of forcing readers"—as well as the biographer—"to a more differentiated conception of the subject."[4] Thoreau is someone who provokes strong emotional responses, both positive and negative, from readers, and it is all the more critical to work toward a less reductive conception. It is in the interests of attaining "disciplined subjectivity," of becoming as conscious as possible of the psychodynamics of my evolving relationship with Thoreau and thus approaching closer to the "truth," that I embark on this history, or psychohistory, of my "joining" with Thoreau.

This exploration of subjectivity raises the question of just how honest or personal one can or should be when addressing an audience of scholars, or the general public for that matter. I know of no way in this case to be reasonably honest, accurate, and enlightening without being confessional to some degree. Clearly, being confessional is a risk—it can cause discomfort both for writers and their audience, and it certainly challenges whatever mystique or persona the writer has consciously or unconsciously cultivated. This is not to claim that writers escape subjectivity even in their attempts to be more "objective" about their subjectivity. The analysis, for various reasons, may well remain unavoidably selective, and may even be intentionally or unintentionally self-serving. Also involved is the question of ethics—the perceived obligations to protect other people who have played a part in one's life history. Moreover, a strategy involving autobiographical probing may be regarded as a challenge to the assumption that "intellectual" judgments are only a function of "pure" intellect and that personal (or cultural and historical) factors can be purged completely as one seeks the "truth." It strikes me that, as a complement to the sociology of knowledge, there is a need for a "psychology of knowledge" which is sensitive to the private worlds from which intellectual perspectives and discoveries emerge. Whatever the risks of self-disclosure in coming to terms with one's own subjectivity, I am convinced they are worth it.

Unable to find, in the hinterlands of East Lansing, a psychotherapist with the time and inclination to collaborate in the systematic manner pioneered by Carl Pletsch and George Moraitis,[5] I have had to rely heavily on other resources, most especially introspection. My introspection, however, has been aided by experiences with therapy (about five months in 1980 and about nine months in 1975 and 1976); by relatively brief discussions with three local therapists about my relationship with Thoreau; by a men's group I have been involved with for about a year; by a "Journal Workshop" in June 1981 (making use of humanistic psychologist Ira Progoff's "intensive journal" method)[6] and other activities that promote psychological sensitivity. Introspection has been an ongoing part of my work on Thoreau, and several years ago I wrote a paper, recently published, which begins to deal with the issue of subjectivity in my work.[7]

Memories of my first exposure to Thoreau are vague. Although we must have read some short excerpts from *Walden* in my tenth-grade

English class, I cannot remember concretely my response to him. That I had a primarily positive reaction to this high school Thoreau— no doubt presented chiefly as a solitary woodsman and lover of nature by the text and teacher—is quite likely. My own attachment to nature had been established through many deeply pleasurable week- ends spent at my grandmother's house in a still-rural town in central Massachusetts, only a short drive from the medium-size city where my family resided. The house and environs had once been a farm, and there my father and his siblings had grown up. Next to the small, rustic house, the abandoned chicken coop, and the unmown field was a horse stable, and the area was still rich in what to me were uncharted forests, where I often rambled by myself. Across the street from the house was a drive-in movie theater, behind which was an old quarry which I explored again and again. Aside from my intox- icating experiences with nature on the farm, I was sent by my par- ents—probably with the hope I would become interested in science and perhaps medicine—to the Nature Training School in a nearby town during my elementary and junior high school years. Although I was not a particularly serious student of nature at this summer camp (I was more concerned with being a star athlete), I clearly absorbed a love and appreciation of nature in this setting, and at the end of tenth grade I worked as a nature counselor at a local YMCA camp. I fre- quently camped out with friends in the central Massachusetts woods. Thus I already had a strong feeling for nature when I came upon Thoreau in tenth grade, and it is probable that my first contact with him had some resonance.

By eleventh grade I had begun writing poetry and short stories, playing guitar, and writing my first songs; creativity was becoming an important part of my incipient identity. Moreover, inspired by my junior-year Honors English teacher, in my last two years of high school I gravitated increasingly toward literature—especially English literature—and was starting to entertain the idea of becoming an English teacher. My combined interest in nature and art culminated in the summer before college—I remember hearing news about the Gulf of Tonkin on the portable radio I took along when I camped out by myself for three days at my "special campsite"—my own Wal- den—on a hill behind the nurseries owned by a relative. I brought with me pencils and a notebook, kept a journal, and wrote some poetry and song lyrics. It is difficult for me to believe that I wasn't somehow influenced by the model of Thoreau's Walden experiment, though, curiously, I simply cannot remember thinking about Thoreau at the time.

I did not meet up with Thoreau again until the fall of my sophomore year, in Reginald "Doc" Cook's American literature course at Middlebury College. I remember responding enthusiastically—if still superficially—to Cook's enthusiasm for Thoreau (he had even written a book on him!),[8] and I was drawn this time not only to Thoreau's love of nature but also to his emphasis on nonmaterialistic values, the necessity of loving one's work, the legitimacy of noncommitment, and (with our growing entanglement in Vietnam) the need for civil disobedience. At this point I was an English major, but I was on the verge of questioning my commitment to English. I was taking my first sociology course and was intrigued by it. Moreover, I was disenchanted with the rather doctrinaire "New Criticism" approach promoted by the English Department at the time, which I found stifling and inimical to my burgeoning interest in the lives of writers and the profound issues they addressed. It is possible that Thoreau helped give me permission to consider changing majors—not to fear being uncommitted for a time and, even more surely, to stick with my inclination not to go into law (a profession my parents gently hinted I should consider) or any other profession just for the sake of status of financial reward. Only later would I discover how Thoreau himself had to struggle to resist perceived pressures to become a conventionally successful professional.

Before the end of the fall term of my sophomore year, my grandmother died, and I knew that those summer weekends on the farm were forever lost to me. I recall smelling the pines at Middlebury and feeling nostalgia for that same smell, so much a part of my earlier experience in the countryside. Already I had a strong sense of loss. I had experienced an unexpectedly severe case of homesickness in my first year at Middlebury, no doubt linked partly to my sense that I was leaving childhood behind. But even during childhood I felt loss. Before starting the fourth grade, I had rheumatic fever, spent a week in the isolation ward of a hospital, and was in bed at home for seven months. I have been told that I became a less extroverted, confident, upbeat person after that illness, and the very fact that I was outside the mainstream for a time probably deepened my sense of separation from peers and dependence on parents. The summer after fourth grade, when I was sent away to overnight camp, I became so homesick that my parents had to take me home early. Thoreau, too, I would later learn, had experienced intense homesickness—for example, when he moved briefly from Concord to Staten Island in 1843. It is quite likely that my own sense of loss would eventually sensitize me to the issue of loss in Thoreau's life and writings. In my early college years, I believe, Thoreau provided for me, as he would in the future, a means of regression back to youth; back to the relatively innocent, carefree days at the farm, the nature camp, and home; perhaps even back to the lost paradise of the infantile past.

I would read very little of Thoreau again until graduate school, but our "joining" had already begun. By the spring of my sophomore year, I was a sociology-anthropology major, though continuing to take literature courses. Between my sophomore and junior years there was a traumatic family crisis—the harbinger of my parents' divorce eight years later—which left me shaken, confused, disillusioned, feeling isolated and singled out, fearing intimacy and searching for values other than the conventional. I felt that I could never truly go home again, though I was not psychologically prepared to leave. I had finally, by the end of my sophomore year, become more socially confident, relaxed, and self-assured, but the secrets and burdens of that summer—which I felt I could share with no one—exacerbated my tendencies toward introversion and being something of a loner. There was, however, one exception to my move away from social relations. I became involved that traumatic summer with a young woman and, largely due to my need to escape my family, I found myself—to my astonishment—informally engaged by October of my junior year. We shared a love of nature, and I am certain that I invoked Thoreau's name in our intense discussions and frequent walks in the woods. Undoubtedly, one of the landmarks of my relationship with Thoreau was during that summer when my woman friend and I went to Concord. It was my first trip to Concord, and I think that it forcefully strengthened my bond with Thoreau. After my "engagement" broke up the following year, I still reminisced fondly about my first walk around Walden Pond with this woman. Thoreau became associated for me with my first serious romance, and this association—laced with nostalgia and loss—became a basis for my romance with him. When I think of Thoreau today, one image that still comes to mind is walking past the gravestones in the Concord village cemetery with my first real love.

My genuine scholarly interest in Thoreau began when I was in the M.A.T. in English Program at Harvard. After having majored in sociology and anthropology at Middlebury, I had decided—or con-

vinced myself—that I wanted to become a teacher of English at the
high school level. The decision was a complex one, involving my
reluctance to leave literature behind; my longstanding desire to become a teacher first and foremost (Thoreau himself trained at Harvard
to be a teacher); my interest in the sociology of education (my senior
thesis had been on the problems of urban education); my fear of
academic failure after the pressures of my undergraduate years; my
ambivalence about teaching on the college level, which seemed to be
more of a challenge or threat than I was ready for at the time; and my
hope that being in education might help me avoid the draft. I also
believe that in some way my decision constituted a rebellion against
the expectations of upper-middle-class culture and my own family—
my father was a neurologist and psychiatrist, my mother a clinical
psychologist. Indeed, though family, friends, and teachers were supportive and proud that I was going to Harvard, they questioned why
I, valedictorian and summa cum laude at Middlebury, would want to
become a high school teacher. I was all too aware that I was doing the
unexpected.

In the fall of my first year at Harvard, I was fortunate to enroll in
Erik Erikson's "Human Life Cycle" course and had Robert Coles as
my section leader. In Erikson and Coles I found the father-figures and
identity models I was searching for. Certainly, such concepts as
"identity crisis" and "moratorium" spoke to my situation as I perceived it. At the same time, I had a course, "Teaching English," that
required each of us to prepare a "unit" appropriate for high school
students. I chose to do my unit primarily on Thoreau, Ralph Waldo
Emerson, and the Transcendental values they espoused. In my paper
I referred to *Walden* as "a book I love," and I clearly intended to offer
to my students an alternative to the materialistic, capitalistic "rat
race" of American society, where the "mass of men lead lives of quiet
desperation." The education professors who evaluated my unit argued that I was advocating too ardently and openly the values embodied in *Walden*, that it was hopelessly idealistic to expect to "undo
eleven years of teaching and to effect an almost overnight value orientation." Reviewing this unit and the professors' comments now reveals to me the substantial investment I had in one particular, idealized version of Thoreau, with whom I clearly wished—and
needed—to identify.

This was the period when the anti-war movement and counterculture loomed large in the consciousness of many late adolescents and
early adults, including me. Thoreau seemed to me to be one of the

founding fathers or patron saints of the counterculture, a genuine hero who denounced shallow materialism, who "turned on" to nature, "tuned in" to the cosmos, and "dropped out"; who provided a model for how to resist—nonviolently—militarism, imperialism, oppression. Though committed to contributing to the public sphere (I had been greatly influenced in the early 1960s by President John F. Kennedy's call to service) and though deeply engaged with the political and cultural radicalism of the late 1960s, I was uncomfortable being part of a collectivity in which there were increasing pressures to countenance, and even participate in, violent activities. I thought of myself as radical in my own way, and professed to express my radicalism through my teaching, research, and creative efforts. Moreover, at the time I was drawn—not without ambivalence—to a world-view, endorsed by the poet Robinson Jeffers, which deemphasized the social and anthropocentric, which saw society as artificial, superficial, transient, and nature as real and enduring. Thoreau, with his stress on individual action, nonviolence, and the preeminence of the natural, was highly compatible with my ideological and emotional needs. I clung to him as one who provided support for my decision not to go into the highest-paying professions, my reluctance to commit myself to any work I did not love, my desire to put off *any* binding commitments. Perhaps a song, "The Cost of Living," which I wrote while at Harvard (I had written close to fifty songs by that time and had done some performing at a Cambridge coffeehouse) testifies most eloquently to how completely Thoreau, at least my idealized conception of him, had permeated my identity and ego ideal:

> Sometimes I get lonely, and wish I had a home
> But I wouldn't be any other man, and sit on costly cushioned thrones
> I wander through forests thick with thorns, so tangled and blinding green
> It's the life I must lead even though I know I'll have to bleed
> If I want to be free
>
> *Chorus*: That's the cost of living
> That's the cost of living
> That's the cost of living
> The way I do
>
> My thing is so many things, I can't confine myself to one
> With so many colors yet to see I guess that I've just begun
> I won't labor at what I do not love

It's hard work just to live
Time is a treasure that I wouldn't want to waste struggling to be
safe
I'm on the edge of the cliff
*Chorus*

Sometimes I'm sad walking through a crowd on the cement
secret streets
Clinging couples dance upon their clouds, gliding over concrete
I'd love to join the lovers on their clouds—wish I had someone
to meet
But I won't sell out just to pacify my doubts
I've got my promise to keep
*Chorus*

Some say I should settle down to domestic tranquility
But I won't trade the rainbow in just for security
Guess I'm not ready to grow old, and I may never be
And if my home ever comes she will always be young
And she'll want me to be free
*Chorus*

The references to women in the song point to another facet of
Thoreau that became absolutely crucial to me in my early graduate
school years: his celibacy, his quest for purity, his apparent ability to
live happily in solitude. At this stage of my life I was ambivalent
about intimacy and uneasy about sexuality, no doubt due in part to
family influences, early experiences with women, and the repressive-
ness of the '50s and early '60s culture in which I grew up. My painful
experiences with two women in the spring of my first Harvard year
left me with real doubts about my sexuality and seriously undermined my sexual confidence. Thoreau made life more bearable for me
during this period; in some respects he was literally a lifesaver. He
provided a glowing example of a man who lived a rich, full, joyous,
and creative life without sex, marriage, or children. By identifying
with him and idealizing the pure, chaste life he led, I was able to feel
somewhat better about myself. That summer I worked as a nature
counselor at, of all places, Camp Walt Whitman in New Hampshire,
and I can recall turning many times to *Walden* and to essays like
"Walking" and "Life Without Principle" for solace and strength. It
was at that time that I made a "Walden III" sign that now sits on the
mantle over my fireplace. During a very troubled summer at Walt
Whitman, I spent as much time as possible off by myself in the

woods, and—because I desperately needed to—more and more I was
intent on seeing similarities between myself and Thoreau. By the end
of the summer, I had half-convinced myself that I wanted to become a
poet.

In the fall I commenced a full-year internship in teaching English at
a high school in the suburban Boston area. In contrast to the previous
several months, this was one of the happiest, most social, and most
"growthful" times in my life. Images of golden autumn leaves and
warm sunshine come to mind. I felt appreciated and needed as a
teacher and as a person. I was, magically, more of an "adult" than I
had ever been before in this, my first full-fledged professional position. At the same time I was perceived as being unusually close and
sensitive to the students. I early developed the reputation among
students and colleagues of being a warm, sharing, creative person
who often sang songs and played guitar in his classes and used innovative approaches to poetry and other literary genres in the class-
room. I was considered to be a "radical" but not intimidating teacher,
who truly cared about his students and was committed to making
education and society more responsive to people's needs. That fall I
also became involved in a promising relationship with a woman.
Colleagues and students alike assumed that I had very exciting weekends. During these months, Thoreau was less important to me. I no
longer needed to identify so strongly with his solitary and chaste
existence; my own sense of self now relied more heavily on engagement with the social world.

But as the school year progressed, my relationship with the woman ended and I became restless with the prospect of teaching indefinitely in a high school environment that did not fully challenge me
intellectually and was characterized by many institutional constraints
and frustrations. When I applied to, and was accepted by, the graduate program in sociology at Brandeis, I thought I could combine my
background in sociology and education to become a sociologist of
education and an advocate for reform of the educational system. I
was aware, at the time, that I was leaving behind Thoreau and literary
creativity for more "social" concerns, but the promise and prestige of
going to Brandeis, whose unusually humanistic sociology program I
had dreamed of entering while still in college, overcame my doubts.

For various reasons, however, I became dissatisfied at Brandeis. I
found myself missing teaching (and my "image" of myself as a teacher) immensely. As a relatively "younger" student with no established

social life, I frequently felt isolated and out of place, and I was some-times intimidated by the intensely social, self-revelatory, and politi-cally charged atmosphere. I came to recognize—or rationalize—that, although I did not want to give up social science, I also could not abandon my love for literature and my gift for teaching it. Even though, in late fall, I met the woman I would one day marry, my level of comfort with intimacy and sexuality was again at low ebb.

Looking for a "way out" of Brandeis, I decided to apply, among other places, to the newly established American and New England Studies Program at Boston University. I was acutely aware that, at least from the outside, it looked as if I could not commit myself to anything and I had better make the right decision because time was running out. I felt an unexpectedly urgent desire to "settle down." In early spring I spent many hours walking in the fields and woods near my apartment, trying to decide. One major appeal of the B.U. pro-gram was the emphasis on New England Studies. As one who had experienced a prolonged identity crisis, I was drawn to the prospect of defining myself, once and for all, as a rooted New Englander. Moreover, being in New England Studies would give me the oppor-tunity to return decisively to Thoreau, other New England writers, and, indeed, to my own youth and creative aspirations. Thoreau—with whom I was again identifying strongly as I sauntered around Waltham—was very much on my mind. I vividly remember my fear that I would never have children and how Thoreau calmed that fear. I also was conscious of the sense in which New England Studies was a way of identifying with my father, whose roots were in the New England soil. More generally, I saw American Studies not only as a way to combine my interests in American literature and the social sciences but also as a way to mediate between, and reconcile myself with, the divergent world-views of my parents—my father being more "romantic" and nature-oriented and my mother more "real-istic," pragmatic, and socially oriented.

During this period of decision making, I was doing an independent study on Erikson, an intellectual father-figure to whom I had re-turned at Brandeis. Wandering around the Brandeis library in late winter or early spring, contemplating going into American Studies and browsing in the American literature section, I either came upon or sought out books by and about Thoreau. I had never read a biogra-phy of Thoreau—I had heretofore been content with his self-representations, public image, and my own idealizations of him. But coming upon Walter Harding's *The Days of Henry Thoreau*,[9] my curiosity was aroused. Reading this detailed biography was a revelation. Almost immediately, facts jumped out at me and demanded an interpretation: for instance, Thoreau's pattern of avoiding or rejecting opportunities for conventional success after his graduation from Harvard in 1837; his characterization of himself in 1837 as a "parcel of vain strivings"; his tearful response when his mother told him, "You can buckle on your knapsack and roam abroad to seek your fortune"; his fervent adoption of Emerson as a father-figure and Transcendentalism as an ideology just when he needed someone and something compatible to believe in; his extended sibling rivalry with his beloved elder brother John, who also seemed to be a father-substitute (his father was named John); his rivalry with John for the affection of Ellen Sewall and John's subsequent death from lockjaw in 1842; Thoreau's own attack, soon thereafter, or "sympathetic lockjaw" (from which, it seems, he almost died); his setting on fire of almost three hundred acres of Concord woods in 1844 and his refusal to help put out the fire; his late blooming as a writer only after the beginning of the Walden experiment in 1845; and, even while he was living at Walden, his frequent visits home and raids on the family cookie jar, and the weekend visits of his mother and sisters, who often brought "care packages" with them.

One of my first responses to these facts, I recall, was astonishment—not only that the facts begged for an interpretation but also that Harding (and, I soon discovered, most other biographers) had not made more of these facts. Later I would learn that Raymond Gozzi's Freudian dissertation on Thoreau and Leon Edel's biographical monograph did draw on these facts for their psychological analyses.[10] Having been immersed in Erikson, I sensed that such Eriksonian concepts as "identity crisis" and "moratorium" could be readily and helpfully applied to Thoreau, and I suspected that such a project would be especially appropriate under the rubric of American Studies. Indeed, my encounter with Harding's biography and my conviction that an Eriksonian approach to Thoreau would "work" helped sway me to American Studies. It would soon become evident that, even with the widespread popularity of *Young Man Luther* and *Gandhi's Truth*,[11] few Americanists had attempted Eriksonian psychobiographies or psychohistories. Thus, the time seemed right to undertake a study that would serve as a vehicle for my entrance into, and acceptance by, the professional community I aspired to join.

As I got deeper into my Thoreau project at Brandeis and then at B.U., I came to realize that the time was also right to study the "young man Thoreau" because I, too, was a young man struggling with dilemmas of identity, vocation, and intimacy so often associated with that stage of life. Even in the early phases of my work on Thoreau, I do not remember being particularly disappointed that he was not the mythical, ideal figure I had previously thought him to be. From late spring at Brandeis on, I was becoming more confidently and solidly involved with my wife-to-be, and perhaps I did not feel the desperate need for Thoreau to provide me with all the answers or an escape from intimacy. I was not as demanding that he be perfect. I could still be grateful for how he had helped me in the past, could still love and admire his achievements, but I did not have to worship him. In fact, I was relieved that Thoreau was all too human and that his life was not the unattainable ideal I once thought it was. I appreciated his accomplishments all the more because they were not come by without struggle. His humanness made it easier to identify with him, and I became excited by the possibility that, in coming to terms with Thoreau, I would have the chance to work through my feelings about myself, my life, "significant others," and American society. Working on Thoreau might be good therapy. In the summer between Brandeis and B.U., my wife-to-be and I trekked on foot from Waltham to Walden Pond, and that became another memory-bond linking me to Thoreau. With the exception of two brief periods of hesitancy (the second after orals at B.U., when I feared that I might be investing too much in my Thoreau work and that I would be competing with—and challenging—well-known scholars and Thoreau worshippers), my "marriage" to Thoreau was more or less firmly established.

Since I identified with Thoreau in many respects, I was concerned that I might be reading too much of Lebeaux into Thoreau. Indeed, I was struck right from the start with the similarity in our names and the fact that my wife-to-be, like Thoreau's one romantic interest, was named Ellen. Thus, I had to monitor my responses to the facts of Thoreau's life to make sure that my identification with him was not seriously distorting my interpretation. I think my developing awareness of at least some of the identifications, as well as my marriage and my increasing concern with the social, helped provide me with some much-needed distance from my subject. There was little doubt in my mind—and less now—that my own experience, and the perceived parallels with Thoreau, had predisposed me, or enabled me, to see certain aspects of his life and personality that other scholars—and certainly members of the "cult" that swallowed his persona whole—could not see or had overlooked. (I remember once saying to someone that what I had to contribute was an urban Jew's perspective on Thoreau!) And these perceived parallels between myself and Thoreau helped me to accept certain things about myself. The similarities led me to be more compassionate toward him and, ultimately, toward myself. Just as I resisted considering myself a "patient," so did I resist reducing Thoreau to a psychiatric "case." Moreover, to the great extent that I continued to respect and revere Thoreau, he granted permission and legitimacy to my own experience, behavior, and values. My self-monitoring, the widespread acceptance of Eriksonian and other psychoanalytic concepts, and the enthusiastic response of early listeners and readers provided validation that my interpretation of Thoreau was far from idiosyncratic. On the other hand, I am sure that, for better or for worse, not only the content emphasis but also the tone of my biography is informed by subjective elements.

My recognition of influential identifications with Thoreau, though there from the start, became more differentiated the deeper I got into my research and writing. For example, I saw myself as having been, like Thoreau, a sensitive, idealistic, and gifted youth who was unhappy with the materialistic, militaristic directions in which America was going and who was having trouble finding an appropriate niche in society. I realized that I, like Thoreau, had relied heavily on a persona—a presentation of self to the world and an ego- ideal—which did not always jibe with reality. My songs, for instance, presented an image of me as romantically sophisticated and confident which misled some people, particularly women. Much like Thoreau, I had depended heavily on sublimation as an escape from, and alternative to, intimacy and sexuality. I, too, tended to proclaim loudly my independence and inner-directedness while remaining in important ways dependent on home and mother. I wanted to consider myself an adventurous person without leaving Massachusetts, as Thoreau wished to see himself as a "traveller in Concord." I wondered about the extent to which my own rebelliousness, like Thoreau's, was a militant response to underlying feelings of dependence and a sense of anger at having been "let down" by significant others.

I, too, had ambivalent feeling about my parents. I perceived myself as having received some pressure from them to go into a more prestigious, lucrative profession. Like the subject of my biography, I also had had difficulty committing myself; had needed to create a moratorium for myself (including, I now realized, my Harvard years); had resisted temptations for "success without identity"; and was only now, a "late bloomer," coming into my own vocationally and personally, in the process of working on Thoreau, getting my Ph.D., and getting married. Just as Thoreau was able to commit himself at Walden and in *Walden* to a form of constructive noncommitment, so could I commit myself to Thoreau because he legitimized noncommitment. I could argue that *Walden* was, in fact, an archetype of the moratorium and suggest to readers, as Thoreau did, how crucial a moratorium is for growth. My own traumatic experience had sensitized me to the enduring and transforming significance of trauma in Thoreau's life, especially the death of his brother.

Another area of identification involved issues of success, guilt, and the quest for purity. A critical facet of my argument centered on Thoreau's aversion to conventional success, which resulted from his reluctance to surpass his less-than-successful and, by stereotypical standards of "masculinity," relatively "passive" father, just as he suspected he had won his "strong" mother from his "weak" father during the oedipal period. His need for purity, then, was linked to the guilt he felt with respect to his seemingly successful initiative in the oedipal project. Moreover, he experienced guilt vis-á-vis his elder brother, also a father-figure and rival for his mother's affections. He, rather than John, had been chosen by his mother to go to Harvard and follow in the footsteps of her father, and John even helped work Henry through college. In young adulthood Thoreau also became locked in a series of fateful, if not always consciously acknowledged, rivalries with the brother he loved and admired: while teaching in the same school and competing for student and community approval and, most crucially, when courting the same woman. The hostility aroused by these rivalries intensified Thoreau's guilt, called further into question his ambitions and initiative, and made the search for purity a progressively more urgent one. John's subsequent frail health and his death from lockjaw in 1842 made the prospect of conventional success even more a source of guilt and anxiety for the surviving brother. Torn between ambition and guilt, he sought to redefine "success"; if he were to achieve "greatness," he would have to do so in a manner that would not call forth comparisons with, suggest competition with, or involve "defeating" his father or brother. He became in many respects more comfortable with failure than conventional success, and sought "greatness" as a writer—a profession that certainly did not promise success in nineteenth-century America.

As I contemplated these aspects of Thoreau, I gained insight into some of my own motivations. In contrast to Thoreau's father, mine was a highly respected doctor, and it became clearer to me that one reason I avoided the more prestigious professions was because I feared I would be competing with my father and might not "measure up." Moreover, I had learned that being a successful professional by no means guaranteed happiness. To the extent that I perceived myself as being (or wishing to be) close to my mother and as challenging my father, I was no doubt subject to oedipally related guilt and fear.

Perhaps even more relevant to my identification with Thoreau, however, was the fact that my brother, three years my junior, was going through a difficult period. At the time I was working on *Young Man Thoreau*, he was, among other things, having problems finishing college, and in fact had dropped out on more than one occasion. (He has since finished college and has recently received a Master's in counseling.) My own ambitions, I recognized, had been tempered or modified by my sense of my brother's situation. When things seemed to be going well for him, I seemed to feel freer to be successful; when he was not doing well, I felt dragged down, uncomfortable with ambitiousness. Perhaps this dynamic—the guilt and anxiety aroused by the prospect of being more successful than my brother—helped to explain some of my own career and identify conflicts. To a degree, my brother was closer to my father than I, and it is possible I associated my brother with my father, thus introducing an oedipal element to the equation. During this troubling period, my brother and I had difficulty communicating; we had a painful falling out and I feared I had hurt him or let him down. In some sense I felt that I had lost the brother whom I admired as having been more independent and extroverted than I, to whom I had once been close and shared many good times. As I would learn later, there had been more sibling rivalry between us than I was aware of or consciously acknowledged, and my ambivalent feelings toward him may have exacerbated my guilt and made me unusually uneasy about competition. One of the first things that struck me in Harding's biography had been what appeared to me to be the rivalry between John and Henry for Ellen Sewall's affections, John's death soon thereafter of lockjaw, and Henry's extraordinary attack of psychosomatic lockjaw. Obviously, as I realize even more clearly now, my own relationship with my brother at the time helped me to see what, amazingly, other Thoreau biographers did not; my own experience sensitized me to these events and their implications, and probably led me to perceive the significance of guilt in Thoreau's psyche and development. That other scholars have frequently concurred with my conclusions about Thoreau and his brother—often characterizing them as my most original contribution to Thoreau biography—suggests that, whatever the subjective origins of these insights, they are likely to embody considerable "objective" truth.

In working through personal issues as I was working on Thoreau, I ultimately became conscious that the process of transference accompanied that of identification. In some ways, he had evolved into a father-figure and brother-figure for me. Of course, to the extent that he could provide me with a model for how to live my life, he was a father-substitute, a mentor. The courses I designed and taught at B.U., under the rubric of "New England Writers: How Is A Life to Be Lived," encouraged me to consider how Thoreau could serve as a "father" to me. (Perhaps my anger and frustration when I realized Thoreau's limitations may be partially explained by the strength of my transference.) More critically, in coming to terms with Thoreau, I was seeking to come to terms with my own brother and father; even while acknowledging their flaws and limitations, I could not only identify with them, but also love them, be close to them, express compassion for them. Thus I could work toward resolving my ambivalence toward these significant male figures in my life. It is likely that the desire to see Thoreau as a "brother" (as well as a "father") helps account for the fact that, though I do much demythicizing and humanizing of Thoreau, even many ardent Thoreauvians perceive me not primarily as a reductive debunker but as one who is sympathetic and even affectionate toward him. In the wake of the loss of his brother, and the uneasy feelings it provoked, Thoreau sought to perform much-needed "grief work" in an effort to assert his closeness to and love of him. His deepening immersion in nature and Indians, for instance, was part of this effort to reconcile himself with his brother. I believe that, in tracing his responses to John's death, I, who feared that he had lost a brother, was also dealing with emotions of guilt, grief, and alienation and seeking some form of reconciliation. The tone, if not the substance, of my biography probably owes much to these private motivations.

I was certainly able to identify with Thoreau's attachment to Emerson as a father-figure and Transcendentalism as an "ideology." Emerson obviously became the father-substitute he so desperately needed. Indeed, Emerson had become a mentor for me at a time when I needed him, and unquestionably my discussion of Emerson is not without both positive and negative father-transferences. But perhaps the most obvious father-figure in my work is Erik Erikson. The white-haired, wise, gently paternal Erikson, also a mentor of Robert Coles—who remains a real hero for me—provided me not only with an identity model but also with a coherent and positive view of human development. He is at once a social scientist and a humanist. In *Young Man Thoreau*, there is very little challenging or questioning of Erikson's model and, especially in the first three chapters, I rely heavily on Erikson for a framework in which Thoreau can be understood. This full-scale acceptance of Eriksonian psychology was partly due to my work's original status as a dissertation. Such work tends to emphasize (and sometimes overplay) scholarly debts and over-scrupulous use of footnotes. Moreover, as a dissertation, the stress was—properly, I think—on *demonstrating* the explanatory efficacy of Eriksonian analysis applied to a literary figure. Another reason for the deference to Erikson was my anxiety about challenging the authority of other Thoreau scholars, psychohistorians, and my dissertation committee; I felt that I needed the ideas and words of "father" Erikson to validate my conclusions, to "protect" me, even if I was not as indebted to Erikson for insights as my frequent bows would indicate. Indeed, I may have been afraid that I would let down or anger Erikson if I did not give him full credit. In any case, I *had* adopted Erikson as a father-figure and embraced his psychology with "born-again" zeal. I therefore paid homage to him whenever possible.

Toward the middle of my book, my confidence grew, and I realized that Erikson's insights alone would no longer be sufficient or appropriate. In the second half of the book, and in my more recent work, I felt freer—though not without some anxiety—to explore alternative or complementary psychological perspectives and to speak more confidently in my own voice. In the past I have had the tendency to regard authority either with excessive deference or with disillusionment, disappointment, and rebelliousness. Having gained more insight into that process, I am able to be more balanced, selective, and eclectic in my use of "authorities" and not as likely voluntarily to put on blinders or a harness in an effort to placate my "fathers." Having said this, I must add that I continue to view Erikson as a key intellectual "father" and to find Eriksonian psychology a helpful, meaningful, and valid intellectual perspective.

Toward the end of my introduction to *Young Man Thoreau*, written after the book had been accepted by the University of Massachusetts Press in 1976, I wrote:

> Thoreau clearly has limitations as one who, by his words, thoughts, and deeds, can guide or lead us today. For instance, I have deep reservations about his relative disinterest in, and apparent devaluation of, human relationships and "social facts." Our fulfillment and very survival depend in large part, I believe, on our sensitivity to the needs of other people, our respect for their experience and aspirations, our willingness to put into action our care and compassion, and our recognition that, as human beings having so much in common on this miraculous and threatened planet, we need each other.[12]

While I added in the next paragraph that it was "important to consider how he might speak constructively to us," these remarks reveal my sense of having distanced myself from Thoreau in certain significant ways at the same time that I continued to respect and admire him in others. One profound change that had reduced my need and inclination to identify so strongly with Thoreau was, as I have already suggested, the deepening of my relationship with my wife-to-be and our marriage in 1973, when I began writing *Young Man Thoreau*. As interpersonal intimacy became a real, gratifying, and very prominent part of my life, my priorities and sense of self gradually shifted. I was now more of an "adult" in my own eyes, and Thoreau no longer seemed able to speak to all my concerns. Indeed, the more involved I became in friendships and the relationship with my wife, the more limited he appeared. That I was now more comfortable and confident in my sexuality also increased my distance from, and skepticism about, Thoreau, who, after all, had never married or, as far as we know, been sexually involved with another person. Another factor was the ever-higher priority, no doubt encouraged by my social worker–political activist wife, that I was coming to attach to the social and political realm. I was now more fully prepared to acknowledge the reality of "social facts" and more comfortable with the prospect of being involved in a collectivity. Feeling more independent, I was no longer afraid to accept that I needed other people; in fact, partly due to such books as Philip Slater's *The Pursuit of Loneliness*,[13] I now became mindful of the potential destructiveness of excessive individualism and independence and the benefits of dependence and interdependence. I had always been uneasy with Thoreau's attacks on compassion, philanthropy, and reform movements; now I was even more impatient with him. Further events contributing to my shift in perpective were the actions of the Nixon administration; George McGovern's campaign and defeat; Watergate; my parents' divorce; my difficulties finding a job after getting my Ph.D. (which crystallized and deepened my anger at a "system" that frustrated human potential); my positive experiences teaching at B.U., and, during 1975 and 1976, at Forest Park Community College in St. Louis, an urban community college in which I was able to put my convictions into action. The move to St. Louis from Massachusetts also represented a decisive step toward independence and away from reliance on family and region for self-definition.

In the years immediately following the publication of *Young Man Thoreau*, I kept Thoreau at some distance, and I was hesitant to continue working on him. Although I still valued him and was grateful to him for helping me land a tenure-track job in academia, I was reluctant to be identified with him too closely and considered devoting myself to other academic pursuits. Aside from the understandable desire for a change of pace, at least a hiatus in my Thoreau work, there were many reasons for this "trial separation." Perhaps he reminded me of parts of my past—and past self—that I wanted to leave behind. Certainly I was afraid of becoming overcommitted to Thoreau; I was anxious to get on with something new and not be labeled as the "Thoreau expert" forced to maintain and defend, again and again, the same interpretation. There were, after all, so many things I could be doing. Although my book received numerous favorable reviews, the inevitable criticisms of my controversial work increased my anxiety about working on Thoreau and using psychological methodology. I was weary and wary of the prospect of competing with other Thoreau scholars, authority figures, and fearful that someone else would preempt any discoveries I might make. The fear that my future work on Thoreau could not live up to what I had already done—that I could not "bring off" a sequel—also clearly played a part in my reservations about continuing. I tended, furthermore, to see Thoreau as drawing me away from, draining energy from, my creative writing—especially song writing.

Another issue that militated against my continuing work on Thoreau was my growing involvement, both intellectual and personal, in feminism and men's liberation. It was apparent to me that Thoreau was a misogynist, and I was ambivalent about devoting so much of my life to—or being identified with—a man with such sexist views. It appeared to me, in fact, that my psychoanalytic approach to Thoreau and his family (especially my portrayal of his "strong" mother and "weak" father) contained elements of sexism, and Erikson himself was being accused by feminists of sexism for such concepts as the "inner space." As one whose wife is an active, committed feminist; who considers himself a feminist; and who was beginning to teach women's studies courses, I was not at all comfortable with what I perceived as the sexism in Thoreau and psychoanalysis. Before too long I did come to realize that my depiction of Thoreau's parents validly reflected how Thoreau, conditioned by nineteenth-century American gender stereotypes, would regard his parents, and I began to see how sex-role analysis might shed light on his psyche and problems, showing how he was himself trapped by sex roles and oppressive masculine stereotypes. One further concern that kept me uneasy about Thoreau was his contempt for "big government"; especially with the advent of Proposition-13 conservative mentality, I saw Thoreau's potential as a legitimizer of a retreat to privatism and a dangerous brand of conservatism (though I strongly suspected he would disapprove of many of the actions taken in the name of so-called conservativism).

On the other hand, many factors and circumstances soon began to draw me in the direction of going ahead with a study of Thoreau's later years. Walter Harding invited me to participate in an April 1978 conference on Thoreau and psychology, and I decided to use this invitation as an opportunity to explore what I might have to say about Thoreau in the post-Walden years. Indeed, I found that such Eriksonian concepts as "generativity versus stagnation" helped immeasurably to understand the later Thoreau. The response of Harding and other scholars to the paper was quite enthusiastic and encouraging. Moreover, this was a period when books about adult development—including "mid-life crisis"—were published in abundance and re-

ceived widespread critical attention. Such works as Gail Sheehy's
*Passages,* Daniel Levinson's *The Seasons of a Man's Life,* Roger Gould's
*Transformations,* and George Vaillant's *Adaptation to Life*[14] furnished
me with promising perspectives—complementary to Erikson's—and
suggested that the time was propitious for a study of the "middle-
aged Thoreau." Letters, remarks, and reviews from scholars, non-
academics, and the director of the University of Massachusetts Press
further emboldened me to write a follow-up book. From the standpoint of my academic career (which had assumed great importance),
this project seemed a logical and potentially prestigious step, which
might give me more choices. In continuing my work on Thoreau, I
would be maximizing my chances for publication. A colleague at
Michigan State, who had become a sort of father- and elder-brother-
figure and whose opinion I valued highly, advised me to go ahead
with the Thoreau book. Spurred on by all the encouragement and
career considerations, though still ambivalent about taking on such
an enormous project, I resolved to write a prospectus and submit it to
the University of Massachusetts Press. On the brink of mailing in the
completed prospectus, I came down with a virus that left me weak,
feverish, and not tasting or smelling properly for over a month.
Rarely having been seriously ill in previous years, I wondered if my
body was trying to tell me something, if perhaps I remained too
ambivalent about the project and the monumental commitment in
time and energy it would entail. At the beginning of the summer of
1979, however, I took a deep breath and submitted the prospectus; by
September 1979 I had agreed on a contract with my publisher.

There were, in addition, life-cycle-related issues at work in my
decision. At this time, settling down, establishing roots, was a prominent concern in my life. In the summer of 1979, we bought a house,
and I recollect thinking that the parameters of my life were probably
defined for the next five years—house, quite possibly children, work
on the Thoreau book. Although my emotional investment in a house,
marriage, children, and career constituted, I believed, an obstacle to
close identification with Thoreau, I was in the process of discovering
how crucial certain issues of adult development were to me, someone
who could soon anticipate entering middle age himself. Following
Thoreau's passages through adulthood would put me in touch with
issues I was already facing and prepare me to deal with concerns I
would soon be confronting. Studying Thoreau, I realized, would contribute to my own growth. And, as my work on the paper for Harding

and on the prospectus suggested, I might well find new, unanticipated grounds for reconciliation with Thoreau.

In the past few years, my "marriage" to Thoreau *has* evolved in new, unexpected directions, though it has not been without its quarrels and reservations. Working in recent months on "dialogues" between myself and Thoreau and between myself and my "work" on Thoreau—begun in June 1981 as part of a "Life Context Workshop" (an introduction to Progoff's intensive journal method)—has revealed much to me about these directions in our relationship.[15] Such dialogues may well be a valuable source of insight on subjectivity for other biographers.

When I first worked on the dialogues, I had a sense, inspired by the possibility that my wife and I might be pregnant, that I was on the verge of a new period of my life. With the confirmation that we were indeed going to have a child, I have unquestionably entered a new phase, a new life within my life. I wonder now whether, or how, my relationship to Thoreau will be modified as I become involved in parenting. Surely, the relationship *will* change. However, as I review the history of our relationship, with its separations and subsequent reconciliations, I am convinced that it will continue to grow as I do, and that I will have reason to feel close to, and grateful to, Thoreau again in the future. I suspect that he will provide me with other Waldens, other inspirations and consolations, other reinvigorating perspectives, as I plunge deeper into the mists of adulthood. I am, then, hopeful that I can maintain and nurture an enduring I-Thou relationship with Thoreau. Wherever I go now, I have a feeling that he will be by my side, perched on my shoulder, inside my head, ready to engage in a constructive dialogue with me. He will continue to be, I expect, an old and cherished companion—human, fallible, admired, loved, a part of me.

## NOTES

[1]Bernard Malamud, *Dubin's Lives* (New York: Avon Books, 1980), pp. 20–21.

[2]Henry David Thoreau, *The Writings of Henry D. Thoreau, Walden,* ed. J. Lyndon Shanley (Princeton: Princeton University Press, 1971), p. 323.

[3]Erik Erikson, "On the Nature of Psycho-Historical Evidence: In Search of Gandhi," *Daedalus* 97, no. 3 (Summer 1968): 695. See idem, pp. 695–730, for an important discussion of subjectivity and methodology in psychohistory.

[4]Carl Pletsch, "An Experiment in Collaboration in Psychoanalysis and Biography" (unpublished), p. 320.

[5]See George Moraitis and Carl Pletsch, "A Psychoanalytic Contribution to Method in Biography," *The Psychohistory Review* 8 (1979): 72–74; George Moraitis, "A Psychoanalyst's Journey into a Historian's World: An Experiment in Collaboration," *The Annual of Psychoanalysis* 7 (1979): 287–320 (reprinted here as Chap. 3).

[6]See Ira Progoff, *At a Journal Workshop* (New York: Dialogue House Library, 1975); Robert Blair Kaiser, "The Way of the Journal," *Psychology Today*, March 1981, pp. 64–76.

[7]Richard Lebeaux, "Searching for Thoreau: Some Methodological and Personal Reflections," *American Examiner* 7 (Spring 1980): 66–81. See *Young Man Thoreau* (Amherst: University of Massachusetts Press, 1977).

[8]Reginald L. Cook, *Passage to Walden* (Boston: Houghton Mifflin, 1949).

[9]Walter Harding, *The Days of Henry Thoreau* (New York: Knopf, 1965).

[10]Raymond D. Gozzi, "Tropes and Figures: A Psychological Study of David Henry Thoreau" (Ph.D. diss., New York University, 1957); Leon Edel, *Henry D. Thoreau* (Minneapolis: University of Minnesota Press, 1970).

[11]Erik Erikson, *Young Man Luther* (New York: Norton, 1958); idem, *Gandhi's Truth* (New York: Norton, 1969).

[12]Lebeaux, *Young Man Thoreau*, pp. 7–8.

[13]Phillip Slater, *The Pursuit of Loneliness* (Boston: Beacon Press, 1970).

[14]Gail Sheehy, *Passages* (New York: Dutton, 1976); Daniel J. Levinson et al., *The Seasons of a Man's Life* (New York: Ballantine Books, 1978); Roger Gould, *Transformations* (New York, Simon & Schuster, 1978); George Vaillant, *Adaptation to Life* (Boston: Little, Brown, 1977).

[15]Though space limitations prevent me from including a portion of the dialogues as part of this essay, I hope eventually to discuss these dialogues elsewhere and how they (and, more generally, journal writing) may be useful to biographers.

# 12

# *A Stalin Biographer's Memoir*

## Robert C. Tucker

THE OLD MAXIM *cherchez la femme* can do duty in this case, where the question is why someone who never intended to be a biographer became one, although reluctantly and after long delay. The *femme* was the revisionist of psychoanalytic thought, Karen Horney, with whose writings I became acquainted around 1940.

When her last and synthesizing book, *Neurosis and Human Growth*, was published in 1950, I was serving in the American embassy in Moscow.[1] Having procured a copy from Brentano's via the diplomatic pouch, I read it repeatedly. Despite its lucidity of expression, it is not an easy work to comprehend thoroughly and to use, yet it deeply influenced my thinking.

Horney's subject was the "neurotic character structure." To summarize the core of her argument: a person who experiences "basic anxiety" resulting from adverse emotional circumstances in early life may seek and find a rock of inner security by forming an idealized image of himself or herself. The content of the self-image will depend on the direction the child takes in relations with others—moving against, toward, or away from them. One whose tendency is to move against others may idealize himself as a great warrior, while one whose tendency is to move toward others may imagine himself to be saintlike. Gradually and unconsciously, if the anxiety-causing conditions do not change, the child moves from self-idealizing to the adoption of the idealized image as an *idealized self*, the imagined real identity. Then the energies available for growth toward self-realization are invested in the quest to prove the idealized self in action. Horney calls this the "search for glory."

Because the idealized self is free of the faults, blemishes, and limitations that go with being human, it cannot be actualized. Hence, the individual begins to feel estranged from and to accuse, hate, and condemn the fallible, merely human, "empirical self" he is in practice. The drive to enact the idealized self, however, is compulsive, with painful anxiety and self-condemnation as the price of failure. Consequently, the inwardly conflicted individual develops a system of unconscious defenses against the experience of failure. These include repression of the disparity between the idealized and empirical selves, various forms of rationalization, the search for affirmation of the idealized self by significant others, and the projection onto still others—who can realistically be condemned and combatted—of both the repressed faults and the self-hatred they arouse. Repressed self-hatred is then experienced as hatred of others. The particular others onto whom the self-hatred is projected are likely to be those who have incurred the neurotic person's animosity by failing somehow to affirm him as the idealized self he takes himself to be. A "need for vindictive triumph" is therefore a regular ingredient, according to Horney, of the search for glory, especially in those whose tendency is to move against others in a drive toward mastery.

When I was reading and rereading this book, my work consisted in directing a translation bureau operated cooperatively by the British, American, and Canadian embassies. It produced a daily bulletin of translations into English of articles I selected from eight Soviet daily papers, as well as from periodicals ranging from the Central Committee monthly *Kommunist* to journals on history, law, philosophy, and the arts. Because my Russian wife, whom I had married in 1946, was not given an exit visa to accompany me back to the United States, I was, so to speak, serving an indefinite sentence in Moscow.

The cold war, raging fiercely at the time, received ample domestic as well as foreign coverage in the Soviet press. Thus, a play running in Moscow theaters, called *The Mad Haberdasher*, featured a thinly disguised villain who was a Hitler-like, younger Harry Truman. The highly favorable press reviews of it were vintage cold-war material. But if hatred for enemies was one pervasive press theme, love was another. Love of Soviet citizens and all people of good will abroad for the Soviet regime as personified by Joseph Stalin. What would one day be called the "cult of personality," with Stalin as the centerpiece, was at its zenith. Unlike George Orwell's Big Brother, Stalin really existed. But he was a recluse and hardly ever appeared in public, save for the parades in Red Square on May Day and November 7. Still, a heroic portrait of him, usually in generalissimo's uniform, appeared almost daily on the papers' front pages, and in myriad other ways Stalin symbolically figured in Soviet public life as an object of reverence.

Two years earlier, in 1949, the cult of Stalin had reached a climax when the celebration of his seventieth birthday resulted in what can only be described as his virtual deification. Although the birthday fell on December 21, the press and radio prepared for it long in advance with a mass of material on Stalin's greatness as a revolutionary and as a Russian Soviet statesman of world-historic stature. Plays were staged, for example, about heroic episodes out of his early life as a revolutionary in Georgia. Reports filled the press on presents coming in from all over Russia and distant countries, and afterwards a special "Museum of Presents to J. V. Stalin" was created to display these gifts to the public. On the birthday itself the Politburo members and others contributed laudatory articles, and there was an evening meeting in the Bolshoi Theater to mark the occasion. To keep the momentum going, every day for over a year, *Pravda* carried, under the headline "The Stream of Greetings," long lists in fine print of the names of organizations that had sent birthday congratulations to Comrade Stalin.

One Saturday afternoon in 1951 I had been browsing in the Academy of Sciences bookstore and was walking down Gorky Street toward the U.S. embassy on Mokhovaia. In full view below was the Red Square and, off to its right, the Kremlin. It may have crossed my mind that Stalin was at work there. Suddenly I had what struck me as a momentous thought in the form of a question: What if the idealized image of Stalin, appearing day after day in the party-controlled, party-supervised Soviet press, were *an idealized self in Horney's sense*? If so, Stalin must be a neurotic personality along the lines portrayed in her book, except that he possessed a plenitude of political power unprecedented in history. In that case, the Stalin cult must reflect Stalin's own monstrously inflated vision of himself as the greatest genius of Russian and world history. The cult must be an institutionalization of his neurotic character structure. So the Kremlin recluse, this ruler who was publicly so reticent about himself, must be spilling out his innermost thoughts concerning himself in millions of newspapers and journals published throughout Russia. He must be the most self-revealed disturbed person of all time. Finding out what was most important about him would not require getting him onto a couch; one could do it by reading *Pravda*, while rereading Horney! I

began to do just that, and in the process grew more and more convinced of my hypothesis.

At that time, the members of the small colony of Westerners living
in Moscow attached no serious importance to the adulatory publicity
surrounding Stalin. Everyone knew that a Stalin cult existed and
accounted for a large share of the material in the Soviet press. Everyone assumed that this press was regime-managed, regime-censored,
and regime-controlled, down to the minutiae that were pondered for
potential insight into Soviet policy. But these two facts were not seen
as meaningfully related, partly because the regime was not understood to be a personal one. Statesmen who negotiated in Moscow,
such as General George Marshall in 1947 and others (although they
were very few), sensed that Stalin's was the final world on foreign
political issues. But that in itself could be and was interpreted as
signifying that he was the ultimate spokesman of a Politburo consensus, and not necessarily a controlling figure in creating the consensus. To illustrate: in an autobiographical account of his ambas-
sadorship between 1946 and 1949, *My Three Years in Moscow,* General
Walter Bedell Smith expressed the opinion that Stalin should be seen
as a chairman of the Politburo board; and in taking this view, he was
certainly relying on advice from embassy officers and Russian specialists in the U.S. government.[2] The received view was reflected in,
and perhaps influenced by, a small book published in 1949, *The Operational Code of the Politburo.* Its author, Nathan Leites of the RAND
Corporation's Social Science Division in Washington, interpreted the
decisions then being made in Moscow as decisions of a group, the
Politburo, which was guided by an operational code implicit in Bolshevism as a body of thought.[3] The book gave no inkling that Stalin
rather than "the Politburo" might be making the key decisions. I
heard later that Admiral Joy, the negotiator for the U.N. side in the
long, drawn-out talks with the North Koreans in Panmunjom for an
armistice in the Korean war—negotiations that were not successfully
concluded so long as Stalin lived—used to take *The Operational Code*
with him on his helicopter trips to the conference site.

What, you may be asking yourself, did we foreigners in Moscow
suppose was Stalin's attitude toward his cult? I believe the general
view was that he simply *tolerated* it as a pragmatic political device for
providing a father symbol ("father and teacher of the peoples" was a
phrase regularly applied to him in cult articles) for a population that
historically personalized authoritarian rule in a *tsar-batiushka* (father-

tsar). Very likely, one reason why knowledgeable observers understood the matter in this way was that Stalin himself had given the cue
for it in an interview with the German writer Lion Feuchtwanger,
who duly recorded the comment in his *Moscow 1937*.[4] It appeared
from Feuchtwanger's account that an indifferent and even somewhat
bemused Stalin felt he had to make a concession to his backward
people's persisting need for a ruler cult as a personalization of Russia's present regime. Some foreigners living in Moscow in the 1940s
and early 1950s had read *Moscow 1937*. Much later, Edgar Snow,
standing beside Mao Zedong on the reviewing stand in Peking when
the Mao cult was close to its orgiastic climax, asked the chairman a
question like Feuchtwanger's, and received an answer not very different from Stalin's. What do journalists who ask such questions of
rulers surrounded by personality cults expect them to answer? If such
a man supported the cult because he craved it, as well as for reasons
of *realpolitik,* would he—could he—say: Because I like being adored?

Not surprisingly, my novel hypothesis found little favor with the
few acquaintances in the Anglo-American colony in Moscow to
whom I confided it. They dismissed it as improbable, or they pooh-
poohed it with comments like: "Stalin doesn't give a hoot for the cult,
he simply countenances it as a useful propaganda tool in Soviet domestic affairs." After a few such exchanges, I gave up propagating
my idea—but I didn't give up the idea.

In the summer of 1952 I flew home for a short leave. While in the
United States, I was asked by the State Department to consult with
Russian specialists at the Voice of America, which then had head-
quarters in New York. Two episodes stand out in my memory of the
two days spent in New York. One was a remark by Bertram D. Wolfe,
who was them becoming famous as the author of *Three Who Made a
Revolution,* [5] while also serving as a part-time consultant with the
Voice of America. After a morning of discussions with the Russian
section's staff, he and I stopped in the washroom on the way to a
lunch that had been arranged. There he told me the following story.
An unknown man had contacted the State Department and suggested that much of Russia's enigmatic behavior in the cold war
might become explicable if one took account of the possibility that
Stalin was paranoid. "The department didn't know how to get rid of
him and sent him to me," Wolfe said with a wry smile, "and I got rid
of him." Not knowing much about paranoia but realizing that the
unknown man and I were on the same general intellectual wave-

length, I felt leaden inside. From the point of view of people like Wolfe, not to mention the Department of State, the unidentified person and I were both crackpots.

The other memory is of a conversation with an academic who, by arrangement with the State Department, came for an interview in my New York hotel room. He introduced himself as Walt Rostow of the Center of International Studies at the Massachusetts Institute of Technology, and explained that he was in charge of a collaborative project about the Soviet system. On the advice of the State Department Russian specialist Charles Bohlen (whom I knew and much respected), the group was proceeding on the premise that the Soviet system's behavior could be explained in terms of the regime's drive to preserve, consolidate, and increase its power. What did I think of that? I don't recall exactly what I said to Professor Rostow, only that I was unenthusiastic about his approach. The Rostow study was subsequently published as *The Dynamics of Soviet Society.*[6] However widely read it was in its time, today it is one of the forgotten works in the field.

The conversation with Rostow proved useful, nevertheless, in that it set me thinking more in "system" terms than before. I began to see possible ramifications of my hypothesis. Books were being published in those days about totalitarianism—among them, Hannah Arendt's *The Origins of Totalitarianism.*[7] On returning to Moscow, I began to study this literature. Interesting though much of it was, I found it deeply flawed because the dictator and his psychodynamics were missing from the picture of totalitarianism. Arendt, for example, thought that totalitarian regimes were actuated in their total terror by an "ideological supersense," one not located, so far as her reader could tell, in anyone's individual psyche. Perhaps, I thought, the dictatorial ruler of a totalitarian state could politically institutionalize the inner defenses of his ever-threatened idealized self. If all-powerful, he could then mobilize a vast apparatus of repression to visit revenge not only on individuals whom he had come to perceive as enemies but on entire social groups so perceived. Thus the Holocaust might have been Adolf Hitler's enactment of vindictive hostility stemming from neurotically generated self-hatred projected onto the Jews as a group. This would not absolve those who carried out his lethal orders of responsibility for their actions, but it could help explain some "system" behavior that the theoreticians failed to explain convincingly to me. In 1965, I finally set forth this reasoning in an article on "The Dictator and Totalitarianism."[8]

To return to Moscow in late 1952 and the fear-filled early months of 1953: the Soviet press was then printing ominous stories about Jewish "doctor-murderers," who allegedly had conspired with the Anglo-American intelligence services and the American-Jewish Joint Distribution Committee to shorten the lives of Soviet leaders. For my part, I was coming to the conclusion that if Stalin, then in his seventies, were to die, major changes might occur rather suddenly in the Soviet regime's conduct. If the regime were acting out a neurotic personality's political needs, it might no longer be compelled to do so once he was dead. Theoretically, another individual of like character could assume dictatorial power and pursue the same sort of politics. But it was unlikely that a highly neurotic Stalin would tolerate the presence of an individual of his own psychological makeup in his entourage; rather, he would surround himself with steady, pliable, nonthreatening types, unafflicted by compulsions like his own. If Stalin were to die, maybe the regime would call off the terroristic new purge apparently in the making, with preparations for the trial of the "doctor-murderers." Then, in other ways, the Soviet government might stop acting against its own interests (Karen Horney had observed that every neurotic tends to act in ways contrary to his own best interests). For example, early in 1953 the Soviet government was pressuring the American and British governments to move their embassies some distance from their longstanding locations on either side of the Kremlin. Why was this happening? Might Stalin, neurotically enraged against the Anglo-Americans, want the embassies moved out of sight of his Kremlin workplace, whence their flags could be seen flying on special occasions like the Fourth of July?

Such deductions from my psychological hypothesis were very relevant to me personally, because of the denial of an exit visa to my wife. It had never been easy for foreign governments to secure permission for Soviet wives of their nationals to leave Russia. Yet, however grudgingly, a handful of visas were usually issued about once a year. The last time that had happened was early in 1946, shortly before our marriage. Then, in 1947, the official legal gazette published a governmental decree announcing laconically: "To prohibit marriages between Soviet citizens and foreigners." Ever since, Soviet citizens already married before the decree's passage were denied exit visas, even though the anti-marriage law was not explicitly retroactive. Numerous high-placed foreigners had interceded with the Soviet government on behalf of the few women married to foreign nationals, but to no avail. At that time, there were six Americans in Moscow

with Russian wives (two embassy employees and four press corre-
spondents). When a foreign ambassador took up the matter with
Foreign Minister Andrei Vyshinsky, the latter would get red in the
face and declare that his government considered it a closed question.
Clearly, it was contrary to Soviet government's best interests to allow
such a trivial matter to fester in relations with our own and other
foreign governments. Why was this happening?

A Horneyan explanation occurred to me. If the public cult of Stalin
was an institutionalization of a neurotically idealized self, then given
that he was ruler of the Soviet Union, the idealizing must extend to
his realm as well. Logically, then, any criticism of the Soviet state over
which the idealized Stalin presided, would, by implication, demean
him, the all-wise, beneficent genius-leader that he took himself to be.
The Soviet press daily provided an image of the Soviet realm that fit
with this interpretation: it idealized life in Stalin's Russia, except insofar as enemies tried to harm the state and society. What, then, would
have been the aging, neurotic Stalin's response to a statement in, say,
1947 that the foreign ministry was prepared to issue exit visas to some
Soviet women married to foreigners? He would have reasoned that
the women's willingness to leave Soviet Russia to live abroad was an
implicit derogation of his, Stalin's, state. This would have made him
furiously reject the proposed issuance of visas and add: "There must
be a law against these marriages!" If that was how the matter stood,
then Stalin's death might open the way for our departure. One night
when my wife and I went out for a walk, I explained this line of
thought and predicted: "If Stalin dies, I bet they'll let you go." Dis-
couragingly, she replied: "Georgians are long-lived, he'll probably
outlive you and me."

On March 3, 1953, I arrived at my office at the normal time. The
Soviet newspapers were late that morning—usually a sign of an especially important item of news coming up. I thought it would be an
announcement that the trial of the "doctor-murderers" had begun.
Just then I met one of our American typists. Ashen-faced, she reported that she and her husband had heard on Moscow radio that
something was the matter with Stalin. A few minutes later the papers
came. A front-page announcement said, "Comrade Stalin is gravely
ill" and gave details about the stroke he had suffered. This meant that
Stalin was dead or as good as dead. The thought crossed my mind
that some person or persons high in the regime who felt threatened
might have acted to shorten Stalin's life to prevent the trial from
starting and the purge from taking place.

But what I mainly want to record is that never in my life, before or since, have I experienced such intense elation as I did at that moment. It was compounded of joy that one of history's awful evil-doers was meeting his end, hope that this might mean early release for my wife and me from a stay in Russia that had now lengthened into nearly nine years, and excitement that my hypothesis was going to be tested. Would Russia after Stalin change in the ways that I anticipated? The answer was not long in coming, and it was affirmative.

For about two weeks, Russia's public life focused on the ceremonial send-off. There was a final burst of the Stalin cult in the press tributes. He was praised in three funeral speeches that were broadcast over the radio, but it was notable that only V. M. Molotov sounded broken-hearted. Georgi Malenkov came across calm and collected, and L. P. Beria was briskly upbeat. Once the leave-taking ended, a deep change came over Soviet public life. The terror-tinged atmosphere of the first months of the year evaporated like mist in the morning sun. The threatened purge never took place. The Ministry of Internal Affairs, now again under Beria, issued a sensational public statement in mid-April denouncing the doctors' affair as a frame-up (it did not say by whom). Beria also revealed that "inadmissible methods," meaning torture, were used to extract from the hapless doctor-victims confessions of guilt for nonexistent crimes, and not all of them had survived the ordeal. In conclusion, the statement assured Soviet citizens that now they could ive and work in security. This was a thinly veiled reference to the general insecurity of only two months ago, and it took no Kremlinological expertise for politically literate citizens to grasp the implicit indictment of Stalin. By then his name already was hardly to be seen in the Soviet press; the Stalin cult was a thing of the past. Spring 1953 in Moscow reminded me of Spring 1945, when victory, peace, and hope for the future came to Russia all at once. Ilya Ehrenburg captured the spirit of that time in the title of his novel *The Thaw*.[9]

The change was felt no less quickly in foreign relations. The American and British embassies were informed that they would not need to move to new locations. Steps began to be taken toward winding up the cold war, notably by reviving talks that soon led to an armistice in Korea on terms that the Communist side had stubbornly rejected so long as Stalin lived. In May, when Charles Bohlen arrived in Moscow to take up the post of ambassador, he decided to raise the question of the Russian wives of Americans to test the new atmosphere. Molotov now headed the Foreign Ministry. Instead of angrily refusing to consider the question when Bohlen raised it, he calmly said that he would look into it. Three weeks later, visas that had been denied for seven years were granted, and before the end of June my wife and I were on our way West. Later in 1953, the anti-marriage law of 1947 was repealed in a governmental decree as laconic as the earlier one.

Back in the United States after an interim assignment to Paris, I held a job with the Social Science Division of the RAND Corporation while working at night to complete an interrupted doctoral dissertation on Karl Marx and German philosophy. RAND wanted me to write interpretive studies of Soviet internal and external policy after Stalin. In order to clarify what was new in Soviet policy after Stalin, I had to go into Stalin's influence on earlier policies, and this inevitably led me into psychological analysis. The Social Sciences Division under Hans Speier was generally supportive so long as I devoted primary attention to developments *after* Stalin, and I wrote a few studies, subsequently published in scholarly journals, which touched on my psychological interpretation in the course of seeking to explain post-Stalin policies. But my thesis that a really profound change had occurred with Stalin's death *because* of the psychological factor at work while he lived met with resistance. I was advised not to focus on history. Besides, what had really changed? Of course, there was the armistice in Korea and, in 1955, the Austrian peace treaty that Stalin had withheld, and some other smaller steps. But might not all this be explained by pressures on the Soviet regime? Or, might it not be simply "tactical," the politics of a younger, more "flexible" Soviet political leadership? Might not the new Soviet politics for that reason by more dangerous to the West than Stalin's implacable cold-war policies?

I was now experiencing the problem of historical evidence, the circumstance that whatever happens in history is subject to differing interpretations depending on one's assumptions. From my psychological point of view, a small political act like the release of the wives was highly significant, apart from the meaning it had for the few persons immediately affected. Like little changes in a person, it manifested change in the character of the actor—in this case the Soviet regime. Minds trained in the political and social sciences didn't seem to see it that way. They were inclined to reason that small changes in the regime's behavior had best be thought of as having small causes, whereas large changes would stem from large causes. I disagreed, but not persuasively, except to a few friends who found my reasoning plausible albeit undemonstrable. Without knowing it, I was on my way to becoming a historian of the Stalin era. However, the idea of writing a biography was still remote from my mind. I simply wanted to produce a study of a totalitarian dictatorship that would disclose the personality of the dictator as a motor force of the regime's politics.

Another major problem of evidence confronted me: How could I demonstrate that Stalin really was a neurotic personality? We knew so little of him as a person. In his infrequent public appearances, he had seemed modest, unassuming, oblivious of his own personality. To read his psychological makeup through the public Stalin cult was questionable, to say the least, because the evidential value of this material turned on its meaning to him, and that we didn't know. Then came an unexpected windfall in the form of Nikita Khrushchev's secret report about Stalin to the Twentieth Party Congress, a copy of which came into American hands and was published in the *New York Times* on June 5, 1956. In this lengthy document, significantly entitled "On the Cult of Personality and Its Consequences," a one-time admiring protégé, one of the dictator's lieutenants who had observed him a close hand from the later 1930s to his death, offered abundant first-hand testimony of his former boss. He depicted Stalin as a man of colossal grandiosity, along with profound insecurity that caused him to need constant affirmation of his imagined greatness. Khrushchev protrayed a neurotic personality precisely in Horney's sense, an example of the "arrogant-vindictive" type described in *Neurosis and Human Growth*. A self-idealizer, insatiably hungry for the glorification that the public cult provided, Stalin was easily aroused to vindictive hostility by whatever appeared to detract from his inflated vision of himself as a leader and teacher of genius. His aggressions, typically expressed in purges—it followed from Khrushchev's account—were the other side of his self-glorification.

To give the reader a more concrete picture of Khrushchev's testimony, I will cite some examples. Stalin personally edited the adulatory *Short Biography* of himself published in 1947, according to Khrushchev, and in doing so he "marked the very places where he thought that the praise of his services was insufficient." He therefore inserted the following sentence: "Although he performed his task as leader of the party and the people with consummate skill and enjoyed the unreserved support of the entire Soviet people, Stalin never allowed his work to be marred by the slightest hint of vanity, conceit or self-adulation." He also added this testimonial: "Comrade Stalin's genius enabled him to divine the enemy's plans and defeat them. The battles in which Comrade Stalin directed the Soviet armies are brilliant examples of operational military skill." Stalin, Khrushchev testified, doted on a 1951 film about the civil war, *The Unforgettable Year 1919*, "in which he was shown on the steps of an armored train, practically vanquishing the foe with his own saber." He diminished Lenin as he magnified himself. The draft text of the *Short Biography* said at one point: "Stalin is the Lenin of today." That seemed insufficient to the editor, who altered the sentence to read: "Stalin is the worthy continuer of Lenin's work, or, as it is said in our party, Stalin is the Lenin of today." He created Stalin prizes but no Lenin prizes, Khrushchev said, adding that "not even the tsars" created prizes named after themselves. While Stalin kept postponing the decision passed long ago by the party to build a Palace of the Soviets as a monument to Lenin, in 1951 he signed a resolution of the USSR Council of Ministers for the erection of an impressive monument to himself on the newly built Volga-Don Canal.[10]

My surmise about an organic link between the cult of Stalin and the official idealization of Stalin's Russia found confirmation in Khrushchev's report. He noted that Stalin had last visited a village in 1928, when he went to Siberia to speed up grain collections. But in later years he needed to believe that Soviet agriculture was prospering under his beneficent rule, and films were produced to demonstrate the same. "He knew the country and agriculture only from films. And these films had dressed up and beautified the existing situation in agriculture. Many films so pictured *kolkhoz* life that the tables were bending from the weight of turkeys and geese. Evidently, Stalin thought that it was actually so."[11]

More evidence of this kind was to appear in Soviet publications during Khrushchev's tenure in power, and still more in the memoirs that he dictated following his ouster in 1964. But the secret report was the crucial source of evidence. My hypothesis was now confirmed to my own satisfaction, and the task was to get on with the study. In 1958 I finished and defended my dissertation on Marx and became a teacher of Soviet politics and related subjects, first at Indiana University and later at Princeton. Finally, between 1964 and 1965, I had a year of academic leave at the Center for Advanced Study in the Behavioral Sciences at Stanford, and with it the opportunity to work on Stalin. There was only one problem: I didn't know how to carry out the task. My aim was to write a political scientist's tract on dictatorship from a psychological perspective, not a Stalin biography. There was and is, so far as I know, no example of such a work. G. M. Gilbert, the American court psychologist at Nuremburg, produced an important study, *The Psychology of Dictatorship*, based largely on what he learned about Hitler from that dictator's surviving ex-associates on trial.[12] It was valuable because it showed that the dictator's personality can be immensely influential in the behavior of a dictatorial regime. But, for various reasons, it was not a model for my projected study.

The idea came of constructing the study as a scholarly whodunit, and I wrote a fifty-page first chapter entitled "The Making of a Dictator." Starting with Stalin's rise to supreme leadership in 1929, it showed how he made himself an autocrat by his terroristic purges of the 1930s. To prove that he was not yet a dictator in 1929, I had to clarify the origin of the role of leader (*vozhd'*) in Russian Communism. Despite the existence of a large literature on Lenin and the early years of Soviet power, I found no study of the leader role that Lenin created as the founder of Bolshevism at the start of the century. Chapter 2 addressed that question, arguing that Lenin could lead the Bolshevik party without being a dictator because he had acquired charismatic authority in the Bolsheviks' eyes from the time of their movement's formation and by the crucial part he played in the party's coming to power in 1917. Why the Bolshevik regime underwent transformation into an autocracy under Stalin became the issue. An important factor favoring that outcome, it seemed, was historical: the political culture of pre-revolutionary Russia as a system of autocracy. I knew something about that from my reading in old Russian history books that I had found in second-hand bookstores while in Moscow. So I wrote a third long chapter, "The Tsarist Autocratic Tradition," not realizing at the time that much of this material was destined to become a part of the second volume of a study that would turn into a trilogy.[13]

Now, paradoxically, what was to have been a personality study in its fundamental character was shaping up as something else. Save for the introductory chapter, Stalin as a personality hardly entered the picture until the last part of what would become the first volume of the trilogy. There, in discussing the rise of his personality cult in 1929, I went back to his early life as a revolutionary in order to show the ways in which it was touched up and in places falsified in the idealized Stalin image that formed the cult's centerpiece. So, when the draft of the volume, (later published under the title *Stalin As Revolu-*

*tionary 1879–1929: A Study in History and Personality)* was finished and submitted to the publisher in 1971, my two editors, having read it, returned it to me with a gentle but clear indication that major revisions were needed because something was wrong with the book's structure. The task was unavoidably mine to solve. A trip to Europe in the summer of 1971 afforded some leisure for thinking, and by fall, when it was my good fortune to have a semester of academic leave, a program of revision was becoming clear in my mind. By now I saw that chronology could not be cavalierly disregarded. At the very least, Stalin's early life and early revolutionary career would have to be treated early in the book. I think this was the point in my own life at which biography as a genre grew interesting to me, or at any rate not something from which I instinctively shrank as outside my ken.

The solution to my structural problem proved rather easy, once my mind was open to the possibility and desirability of being biographical. The chapter on Lenin as the founder and leader of the Bolshevik movement led me naturally to ask: how did a young Georgian of lowly origin named Iosif Djugashvili become a follower of Lenin early in the century? There was no way to answer this question with generalities; an interpretation of my subject as an individual young person became unavoidable. Nor would it help to describe Horney's profile of the "arrogant-vindictive" neurotic personality type, and then try to show that Djugashvili was a case in point. True, his wretched early family life, the brutal beatings inflicted on his mother and on him by his drunken father, would easily have produced the basic anxiety from which a neurosis can grow. Biographical interpretation could and should take this into account. Further, what was known of Djugashvili's boyhood showed a definite streak of self-idealizing, which continued during his years in the Tiflis theological seminary when he entered the local revolutionary underground, and subsequently as well. He *was* neurotic, it seemed.

Instead of dealing in such abstract categories from a book of psychology, however, I was now using that book as guidance in a *biographer's* effort to portray his subject as an individual. Further effort brought to light Djugashvili's discovery, in the far-off charismatic figure of the party's leader, Lenin, a heroic identity figure who inspired him to adopt a Lenin-like revolutionary pseudonym, "Stalin," or man of steel, as the symbol of his idealized revolutionary self. Here I was making use of Sigmund Freud's concept of "identification," a process that "endeavors to mold a person's own ego after the fashion of the one that has been taken as a mode."[14] But, again, the concept was being applied in the context of life-writing.

The Lenin identification carried momentous implications for an understanding of Djugashvili's personality, among them the fact that he would feel driven one day to match or outdo his identity figure in revolutionary accomplishment of world-historic importance. Before then, the Lenin identification resulted in the Russification of Djugashvili's national self-consciousness. Since the identity figure was a Russian revolutionist, *he* must be Russian too, and yet the Russian revolutionary *persona* that he thus fashioned for himself as Stalin was inevitably going to conflict all his life with his ineradicably Georgian empirical self as Djugashvili. This was an inner conflict of the sort that Horney had found to be one of the normal accompaniments of neurotic life experience.

Now one could begin to see how Stalin would necessarily come into murderous collision with many others who were aware not simply of his original national identity but, more important, of the spotted actuality of his character and his revolutionary past. One could see how he would be driven to have history rewritten to conform to his idealized Stalin self, for which purpose unchallengeable power was a prerequisite. This is how a work took shape that might be described as *biography-centered history*. It fortunately never became the political science tract that it started out to be, but neither did it become a conventional piece of life-writing about a historically influential person. It became a study in history and personality designed to show how history shaped an individual who, in turn, greatly influenced the history of Soviet Russia and the world. In producing this study, the author became, *malgré lui,* a sort of biographer.

The reader will doubtless be interested in my attitude toward a figure who has absorbed so large a part of my scholarly lifetime that friends have begun calling me Stalin's last victim. I think it proper here to take the advice of Erik Erikson, who has stipulated as "the first rule of a 'psychohistorical' study, that the author should be honest about his own relations to the bit of history he is studying and should indicate his motives without undue mushiness or apology."[15]

From the start, as I think this memoir shows, it was intellectual fascination with an unusual hypothesis that inspired me. But by 1950 or so I was also clear in my mind that Stalin was an evil-doer. Have I not been impelled to take biographical revenge upon a man who caused me great personal anguish in the seven years that intervened between my marriage to one of his subjects and her release from Russia, who made us live with the constant possibility that she would disappear one day, as many other Soviet citizens had done? Maybe so, but let us consider the happy outcome.

I shall not forget something Hans Spier said when he interviewed me in 1953 for a position with the RAND Corporation. I was about to say, "I realize that my overextended stay in Moscow is a big handicap, but I think it is one I can overcome," when he remarked offhandedly, "That long stay in Russia is a big advantage for you." I kept quiet and took the job. Those seven Stalin-caused years proved a career boon. Not only Speier but Indiana University's Department of Government took them as the equivalent of the graduate school education in political science and Russian studies I never had. My sole relevant study in college was an intensive course in the Russian language. Thus my ability to establish myself in academia in the later 1950s was due in part to Stalin. Not that he deserves gratitude for having been my benefactor in the strange way that he was. But who can avoid being influenced by such pranks of fortune?

This said, the fact is that I consider Stalin a loathsome man, and the better I have come to know him as my biographical subject, the more intense the feeling has become. Especially in working on the second volume of the projected trilogy, dealing with Stalin's transformation of Soviet Russia in the 1930s by a "revolution from above," I have come to consider him detestable as I never did during the Moscow years or the post-Moscow years when the study was getting under way. Then I was above all conscious of the formidable intellectual challenge of the task being undertaken. I never mistook my subject for a decent man, but the bottomless depth of his villany was not clear to me. Now it is.

I believe with R. G. Collingwood that history is the reenactment of past thought. Its aim is "the discerning of the thought which is the inner side of the event." Historians' proper task is that of "penetrating to the thought of the agents whose acts they are studying."[16] Now that I have been living through the 1930s with Stalin, trying to reconstruct his acts as they first took shape in his mind, I believe that I know him well enough to be able to think things out as he did and, in that sense, to *be* Stalin in the process of reaching key decisions and acting to implement them.

This has led me to comprehend, far more clearly than before, the depth of his duplicity, his capacity to deceive both individuals and large groups, and to lull intended victims into a false sense of security. I have likewise come face to face with Stalin's all but unbelievable indifference to the suffering that he caused, and his ability to take delight in inflicting torment upon people he saw as enemies and upon others whose only guilt lay in association with those "enemies." Khrushchev testifies in the secret report—and this is amply documented in other sources—that on January 20, 1939, Stalin dispatched a coded telegram to high party and police officials throughout the country. It ordered that "physical pressure should still be used obligatorily as an exception applicable to known and obstinate enemies of the people, as a method both justifiable and appropriate."[17] "Physical pressure" meant torture. Stalin was determined that those labeled enemies must be tortured. If, as I believe, the worst of human vices is cruelty, this man must have been one of the most vicious individuals ever to wield power.

Stalin's thoughts and actions have become intelligible to me. The real mystery is why some of his old associates failed to lift a hand against him while it was still possible to prevent his murderous assault upon Soviet society in the later 1930s. Alongside such creatures of Stalin as Lazar Kaganovich and Klim Voroshilov, there were in the Politburo of 1934 such men of independent mind and standing as Sergei Kirov, Valerian Kuibyshev, and Sergo Ordzhonikidze. They were tough Bolsheviks but not evil-doers of Stalin's stripe, and they could not have wanted him to succeed in finally wrecking what was left of the Revolution. Kirov may with difficulty be forgiven his own inaction. But when he was assassinated on December 1, 1934, an act that perceptive men of the inner circle could see must have been Stalin's doing, I cannot comprehend the failure of Ordzhonikidze and Kuibyshev to respond. They must have known then that Stalin, like a mad dog, had to be destroyed. They still had access to him; they sat around the table with him at Politburo sessions. Sometimes in the quiet of my study I have found myself bursting out to their ghosts: "For God's sake, stab him with a knife, or pick up a heavy object and bash his brains out, for the lives you save may include your own!" (Kuibyshev died under mysterious circumstances in early 1935, and Ordzhonikidze was forced by Stalin to commit suicide in early 1937.) Untold hundreds of thousands of lives could have been saved, and untold damage to Soviet Russia averted. Or consider the behavior of Mikhail Tomsky, to whose apartment Stalin went with a bottle of wine in 1936, very probably to solicit help in his contemplated purge trial of Tomsky's ex-rightist associates Nikolai Bukharin and Alexei Rykov. Tomsky showed Stalin to the door with curses, went back to his study, and shot himself to death.[18] Why didn't he shoot Stalin first?

I cannot answer such questions, but I think the fact that I ask them discloses the nature and strength of my feelings. The issue is whether they impair what capacity I otherwise may have to produce a sound biography-centered study of the Soviet 1930s. In *apologia*, let me revert to my original design to write the work as a scholarly whodunit. It suggests that for a long time I had thought that I was on the track of a criminal and his crimes. Pursuing the analogy, what is or should be the detective's attitude toward his quarry? Like a Collingwoodian historian (following Collingwood's view of history-writing in a section of *The Idea of History* entitled "Who Killed John Doe?"), he must, it seems to me, do everything possible to reenact the thought underlying the criminal deed and then project himself into the fugitive's mind to such an extent that he can divide the man's likely pathways of escape and present whereabouts. Will the detective's horror at the crime and hatred of the criminal cripple his capacity to fulfill his professional duty? My own view is that they will not. But is the analogy itself, the idea of Stalin as a criminal and some of his key historical actions of the 1930s as crimes, misleading? Might it not blind one to the constructive accomplishments of that decade under Stalin's leadership? It could, but it need not, for even criminals, the biggest ones in fact, can make positive contributions to the community in their careers of crime.

A final qualification is in order. Stalin was despicable as man and ruler, but he did not see himself as the villain of history that he was— or so I believe. The Stalin biographer must therefore be careful not to attribute to his villain a consciousness of his own villainy. In the effort to reenact the villian's thought, he must attempt to understand, and if possible to show, how the villain managed to reconcile his duplicities and atrocities with his inner picture of himself as a righteous man and a good and noble ruler. This takes a bit of doing, but the whole meaning and worth of the scholarly enterprise rest upon it. Why this postulate is so important to me probably goes back to the strange way in which I first became involved with the Stalin question. If Stalin's personality cult was a public, institutionalized expression of a private cult of himself as an ideal being, how could he ever have admitted to himself that he was other than a righteous ruler?

## AFTERWORD

The process of collaboration between biography and psychoanalysis was a theme of the symposium for which this paper was written. No systematic collaboration of that kind has been a part of my experience as a biographer, although I have benefited from contacts with psychoanalysts who showed interest in my project, among them Robert Wallerstein, Erik Erikson, Otto Kernberg, and Joseph Slap; and my intellectual debt to Karen Horney will have been evident all through these pages. But the conference itself proved a very valuable forum for interchange with participating psychoanalysts (Joseph Lichtenberg, George Moraitis, and Arnold Rogow) as well as with nonpsychoanalyst biographers. I address the afterword to the psychoanalysts' observations and my reactions.

They showed special interest in the paper's report of my attitude toward Stalin, specifically my loathing of him. Arnold Rogow asked: How, if you are so angry, can you do justice to Stalin in your role as biographer? I did not have any ready answer other than what was in the paper about the detective analogy and Collingwood. Joseph Lichtenberg, however, responded, on my behalf, that there can be a "work dynamism of carefulness" that allows a biographer to "factor in his affect," even if it is intense, provided he is aware of it. This gave me the benefit of the assumption that the dynamism was operative in my case. Dr. Lichtenberg also observed, apropos Arnold Rogow's suggested analogy between the biographical and therapeutic situations, than an analyst *can* feel anger toward an analysand.

George Moraitis thought the place to begin was not with anger but with the theme of *cherchez la femme,* and he invited attention to the presence in the story of a *femme* other than Karen Horney, namely, my wife. Instead of seeing only the villain in the piece, Stalin, we should take account of my wife as a potential victim who was in need of being rescued and, indeed, of my need to avoid becoming a victim myself. In the background of this biographical effort, then, lay the experience of the future biographer, as a young man, being in the position of responding to a threat of victimization. His violent response to the threat of victimization was manifest in his reported outburst to Kirov, Ordzhonidize, and Kuibyshev: Why didn't you kill Stalin and thereby avoid falling victim to him? Dr. Moraitis suggested that my "Kill him!" to Kirov and the other victims-to-be was the voice of "the Stalin in you" (i.e., in me), meaning (I take it) my readiness to resort to violence in a situation of threatened victimization.

My immediate response to this is worth reporting. Dr. Moraitis was shifting attention to me and my own *femme* and the predicament we were in at the time, but my first thought was of Stalin. I was moved to say something to my fellow conferees about what I am doing in the second Stalin volume. One of the themes of the second volume is that Stalin had a driving fantasy of being the rescuer of Russia from the threat of victimization from without by a hostile capitalist encirclement. It was a fantasy, I speculate, with a source in Djugashvili's childhood memories of wanting desperately, but vainly, to save his mother from being victimized by the beatings that his violent father inflicted on her. I believe that this was one of Stalin's motivations to become a revolutionary from above in the war-oriented industrialization drive of the 1930s.

Even though it has only been in the course of later research that this idea has entered my mind and it was not there at the time of my own need to rescue my wife from victimization, it seems possible, in the light of Dr. Moraitis's interpretation, that my earlier experience sensitized me later, in the biographer's role, to the evidence that Stalin had a fantasy, or a hero-script as I like to put it, of being the savior of still another *femme*—Mother Russia—from victimization by dangerous forces outside her. All the more so as this manner of reading Stalin's motivation is not something found, so far as I know, in the existing biographical literature.

But this treats "the Stalin in me" as the would-be savior of a *femme* in distress, and not as the violent feeling to which Dr. Moraitis made reference when he referred to my "Kill him!" as the Stalin in me. And so, in conclusion, I want to return to the issue of my loathing of Stalin (an emotion related to but not identical with that of anger, it may be noted) and try to confront, as best I can, the possibility that it may in some measure disqualify me from fulfilling the role of biographer in accordance with the requirements of objective scholarship. The concluding part of the paper presented an *apologia* on this count. Here I will enlarge upon it from a different perspective.

If one surveys the field of Stalin biography, most of the relevant works can be classified, broadly, as "pro" or "anti," positive or negative, in their portrayal of Stalin. This is a very rough classification. The works that fall into the positive category differ in the degree of positive assessment and also in their basis for taking a positive view of Stalin as a historical figure. Thus there was, in Stalin's time, a literature of the personality cult that was unabashedly adulatory, ranging from E. Yaroslavsky's *Landmarks in the Life of Stalin* to Henri Barbusse's *Stalin: A New World Seen Through One Man*. One would also place Isaac Deutscher's *Stalin: A Political Biography* in the positive category, but it is a genuine work of biography, not a cult work of idealization.[19] Similarly, the studies that fall in the negative category cover a wide range. Some among them are extreme cases that might be described as demonological biographies.

An example is the book by Anton Antonov-Ovseyenko, *The Time of Stalin: Portrait of a Tyranny*. It is the portrait of a demonic Stalin, of whom the author writes:

> Stalin was a genius, if that word is applicable to political brigandage. A genius of behind-the-scenes maneuvers, a man of satanic cunning. No "gray blur" or blockhead could have woven the complex webs of his Kremlin intrigues. Nor just a paranoiac.[20]

There is considerable valuable information, gleaned by oral history methods from survivors of the Stalin years, in this book. Yet, it seems a poor biography because it portrays its subject solely under the aspect of criminality, the drive for total power, and savage persecution of all who failed to be utterly submissive to him. The author cannot see Stalin as a political figure who, for all his egomania, his blunders in politics, and his cruelty, had a sense of his role in history, of a mission to lead Russia toward certain programmatic goals. This is a cult biography in reverse. Now Antonov-Ovseyenko, a Soviet citizen who wrote his book knowing that it could not now be published in Russia, is a multiple victim of Stalin's: his father, a prominent Old Bolshevik, was a victim of Stalin's terror of the 1930s, and the author himself was arrested as the son of an "enemy of the people" and spent awful years in a concentration camp before being freed, after Stalin died, and given an apartment and a job as a historian in Moscow. He is filled with fury against Stalin, and his book reads like an act of revenge against an object of insensate hate. Very likely this is why he rejects the idea that Stalin might have been psychopathological. To a biographer consumed with the desire to condemn his subject as a monstrous miscreant, nothing can be permitted to cloud that individual's full moral responsibility for his criminal acts.

What it all suggests is how important it can be whether or not one has in fact been victimized, as distinguished from living under the threat of victimization. By the accidents of fortune, Antonov-Ovseyenko was a victim and I was not. Our story, unlike his, had a happy ending rather early on. The fortunate fact of Stalin's stroke (whatever sort of stroke it was that finally ended his life) saved us from likely personal tragedy. Had it been otherwise, had I, for example, been compelled to leave my wife behind to victimization in Stalin's Russia, this could have incapacitated me ever to take up the Stalin *problematique* with the basic measure of open-mindedness that authentic scholarship demands. Even Russian studies as a profession might have proved too psychically painful an option to pursue.

What happens to us in life, or doesn't happen, makes a difference. Let me then conclude: I am not exactly angry at Stalin, and certainly not blinded by rage. He is someone I have learned to loathe.

One final consideration is in order. When one spends a large part of one's scholarly life seeking to puzzle out the behavior of an infinitely evil person, like Stalin, and that of others around him and people in his society, something can develop in the course of the biographical process that might almost be described as the passion of curiosity. One's inquisitiveness, the urge to illuminate what went on inside the man that led him to act as he did, the need to explain to oneself as well as others, to comprehend and communicate things that may have evaded understanding, can become a dominating drive, and this drive can counteract the simplifying mental tendencies that hatred of the subject may generate. I think that something of this sort has happened in my case. Stalin is a loathesome figure to me. But the complexity of the thought processes which, as a Collingwoodian historian, I am bound to try to reenact, presents so great an intellectual challenge that I may be protected from the effects of my moral condemnation of the man (the work itself will have to show whether I am right or wrong about this). In brief, when you seek to penetrate the heart of darkness, it is very important that the project be interesting from the scholarly point of view.

## NOTES

[1]Karen Horney, *Neurosis and Human Growth* (New York: Norton, 1950).

[2]Walter Bedell Smith, *My Three Years in Moscow* (Philadelphia: Lippincott, 1949).

[3]Nathan Leites, *The Operational Code of the Politburo* (New York: McGraw-Hill, 1949).

[4]Lion Feuchtwanger, *Moscow 1937* (New York: Viking, 1937).

[5]Bertram D. Wolfe, *Three Who Made A revolution* (Boston: Beacon, 1948).

[6]Walt Rostow, *The Dynamics of Soviet Society* (New York: New American Library, 1954).

[7]Hannah Arendt, *The Origins of Totalitarianism* (New York: Harcourt Brace, 1951).

[8]Robert C. Tucker, "The Dictator and Totalitarianism," *World Politics* 17, no. 4 (July 1965).

[9]Ilya Ehrenburg, *The Thaw* (Moscow, 1954).

[10]See *New York Times*, (June 5, 1956).

[11]Ibid.

[12]G. M. Gilbert, *The Psychology of Dictatorship* (New York: Ronald Press, 1950).

[13]Robert C. Tucker, *Stalin as Revolutionary* (New York: Norton, 1973); idem, *Stalin's Revolution from Above* (in progress); idem, *Stalin and the Cold War* (in progress).

[14]Sigmund Freud, *Group Psychology and Analysis of the Ego* (New York: Norton, 1960), p. 47. For a full discussion of the identity concept's uses for a Stalin biography, see Robert C. Tucker, "A Case of Mistaken Identity: Djugashvili-Stalin," *Biography* 5, no. 1 (Winter 1982), pp. 17–24.

[15]Erik Erikson, Review of *Thomas Woodrow Wilson: A Psychological Study*," in *The International Journal of Psycho-Analysis* 38, (1957), p. 464.

[16]R. G. Collingwood, *The Idea of History* (London: 1974), pp. 222, 228.

[17]*New York Times*, June 5, 1956.

[18]Roy A. Medvedev, "New Pages from the Political Biography of Stalin," in *Stalinism: Essays in Historical Interpretation*, ed. Robert C. Tucker (New York: Norton, 1977), p. 213.

[19]E. Yaroslavsy, *Landmarks in the Life of Stalin* (Moscow: Foreign Languages Publishing House, 1940); Henri Barbuse, *Stalin: A New World Seen Through One Man* (New York: International Publishers, 1935); Isaac Deutscher, *Stalin: A Political Biography* (New York: Oxford University Press, 1967).

[20]Anton Antonov-Ovseyenko, *The Time of Stalin: Portrait of a Tyranny*, trans. George Saunders (New York: Harper & Row, 1981), p. 52.

# 13

# T. E. Lawrence and the Psychology of Heroism

John E. Mack

---

IT CANNOT BE SAID that there has been from the beginning a deliber-ateness of purpose, structure, or psychohistorical interlacing in my work on T. E. Lawrence. On the contrary, the study began late in 1963 when upon getting up from seeing the film *Lawrence of Arabia*, I remarked to my wife, "I don't believe he was like that, but he was a very interesting person. Someone ought to do a study." The work developed piecemeal after that and was tended to intermittently when time permitted. A systematic or cohesive view of the subject seen in a historical context evolved gradually over a period of several years.

My ultimate motive for choosing to study Lawrence's life and per-sonality is undoubtedly "rooted," as Bernard Meyer has suggested of such efforts, in this "writer's remote past."[1] To plead, if not executive privilege, at least privileged communication on that score, there were and are more particular reasons why I thought Lawrence would be a fascinating and suitable subject for psychohistorical study. In the first place, he seemed to me unique among men of action (an indisputable quality in himself which he steadfastly denigrated) in his need to explore himself and the motives for his action. Other soldiers have written their personal memoirs, but none, I believe, has ever probed so deeply, with such psychological acumen, in published works or in

Excerpted by permission from John E. Mack, "T. E. Lawrence and the Uses of Psychology in the Biography of Historical Figures," in *Psychological Dimensions of Near Eastern Studies*, ed. L. Carl Brown and N. Itzkowitz (Princeton: Princeton University Press, 1977), pp. 27–59.

letters, the inner sources of his actions, or revealed so fully the consequences of the actions upon his subsequent mental state.

Men who act in the public domain rarely care to explore why they do so. They were born to serve; duty called; their country needed them—these and other justifications are offered, suggesting a general coming together of an individual's availability with historical exigency. When they write their memoirs they may, like Lyndon Johnson, bend history to justify their actions, rarely if ever examining the psychological determinants of the courses they chose.[2] Generally, it is unusual for an historical figure to examine deeply and objectively not only those motives for action that are congenial to self-esteem, but also those less conventionally creditable purposes that underlie much of what we do. This is what Lawrence undertook.

To be sure, Lawrence's writings, particularly *Seven Pillars of Wisdom*, are written with a public in mind and contain a great deal of self-examination, much of it self-condemnatory, that strives for ultimate vindication, both private and public. But they contain much more. They seek to explain the source of the willingness to sacrifice himself in an alien cause for reasons that lay not only in the circumstances of the Arab campaigns, but in a characterologically rooted need for self-immolation, moral masochism, and other personal conflicts made evident in the soul searching precipitated by the traumas and torments of the war experiences. "To endure for another gave a sense of greatness," Lawrence wrote of his self-sacrificing role in the Arab revolt. "There was nothing loftier than a cross, from which to contemplate the world. The pride and exhilaration of it were beyond conceit. Yet each cross, occupied, robbed the late-comers of all but the poor part of copying: and the meanest of things were those done by example. The virtue of sacrifice lay within the victim's soul."[3]

I was also drawn to Lawrence by my interest in the problem of heroism and its cultural contingencies. Definitions of heroism can embrace centuries, but are bound nevertheless in cultural terms. Lawrence in this respect appears to be a transitional figure between the romanticism of nineteenth-century heroism, rooted in a revival of medieval heroic idealization, and the cruel complexities of the twentieth century, in which we have come to demand of our heroes not only that they act decisively but that they take full personal responsibility for the consequences of these actions. Lawrence's exaggerated, almost grandiose, assumption of responsibility might in a limited sense be said to have neurotic origins, but its historical importance lies in the evolving consciousness of what is expected in the twentieth century of its heroes.

Finally, Lawrence seemed to offer an unusual opportunity for psychohistorical research as a result of the fact that he was near enough to being a contemporary figure to have living relatives, friends, and acquaintances who might be interviewed or could otherwise assist me in my efforts. In fact, my contacts with members of the Lawrence family, and with his friends, especially those from boyhood whose closeness had grown naturally and depended little, if at all, upon their knowledge of "Lawrence of Arabia," has been one of the most rewarding aspects of this study.

## APPROACH AND METHOD OF STUDY

Lawrence's Arabic teacher, a Syrian woman, when in her late eighties wrote to a friend, "Lawrence seems to me like an oyster which has, through pain and suffering all through life, developed into a pearl which the world is trying to evaluate, taking it to pieces layer by layer without realizing the true value of the whole."[4] There is contained in the simile of this wise woman certain principles of psychohistorical research which I have tried to follow in my work. It was Lawrence's suffering which originally affected me deeply and with which I could most readily identify. It moved me sufficiently to try to understand it further. My strongest interest has always been in how Lawrence dealt with his pain and conflict, in how he tried to surmount or transform the personal struggle in his actions, or through his writings.

In my first approach to the Lawrence family—to his older brother, a retired physician—I wrote in these terms: I had read much by and about Lawrence and had "developed a warm and sympathetic interest in him as a person. . . ." I wrote, further—as one physician to another, "Particularly real and moving to me have been the conflict and suffering he experienced in his life . . . I have the deepest respect for the full range of his fine qualities and have in mind no 'pigeon holes'." He, in turn, replied, "I will be very pleased to see you when you come over," and concluded, "I am not in practice now."[5]

Despite what I felt to be the awkwardness of my approach to Dr. M. R. Lawrence, the emphasis suggested in this first letter to the

Lawrence family has persisted. My interest has remained in the integration, in the creative surmounting of pain or guilt, in the adaptation
of a personal need to the sociopolitical realities of another people. In
some sense it has reamined "physicianly." The interest in the childhood or developmental background—I stop short of saying "sources"—of Lawrence's adaptations has been to obtain a more complex
picture of the pearl, not to reduce it to its mineral or chemical origins.
It is in the times when a man's external and internal adaptations fail
that other people may have access to the inner life, to the psychic
components of personal conflict that heretofore were not detectible in
the smooth surface of a well-functioning individual. This is true in a
sense when a troubled individual seeks out a psychotherapist. It was
equally true for Lawrence when the experiences he underwent during the war undermined the ambitious integration of personal need
and historical opportunity that he had tried to achieve in his involvement in the Arab Revolt. He did not seek psychotherapeutic help.
What he did do was to attempt to organize and communicate his
involvement in the Arab Revolt in a personal justification set in the
epic mode.

   *Seven Pillars of Wisdom*, not published in a public edition during
Lawrence's lifetime, is a highly personal document, written anew
three times between 1919 and 1922, the very writing of which was
filled with symptomatic acts that reflected the author's ambivalent
attitude toward the work. He "lost" in 1919 the first version, written
in great heat earlier that year, having left the manuscript unguarded
*in a bank messenger's bag in Reading Station* ("the thing they carry the
gold in"), which surely invited theft.[6] Lawrence acknowledged that
unconscious factors might have been at work and suggested he could
"involuntarily" have contributed to the loss. The second version,
written in three months during the winter of 1919 to 1920, left Lawrence equally dissatisfied, and two years later he burned it virtually in
its entirety.[7] Only the third version, rewritten more slowly during
1921 and 1922, survives.

   Lawrence's attitude toward this work remained highly conflicted
owing to its personally revelatory nature. "The reason that *Seven
Pillars of Wisdom* is not published," he wrote in a note to one biographer in 1927, "is because it is a full-length and unrestrained portrait
of myself, and my tastes and ideas and actions. I could not have
deliberately confessed so much in public: and so could not have written the book had there been any chance of its coming out. Yet to tell

the whole story was the only justification for writing anything at all."[8] The first two manuscripts were presumably even more "unrestrained," as they have not survived at all. Having completed this third version, Lawrence entered the Royal Air Force in August 1922 as an airman of low rank. A full exploration of the motives for Lawrence's retreat into the ranks is not in order here. One clear purpose, however, was to withdraw from public life, to reduce the scope of his powers, and to reduce his activities to a scale and context commensurate with his sense of personal failure. In some of his letters, particularly those written to his friend Lionel Curtis and to Mrs. George Bernard Shaw, Lawrence continued to try to explore the motives of his actions and the developmental origins of his vulnerability and intermittent despair.[9]

The foregoing and other documents, some of which are published and some not, together with many interviews of those who had personal contact with Lawrence (including several Bedouins), and other written data made available by the executors, have furnished the principal materials for my study. As I became more familiar with the data, and came to appreciate the protean quality of Lawrence's personality and the degree to which he was constantly engaged in influencing others, the character of my study changed. Originally I was grateful for the richness of the psychological materials available to me, particularly concerning childhood influences, and had thought to do a "psychological" study. But increasingly I found that the material was embedded in a multiplicity of sociohistorical contexts; that revelations seemingly of a purely personal nature were aimed at posterity as well; that actions and events in which Lawrence played a part had not only a personal meaning for him, but were difficult to understand apart from various political, cross-cultural, and other historical realities; and, finally, that the way in which I cast the whole interrelated mass of material was highly reflective of my own psychology and view of history. I have found myself becoming less a psychologist or, perhaps more accurately, less exclusively one, and more predominantly a biographer and historian, using psychological materials to deepen and broaden the view of the interrelationship between an individual and certain historically significant events in which he took part—with resultant consequences for history as well as for the individual.

Furthermore, the answers to many psychological questions, such as matters of motive, the analysis of action, and the assessment of character are dependent on certain assessments of a purely historical nature—i.e., the psychology takes on a different perspective, depending on matters of historical fact. For example, the analysis of *why* an Oxford graduate of Anglo-Scotch-Irish descent, such as Lawrence, should plunge himself so totally into the service of an alien people is contingent upon the assessment of whether he was or was not actually devoted to the cause of Arab freedom. It is pointless to set about explaining something that was not so. There are writers who deny Lawrence's dedication to the Arab cause, and claim that he was following motives entirely of self-interest, or was simply carrying out prescribed British war policies. A responsible opinion on this question, which is one of considerable importance for *any* biography of Lawrence, not only requires a careful review of Lawrence's own statements but a sufficiently thoroughgoing review of the relevant historical documents to permit a balanced judgment. My own conclusion is that Lawrence's motives were complex and multifaceted, a mixture of personal and political purposes, an opinion which he confirms most concisely in a 1919 letter that has recently come to light, written to a British Foreign Office official during the Paris Peace Conference:

Dear——,
You asked me "why" today, and I'm going to tell you exactly what my motives in the Arab affair were, in order of strength:
(i) Personal. I liked a particular Arab very much, and I thought that freedom for the race would be an acceptable present.
(ii) Patriotic. I wanted to help win the war, and Arab help reduced Allenby's losses by thousands.
(iii) Intellectual curiosity. I wanted to feel what it was like to be the mainspring of a national movement, and to have some millions of people expressing themselves through me: and being a half-poet, I don't value material things much. Sensation and mind seem to me much greater, and the ideal, such a thing as the impulse that took us into Damascus, the only thing worth doing.
(iv) Ambition. You know Lionel Curtis has made his conception of the Empire—a Commonwealth of free peoples—generally accepted. I wanted to widen that idea beyond Anglo-Saxon shape, and to form a new nation of thinking people, all acclaiming our freedom, and demanding admittance into our Empire.

There is, to my eyes, no other road for Egypt and India in the
end, and I would have made their path easier, by creating an
Arab dominion in the Empire.

I don't think there are any other reasons. . . . You are sufficiently Scotch to understand my analysing my mind so formally.[10]

The relevance of dissecting the psychological determinants of particular action is, of course, also dependent on whether or not the
events under consideration actually occurred, and upon a more or
less accurate knowledge of the subject's role. In order to understand
the effectiveness of Lawrence's actions during the Arab Revolt of 1916
to 1918 one must assess carefully the actual nature of his role therein.
A writer who claims as much as Lawrence did in his narrative of the
Hijaz and Syrian campaigns is legitimately subject to the charge of
charlatanism if, in fact, these claims are shown to be spurious. This
question has been sufficiently controversial to force me not only to
review carefully his own accounts, but to form my conclusions after
reviewing as many independent versions of what occurred as possible, drawing on published and unpublished European writings and
responsible Arab sources as well.

In my opinion, Lawrence's account of the events of the Arab Revolt, and of his role in it as the principal organizing and guiding force
of the Bedouin campaigns, is, with some allowance for the dramatiza-
tion, exaggeration, and self-deprecation which was part of his literary
style and character, accurate in its *fundamentals.* I have reviewed some
of the evidence for this conclusion elsewhere and will not supply it
here.[11] Other historians, studying the same data, may naturally come
to different conclusions. Lawrence *felt* he was acting the role of a
charlatan, not merely because he took part in inspiring his Arab followers with promises of freedom he could not fulfill, but because he
considered the very process of working out highly personal conflicts
and needs through the medium of another people's political destiny
to be a false one. Thus, however valuable in reality he may have been
to the Arab cause, he remained in his own eyes a charlatan.

Knowledge of character, or of the previous patterns of action of a
particular individual, may help to point to where historical "truth"
lies. The well-known episode of the killing of Turkish prisoners in
September 1918 before the capture of Damascus provides a useful

case in point. The evidence regarding the incident, and Lawrence's role in it, will be examined in detail not because the episode is of great historical significance, but because I believe it to be illustrative of the kind of event which, because of its *emotional* aspects, is particularly prone to distortion according to the biases, allegiances, and other partisan purposes of both the participants and their biographers. A psychologically minded biographer who is alert to these undercurrents is by no means exempt from such distortions.

In *Seven Pillars of Wisdom*, Lawrence told in vivid, gory detail how the retreating Turkish columns had bayoneted or otherwise massacred the citizens of the Syrian village of Tafas, pregnant women, children, and babies included. Talaal, an Arab leader of this region, whose village it was, rode suicidally into the Turkish ranks and was cut down. The other Arabs, "the flame of cruelty and revenge . . . burning in their bodies," avenged themselves upon the Turkish columns, led by the desert warrior, Auda Abu Tayi. "By my order we took no prisoners, for the only time in our war," Lawrence wrote, and "in a madness born of the horror of Tafas we killed and killed, even blowing in the heads of the fallen and of the animals: as though their death and running blood could slake our agony." One of the Arab groups evidently had not heard that no prisoners were to be taken and had captured 200 men. Lawrence described luridly how one of the Arabs, Hassan, had been brutally bayoneted by these Turkish soldiers "into the ground, pinning him out like a collected insect."[12] Then, presumably under Lawrence's supervision, the prisoners were executed. The film *Lawrence of Arabia* shows Lawrence (5'5") played by Peter O'Toole (about 6'2") with his arms covered with blood, having gleefully taken part in the slaughter.[13] Lawrence's debunking biographer, Richard Aldington, ready always to believe the worst about Lawrence, wrote: "The spectacle of a British officer encouraging a mass slaughter of prisoners is deplorable."[14] Suleiman Mousa, a press and public information officer in Amman, and the only Arab author of a full-length biography of Lawrence, discounts the tale of Turkish atrocities on the basis of a verbal testimony of the son of one of the chiefs of the region who had served in the Turkish army.[15]

Lawrence's role in this horrible episode, as depicted in his own account, did not seem consistent with the picture of his character I had formed, which included a genuine disgust with the bloodshed of war and a deep concern for human life. Although he developed a complex masochistic disorder after the war (not the silly burning of his fingers with a flame because he supposedly liked the pain, as shown in the film), I had not come across any instances of overt cruelty or even sadistic fantasies in others of Lawrence's history or writings. Alec Kirkbride, another British soldier who fought with Lawrence near the end of the campaign, wrote to Liddell Hart on this point at the time the film was produced: "I can say with certainty that it is complete nonsense to describe him [Lawrence] as having been either sadistic or fond of killing. (These are not always the same thing.) He once told me that his ideal of waging war was based on the professional *condottieri* of medieval Italy. That is to say, to gain one's objectives with a minimum of casualties *on both sides.*"[16]

Puzzled about the question of Tafas, I contacted A. W. Lawrence to see if he could shed any light on the matter (this was before the publication of Mousa's book in which A. W. Lawrence wrote a rebuttal of Mousa's version of the Tafas incident).[17] He too had been troubled about the film's depiction of his brother as a "bloody sadist," and had contacted Colonel F. G. Peake ("Peake Pasha"), a British officer in the desert campaigns who had taken part in and witnessed the events around Tafas, and later developed and commanded the Arab Legion in Transjordan. Peake wrote that Lawrence used the "we" as a general would, referring to what his men were doing. According to Peake, Lawrence, contrary to his own account in *Seven Pillars*, used his influence with the sheikhs to attempt to stop their followers from killing the Turkish soldiers, but their fury was so great that they would not listen to him. Peake wrote of his regret that a film about Lawrence should give the impression that he was a callous person or "enjoyed seeing such horrible scenes. It would have been no less interesting and far more truthful had he been shown rushing about on foot trying to persuade the Sheikhs to call back their men."[18] When A. W. Lawrence called the proofs of Mousa's book to Peake's attention in 1965, the latter wrote his own first-hand recollections of the villagers who had been massacred by the Turks and of the Bedouins out of control in their thirst for vengeance.[19]

In his account Peake wrote that Lawrence had come running to him and asked for his help in restoring order as soon as possible. Peake was able to do so by dismounting 100 men and marching them with fixed bayonets on the village. The sight of this disciplined body of soldiers was apparently enough; the furor died and the Bedouins rode off northward "in the hope of catching up with the Turks, who had already retreated." Peake states further that he was ordered by Lawrence to collect and guard all Turks as they arrived from the battlefield in Palestine.[20]

In his earlier account, Peake stated his opinion that Lawrence wished to assume responsibility for an occurrence that neither he nor anyone else could at that time have prevented. He knew, Peake wrote, that in the future "it would be severely criticized," but as he had originally stirred the Arabs to rebel against the Turks, it was only just that he and not the Arabs should be blamed.[21] A. W. Lawrence, however, has acknowledged that in a conversation with him, "T.E.L. gave me clearly to understand that he had himself given the order to execute the 200 captured Turks who had pinned down Hassan; that he had then regarded it as an execution was unmistakable."[22] Elsewhere, A. W. Lawrence has written, presumably on the basis of other conversations with his brother, that "unquestionably he afterwards suffered deeply over his loss of control" in this episode and that this largely accounted for his "insistence, throughout the rest of his life, that no Englishman could so serve an alien race without prostitution."[23] More recently he has written to me, "I merely guess that T.E. reacted *as an Arab* to the sight of the Tafas villagers, and was thereby forced to realize he had become an alien to his own people. Hence, in part, his depression at Damascus . . . and continued aversion to anyone's service to a foreign race."[24]

If, as these passages suggest, Lawrence did lose some control in this episode as a result of his overidentification with the anguish and desire for revenge of the Bedouins, then his subsequent guilt about his behavior is not surprising. His treatment of these events after Tafas in *Seven Pillars of Wisdom* is consistent with this guilt, as he assigns to himself an exaggerated personal responsibility for the killing, downplaying the uncontrollable nature of the Bedouins' thirst for vengeance, and covering up for Auda. This indeed left him open to criticism and allowed a sensational interpretation to be made, as in the film, that he personally took part in the slaughter, damaging thereby his historical reputation. It is quite consistent with Lawrence's state of mind at the time when he wrote this passage, filled with guilt as he was, that at an unconscious level he was trying to do just that—to punish himself by casting his actions in these incidents in a light that would serve to discredit himself further.

## THE USE OF CHILDHOOD MATERIALS AND THE
## PROBLEM OF HEROISM

That T. E. Lawrence should so compel continuing attention is as fascinating to his biographers, and to a sympathetic audience, as it is irritating to his detractors. His genius as "the mainspring of the Arab movement"—the phrase of his commander, Edmund Allenby—was recognized by virtually all of the British officers and soldiers who worked with him in the years of revolt. This, however, is only part of the story. Lawrence's role in the post–World War I political settlements remains controversial, and the historical judgments are not all in. Even so, a careful study of his participation during these years demonstrates that he worked indefatigably for the cause of freedom for the Arab people. Through a steady stream of newspaper articles, essays, and personal supplications, he embarrased and otherwise influenced the British colonial establishment to change its mandate policies in the direction of greater autonomy for the Arab people in the Middle Eastern areas under its control.[25]

But it is not Lawrence's direct military and political activities alone, or even his writings, that account for our continuing interest in him. This lies rather in our fascination with heroism, a subject that has no definable historical beginning—man has always striven to define what he most admires in himself—and will have no end as long as men continue to yearn for identification with an idea or a person of the highest value. Lawrence's central interest for our time lies in his place as a peculiarly contemporary hero, embodying some of the central dilemmas and conflicts of our century.

Irving Howe, in his perceptive essay "T. E. Lawrence: The Problem of Heroism," wrote: "For better or worse, the hero as he appears in the tangle of modern ife is a man struggling with a vision he can neither realize nor abandon, 'a man with a load on his mind.'" Howe, in an Eriksonian phrase, feels that "what finally draws one to Lawrence, making him seem not merely an exceptional figure, but a representative man of our century, is his courage and vulnerability in bearing the burden of consciousness."[26]

Lawrence's claim on our attention as a contemporary hero lies in the genius of his courageous leadership in a modern guerrilla war of national liberation, his idealistic self-sacrifice in the service of the freedom of a colonized people, his "absolute unwillingness to sell out" (Howe's phrase) in the peace settlement, his renunciation of all personal gain for his efforts, and finally his willingness to face fully the psychohistorical complexities of his own role. This willingness was best expressed in *Seven Pillars of Wisdom*, which in its peculiar mixture of lofty idealism, frank treatment of the conduct of men in war, paradoxically combined with romantic embellishment of their deeds to the point of myth-making, and honest self-exploration comes close to being a contemporary epic. In Howe's summation, "He left his name entangled with a cluster of unanswered questions, this prince of our disorder."[27]

The problem of heroism is perhaps uniquely psychohistorical. Its understanding requires an appreciation of a series of psychosocial or psychohistorical interrelationships. Foremost among these are the connections between the psychology of the individual as an adult, with his own childhood and with his family background, and his more general national, or cultural, background; the associations between the psychology of the adult hero and his immediate followers or contemporaries; the relationship between the individual and a society viewed collectively and over time; and finally, the relationship between the biographer or other chronicler and the hero-figure, since the biographer may contribute to the definition, or even creation, of a public hero. In the paragraphs that follow, I will illustrate some of these interrelationships as they apply to Lawrence's case.

In April 1911, shortly after arriving at the archaeological site of the ancient Hittite city of Carchemish on the upper Euphrates, Lawrence, then twenty-two, wrote to his family: "Poor father! his sons are not going to support his years by the gain of their professions and trades. One a missionary: one an artist of sorts and a wanderer after sensations: one thinking of lay education work: one in the army, and one too small to think. None of us can afford to keep a wife: still the product of fairly healthy brains and tolerable bodies will not be worthless in this world. One of us must surely get something of the unattainable we are all feeling after."[28] Lawrence never seems to have had much doubt as to who the "one of us" might be. From earliest childhood there seems to have been an expectation in the Lawrence family that the second son, Ned (as T. E. was called), was destined for some special mission, a deep conviction he evidently internalized. Even childhood friends became aware that there was something special about him. One such friend, a woman, recalled crossing the English Channel with him when they were small children. A soothsayer, pointing to Ned said, "Someday that baby will have a price on his head."[29] Lawrence as a small child seemed to another friend "to be inuring himself to hardship, as if he'd got some premonition that fate had got something in store for him. . . . right from a boy he was preparing himself for some big thing."[30] Lawrence, born on the same day as Napoleon, teased this friend in the fourth form at school that since the latter had been born two days earlier he was out of luck. None of the half-dozen childhood friends I interviewed ever resented this quality in Lawrence. One must acknowledge the possibility of distortion based on the retrospective falsification of memory and the influence of subsequent events. But even with these possible distortions in mind, it is to me still significant that each friend made clear to me his recognition that Lawrence was different and *special* even as a child, "a genius," "strange," preparing himself, "reaching out for greatness."

The relevant individual history of such a child begins with his ancestry and its circumstances, and with the situation of the parental union and early family situation. The father's family, originally merchants in the English midlands, settled on an estate in Westmeath near Dublin in Cromwellian times, where a baronetage was established in the eighteenth century. Thomas Chapman, who became the seventh baronet late in his life, fathered four daughters by a cousin, to whom he was obviously not very much attracted (the Anglo-Irish settlers almost invariably intermarried). Lawrence's mother's origins were less well known. She was born Sarah Junner, the illegitimate daughter of a ship construction worker in Durham county in the north of England,[31] was raised in Scotland by strict relatives, and was brought at about eighteen as a nursery governess to help Mrs. Chapman look after the increasingly large family. Sarah in her late teens and early twenties was already highly capable, attractive, and strong-willed, and Chapman was drawn to her. Despite strong religious scruples, especially on Sarah's side, they eloped, changed their name to Lawrence, and began the raising out-of-wedlock of a family of five boys, of which Thomas Edward was the second. "They thought always that they were living in sin," Lawrence wrote in a letter to Mrs. Shaw in 1927,[32] and worried lest their children or anyone else found out. After living in several port towns in Wales (where Lawrence was born), Scotland, the Isle of Jersey, and Brittany, the family settled in Oxford when Lawrence was eight.

The original seeds of heroic myth-making in Lawrence's case were laid in these ancestral circumstances. The *capability* of performing deeds of heroic character is a product of the biological gifts that the child possessed and the nature of his upbringing, especially of the parental investment in his development and future. The *opportunity* to play a heroic part in actual events requires a wedding of this capability with historical circumstances. His acceptance or *espousal* as an authentic hero by the culture is the product of the coming together of the actuality of great accomplishments, the myth-making that accompanies them (on the hero's part as well as on that of his audience), and a response from a people yearning to identify with such deeds. The epic hero is, above all, a person with whom a people (and a biographer) can rewardingly identify, however painful or poignant this identification may be. In Lawrence's case, the very conflict itself, with its dimensions of renunciation and devotion to the dictates of individual conscience, and the unusual assumption of responsibility for the making of war, could furnish the heroic-idealistic example with which a wide contemporary audience might identify.

The complex family origins—Lawrence delighted in spinning mysteries about his shrouded, multinational ancestry—and the need of the parents to keep their situation secret, led to the beginning of family myth-making even before Lawrence was born. On the children's birth certificates the parents had always to give false information, and invented names and places for their own ancestry and alleged marriage so that the secret would not come out. To compensate for what they felt was sinful, the parents, especially the mother, insisted on a strict, religious upbringing which, needless to say, caused considerable confusion in Lawrence as he gradually pieced together the facts of his illegitimacy and the discrepancy between the principles by which he was being raised and the facts of his parents' union.

All of the children were meant to redeem the mother's fallen state by good Christian works or great deeds. Lawrence, as the most gifted child, was the object of the greatest parental investment for the future. Precocious and unusually intelligent, Ned was the son to whose great deeds—of a religious nature, it was hoped—the mother looked for her vindication and salvation.[33] The disappointment provided by the secular direction of Lawrence's life's work was perhaps outweighed for his mother by the extraordinary nature of his achievement. There are many myths about Lawrence's precocity as a child— as a reader, climber, and cyclist, for example. It is difficult often to separate fact from fancy in these tales. My own estimation, based on the facts of his later life, is that Lawrence's childhood exploits were mostly true.

The important point, however, is that within the family there was, regardless of how extraordinary or capable Lawrence may in fact have been, a need to mythologize, which he internalized, and which remained for Lawrence himself a part of his psychology throughout his life. The need derived from his internalization of the parental sense of sin, the conviction (certainly not conscious until his war experiences) that no matter how self-sacrificing or noble he might try to be, no matter how courageous his deeds, he remained the product of this sin, and, despite his later rational rejection of conventional Christian notions, identified with it. Such mythologizing is intended to reverse this *psychic* reality, as it inspires in the hearer, witness, audience, beholder, reader, biographer, or whoever is to receive and transmit the material of the myth, the belief that the character behind the myth is special and transcendent. Facts and realities about which the individual is ashamed that might be traced to deeper private sources of shame and guilt are overshadowed and clouded in a web of mystery. The sense of shame remains, of course, and in Lawrence's case laces many of his writings after the war.

The need to treat himself as a mythic or mystery figure is evident in Lawrence to a far lesser degree before the traumas of the war years evoked deep inner currents of shame and guilt. It is suggested in a certain aloofness which his friends observed, and in a seemingly unnecessary need for anonymity, as when he signed a short piece for his college magazine, sent from Carchemish in 1912, "C. J. G."[34] After the war this weaving of mystery and legend became for Lawrence almost a matter of personal philosophy, especially when dealing with any matter linked to his past. In correcting a typescript in 1934 of Liddell Hart's biography, Lawrence wrote: "There are (as I hinted at Hindhead) things not quite desirable in this. Without wanting to censor I suggest alternatives—written with the allusiveness that hints at knowledge refusing to betray itself between the lines."[35]

Lawrence seemed almost to relish leaving his biographers puzzles and mysteries about him to fathom. They have approached this with a humorless dutifulness, the search for the identity of the object of the dedicatory poem of *Seven Pillars of Wisdom*, "To S. A., " being the best-known case in point. Each biographer of Lawrence, depending on what he wishes to emphasize, has chosen his own favorite scavenger hunts in Lawrence's history or character.

There is an idea, or system of ideas, common during early childhood, that might be called the *hero fantasy*. It derives from the limitations of being a child, with powers and authority far more restricted than those of the parents, who seem to be the cause of the frustration of the child's wishes. The fantasy enables the child to transcend these limitations. In this fantasy the child determines that the parents with whom he is living are impostors who are looking after him as a result of some unusual set of circumstances. They are not his real parents. These impostors fail to appreciate fully the child's potentialities as would his real parents, who are of noble birth (as, of course, is he). The child determines that he will embark on a heroic quest in which he will discover and restore to their rightful place his real parents, eject the impostors, and be reunited in greatness with his true fore-bears, who will recognize and appreciate fully the deserving qualities of the child-hero. A variation on this fantasy is that the present parents are reduced from former greatness and need to be restored by the child's heroic efforts. Otto Rank, in his classic work *The Myth of the Birth of the Hero*, has examined the ways in which the elements of the hero fantasy, with its many variations, have found expression in the hero myths of Western and Middle Eastern civilization.[36]

A most interesting psychohistorical problem arises when the out-lines of a family's actual situation lend themselves in reality to the forms of this fantasy, as occurred in Lawrence's case. His father, if not of noble birth, had belonged to the landed gentry of Ireland (children do not make so much of these fine distinctions). He had cast off this role and established himself in Oxford with his un-noble wife, and raised their five boys to be respectable, church-going, well-educated, middle-class citizens. Lawrence indicated clearly that he regarded his father as having fallen in status—for which he blamed his mother's determination and ambition—and was much troubled about the ambi-guity of his own status. For Liddell Hart's biography, Lawrence wrote: "Observers noted a difference in social attitude between the courtly but abrupt and large father, and the laborious mother. The father shot, fished, rode, sailed with the certainty of birthright experience."[37] The mother had brought the father down in social status, but to Lawrence this fact had a deeper meaning, as it diminished the father personally in his eyes. To Mrs. Shaw he had written several years earlier: "My father was on the large scale, tolerant, experienced, grand, rash, humoursome, skilled to speak, and naturally lord-like. He had been 35-years in the larger life, and a spendthrift, a sportsman, and a hard-rider and drinker. My mother, brought up as a child of sin in the Island of Skye by a bible-thinking Presbyterian [probably a minister of the

Church of England in Scotland], then a nursemaid, then 'guilty' (in her judgment) of taking my father from his wife. To justify herself, she remodeled my father, making him a teetotaler, a domestic man, a careful spender of pence."[38] Thus the hero fantasy and the reality come together. Both parents are fallen, the father from status and both from grace.

Although his childhood play was filled with adventures against imaginary evil foes[39] and the preparation that we have noted for the achievement of great deeds, there is no surviving expression on Lawrence's part, as a child, of his heroic fantasies. However, his readings as a youth were dominated by his interest in medieval poetry and epic forms, such as the Rolandic and Arthurian legends, in which the heroic and chivalric fantasies reached their classic form. His choice of subject for his college thesis was medieval military architecture, and the Crusades—that curious blend of heroic romantic idealism and ecclesiastical fervor with barbaric actuality—were a dominant interest of his young manhood. Lawrence has left little doubt that his engagement in the Arab campaigns was for him the apotheosis of the hero fantasy, in which he would restore not his family to its proper status, but another people, a downtrodden race, to its original noble place in history. At least, he hoped his father's family would recognize the greatness of his effort. In this he was disappointed. For Liddell Hart, Lawrence wrote near the end of his life, "T.E.'s father's family seemed unconscious of his sons, even after his death recognition of their achievement might have done honour to the name."[40]

There is no contradiction in the fact that extraordinary achievements may, as in Lawrence's case, exist side by side with the conviction of being an impostor. The achievements, or the effort on Lawrence's part to accomplish heroic deeds, are meant, in addition to their immediate military or political purposes, to redeem the fallen self-regard that is at root the result of an early identification with parents who, in the child's harsh system of values, are "fallen" through having betrayed the very ideals they espoused. The clearest statement by Lawrence of this view of his parents, and its relation to his retreat into the ranks occurs in the same letter to Mrs. Shaw that was quoted above:

> One of the real reasons (there are three of four) why I am in the service is so that I may live by myself. She [his mother] has given me a terror of families and inquisitions. And yet you'll

understand she is my mother, and an extraordinary person. Knowledge of her will prevent my ever making any woman a mother, and the cause of children. I think she suspects this: but she does not know that the inner conflict which makes me a standing civil war, is the inevitable issue of the discordant natures of herself and my father, and the inflammation of strength and weakness which followed the uprooting of their lives and principles. They should not have borne children.[41]

This is the "crack in the firing" of which John Buchan wrote; the "diffident, perhaps weak core" to which his brother referred.[42] No deeds, however great or unusual, can undo the meaning of these identifications with the parents. In fact, the personal traumas that Lawrence underwent in the war, the ambiguity of his own position in the Arab Revolt, the sordid aspects of the activities of a people he idealized and meant to uplift (with whom he also identified himself too deeply), all confronted him with the contrast between the reality he came to experience and the heroic fantasy he had pursued so intensely. It is this contrast, the inner awareness of the discrepancy between the ideals and the actuality, that leads Lawrence to feel he is an impostor, that he has acted under false pretenses. In his heart he knew he had sacrificed himself for deeply egoistic motives in a cause that was not his own and was not, in reality, very glorious. Acclaimed as a hero, and wishing to be great, he retains the conviction of his debasement.

Lawrence was in no real sense an impostor or a charlatan from the *external* standpoint. He did the best he could for the Arabs in the revolt and on their behalf in the postwar settlement, and in the process he committed some political errors as he tried to serve as an intermediary between Arab national interests and the colonial policies of the Western powers. It has been the tendency of Lawrence's detractors to obliterate the distinction between external reality and internal conviction, and to use Lawrence's assessment of himself as an impostor as evidence that he did not achieve what he claimed. This is also a misuse of psychological materials in psychohistorical research.

In the desert campaigns Lawrence was able for a short historical moment to bring boyhood dreams together with sociopolitical realities and to galvanize the Arab Revolt. His ability to work as effectively as he did with the Arabs is itself a psychohistorical problem of considerable interest and can only be touched upon briefly here. It has been best described by the senior officers who worked most closely with him, especially W. F. Stirling and Pierce Joyce (observations of the latter being contained in unpublished statements made in 1939 and 1941 in BBC broadcasts).[43]

Lawrence's success lay in the demonic intensity of his will, and his capacity to transform himself, in his brother's phrase, "from a man into an instrument of victory." His genius was implemented in the attention he gave to an infinite variety of necessary details. Above all, he was capable of grasping and representing to the Bedouin tribes their own longings for freedom, and to organize the fragmented drives of the Arabs of various tribes into a sustained guerrilla effort, adapted to the terrain, the awkward nature of the common enemy that had exploited their lands and people for centuries, and the problems of supply and the great distances involved. It was in fundamental respects a psychological achievement. Fluid and protean as he was in his own psychological identities, Lawrence had, in Stirling's phrase, "the uncanny ability to sense the feelings of any group of men in whose company he found himself," and the "power to probe behind their minds and to uncover the well-springs of their actions."[44] Joyce, Lawrence's immediate superior, in one of his broadcasts said:

> At dozens of conferences we attended together, Lawrence rarely spoke. He merely studied the men around him and when the arguments ended as they usually did in smoke, he then dictated his plan of action which was usually adopted and everyone went away satisfied. It was not as is often supposed by his individual leadership of hordes of Bedouin that he achieved success in his daring ventures, but by the wise selection of tribal leaders and by providing the essential grist to the mill in the shape of golden rewards for work well done.

> His individual bravery and endurance captured their imagination. Initial successes made "Orance," as the Arabs called him, a byword in the desert, and there was always competition among the sheikhs to ride with him on a foray. Like the rest of us he had many disappointments but nothing could shake his determination to win through, or his restless energy in initiating alternative plans when things went wrong, and the whole scheme recast.[45]

Joyce's summary coincides with that of the other officers who actually worked closely with Lawrence: "I have just given these few notes on my personal contact with Lawrence, that mass of contradictions. I shall never meet a greater personality or more inspiring leader."[46]

I was fortunate in 1967 to have the opportunity of interviewing surviving Bedouins of the Ibn Jazi branch of the Howeitat tribe of what is now southern Jordan. These men had participated in the capture of Akaba, and in the battles and raids during the revolt that took place in southern Jordan and the northern Hijaz. They had not been interviewed before, knew no English, did not read, and retained their nomadic ways. The interviews were translated twice—once at the time they were made and then checked in a second translation in this country. As accounts of battles that had taken place fifty years before, the memories, though very clear and quite detailed, were probably not reliable. The memories of Lawrence, allowing for the fact that the men were talking to a Westerner, were, however, remarkably consistent.

What the Bedouins stressed was that Lawrence lived with the tribesmen, slept with them, ate their food, and knew the details of their tribal lives. One said, "He was an Arab—he was talking Arabic. He was living like an Arab."[47] Lawrence planned the raids and taught the tribesmen what to do. He talked to them about "our future, and all in pure Arabic," said one. "He used to think of everything," this sheikh continued. "Now this is what they loved. Because before they went on any expedition he used to know which tribe the expedition was going to consist of. He used to have a big statement—a detailed statement—of every member of that family that was going to go on this expedition, knowing full well how many members of this expedition would stay behind, and he used to give them enough money to buy food, rice, fat, and everything that would keep them going for the full expedition, for what he thought the expedition would last." Lawrence used to talk to the other British officers in front of the Bedouins and tell them that the best way to get what you wanted was "through respect, because they are a very, very proud people and they are a very strong people."[48] They were also impressed with Lawrence's bravery, and described how he would risk his own life to personally save Arabs who had been wounded in raids on Turkish trains. For these elderly men, the revolt in which the tribes had put aside their differences and fought to obtain their freedom against a common enemy, remained, after fifty years, the great event of their lives. For the Arabs of this region, Lawrence was still an important figure, and his name is part of their oral traditions. He helped give them confidence in their own strength. One man told his son, "You should be like I was, strong and courageous in front of Lawrence."[49]

Much has been made both by Lawrence and his denigrators of his duplicity during the Arab Revolt, both in terms of fact and as an explanation of his conflicted state following the war. The falseness lay in his continuing to inspire the Arab tribesmen to fight in the Allied cause when he was aware that settlements had been made between the British and the French that planned control by the great powers in Arab regions following an Allied victory. But what alternative course could be suggested? Surely it was to the advantage of the Arabs to be relieved of the Turkish oppression, to place their hopes in working after the war with Lawrence and whatever other allies to the cause of self-determination or freedom they might find.

The arguments on that issue extend far beyond the scope of this essay. From Lawrence's personal standpoint, his postwar retreat and troubled conscience relate far more to his personal sacrifice in a war whose actuality, far from containing the romantic glory that he sought, was filled with horror, for which he took exaggerated responsibility, and contained also a sadistic sexual assault that left him with a complex flagellation disorder, the details of which are described elsewhere.[50]

From the psychological standpoint, there is no contradiction between the deep conviction of failure that Lawrence felt so powerfully after the war and his own contribution to the heroic myth-making that surrounded him in his own lifetime and has continued since his death. On the contrary, the need to write a narrative in the epic mode in which he was the central figure, and the need to raise the story of the Arab Revolt to the level of an epic heroic quest, are in part acts of redemption, efforts to convert a conviction of personal baseness into the loftiest possible realm. This has little to do with the quality, validity, or importance of the actual deeds that Lawrence accomplished. *Seven Pillars of Wisdom* is a true epic narrative of the twentieth century, a literary embodiment of the conflicted heroism that is the only heroism we can tolerate, a heroism tainted with realism, personal conflict, and responsibility. World War I destroyed, probably forever, the naive kind of romanticism that ran through much of Western culture prior to the twentieth century. No one is blind any longer to the effects of weapons of mass destruction. The experience of loss, atrocity, and death have been communicated to everyone who has not suffered directly. Civilized men can no longer permit the conventional glorification of war. Lawrence, like others who fought in the war, identified the falseness of its glorification and helped to explode its mythology by disclosing in full psychological detail his own shattering experience of first-hand participation in war, while in so doing he set in motion another set of myths which applied to himself. His work and his later life of renunciation of all rewards of war are true to his convictions and values. They have contributed to the transition from a nineteenth-century conception of heroism, which retained much of the medieval chivalric romanticism upon which Lawrence was raised, to a twentieth-century perspective and realism in which heroism must lie in examples of restraint, renunciation, empathy with alien peoples, avoidance of war, and devotion to settling all disputes by other means.

## NOTES

[1] Bernard C. Meyer, "Some Reflections on the Contributions of Psychoanalysis to Biography," *Psychoanalysis and Contemporary Science*, vol. 1, ed. Robert R. Holt and Emanuel Peterfreund (New York: Macmillan, 1972), p. 375.

[2] Lyndon Johnson, *The Vantage Point: Perspectives of the Presidency, 1963–1969*. (New York: Holt, Rinehart & Winston, 1971).

[3] T. E. Lawrence, *Seven Pillars of Wisdom: A Triumph* (Garden City, N.Y.: Doubleday, 1935), p. 551.

[4] Fareedah Akle to Helen Cash, June 12, 1969.

[5] John E. Mack to M. R. Lawrence, June 30, 1964; M. R. Lawrence to Mack, July 3, 1964.

[6] Basil Liddell Hart (1938), in *T. E. Lawrence to His Biographers* (Garden City, N.Y.: Doubleday, 1963), p. 145.

[7] Bodleian Library, Oxford University, Reserved Manuscripts, d. 230.

[8] Robert Graves (1938), in *T. E. Lawrence to his Biographers*, p. 117.

[9] Letters to Lionel Curtis, in David Garnett, ed., *Letters of T. E. Lawrence* (London: Spring Books, 1964), pp. 410–421; Letters of T. E. Lawrence to Charlotte Shaw, British Museum, Additional Manuscripts, 45903.

[10] Bodleian Library, Reserved Manuscripts, b. 55.

[11] John E. Mack, "T. E. Lawrence: Charlatan or Tragic Hero?," *American Journal of Psychiatry* 125, no. 11 (May 1969): 1604–1607.

[12]Lawrence, *Seven Pillars*, 632–633.

[13]Samuel Spiegel and David Lean, *Lawrence of Arabia* (filmscript), p. 237.

[14]Richard Aldington, *Lawrence of Arabia: A Biographical Enquiry* (London: Collins, 1955), p. 337.

[15]Suleiman Mousa, *T. E. Lawrence: An Arab View* (London: Oxford University Press, 1966), p. 199.

[16]Alec Kirkbride to Basil Liddell Hart, December 8, 1962, Bodleian Library, Reserved Manuscripts, b. 56.

[17]A. W. Lawrence, "Comment" in Mousa, *Lawrence*, p. 285.

[18]F. G. Peake, "Some Notes," May 26, 1963, pp. 1–2 (furnished to the author by A. W. Lawrence).

[19]F. G. Peake to A. W. Lawrence, 1965.

[20]Peake to A. W. Lawrence, 1965.

[21]Peake, "Some Notes," p. 1.

[22]A. W. Lawrence, "The Aftermath of Tafas" (unpublished manuscript, undated but probably 1963 or 1964), Bodleian Library, Reserved Manuscripts, b. 56.

[23]A. W. Lawrence, "The Fiction and the Fact" (review of film *Lawrence of Arabia*), *The Observer*, December 16, 1962.

[24]A. W. Lawrence to Mack, August 20, 1973.

[25]Elizabeth Monroe, *Britain's Moment in the Middle East: 1914–1956* (Baltimore: Johns Hopkins University Press, 1963), p. 68.

[26]Irving Howe, "T. E. Lawrence: The Problem of Heroism," in *A World More Attractive: A View of Modern Literature and Politics* (New York: Horizon Press, 1963), pp. 20, 36.

[27]Ibid., p. 39.

[28]M. R. Lawrence, *The Home Letters of T. E. Lawrence and His Brothers* (Oxford: Basil Blackwell, 1954), pp. 147–148.

[29]Janet Hall-Smith, interview, December 17, 1965.

[30]Reverend E. F. Hall, interview, December 16, 1965.

[31]Registrar of Births and Deaths, Sunderland, England.

[32]T. E. Lawrence to Charlotte Shaw, April 14, 1927, British Museum, Additional Manuscripts, 45903.

[33] A. W. Lawrence, interview, December 8, 1965.

[34]C. J. G. (T. E. Lawrence), "The Kaer of Ibu Wardani," *Jesus College Magazine* 4 (1912–1913): 37–39.

[35]Liddell Hart, in *T. E. Lawrence to His Biographers*, p. 78.

[36]Otto Rank (1914), *The Myth of the Birth of the Hero* (New York: Knopf, 1959).

[37]Liddell Hart, in *T. E. Lawrence to His Biographers*, p. 78.

[38]T. E. Lawrence to Charlotte Shaw, April 14, 1927.

[39]M. R. Lawrence, interview, August 24, 1964; A. W. Lawrence, ed., *T. E. Lawrence by His Friends* (London: Jonathan Cape, 1937), pp. 31–35.

[40]Liddell Hart, in *T. E. Lawrence to his Biographers*,p. 78.

[41] T. E. Lawrence to Charlotte Shaw, April 14, 1927.

[42] John Buchan, *Memory Hold the Door* (London: Hodder & Stoughton, 1940); A. W. Lawrence, ed., *Lawrence by His Friends*, p. 590.

[43]W. F. Stirling, *Safety Last* (London: Hollis & Carter, 1953), pp. 245–248; Colonel Pierce Joyce, transcripts of BBC broadcasts, April 30, 1939; July 14, 1941.

[44]Stirling, *Safety Last*, p. 246.

[45]Joyce, BBC broadcast, July 14, 1941.

[46]Ibid.

[47]Sheikh Salem Ibn Nassar, interview, Wadi Rumm, April 16, 1967 (translated by Andrawes Barghout).

[48]Sheikh Aid Ibn Awad Al-Zalabani, interview, April 28, 1967 (translated by Antoine T. Hallac).

[49]Ibid.

[50]John E. Mack, "T. E. Lawrence: A Study of Heroism and Conflict," *American Journal of Psychiatry* 125, no. 8 (February 1969): 1083–1092; idem, *A Prince of Our Disorder: The Life of T. E. Lawrence* (Boston: Little, Brown, 1976).

# 14
# *A Biographical Inclination*
## Steven Marcus

---

Let me begin by observing that although I have never written a complete biography, or a book that was nothing but a biography, almost everything that I have written has a biographical side to it. All of my writing is in some measure biographical and arises out of biographical (and historical) interests and impulses, which are themselves not easily separable from autobiographical circumstances. To illustrate these assertions let me turn to my first book, on Charles Dickens,[1] and recall the circumstances out of which my interest in Dickens arose.

I chose Dickens, I think, long before I began to write the book about him; in some sense, I chose him long before I consciously knew that I had done so. I had read hardly anything by Dickens until I was a senior at Columbia, when, for a course in Victorian literature, I read *Hard Times*. A few years before, F. R. Leavis had published his famous piece on *Hard Times*,[2] and Lionel Trilling, the instructor of my class, said, "Why don't we read *Hard Times* and see if Leavis is right?" We read *Hard Times*, and I was bowled over by it. Later on, as a graduate student, one of the first things I did when I had the time was to sit down and read Dickens's novels from beginning to end; again and again, I was bowled over. At the same time I read a good deal of Dickens criticism, which was then fairly primitive, not yet having become the very urbane and elaborate industry it has since become. Because there were almost no really good, extended modern studies of Dickens, I said to myself that I would, when the time came, write my dissertation on Dickens—and I did. I had to finish the original dissertation in a hurry because it took me a number of years to write and was already 600 pages long, even though I had only gotten halfway through Dickens's career. At that point it was a matter of either completing my degree or losing my job at Columbia. So I called it quits halfway through, saying, "That's enough for the dissertation."

My primary conscious interest in this project lay in the fascinating creativity of Dickens, which is a source of inexhasutible pleasure to anybody who deals with him. His works, after those of William Shakespeare, are the most inventive and creative individual source of the English language and the way it moves. In addition, an interest in Dickens tends to draw one into the entire nineteenth century, because Dickens stands right at the center of so much of it; he's really a kind of crossroads, where multifaceted aspects of nineteenth-century English history, culture, and literature meet. That alone is an immense intellectual convenience.

All this, as well as the fact that at the time this was a relatively unworked field, contributed to my writing on Dickens. Yet behind my interest, I was later to discover, lay something deeper and more resonant. A hint comes in the appendix to my book, called "Who Is Fagin?," which I wrote after I had finished my dissertation, during the first couple of years of my own analysis. I discovered a certain series of illogicalities in the narrative structure of *Oliver Twist* which make sense only if one considers them *as* illogicalities. And I discovered them, if not precisely on the couch, then slightly off the couch or in relation to it—suggesting the depth of my engagement with this book. What struck me was the presence of decomposed elements of the primal scene in *Oliver Twist*, especially in the relation between Oliver and Fagin. I connected this with Dickens's relationship with his father and with his own childhood experiences.

The personal significance of these facts is intimated by the following autobiographical circumstance: I learned to read when I was very young. I can't remember when I couldn't read. My mother, who taught me how to read, told me that I was already reading at age two or three. I recall that the first book she gave to me—for Christmas, when I was about five or six years old—consisted of a series of condensed versions of Dickens's novels. The chapter I read at once and remembered thereafter very clearly was the one on *Oliver Twist*. An illustration by George Cruikshank depicted Fagin and Oliver's stepbrother, Monks, staring through the window at Oliver while Oliver was asleep. Then Oliver wakes up, and there follows a terrible scene of castration threats and fear. Although that is one of the early books I remember reading, one my mother gave to me, the experience went underground in me and didn't come out again until after I had finished writing my dissertation. That is, the meaning of what was going on in *Oliver Twist* and the meaning of part of my deep interest in Dickens were not revealed to me until after I had finished the dissertation and was in the midst of my own analysis.

Of course, what comes back to mind now is the recollection of myself as a small boy being presented with this book by my mother, reading it to myself in bed to put me to sleep, and being quite frightened by this particular scene. So I can conjecture this reconstruction: that my interest in Dickens was profoundly prepared for by this early experience, that it is closely connected with my own early life experiences. This makes the clearest kind of sense to me. For what other explanation could there be for engaging oneself for years on end with great passion and with all one's force with a single figure, except that it answers to certain of the most primordial resonances in one's own life?

There is, I believe, a symmetry between the castration anxiety that I experienced in reading the story as a child and the assertion at a later date of potency and creativeness in writing a book about the figure that had been the literary locus of that memorable experience. In this sense I think one can say that any critic—and by "critic," I mean the biographer as well as the literary critic—anybody who is dealing analytically with a literary or historical figure of this power—identifies, both consciously and unconsciously, with that figure. The biographer identifies with the creative triumphs of his subject, including his triumphs over, let's say, a parent or adversities or his deepest fears and inhibitions. There is no question in my mind that whenever I deal with Dickens, whenever I write about him or teach him, I profoundly identify with him.

But there are further historical conditions attached to my choice of Dickens as the subject of my extended study. All of Dickens's novels are about society, but *Hard Times*—the work that led me back to Dickens—has a peculiarly acute saliency when one thinks of literature as a systematic imagination of society or of using literary texts as social or cultural documents. At the time I decided to devote my efforts to work on Dickens, the idea of writing directly about the relations between literature and society was not the most academically approved or widely accepted thing to do. It was the heyday of the New Criticism, and one of my many purposes in writing on Dickens was polemical: to show that the New Criticism was quite an inadequate vehicle for dealing with writers like Dickens, that a phenomenon like Dickens was much more substantial than the academic formalism of New Criticism allowed. For criticism to touch on the greatest literature, in my opinion, it had to be able to approach someone like Dickens on his own broad terms. In deciding to write about Dickens in the broadest way possible, I was countering the views of many of my elders and virtually all my fellow students.

Here, however, I ought to mention the part taken by Lionel Trilling in this project. Trilling, my teacher and therefore my surrogate father, entirely supported my notion that Dickens was a supremely great writer, that he had been woefully neglected, and that it was precisely the right time to write about him. Indeed, he never wavered in his conviction that I had made the right choice, that I was on the right track. The one other person who approved with a similar force was the historian Jacques Barzun, one of my primary readers and an admirer of Dickens, too.

This attitude contrasted sharply with that of F. R. Leavis. Leavis had indeed praised *Hard Times*, but he had also said that it was the only book by Dickens worth serious study. When I went to Cambridge on a fellowship and listened to Leavis, I was just beginning my own work on Dickens. Leavis's convictions had not changed: he dismissed me by claiming that *Hard Times* was still the only book worth reading. My response was: "Well, I'm going to show you."

Something should be said about my not having fulfilled my ambition of writing on Dickens's entire career. It took about ten years to write the first volume, and Dickens's later novels are much more complex than the early ones, necessitating an even longer period of study. Besides, the second half of Dickens's career has been much more written about than the first half, so one would have to find new ways of dealing with it. But there is a larger significance to my concluding my book halfway through than these remarks may indicate. At the point I break off Dickens is just entering the great crisis of his life, a complex personal and cultural crisis. The personal aspect involves the breakup of his marriage, and the cultural one, his despair about the nature of contemporary society. My own first marriage was breaking up at precisely the time I came to Dickens's crisis. I believe that a certain inhibiting residue remains from the confluence of those two circumstances. Moreover, as I've already indicated, the second half of Dickens's career is very intimidating and requires an enormous engagement of sustained energy. I have not been able to sit still in one place as I could when I was a graduate student. But these statements may simply be rationalizations for all sorts of other things I'm not in touch with that have prevented me from sitting down and doing what I intended to do, to write a second and perhaps even a third volume.

Yet there is something else, I think, that has kept me, as it were, riveted to Dickens's early career. As I remarked, he went on to write novels that are more structurally complex and more integral than such early works as *Pickwick Papers*, but he never again achieved what I call the transcendence, the supreme comic happiness and well-being that one finds in *Pickwick Papers*. I am not sure what biographical or personal bearing that consideration has for me. I can only point out that a similar circumstance is true for Friedrich Engels, about whom I have also written.[3] Admittedly, the situation is very different because Engels's first book really *is* his best book, while one can't say that *Pickwick Papers* is Dickens's best book—works such as *Bleak House* and *Little Dorrit* are clearly much greater. But Dickens never wrote a happier book. And I don't think it is an accident that I chose to deal biographically with two writers who did something spectacular at the very beginning of their careers, although neither was a flash in the pan. Both, in fact, were steady long-distance runners, with an extended, complicated development. But both started out with a big bang, and that, for me, is significant.

One of my interests—and I think this shows in a number of other works that I've done—is in how young men, particularly writers, initially get to be what they are. When I look over my own writings, I find that my greatest interest is in the arc of development up to what is usually their first great triumph.

An exception seems to be my interest in Sigmund Freud, for I have written not simply about the young Freud or even the first half of Freud, but the whole of Freud.[4] Nevertheless, many of my essays are about the first part of his career, dealing with the letters to Wilhelm Fliess, the *Three Essays on the Theory of Sexuality*, and the Dora and Rat Man cases. So some of my writing on Freud does fall into this category, especially the essay on the Fliess correspondence. Here, too, I am interested in following the development of a young genius up to the point of self-definition in action, the point where he breaks out publicly and determines by some kind of intellectual, conceptual success in writing what his identity will be.

This theme is a recurrent pattern in my writing, and I think that it is a refraction of something in my own life. In my own development an important step was my decision in college, against my father's wishes, not to pursue a premedical course but to become a student of literature. That was the great early crisis in my career because I lost my father's support and had to go ahead on my own. It was the one turning point in my life where I felt that I had nothing to rely on except an intuition of a certain gift of my own, which lay in reading and writing about literature. It was through this decision that a large part of my identity and future was defined. This is the similarity I see between what happened to me as a very young man and the sections of the biographical arc that I have pursued.

There is something else to be said about the connection between my interest in Dickens and my interest in Freud, however. I first read both at about the same time. I was about eighteen when I read Freud's *Introductory Lectures on Psycho-Analysis* of 1916 to 1917. It was something like an experience of revelation, as if somebody had turned the lights on for me. I read the book not so much with a quasi-religious sense of conviction as with the kind of conviction in the essential truthfulness of its insights that one very rarely gets in life outside of the works of great novelists like Dickens or great poets like Shakespeare. Moreover, I think that it was in part Dickens and in part my early reading of and deep feeling for Freud that gave me the inner permission to write about things that were not at the time within the standard purview of an ambitious graduate student in English literature. A great many hints and cues for my unorthodox inclusiveness came from my reading of Freud, who was not afraid to include anything.

My active work on Freud began with the collaborative editing and abridging, with Lionel Trilling, of Ernest Jones's three-volume biography.[5] Here, too, an unconscious biographical inclination can be seen at work—for I must confess that I was not conscious of any special interest in biography at the time. Our task on the Jones biography was really one of critical editing, of reducing three volumes to one; it was a weeding out of the three volumes, the last two of which were written when Jones was sick and dying of cancer, and were therefore not as shapely as the first volume. In this, we had two main concerns: to bring this material to a wider audience and to bring coherence into Jones's biography, which was dispersed in various ways. We hoped to make what we considered to be a great life and a very distinguished biography more accessible.

I was not aware then, nor am I aware now, that there was any particular crossover between my interest in Dickens and my interest in Freud at the time. The interests ran parallel to each other. Later, however, they did converge—in my third extended project, *The Other Victorians*.[6] In that book an interest in Victorian culture and writing and an interest in psychoanalysis are inseparably compounded. In point of fact that compounding was what made the book possible to write. And it seems no accident that the central chapters of that work are a biographical reconstruction on my part of the life of the anonymous author of *My Secret Life*. No, it can hardly be an accident.

But to return to my books on Dickens and Freud: the biographical shapes of the two projects are different. This raises the interesting question of whole as opposed to partial lives, since I've been involved in both kinds of undertakings. The point about both Dickens and Freud and why one likes to see the grand sweep of their lives is that they're both essentially heroic characters, Freud a hero of thought and Dickens a hero of literature. Moreover, both were aware that they were heroes, that they had heroic destinies and heroic mythological structures in their lives. So, in reading about their lives, one wants to see how the fate of the hero is played out in detail, through all his terrible defeats and recoveries, as well as in the mythology that accrues about him. Perhaps this is one of the reasons for my parallel interests in Dickens and Freud—that both are heroic figures—for I certainly am most interested in the nature of heroes in culture and civilization. Whether our public at present can still take heroes whole is another matter. In recent years it's obviously not been the case. If one asks, "What is the biography that has had the greatest influence on numbers of intellectuals in the past twenty-five or thirty years?," I suppose one of the first books one would look to would be Erik Erikson's *Young Man Luther*[7]—and that's not taking the man whole at all. Only a piece of Luther is there.

Let me advert once again to Dickens, for I did make a second return to his early work, well after the first psychoanalytic return that I made with *Oliver Twist*. Before 1970, the centenary year of Dickens's death, I had never taught a seminar on all his novels. In that year, to celebrate the centenary, I decided to teach a graduate seminar in which all Dickens's novels would be read. I started from the beginning, from *Pickwick Papers*, and I discovered that each of the novels that I had written about in my book now appeared in a different light to me. All my interpretations now seemed inadequate, and I found that, were I to write a second book on those novels, my interpretations of each would differ substantially from and, I think, strike at a deeper level than my earlier ones. Indeed, when I was invited to give a paper at one of the centennial conferences, I wrote an essay on *Pickwick Papers* that is entirely different from my original chapter on this work.[8] It comes at the novel at a more primitive, more primordial pitch, because it deals with the novel as a kind of linguistic activity in itself. I believe I could do something similar for all the early novels. This is both pleasant and unsettling, because it shows not only that my own mind remains responsive but also how exceptional Dickens really is, that he changes as the observer changes.

Again, one is confronted with the depth and complexity of Dickens's works. They are like Shakespeare's writings in the sense that they are almost literally inexhaustible in their richness and linguistic complexity. It was indeed an odd experience: I had invested an enormous amount in that first reading of *Pickwick Papers*, yet eight or nine years later, when I undertook to teach it for the first time, I came up with a reading that undercuts the first one (although it includes it, too). I have been congratulated on this, but it is a chastening experience, too. It represents for me something of the depth of my engagement with Dickens and stands in contrast to my relation to Engels, to whom I feel no urge to return. The Engels book caught me for a few years, but its origins had to do with my harbored or accumulated polemical response to some of the events of the late '60s and early '70s rather than with events located in the early matrix of my own life. The Dickens commitment is much deeper.

In the first reading of *Pickwick Papers*, I had not yet sufficiently neutralized certain things, in particular the idealized relation between father and son, between Sam Weller and Mr. Pickwick. Only after that relation had become relatively neutralized in my mind could I shift my focus and re-see the book as a whole. Suddenly, what struck me was the overwhelming presence of linguistic play in the book and how that becomes gradually transmuted in the course of the narrative. There's little question in my mind that it was in large measure developments in my own internal life that permitted me to undertake this essentially new reading of the same work. This event was the equivalent at a later stage of my development of what had happened to me earlier with *Oliver Twist*. My analysis had led to a breakthrough in my reading of Dickens, just after I had finished the text of the book on Dickens. It was a matter of considerable importance to me. Not only did it lead to a second and new reading of a complex text, but it helped me to understand a part of my own life in a way that I had never understood it before. It was a sort of liberation for me. It was one of those rare experiences when a whole area of one's early life becomes accessible, understandable, and coherent, and can, in fact, be put to creative use—in this case toward understanding a previously obscure text.

There is another event in my writing life that seems roughly parallel. One of my favorite pieces concerns the Irish famine.[9] It is an essay on hunger and ideology, but it has some relation to my childhood. I was raised in an Irish Catholic neighborhood in New York, where, as one of the few Jewish boys, I came in for a good deal of abuse from Irish boys. I therefore built up a considerable measure of unexpressed hostility toward them. But I didn't realize at the time how much I really liked them and how much they had suffered historically; I came to feel that personally I owed them something and should repay my debt to them, even though they had beaten me up and abused me when I was a boy (although "beaten me up and abused me" is really an excessive term for just being pushed around and called bad names). And so in writing about how the Irish suffered at the hands of the English and in doing justice to them, I was, in a measure, coming to terms with a part of my childhood and with an aggression and vindictiveness that I had never been able to vent. In writing about the Irish as I did, I think I was indicating that I identified not with the aggressors but with the Irish as victims, as I had been their victim earlier. I saw them in their historical plight as being, in some sense, prototypes for Jews a hundred years later. In fact I literally said that in my piece. I made it a point to put that essay on hunger and ideology as the opening article in my book of essays. For it was also the piece in which I could most easily point to how I typically deal with things.

Yet if I identified with the Irish (though to a lesser degree than I did with Dickens), I also have to say that I didn't really identify with Engels, except insofar as he was a young foreigner writing about England, too. I wrote the Engels book in complex circumstances. I came back from a year's leave in Europe in the late '60s to the aftermath of the riots and disorders at Columbia and heard a lot of my students proclaiming that they were radicals. Their radicalism consisted in a series of impulsive, expressive activities that seemed to me essentially incoherent and sometimes self-destructive. They were often only obliquely political. I had a nagging intuition that I ought to do something about this, not directly but in my capacity as a teacher of literature. I didn't know at first why I did it; I hadn't read Engels's *The Condition of the Working Class in England in 1844* myself since I had been a graduate student some fifteen years earlier. It was entirely intuitive behavior on my part. We read it, and to my surprise, I suddenly realized that I had assigned this book out of a polemical impulse in relation to my graduate students; the impulse could be translated thus: "Well, if you want to be a radical, I think you ought to take a good look at a real radical. And what is he? He's just like you. He's an absolute member of the middle class, but he doesn't pretend to be anything except a member of the middle class, and he is capable of a lifelong dedication to radicalism and revolution. This is the real point, and I would like to rub your noses in it." The responses of my students were mixed, but the positive responses only increased my own acerbity and acidulousness. So I sat down and wrote the book. The book was really written in a warm polemical spirit vis-à-vis my own graduate students who had gone in for the radicalism of the era and who, by the time I finished the book, had, most of them, long since ceased to be radicals. But it was also written out of a strongly critical impulse to respond to what my graduate students had felt to be their own radicalism.

For my own part, it was clear from the outset that I was not a radical either in the sense that my students were or in the sense that Engels was. That is, I'm not a committed revolutionary, which he was. There was never any question in his mind that he was an active revolutionary. Insofar, however, as a radical questions the disparity or the discrepancy that always exists between the professed ideals and the actualities of a society, then I think that there is a continuity between the radicalism of figures like Engels and Karl Marx in the nineteenth century and the kind of activity that nonrevolutionary but nevertheless pointed social and literary criticism can make in the present. It seems to me that one of the responsibilities of criticism is precisely to reveal continually the discrepancy between the ideals people profess and how these ideals are implemented in actuality. This operates at the level of literature, at the level of criticism, as well as in relation to society as a whole. In that sense I do feel that there is a continuity between the great radical figures of the nineteenth century and the kind of criticism that some of us carry on today.

One final word about the book on Engels. Writing it added to my confidence. I don't think it was as profound an experience as my engagement with Dickens or Freud, but it gave me confidence that I could deal with another body of material and with an audience of another generation. The book was also a partial demonstration of my own characteristic way of dealing with things. I was saying, "I am going to deal with Engels in exactly the same way I deal with Dickens. Here is a nonliterary text, but I'm going to treat this extra-territorial text with the instruments of literary criticism; I want to see how literary criticism, if appropriately pursued, can bring what has not been seen in this work into relevant focus and therefore revive the text as a document of importance and pertinence to our own time."

Finally, I suspect that in writing about Freud, Dickens, and Engels, I've been writing about three figures who fit into a particular kind of description. All three are characteristic of the heroic style of the social critics of the nineteenth and early twentieth centuries—a style that seems to be found only rarely today.

## NOTES

[1] Steven Marcus, *Dickens: From Pickwick to Dombey* (New York: Basic Books, 1965).

[2] F. R. Leavis, *The Great Tradition* (London: Chato & Windus, 1948).

[3] Steven Marcus, *Engels, Manchester and the Working Class* (New York: Random House, 1974).

[4] Steven Marcus, *Freud and the Culture of Psychoanalysis: Studies in the Transition from Victorian Humanism to Modernity* (Boston & London: Allen & Unwin, 1984).

[5] Ernest Jones, *Life and Work of Sigmund Freud*, ed. and abr. by Lionel Trilling and Steven Marcus (New York: Basic Books, 1961).

[6] Steven Marcus, *The Other Victorians* (New York: Basic Books, 1966).

[7] Erik Erikson, *Young Man Luther* (New York: Norton, 1958).

[8] Steven Marcus, "Language into Structure: *Pickwick Papers*," in *Representations: Essays on Literature and Society* (New York: Random House, 1976), pp. 214–246.

[9] Steven Marcus, "Hunger and Ideology," in *Representations*, pp. 3–16.

# 15

# *Notes on Researching James Forrestal*

Arnold A. Rogow

---

THAT MONDAY MORNING, May 23, 1949, still in pajamas and bathrobe, I retrieved the *New York Times* from the front steps, as I did every morning while I was a graduate student at Princeton. But I did not immediately go back into our small "barracks" apartment, for I was transfixed by the most prominent news story on the front page. James Forrestal, the *Times* reported in its lead column story headed by large black type, the nation's former Secretary of Defense, had fallen to his death from the sixteenth floor of the Bethesda Naval Hospital. According to the *Times,* Forrestal since early April had been a patient at the hospital, where he was under treatment for "exhaustion." The *Times* coverage of Forrestal's suicide concluded with appropriate statements of sadness and regret by a large number of luminaries, among whom President Harry Truman was the most prominent.

Forrestal's hospitalization had been a shock to many in the Princeton community, but I think it fair to say that no one was prepared for his tragic death. Before his suicide there were recurrent rumors that Forrestal, who had attended Princeton as an undergraduate and who usually was referred to in university publications as "Class of 1915" (although, in fact, he never graduated), was to be the next president of the institution. Not only that: as far as I and most other Americans knew, the life of James Forrestal, whose career encompassed conspicuous achievements in Wall Street and Washington, was an all-American success story. His government service, to be sure, had been a stormy one, but its disappointments in and of themselves did not seem to me sufficient grounds for Forrestal's taking his own life.

I remember thinking that someone who had known Forrestal—I guessed it might be a professor in the Department of Politics who claimed a close friendship with him—would and should try to ascertain what had gone wrong. If I myself had been at the end instead of near the beginning of my graduate work, perhaps I would have considered a venture in that direction. But perhaps not. Certainly I was interested enough—I suppose curious is a better word—but I doubt I was self-confident enough at that time to undertake such a project. Ten years later, when there still was no Forrestal biography and I resolved to see what could be done, I encountered opposition and obstacles so formidable that had it not been for a certain stubborn defiance as well as confidence, I would have abandoned the research more than once.

Almost at the outset I discovered that some knowledge of character disorders and psychopathological states was required, and before I was very far along I knew I would have to become familiar with the causes, diagnosis, and treatment of mental illness, in short, familiar with psychiatric theory and practice. Like most other educated persons I had read some Freud, but I had no clinical knowledge of psychiatry, much less any comprehension of the illnesses of psychotic depression, involutional melancholia, and paranoid schizophrenia, the symptoms of which, various psychiatrists alleged, Forrestal manifested in the final months of his life.

I also was advised by almost everyone that a biography of Forrestal was an impossible undertaking. For one thing, these nay-sayers asserted, he had been a VIP and therefore no one in Washington would talk. (Fortunately they mostly were wrong about this.) For another, the family would not cooperate. (Unfortunately here they were mostly right.) Third—and this argument against the book was much more a challenge than a discouragement—there were hints from all sorts of people that the "real" or "true" story about "Jim" Forrestal could not, and certainly should not, be told. It was some time before I learned what part of that story was, and the full story I did not know until some years after the book was published. But let me quickly add that the information missing from my book, while important, does not substantially alter the interpretation put forward of Forrestal's life and death.[1]

Soon after I started work in the summer of 1959, I learned that two other biographies of Forrestal were under way, both by well-known journalists, one of whom was a close friend of Forrestal's widow. I retain a sharp memory of sitting in this gentleman's apartment, gazing dejectedly at three tiers of file drawers, fifteen in all, which I was told were filled to overflowing with Forrestal material. Probably aware that I was discouraged, this putative biographer advised me to abandon my efforts then and there; after all, he told me smilingly, Forrestal was not worth two biographies.

The fifteen file drawers loomed very large indeed, but I do not recall giving any serious thought to abandoning the biography. (Had I done so, there might not have been *any* Forrestal biography since, up to the present, mine is the only one that has appeared.) But considering the difficulties in the way, the question is: Why did I not give up and write something else?

My initial decision to do a book about Forrestal and my adherence to that decision were, like most choices in life, overdetermined. The intellectual determinants, so to speak, included Forrestal's importance in the origins and conduct of the cold war, and in the reorganization of the military services that culminated in the establishment of the Department of Defense (of which Forrestal was the first secretary). In committing suicide he became the highest-ranking American in either government or politics to take his own life, and I was interested, among other questions, in whether the pressures of public life had played a significant role. I also wanted to know at what point in his life Forrestal had begun to manifest symptoms of mental illness. Was it possible, I wondered, that this illness had contributed to his intense distrust and suspicion of the Soviet Union, and was it therefore accountable, at least in part, for his reputation in Washington as one of the foremost "hawks" in the entire free world? Finally, assuming that Forrestal had become ill before he left office in late March 1949, I hoped that a detailed study of his career would illuminate the causes and consequences of mental illness in public life, and show, too, how such illness could be, if not prevented, at least detected before it could have any significant effect on public policy and/or become life-threatening to the individual involved.

My choice of Forrestal as a biographical subject was also influenced, as I suspected at the time and confirmed later during the course of a psychoanalysis, by certain identifications. Like him, I was from a family that had middle-class aspirations and even pretended middle-class status. My mother, like Forrestal's mother, was extremely ambitious for her two sons, and because my father was dead, she was the commanding parent. Although I was not from a Catholic religious background (as was Forrestal), I was a Jew and, like him, an outsider at Princeton, which—in 1948 to 1952, when I was in graduate school—was much more WASP-ish than it is today. (At that time I also began to collect first editions of F. Scott Fitzgerald, another Princeton outsider with whom I felt some connection.) I shared with Forrestal a good deal of that ambivalence he displayed toward the well-born and rich, and like him I was sensitive to the subtle and not so subtle discriminations against minorities of all sorts practiced by the university, no less than the town.

Late in my analysis I made the startling (to me) discovery that Forrestal physically reminded me of a friend to whom I had been closely attached for many years, but from who, for reasons that became clearer in the analysis, I had begun to separate myself. Possibly, but not certainly, the work on Forrestal represented, at some level, an effort to reestablish the relationship that had once existed. That such a hypothesis is not wholly farfetched is supported by the fact that my conscious feelings about Forrestal underwent a substantial change during the research. Because of his extreme (for that time) views about the cold war and his opposition to the establishment of the state of Israel, I regarded Forrestal at the beginning with suspicion and anticipated disliking him even more as I learned more; I assumed, correctly as it turned out, that his private views were even more conservative than his publicly recorded opinions. What I did not anticipate was that Forrestal was as tortured in his political thinking as he was conflicted in his attitudes toward the Catholic church, sex, marriage, and children. His being a Wall Streeter and a Democrat well to the right of the Roosevelt-Truman wing of the party did not preclude certain radical instincts and impulses, such as being a secret reader of and financial contributor to *The Nation* Magazine. Forrestal left Dillon, Read and Company a wealthy man, but as hinted at earlier, he was never entirely comfortable with the wealthy and privileged, and he never completely ceased to look at the world from a vantage point on the wrong side of the Beacon, New York, railroad tracks.

As I learned more about the conflicts and Forrestal's tendency to obsess about decisions and choices, both public and private, I became more sympathetic and even developed, albeit grudgingly, a certain affection for him. I gradually discovered, of course, what everyone who knew him had long since discovered, namely, that the Forrestal who looked tough enough to chew nails for breakfast was in reality a feeling, sensitive, suffering man. Had I then been trained as a psychoanalyst, I also would have become aware of something not known to most of his friends—that Forrestal for a great many years struggled against the depression that ultimately terminated, or was a key factor in terminating, his life.

But while I became more friendly, as it were, toward Forrestal as work progressed, I developed sentiments about many of his former associates and acquaintances that ranged narrowly from ambivalence to dislike. Indeed, during interviews I often was reminded of what Charles Francis Adams, Jr., wrote in his *Autobiography* about the railroad lawyers he had known: that a less attractive collection of men he had never met in this world, and hoped not to meet in the next.[2] Those who were not also anti-Semitic were cold, crafty, and not infrequently ruthless individuals who gave no evidence of any torment comparable to that suffered by their dead friend. One of them wrote Forrestal in 1945 from Germany that the inmates of a concentration camp, which he had just visited, were "filthy dirty," crawling with vermin, and assuredly not the sort of people who should be allowed to come to the United States.

I remember another friend, an attorney, whom I saw on a hot July day in his luxurious air-conditioned office high above Wall Street. Among other questions I asked him about a law suit commenced some years before by Josephine Forrestal, the widow, in connection with a $10,000 insurance policy of which she was the beneficiary. She had sued the company, which had refused to honor the policy on the grounds that it did not apply in cases of suicide. I wanted to know the outcome. "What makes you ask?" the attorney queried. I replied that since Forrestal's widow had been amply provided for, I was surprised that she had instituted the suit. "Oh, if you are implying that Jim Forrestal was a wealthy man," the attorney said, turning in his chair toward the magnificent view of the Battery and entrance to the harbor, "nothing could be further from the truth. If I remember correctly, Jim didn't leave much, certainly not more than a million and a half." I simply did not know what to say and so I sat there in astonished silence. At that time, the summer of 1959, I was an assistant professor earning $4,500 annually, of which I had in my pocket, for the return trip to Philadelphia, about five dollars. I marveled that anyone, let alone someone who lived and worked in New York, could regard a million and a half dollars as not "much," and once again I felt sorrow and some pity that Forrestal had had so many friends like the letter-writer and the attorney.

A long-term consequence of the Forrestal research was a determination to seek psychoanalytic training, and in 1968 I was accepted as a research (non-M.D.) candidate for training by the New York Psychoanalytic Institute, an affiliate institute of the American Psychoanalytic Association. I sometimes wonder how such training (completed in 1978), if undertaken earlier, would have affected the Forrestal book. I think it would have enabled me to probe more deeply into Forrestal's psychopathology, and to that extent I might have been more aware of his underlying depression and its various disguises, such as his compulsive work habits, sardonic and self-mocking sense of humor, heightened awareness of irony, and fatalistic outlook. I probably would have been sensitive to the role in his life of psychosexual conflicts, and less inclined to view certain problems as situational. I also would have been less dependent on psychiatric opinions, some of which, I eventually discovered, were not well informed.

Whatever the effect of psychoanalytic training might have been on the Forrestal project, the value of such training will be demonstrated, I trust, in my current work on the life and thought of Thomas Hobbes, the British political philosopher, who lived from 1588 to 1679. I need hardly emphasize the many differences between Forrestal and Hobbes, not the least of which is an extreme paucity of biographical data on Hobbes. But I also am conscious of at least one important similarity. The Forrestal venture, as mentioned earlier, may have had some relation to a friendship that was foundering, and in connection with Hobbes I have begun to think it more than coincidence that my decision to write about him was made not long after the death of a friend whose life and career were not unlike those of Hobbes in certain respects. Both Hobbes and my friend were geniuses of sorts, both thought of themselves as true scientists of politics (as distinct from political scientists who only fantasize they are scientists), both wrote a good deal that was misunderstood, and both had few doubts that even so-called civilized life was never far from the state of being "solitary, poor, nasty, brutish, and short."[3] In still another resemblance, both lived long and never married. Does the Hobbes effort, in part, reflect a wish to continue a friendship beyond the grave, to bring my friend back to life, so to speak? Does all biography tend to re-create a close relative or friend and that part of oneself that was, or is, reflected in that other self?

Having written one biography and embarked upon another, I begin to wonder.

## NOTES

[1]Arnold A. Rogow, *James Forrestal: A Study of Personality, Politics and Policy* (New York: Macmillan, 1963).

[2]Charles Francis Adams, Jr., *Charles Francis Adams: An Autobiography* (Boston: Houghton Mifflin, 1916).

[3]Thomas Hobbes, *Leviathan* (London, 1651).

# Afterword

# 16

# The Psychoanalyst's Role in the Biographer's Quest for Self-Awareness

## George Moraitis

THE INSPIRATION FOR THIS book derived from the distinct sense of discovery the authors experienced as participants in the conference held at the University of North Carolina in November 1981. The success of the conference should be credited to the participants' willingness to reveal their emotional responses, which was facilitated by a forum conducive to the free exchange of ideas and the absence of an audience other than the participants themselves. The autobiographical papers of the participants had been circulated in advance and provided the necessary background information for the discussions that took place. The conference itself was an intimate gathering. As I have observed in this and other comparable situations, the participating scholars experienced a sense of relief from the restrictions of a formal academic exchange and a feeling of camaraderie powerful enough to overcome at least some of their reservations about putting their humanity on the line along with their findings. Under the influence of psychological forces from within and forces operating as a result of the group interchange, the participants partially, and probably only temporarily, disengaged themselves from the self-imposed censorship that ordinarily governs their sense not only of what they ought to write, but what they ought to think as well. Such controls are shaped by the author's value system, as it pertains to his personal and professional sense of self. At the conference these controls were somewhat relaxed.

Through an interdisciplinary dialogue, the participants extended their thinking beyond the boundaries of their own discipline in an effort to understand and explore perceptions that cannot be accommodated within familiar schemata. In such an enterprise, scholars need an audience that can provide feedback and help them test their perceptions without danger of embarrassment or undue criticism. In my paper "A Psychoanalyst's Journey into a Historian's World,"[1] I described such an audience as the "ideal reader," who may become the author's confidant and function as a buffer between him and the larger public he will eventually face. Such a reader becomes the recipient of a wide range of conscious and unconscious perceptions that are tested on him before the author feels confident enough to present them to the public at large. Of course, conclusions reached as the result of interaction between an author and an ideal reader, or in a small group situation like our conference, could still involve self-deception, and are therefore in need of further validation by the professional group or the public. I do not expect that the sense of discovery experienced by the participants in the North Carolina conference will be reproduced by reading the proceedings or my description of the exchange. I hope, however, that readers will identify in their experiences something that resonates with the experiences and perceptions of the contributors to this volume. Such awareness might create an interest in taking part in a collaborative exchange along the lines presented here. Collaborative interdisciplinary studies in the psychological field must be experienced to be appreciated; descriptions and theoretical conceptualizations alone never suffice.

To enter into a dialogue with a psychoanalyst, a biographer must be prepared to cross the boundaries of his professional discipline. Professional disciplines represent communities, whose existence is supposed to facilitate the professional's capacity to pursue knowledge and utilize it for human needs. Such communities provide boundaries and structure that limit the scope and application of professional activities to manageable proportions. Thus all sciences select and maintain an area of endeavor that becomes their "limited" world. The individual investigator of a given discipline is supposed to operate within these limits. While the laboratory of the scientist represents the tangible boundaries of his limited world, in the human sciences there are no laboratories in the strict sense of the term. There are, however, field studies of different kinds and, more important, academic rules and a code of ethics that determine to a great extent not only what shall and shall not be investigated but also how an investigation should be carried out and reported.

Professional boundaries undergo constant change and redefinition, which may limit or extend them. Important discoveries, however, tend to redefine the boundaries of a given discipline and create new delimitations, which may involve new professional methods or new fields of endeavor.

In every discipline we can identify trends that aim to conserve the integrity of the established limitations as well as trends that aim to overthrow them. The investigator who has found the boundaries of his discipline too narrow to accommodate his individual perceptions and discoveries may seek inspiration from other sciences. Understandably, he is ambivalent about such input because it calls his professional identity and intellectual loyalty into question. It threatens the scholar's relationship to his professional community and raises often realistic fears of being penalized or ostracized. As the reader has already ascertained, all the contributors to this volume have, some enthusiatically, some more reluctantly, come to the conclusion that biographical studies are deeply affected by the biographer's humanity, and that this must be taken into account in assessing the product. As a result, they have all attempted to experience and conceptualize this input and include it, explicitly or not, in their essays. The readiness of these biographers to "go public" probably indicates diminished concern about their professional identities and the reactions of their colleagues. Instead, they have dedicated themselves to studying their subjectivity while maintaining for themselves and for their readers the necessary sense of reality.

In our post-positivistic age it does not require great courage to emphasize the subjective nature of all human perceptions. Investigators in the social and even the physical sciences have come to recognize the degree to which all observations, no matter how controlled, are shaped by our own minds. This trend is evident in the rhetoric of many scholarly publications wherein the author "admits" to the influence of his own humanity and doubts his own conclusions and theses. It is important to keep in mind, however, that such admissions do not always represent a courageous act of humility. Often they constitute a new claim to knowledge or, more accurately, self-knowledge. After attempting for decades to demonstrate their capacity to study others objectively, social scientists are now redirecting these claims in their attempt to illustrate the importance of self-knowledge and the introspection through which self-knowledge is obtained.

Psychoanalysis has contributed significantly to this intellectual climate. Despite Sigmund Freud's strong commitment to the physical sciences and his systematic efforts to locate psychoanalysis within the realm of science, psychoanalytic discoveries have inevitably directed attention not only to the subjectivity of our observations but also to our limited capacity to observe ourselves. From its inception, psychoanalysis has been identified as the science that systematically investigates subjectivity. Personal analysis facilitates an individual's capacity for introspection through the physical presence of a skilled observer. This presence is crucial in the development of the introspective function, as it provides controls and structure that protect the self-observer from deceptive and self-serving assumptions.

When introspection is resorted to as an investigative tool, the scholar may also need a skilled collaborator to provide the structure that will assist him in his introspective function in a way directly relevant to his work. I believe that such an experience could be helpful to all scholars who use introspection in their work, perhaps even those who have already undergone personal analysis. Most of the participants in the conference should be credited with accepting this basic principle and doing whatever they could to put their introspective function under the scrutiny of a collaborating psychologist.

A psychoanalytic model of collaboration, I would emphasize, does not involve procedural rigidity or restrictive rituals. Instead, I propose that the introspective work of the biographer be carried out with the help of another professional in a setting that emphasizes a free exchange of ideas between two professionals who function as experts in their own fields only. The psychoanalyst should under no circumstances attempt to intrude into the historian's function. Instead, he maintains the same respect for his collaborator's autonomy as he extends to his patients in the clinical situation.

Many biographers have been reluctant to turn to psychologists for help, for fear that resorting to psychological theories and formulations will skew the focus of their investigation into the boundless and elusive realm of internal reality. "Boundless" in the sense that it can never be fully ascertained whose internal world is really being explored—that of the observer or that of the observed—and "elusive" in the sense that it cannot be easily described in generally accepted terms. It is important for the collaborating psychoanalyst to respect the biographer's reservations and not to treat them merely as defensive tactics. The biographer cannot be assured of beneficial results in advance. The biographer's motivation for such a collaboration should be an awareness of the need for it rather than the guarantee of results.

By its nature, biography is interdisciplinary. But the interdisciplinary contact between history and psychology in biography must not be understood as the application of psychological theory to historical data. This approach has often created the impression that the biographer's work is no more than a discussion of a case history which confirms the validity of a given psychological theory. It has become increasingly evident that equipping the biographer with psychological theories is not only insufficient to help him carry out his work but often misleading. In order to convey to the reader the inner experiences of his subject, the biographer must have some perception of how his subject has affected him. Such awareness cannot be provided merely by reference to psychological theories applicable to any number of people.

During the last several years I have had the privilege of collaborating with three of the participants in the conference—the historian-biographers Carl Pletsch, Mark Schwehn, and Richard Wortman—who offered me the opportunity to exchange ideas on a more or less continuous basis for periods of months or years. My work began with Carl Pletsch, who had arrived at a similar hypothesis through his own experience. The success of that first experimental collaboration confirmed our hypotheses and provided the impetus for me to repeat the experiment with others. Pletsch persuaded his friend and colleague Mark Schwehn to try the collaboration, and Richard Wortman, who also learned of our work, expressed his own interest shortly thereafter. From these, as well as from other such collaborative efforts, I have discovered that such dialogues go well beyond a simple exchange of ideas between a psychoanalyst and a biographer. They produce complex conscious and unconscious reactions, which have permitted me to study the psychological forces operating behind scholarly activities. I have observed the process of scholarly biographical writing as a psychological phenomenon and tried to integrate it with the basic principles of psychoanalysis.

The biographer's work involves extensive study (of many years' duration), during which he develops his ideas gradually and integrates a wide range of perceptions into coherent schemata. This process involves both conscious and unconscious elements that relate directly to the biographer's perception of himself and the world. When the biographer finally presents his findings to us, he exposes the particular facts and the thesis he has consciously arrived at, as well as (even if unwittingly) his less conscious general sense of reality and values.

In entering into a collaboration with a biographer, I attempt to increase the author's self-awareness with the tacit understanding that I will observe this process, as well as affect it. In my other two papers in this volume, I offered some description and conceptualization of the effects of such a process on both the scholar and the analyst (see Chapters 3 and 6). These and subsequent experiences have reinforced my original impression of the transference nature of such phenomena. They have also reinforced my belief in their usefulness for the study of the psychological process in scholarly writing, which can provide extremely important data for the understanding of creativity. My collaborators' testimony concerning the usefulness of this enterprise for the biographer and his product appears in other parts of this anthology.

It is relatively easy to assume that the presence of transference reactions in the biographer is the result of his intense involvement with his subject. Often these phenomena are described as the biographer's identification with his subject, and pertain to the biographer's psychological need either to perceive his subject as being more or less like himself or to compare his subject with important persons in his own life. Transference phenomena are a mixed blessing for a biographer, however. They may produce intuitive perceptions of great depth and validity, but they can also be the source of major distortions and misperceptions.

In therapeutic psychoanalysis, transference phenomena are facilitated in the analytic process. The past is reexperienced in the present through the analysand's need to mold his perceptions of the analyst into preexisting schemata. Gradually, with the help of systematic interpretation of the transference, the analysand becomes aware of these schemata and is enabled to reevaluate his perceptions in a new light. Who will help the scholar in such a reevaluation? Obviously his subject cannot. It is reasonable to assume that the scholar who has been an analysand has a higher level of self-awareness and that he can put it into the service of his scholarly work. Whether he actually does so is an open question. Self-awareness is an elective process, and the most thoroughly analyzed person is subject to self-deception. Thus, if the interpretation of the transference that results from a scholar's biographical work were left to self-analysis, it would be reasonable to question its reliability, regardless of the scholar's psychological sophistication. Before the investigator can be relatively sure about the nature and effect of the transference phenomena operating during the lengthy period of biographical study, these phenomena should be examined in a controlled situation. As I have already pointed out, the collaboration does not aim to eliminate the influence of the investigator's personality upon his research—this is neither possible nor desirable. The aim is to make these influences more directly observable by bringing them into the context of a relationship with another professional, to facilitate their constructive use.

In discussing my collaboration with Carl Pletsch, I illustrated how, through utilizing the interaction with the analyst, the biographer became more conscious of the transferential aspects of his feelings toward Friedrich Nietzsche from the first dramatic interview (see Chapter 3). My first interview with Mark Schwehn was equally dramatic (see Chapter 6). I will not go into the details of these interviews again, but only point out that the collaborative situation facilitated awareness of transference phenomena concealed in apparently neutral intellectual formulations and made it possible for these two scholars to use this knowledge in their further biographical work. It is important to keep in mind that our ultimate objective was to understand the subject's personality, not the investigator's. I saw my function as helping the biographer to apply certain aspects of self-knowledge within the boundaries of his field of investigation. We were careful not to allow the process to become an open-ended exploration of the investigator's life.

Pletsch expressed open hostility toward Nietzsche, while Schwehn conveyed great admiration for Henry Adams's intellectual work. The diametrically opposite ways in which these two biographers expressed their feelings toward their subjects produced a response that placed me in opposition to their positions. I defended Nietzsche against Pletsch's accusations and attempted to debunk Schwehn's view of Adams by focusing on his psychopathology during my first reading of *The Education of Henry Adams*. I am sure such interactions between two collaborators are not accidental. They represent efforts to disrupt an intense and disturbing negative or positive overidentification of the biographer with his subject. This is a disruption that is intuitively felt as necessary.

Gradually I recognized that many biographers are concerned about the intensity of the bond between themselves and their subject. This

became particularly evident at the conference, where all the participants (with one exception) openly expressed such concerns in one
form or another. In reviewing the papers of the contributors and
reflecting on my recollections of the conference, I realized the degree
to which I attempted to respond to each participant as if he were my
collaborator within the boundaries of the methodological approach I
have already described.

To illustrate to the reader something of my approach, I shall attempt to discuss these papers as if they were opening statements of
scholars beginning a collaborative interaction with a psychoanalyst.
In doing so, I shall focus on these papers to the exclusion of other
material and publications pertaining to these scholars' work. My discussion is not intended to provide a critique of the scholar's intellectual position, but to illustrate an interactional process as it pertains to
the methodological approach I have referred to. Of course the scholars would not agree with all my observations and comments; they
might provide us with responses of their own. In a publication such
as this, however, it is impossible to provide a complete account of the
exchanges between the collaborators. I shall merely attempt to illustrate which type of psychoanalytic response is likely to catalyze a
process that, it is hoped, will increase the biographer's self-awareness
as it pertains to his creativity.

The subject of the conference was the psychology of the biographer, not biography itself. Autobiographical statements were expected from all participants, and this expectation met with a wide
variety of responses, from excitement to discomfort. The request
made of the participants is not inconsistent with contemporary trends
in scholarly writing. Recently, biographers have joined other scholars
in recognizing the influence of their own psyches in shaping their
ideas and conclusions. Vignettes, confessions, and elaborations along
these lines have already appeared in a number of publications.[2] The
better known the biographer, the more interested readers are in such
self-revelations. Despite their appeal, however, such public statements do not provide the evidence needed for a truely systematic
study of the question of subjectivity in scholarly activity. Ironically, in
attempting to study subjectivity objectively, the investigator is bound
to violate his premise that all observations are shaped by the observer's own mind. If, on the other hand, the question is approached
from the standpoint of the investigator's own subjective perceptions,

conclusions take the form of confessions and become suspect of self-deception.

Richard Lebeaux's paper, "Thoreau's Lives, Lebeaux's Lives" (Chapter 11), presents a good example of a biographer who can talk eloquently about his personal feelings toward his subject, with great candor, considerable detail, and little evidence of discomfort. Lebeaux sees parallels between himself and Henry David Thoreau on the level of personal experiences, values, attitudes, modes of expression, etc. He points up these parallels by making remarkable self-revelations and persuasive psychological formulations. There is a good deal more Lebeaux than Thoreau in the paper, but we may suppose this is because the author wishes to illustrate his identification with his subject. Lebeaux has evidently given a good deal of thought to his relationship with his subject and has observed himself very closely over a number of years. His "dialogues" with Thoreau, included in the conference version of his paper, represent a method of psychological investigation directly relevant to his work. The resolution described in the last pages of his paper conveys a sense of closure, with the author relatively free of conflict and ready to undertake a new creative task. When confronted with such a high level of conviction, a collaborating psychoanalyst should refrain from questioning the scholar's findings and insights. Some biographers believe they have a good deal of self-knowledge, and sometimes for very good reason. The collaborating psychoanalyst should avoid playing the devil's advocate with the biographer's perceptions of himself and offering "wild analysis" in place of the author's self-analytic observations. Nothing can be more unproductive than a competitive intellectual exchange in either the historical or the psychological domain.

The intervention of the analyst is effective only when desired by his collaborator. Such a wish does not have to be expressed formally or explicitly. It is conveyed through the form in which ideas are presented, either verbally or in writing. When presented by the biographer, rough drafts, unfinished papers, and verbal reports suggest the author's willingness to rethink his theses, an attitude conducive to a collaborative exchange. Already published papers or papers submitted for publication bespeak the author's high confidence in them and properly discourage a truly collaborative exchange. Lebeaux's paper struck me as the scholar's finished product. In my recollection of the verbal interaction at the conference, however, I had the definite impression that Lebeaux did not want closure, but that he clearly desired a dialogue with the other participants. Although I am not certain of what I said at the time, I can easily describe my thoughts about his paper as they pertain to the response of a collaborating psychoanalyst in such a situation.

I assumed, perhaps erroneously, that the author perceived himself to have formed a symbiotic "merger" with his subject. This close identification was not only comfortable but also enjoyable for the author. He described periodic disruptions of the merger, expecially when he was under other influences, such as arose in his relationship to women and with the ideas of Erik Erikson, who served as a "collaborator" of sorts through his writings. For the most part, it seems, Lebeaux experiences the merger with Thoreau as a useful tool for his work; therefore he welcomes it and, in a sense, is proud of it. As I will explain, I am skeptical of such assumptions. For the time being, I note Lebeaux's high level of conscious awareness of his supposed close identification with his subject. Given this fact, I wonder-How genuinely symbiotic is this relationship? Or, to put it differently, how can he observe himself in this relationship so clearly if he is indeed that close? Questions like this cannot be answered directly. The answer would gradually evolve in the course of a collaborative process, as the psychoanalytic collaborator becomes the author's special reader.

With scholars who are willing to speak about themselves and their personal lives, the collaboration can take the form of a therapeutic process. When the biographer assumes that talking about himself is no different from talking about his subject, it is clear that a state of merger indeed exists in the biographer's mind between himself and his subject. It is the psychoanalytic collaborator's responsibility to bring this to the attention of the scholar and engage him in a process that will, it is hoped, sharpen the distinction between self and subject. Not having collaborated with Richard Lebeaux, I am in no position to draw any conclusions about his relationship with Thoreau. My impression from the conference is that the issue to be addressed is not the existence of such a merger but his contention that such a close identification is indeed a reliable instrument of scholarly investigation.

Joseph Wall's paper—focused on Andrew Carnegie (Chapter 10)—represents, in some respects, a diametrically opposite approach to Lebeaux's. Wall claims to have been "appalled by most psychohistory" and intrigued but disturbed by the questions raised by the conference conveners. He emphasizes that none of his subjects has been of his own choosing. Although he makes few personal revelations in his paper, his statement seems candid and addresses the key issues of a scholarly biography directly. Obviously, Wall is not jumping at the opportunity to "put the 'auto' into his biography,"* but he is an honest investigator ready to listen and reconsider his positions. He identifies himself as an entrepreneurial biographer, But I sensed an apologetic attitude about his choice of subject in both his paper and his communications at the conference. Wall apparently feels some discomfort about his choice for, unlike the intellectual subjects of some of the biographers, Wall's subjects did not produce powerful and original ideas. For him, as for them, introspection did not play a very important role in his conscious thinking, and perhaps in his writing. Wall has primarily studied men of action such as Andrew Carnegie and Alfred I. duPont, not thinkers. As the biographer of extrospective rather than introspective people, perhaps he experiences the desire to tune into his subject's perceptions and motives. Before rushing to criticize Wall for his relative lack of introspection, however, it is important to scrutinize our own value system, which reveres introspection as the primary instrument of knowledge and growth.

When the observer's attention is directed inward, his aim is not necessarily the altruistic pursuit of knowledge and the high ideal of emotional maturity. Introspection is also an instrument of adaptation, particularly effective for individuals and cultures faced with rigid external realities they lack the capacity to alter. Under such circumstances, the turn inward provides a sense of control and mastery in the face of helplessness. When a painful reality cannot be altered, changing the internal perceptions of that reality facilitates a much-needed, although temporary, sense of mastery and provides hope for survival. There is, of course, a price to be paid: introspection for adaptive purposes foments the development of a value system that deemphasizes action and the importance of external reality. Individuals traumatized by prolonged exposure to painful and rigid external realities, which have rendered them helpless or ineffective, could develop a resistance to introspection when, at some later point, they achieve a degree of liberation through outwardly directed activity. To

---

*The original title of Wall's essay was "Putting the Auto- into Biography: Andrew Carnegie and I."

them, introspection may evoke a repetition of past impotence, a regression into passivity to pursue new insights. For such persons, extrospection is more natural because it represents eagerness to experience something new and the freedom to take outwardly directed action.

Few readers of biographies of Carnegie, duPont, Henry Ford, and other self-made men expect a version of their hero's life like *Citizen Kane*. The biographer who is in tune with his prospective readers will be sensitive to their expectations and present whatever introspective data are available by taking into account the specific meaning introspection in the minds of his subject and his readers. In order to do so, he must come to terms with his own dilemma about the use of introspection.

Despite what he portrays as a rather unfortunate beginning of his collaborative experience with the psychologist, Joseph Wall displayed a remarkable capacity to persist in the experiment and benefit from it. An effort to help such a scholar increase his awareness of his subject's internal life will probably require some degree of exploration of the biographer's own humanity. It seems that Wall took important steps in this direction. Then collaborating with such a scholar, a psychoanalyst must keep in mind that it is not sufficient to inform the scholar of the importance of introspection in his investigative work by examples or other means. Even more crucial is the analyst's capacity to appreciate the meaning of introspection for his particular collaborator and project, and, when possible, to demonstrate that introspective data are sometimes collected and used without the investigator's awareness of their true nature.

I have described Lebeaux and Wall as two biographers with opposing attitudes toward the use of psychological insights in their work. The one eager and eloquent, the other reluctant and reserved. Yet both are willing to look deeper into themselves for a better understanding of the nature of their involvement with their subjects. Such fully conscious and intellectually honest intentions, however, are subject to unconscious opposition that is bound to censor their perceptions and the conclusions they will reach. I have attempted to illustrate that the work of the psychoanalytic collaborator should aim to bring this censorship to consciousness and broaden, to whatever extent possible, the biographer's awareness of its effect on the product. In doing so, the psychoanalyst refuses to take at face value the self-revelations the biographer makes, yet carefully avoids being critical and didactic when faced with reservations and criticism. The scholar's resistance to psychological insight is not necessarily or exclusively a manifestation of neurotic conflict. More probably, such resistances spring from the scholar's intuitive need to protect his scholarly investigation from input that would threaten the boundaries of his investigation and the integrity of his product. A collaborating analyst should learn to recognize and respect these boundaries and the scholar's informed decisions about where to draw them.

Isaac Newton's biographer, Richard Westfall, and Joseph Stalin's biographer, Robert Tucker, represent another interesting pair of opposites in their affective responses toward their subjects (see Chapter 8 and 12, respectively). Westfall looks up to Newton as an ideal beyond reach. Tucker loathes Stalin as "the most vicious individual ever to wield power." Westfall defends Newton from the "dark" shadows one previous biographer threw over him. Tucker exposes Stalin to make sure the reader is not deceived by the villain's lies and rhetoric. In doing so, both place themselves at considerable distance from their subjects. Westfall contends that "we deal with figures of major importance, figures who exceed us, their biographers, in intellectual capacity . . . [and] who must in the end elude [us]." Tucker states that his "loathing has grown" as the "bottomless depth" of his subject's villainy became clearer to him.

In other words, in both situations it seems that after a long, systematic study of their subjects, these two investigators experience themselves at a greater distance from their subjects. Newton receded into a still larger world of knowledge and wisdom, while Stalin sank deeper into the pit of villainy. I am sure both biographers can persuasively claim that this emotional response is based on their increased understanding of their subjects and indisputable facts. Newton was indeed a great mind, perhaps greater than the biographer originally thought; Stalin was beyond doubt extremely villainous. A more psychological examination of this phenomenon, however, may lead us in a different direction. Powerful affects are not necessarily or only the product of knowledge and discovery. More often they are an obstacle to it. The strong sense of idealization and the overwhelming sense of moral indignation, even when logically understandable, could be in the service of a psychologically defensive purpose in the scholar's work. It is the psychoanalytic collaborator's responsibility to explore such possibilities, especially, if the scholar believes his affective response has brought his investigation to a premature and predictable closure (which was not the case with Tucker or Westfall).

In his paper "Newton and the Biographer," Westfall states that he managed to conceal from himself something important about his reaction to his subject until the end of his biographical work of twenty years. His realization of this coincided with his writing the preface to his book (a short time before the conference in North Carolina). He felt that Newton had become "a mystery to me," that "he had receded from me, that I knew him less than I had at the beginning."

A statement of this sort can be taken in a number of ways. It could represent a rhetorical device designed to remind the reader that the more we know, the more we realize how little we know. One might, then, raise a question about the finished product and wonder if the author intended to go back to the drawing board. Yet Westfall does not seem to be apologetic about his work. On the contrary, he stands behind his conclusions and defends them. In my opinion, the biographer's statement pertains more to himself than to Newton. Newton had receded from him because the work is finished. Westfall is in a state of mourning over such a tremendous loss. Unconsciously, perhaps, he might like to begin again, but not because he disavows his own findings and conclusions. He simply wishes to prolong his association with Newton, who in twenty years must have become a dear companion. All these years the biographer kept his personal feelings in abeyance to protect his work from excessive influences of psychological forces operating within his own psyche. Now he reveals to us that "the ultimate problem of studying Newton lies in his other activities"—alchemy and theology. It is toward these activities that the author's powerful feelings and personal system of values now incline. Probably it was in this domain that the biographer had to make the crucial distinction between himself and Newton, in order to complete his work. After this distinction was made and maintained and the work was brought to completion, the biographer was bound to experience his subject as receding. Now he relinquishes, partially at least, his claim on Newton as a territorial possession and gives him back to the world. At the same time he can experience a surge of interest in Newton's "other activities." As Westfall pronounces himself a "Presbyterian elder" and emotionally reaffirms his system of values and beliefs, he gives to the reader a powerful sense that he has returned home proud, although sad, from a productive and enriching twenty years' journey. In the process he learned not only "a thing or two about Newton," but also a good deal about himself.

There is no such sense of closure in Robert Tucker's papers. Tucker, with whom I have had the privilege of several lengthy conversations following the conference, reveals his feelings toward his subject at the height of his scholarly investigation, not at the end of it. He thus invites an examination of these feelings not as a historical retrospective but in connection with a complex methodological issue that any biographer of a historical figure like Stalin will inevitably have to tackle.

A tyrant like Stalin, who systematically destroyed millions of people with no sign of discomfort, while boasting about his own greatness, is easy to hate. His cynicism provokes moral indignation in the investigator and demands some form of expression. The biographer, however, must resist the temptation to condemn his subject or risk failing to provide a full understanding of his subject's villainy. For condemnation provides no explanation. Ascertaining the presence of evil inevitably leads to a moralistic closure. Tucker is well aware of this.

In order to avoid such closure and the personal sense of moral indignation that produces it, political biographers have often turned their attention to the historical forces and circumstances in which the tyrant operated. By doing so they tend to blunt their own rage in the belief that, for example, had Stalin not appeared, somebody else would have acted in much the same way he did. This approach, at its extreme, shifts the biographer's attention away from his subject, into a broad and elusive historical context.

Tucker has refused to take this direction. Instead, he has attempted to delve deeper into his subject's personality, primarily through the use of the psychological writings of Karen Horney. The biographer's familiarity with these theories for more than forty years, in combination with his conviction in them, made an impression on me when I first read his paper. If Horney has indeed persuaded the biographer about the psychological profile of his subject, however, how can we explain the intensity of his emotional response? Why is he still so angry?

The investigator who has really been persuaded of the psychological nature of his subject's behavior is bound to deemphasize his evilness and come to better terms with his own sense of rage and indignation. Psychological interpretations, when effective, have a disarming effect, because they alleviate the investigator's anxiety by providing a reasonable and plausible link between observable phenomena and human nature as we know it. A psychological explanation, no matter how persuasive, does not of course constitute an excuse or justification for a given act, yet it places the observer in a position to feel less disturbed by what he observes and capable of avoiding the dangerous path of condemning. At the conference it was my impression that the psychological framework Horney's theories had provided for Stalin's biographer was in need of reinforcement, in the form of a new idea or experience. At the time I took the biographer's *cherchez la femme* metaphor to mean that there was another woman hidden behind Karen Horney whom we should search for. At first we directed our attention to Tucker's experiences in Moscow, when Stalin refused for many years to grant an exit visa to his wife. The incident, as described by Tucker, gave me the impression of a very personal action of a powerful ruler, directed toward a few politically powerless women and their husbands. I admired the courage of both of them to stand up against the wishes of a ruthless and omnipotent tyrant. There is a strong romantic element in this story, whose happy ending is in direct contrast to the experience of millions of others. It must have given the biographer (and his wife) a sense of mastery or victory. By standing up they had not only exposed the tyrant's wickedness, they had also defeated him.

In the process Tucker was persuaded of the personal nature of Stalin's persecutory actions. If Stalin's personal feelings could be aroused by such a trivial issue as granting exit visas to a few Russian women who married foreign diplomats, it would be easy to presume how extremely more personally he must have experienced any suspected opposition and abandonment by those who surrounded him in his political and family life. Accordingly, the persecutions, tortures, and executions of his victims were ordered by Stalin in the spirit of revenge for mostly imagined betrayals and abandonments.

As Tucker's marriage and personal happiness were some time ago in the hands of Stalin, so Stalin's place in history is now in the hands of his biographers. If Tucker wants revenge, he can have it. There is nothing further from this scholar's mind, I am sure, than revenge. In the writing of a scholarly biography, personal motives are superseded by the scholar's sense of professional identity and values that compel him to reveal the facts and their meaning to whatever extent possible. Tucker, as a dedicated scholar, is firmly committed to intellectual honesty and discovery. This commitment is further reinforced by an increased sense of self-awareness, as evidenced in his autobiographical paper. As I have pointed out elsewhere, the investigator cannot eliminate the influence of his personality on his research; this is neither possible nor desirable. The investigator's increased self-awareness, however, facilitates the constructive use of such influences in his writings.

Tucker exposes Stalin's duplicity and villainy so that his subject will not escape the judgment of history under the notion that he was a helpless actor operating under the influence of the historical forces and realities of his time. He identifies Stalin's narcissistic rage as a basic motive behind his behavior, but, even more important, he emphasizes that Stalin's behavior was motivated by passions not by reason. Thus, Tucker disputes the notion that his subject's behavior was that of a "pragmatist" who was "programmed" to the doctrines of Marx and Lenin. Tucker's approach aims at making his subject directly responsible for his behavior by taking away the defensive use of the historical process as an excuse for his villainous actions. However, in his emphasis on justice and responsibility, certain issues arise pertaining to the psychological understanding of his subject and to the place of psychological theories as explanatory propositions in scholarly biography.

Psychological understanding pertains to the search for the unique in human behavior, for that which arises from the individual's private perception and values. In order to grasp the infinite multiplicity of the phenomena observed, the investigator must attempt to make them coherent through the use of logic, reason, and scientific theories. Psychological theories, however, do not represent fundamental truths and ought to be flexible. They are strictly investigative tools, whose influence should be toned down if they interfere with the investigator's capacity to perceive the unique nature of his subject's internal world. To achieve this, the investigator must strive temporarily to set aside not only dominant psychological and scientific theories but personal feelings, memories, and moral convictions. The understanding of another person's sense of reality requires temporarily silencing the investigator's own sense of reality, in order to allow for the registration of the input coming out of the study of the subject's activities and ideas. Stalin apparently persuaded himself that fabricating stories of treason, that killing or torturing and destroying the lives of millions of people, was all for the good of the party and the country, and made him a hero and savior. Naturally, this stance impresses the biographer as irrational and immoral. Yet psychological understanding of this perspective requires that the investigator give his subject the opportunity to persuade him of the validity of his perceptions. Such a temporary surrender to the imagination and private logic of a person like Stalin must of necessity be extremely frightening and repulsive. It requires the capacity to tolerate the regressive perceptions of a primitive individual who lost touch with the common man's intellectual and affective sense of reality.

Of course, in due time the investigator will assess the input generated from such a "surrender" and integrate it into coherent schemata. He will, however, do that under conditions optimally conducive to a reflective examination of the introspective data available. Tucker's earlier experiences in Moscow must have left a memory of entrapment that is bound to play some role in the biographer's anger toward his subject. Such affects are usually an indication that the scholar has placed himself too close to his subject and feels the need for some distance in order to pursue his work.

In my discussions with Robert Tucker since the conference, we have addressed this issue; our dialogue is still in process. I have been persuaded that he shows an intuitive perceptiveness when he draws our attention to Karen Horney at the beginning of his paper in order to explain his feelings about his subject. Karen Horney is not merely a metaphor for somebody else. The power of her ideas has had a pivotal effect on Stalin's biographer. If we assume that the biographer learned something about himself from Karen Horney, his expectation to learn something from her about his subject is understandable. In a sense Karen Horney has been Tucker's collaborator for many years. When I realized how I underestimated her importance at the North Carolina conference, I came to appreciate my competitive feelings toward Tucker's "other collaborator." The psychoanalyst's capacity to recognize his own responses is a crucial factor in the collaborative process. It may very well determine whether or not he will become the scholar's special reader.

Turning to Samuel Baron's paper, "My Life with G. V. Plekhanov" (Chapter 9), one encounters a marvelous historical retrospective from a senior scholar, looking back on his biographical work. He traces the origins of his interest in Plekhanov, the writing of Plekhanov's biography, and the continual evidence of Plekhanov's influence on his thinking long after the biography was published. Although Baron provides few personal vignettes in his paper, he persuasively describes how he came to realize the degree to which he avoided personality issues in thinking and writing about his subject, and how he had rationalized his decision to write "a dispassionate account" of Plekhanov's life and activities. When one reader of his *Plekhanov* was touched to tears by his biography, Baron reacted with surprise because he apparently had no awareness of the emotional impact of his work upon his readers.

Evidently Baron has come a long way since then. His paper reveals a high level of self-awareness, which has enabled him to discover aspects of Plekhanov's personality that were unavailable to him before, such as his military ethos, elitist stance, and abrasive, egocentric character. Obviously Plekhanov is no longer an idealized figure for his biographer, who describes him at the end of his paper as a "self-isolated" man whose "aspirations were frustrated, [who] was politically ineffective, and [who] ended up a general without an army." Baron is perhaps one of the last soldiers to desert the Plekhanov "army" and declare his independence from him.

If Baron's paper is approached as the opening statement of a collaborative exchange, its intensely retrospective character raises some important questions. As a senior scholar, the author shares the fruits of his experiences in biography with others and reminds them of the need for self-awareness and introspection. Baron, however, does not limit himself to the didactic and anecdotal. He obviously wants something important from this experience, important enough to experience collaboration himself, organize a conference, and edit the present volume. His eagerness to retrospect and introspect cannot be explained as a result of having recently completed the biographical work, as seems to have been the case with the biographer of Newton. In Baron's perception, Plekhanov does not recede; on the contrary, the biographer can see his subject more clearly. The idealization has come to an end, and the question for a psychoanalytic collaborator to raise is-What will take its place?

Perhaps one of the most frightening aspects of the biographer's realization that he has identified with his subject is a concern that he has placed himself on a course that will force him to share his subject's destiny. Baron is not prepared to follow Plekhanov, however. With versatility, self-awareness, and hard work he breaks new ground in his professional activities and becomes a pioneer in the field of the psychology of the biographer—behavior that probably would have been anathema to Plekhanov. It is not Plekhanov that Baron now wants to write about. His subject is the biographical and autobiographical aspects of the psychology of the scholar.

As we attempted to put this volume together, I sensed a relatively high level of tension between myself and the two editors of this volume. I did some introspection in regard to this and came to realize that despite the high level of mutual respect and admiration between us, a subtle competitive element had entered into our relationship. The specific issue was the question of who was going to write about the participants and in what form. I insisted on writing this psychological reading of the papers while Professor Baron thought his introduction would suffice. After considerable discussion we finally decided to do both. He opened the discussion; I am closing it. It seems that in writing about the participants in the conference as a collaborative effort, it was hard to maintain the rule that each collaborator act as an expert in his own field only. Inevitably there was an overlap that made it difficult to maintain the boundaries of the methodological approach I have recommended. When these boundaries could not be maintained, competitive tensions emerged that produced tension in the collaborative process. Writing, especially scholarly writing, is a distinctly solitary activity, during which an author must maintain the highest possible level of autonomy. Co-authorship is always problematic, especially when it comes to describing an experience that is conceptually complex and emotionally charged. The contributors to this volume resolved these issues with relative ease, due to their determination to sacrifice some degree of their autonomy in order to present a truly interdisciplinary dialogue.

In this regard, reading the papers of Carl Pletsch, Mark Schwehn, and Richard Wortman has been a particularly gratifying experience for me. They reflect the mutual feelings of appreciation and friendship that the collaborative experience has generated. All of us have tried hard to convey not only the intellectual content of our exchange and its effect on our development as thinkers and authors, but also something of the affective tone and sense of personal communication on which the whole effort is based. The consistency with which these affects appear in all the collaborations I have experienced so far, and the fact that they are sustained for long periods of time, indicate that they constitute an essential part of the collaborative process. This assumption has been further confirmed by observations made at the conference, where the affective response of all the participants closely resembled the sense of camaraderie and discovery already familiar to me in the one-to-one collaborative situation.

It is now some eight years since my collaborative work with Carl Pletsch began, and more than six since my first meeting with Mark Schwehn. My recent rereading of their conference papers made me realize the opportunity they provided for a follow-up study of the experience. This retrospective view of the collaboration can provide some important clues to how the participants integrated this experience into or isolated it from their work, and how they dealt with the affects and self-awareness generated. These two papers show that both biographers maintain a highly positive memory of the application of this method to their work and are eager to persuade their colleagues to repeat the experiment. They give no indication, however, that they intend to reapply the method themselves in the near or distant future. For them, it seems, the collaboration is part of the past. It brought them to a certain level of self-awareness that, according to Schwehn, "enabled me to learn more about myself in the course of learning more about my subject and to learn more about my subject in the course of learning more about myself." Any further learning of the kind apparently will be pursued by other means.

Pletsch's position is comparable. In the version of his paper presented at the conference, he made a clear distinction between past and present by utilizing two typefaces. In one typeface, the author of 1977 describes what he experienced the year before. In the other, the author of 1981 looks back at the "psychological skeleton" of his own "old self-image as an author" and cannot identify with it. Anticipating my reaction, Pletsch accurately predicted that I would attempt to make something of his dramatic statement that in rereading his autobiographical notes on our collaboration, "I see and experience myself as an author then, whereas reading my finished thesis and published work, I find myself receding as an author and emerging as another reader." He has, in a sense, disavowed his old self as a biographer. Apparently, he is in the process of assuming a new sense of his professional self as an author, which he will probably reveal in due time in the finished manuscript of Nietzsche's biography. He amply credits the collaboration with having provided "leverage for building another stage onto my writing about Nietzsche" but has requested no new contacts or feedback from his old collaborator.

The experienced psychoanalyst will feel tempted to connect these observations to the post-termination phase in clinical psychoanalysis,

during which elements of the transference are still active. Considerable time is required before they can be resolved. The post-termination period in clinical psychoanalysis is a period of integration and
consolidation, during which new input from the analyst is avoided
because it could precipitate a regressive episode through the reawakening of transference expectations. Despite some possible similarities, I am reluctant to draw a direct parallel between the post-
termination phase of clinical psychoanalysis and the scholar's attitude
following a successful collaboration. There was ittle evidence of regression during the collaborative exchange to justify such an assumption. I am inclined to compare the scholar's reaction at the end of the
collaboration to that of a post-traumatic period.

Self-awareness is always traumatic because it involves the recognition of the illusionary nature of cherished perceptions and beliefs.
Something must be torn down before anything really new can be
built. Inevitably, pain will be experienced. The intensity of the pain
will be proportionate to the quantity and speed with which new input
is registered. The traumatic effect of such input will be counteracted
through the soothing sense of discovery and the feelings of camaraderie generated. We can assume that the more intense the pain the
stronger the elation and excitement of discovery will be. Understandably, the biographer will carry a disproportionately heavy burden of
trauma and pain. It is primarily his conviction and perceptions that
will be challenged. The psychoanalytic collaborator should expect to
be aware of his partner's discomfort and be in a position to appreciate
the traumatic nature of the process involved.

Schwehn points directly to this when he candidly admits: "I was,
up to a point, seeking to protect myself, and I often resisted our
collaborative investigations by finding excuses for postponing our
sessions. As a result of this resistance, the timing of our meetings was
highly irregular." The psychoanalyst's tact and awareness of the
scholar's sensitivities can make an unavoidably painful process more
tolerable. It is quite important to respect the scholar's wishes with
respect to the regularity and frequency of sessions, and not to interpret delays or postponements as violations of the methodological
rules and procedures. Creativity is always episodic, and so is the
capacity to receive and utilize new stimuli and knowledge. The psychoanalyst should respect his collaborator's need to distance himself
from the process from time to time and avoid turning it into a continual confrontation. It is up to the biographer to decide how he will
obtain the psychological knowledge and self-awareness needed to

master his passionate feelings toward his subject. Perhaps the collaborative experience sets in motion an internal process that can be continued without the presence of the psychoanalytic collaborator.

Not all collaborations involve the mastery of the biographer's passionate feelings toward his subject. My collaboration with Richard Wortman is a good example of that. In contrast to the other two collaborators, he disclaimed any intent to write a biography, and even refused to identify a specific subject of investigation. At the beginning of our work I felt distinctly uncomfortable about this lack of focus, but decided to remain within the boundaries of the methodological structure that respects the historian's choice or lack of choice of a specific focus. We started with Leo Tolstoi's *Childhood,* a beautifully written autobiographical novel, and went on to read *Boyhood* and *Youth.* We also read "The Death of Ivan Ilyich," *Resurrection, The Kreutzer Sonata,* and other works by Tolstoi. Inevitably our attention was directed to the author; and, for a while, despite my collaborator's disclaimer, I thought he was contemplating a biographical study of Tolstoi. My suspicion was reinforced when he shifted the focus to Tolstoi's autobiographical writings, such as his diaries, *The Confession,* and *What Then Must We Do?* We both worked hard to interpret these texts and extract from them whatever we could about the author's internal struggles. It gradually became apparent, however, that Tolstoi was by no means the subject Wortman had in mind.

We have continued our journey into Russian literature, reading Nikolai Gogol, Nikolai Chernyshevskii, Fyodor Dostoyevsky, Maxim Gorkii, V. I. Lenin, and others. In our study of the Russian intelligentsia, we have tried to identify the psychological forces that affected these authors' creative products. To some extent we have explored their personalities, but we have speculated more systematically about the psychological forces operative within their cultural world. Some of the work was done by exchanging tapes, but we have maintained personal contact whenever possible. Since the collaboration has not yet been concluded, I can only offer a tentative psychological formulation about the nature of this long exchange.

In his paper Wortman described our exchanges as "absorbing and informative conversations" that have been "more a way to raise and consider new approaches and ideas than a path to a particular truth." He refers to the experience of "seeing a text anew" and having to "reconsider my initial view of its historical significance."

It should be kept in mind that my collaboator was rereading the texts while I was reading them for the first time. He approached them from the position of an informed reader while I was trying to feel my way into the texts without background information and, for the most part, without any previous exposure. I was not reluctant to reveal to Wortman my reactions to the texts or the ideas I developed after reading them. I am sure some of my observations were penetrating and meaningful to him, while others were less so. But when I read two articles he wrote during the course of our work, one on Tolstoi and the other on the Russian autocracy, I realized how few of the ideas generated by our exchange my collaboator had actually utilized in his writings. It was evident that he had not "plunged into subjectivity," and although our findings fascinated him, he did not trust them enough to include them directly in his writings.

In retrospect, I realize that my objective in this collaboration had been to facilitate Wortman's capacity to choose and "fall in love with" a subject. However, this was not what he actually wanted from me; he had been in search of a more refined method of historical investigation, not a specific subject, biographical or otherwise. My collaborator observed my psychological approach in order to enrich his own historical methodology by learning to take into account the psychological forces in the individuals and culture he studies. My forthrightness in presenting my responses and ideas provided him the opportunity to identify with my function as a psychoanalytic reader and, to an extent, incorporate this into his own method of reading. When our collaboration began, Wortman was intensely distressed at having been denied entrance into the USSR to continue studying the archives on which much of his research depended. These external circumstances may have reinforced whatever internal need he was experiencing for a modification of his method. The void created by the absence of archival data was filled by a psychological approach that enabled him to "see the [old, familiar] texts anew." We often had the sense of discovery, and our friendship and mutual respect have grown with time. We are still collaborating, although our work has become "occasional," given the geographical distance now between us. There has been no sense of closure or post-collaborative period yet. Also, there has been little if any confrontation, for most of the discussion has focused on the texts rather than more personal perceptions and convictions.

The emphasis on reading evident in my work with Richard Wortman provides the opportunity to discuss the reading process as a psychological function. Of course, reading assignments are indispensable because they provide the necessary boundaries and internal structure of the collaborative method. By focusing on a given text, the two collaborators avoid compromising their scholarly aims and entering into a therapeutic exchange. These assignments are not accidentally chosen. In the beginning of my collaboration with Carl Pletsch, he insistently avoided assigning any material from Nietzsche, proposing instead that we focus on Otto von Bismarck and the German nationalistic movement for which Nietzsche had so much contempt. I perceived his suggestion as resistance, an indication of his negative transference to Nietzsche. Mark Schwehn's first assignment was the novel *Esther*, which Henry Adams had published under a pseudonym so that nobody would "profane" it. Schwehn had not even mentioned this book in his dissertation, perhaps in compliance with Adams's wish. More important, however, by excluding *Esther*, he was trying to protect his work from transference reverberations, a protection he did not feel the need for in the presence of the psychoanalyst-collaborator.

To report such observations about my collaborators and myself, however, does not suffice to describe the psychological forces involved in a collaborative exchange. The systematic study of written material is an essential part of the psychoanalyst's work when it extends into interdisciplinary studies. The lack of a generally acceptable psychoanalytic psychology of the writing-reading process represents a fundamental limitation that must be addressed. It is no accident that the writing process has not been studied in psychoanalysis in a way comparable to the study of oral communication. To facilitate the exploration of his patient's internal world, the analyst not only emphasizes oral communication, but also invites his patient to make a conscious effort not to censor his associations. Written material, especially scholarly productions, has been rigorously censored, and, therefore, when viewed as psychoanalytic data, appears unsuitable for investigation. This is particularly true when the writings do not contain biographical information. Yet, although psychoanalysts do not utilize written material in the clinical situation, in their professional life psychoanalysts have made extensive use of written communications. Historically speaking, it was Freud's writings that established psychoanalysis as a scholarly discipline, not his therapeutic successes. The psychoanalytic community puts a high value on authorship. Although analysts often claim that their professional thinking is basically shaped by direct observations made in the clinical situation, there is a good deal of evidence that the reverse is also true. Ideas and concepts communicated through scholarly publications significantly affect how psychoanalytic data are observed, collected, and evaluated in the clinical situation. Scholarly exchange is a major avenue to theory formation, and scholars' dialogues are conducted primarily in writing. The psychoanalyst is no exception. To keep faith with the introspective nature of his work, however, the psychoanalyst cannot simply utilize the writing-reading process as other scholars do, he must also examine it introspectively. Introspective examination of the reading-writing process is needed not simply to provide assistance to other scholars in their efforts to study a given document. More important, it is needed to understand the evolution of psychoanalytic thought, an evolution that has been both reflected in and precipitated by the writing-reading process. The role of introspection is as important for the psychoanalyst in his professional reading and writing as it is in listening and interpreting in the clinical situation. Both functions are integral parts of his professional activity.

In conceptualizing the writing-reading process, I compare the interaction between author and reader to the dialogue between speaker and listener. Oral communications are characterized by repetitions, which provide the listener with many opportunities to perceive the themes contained in the speaker's presentations. The cycles evident in orally expressed thoughts may be brief, occuring rapidly—as we observe them in obsessive individuals—or longer, occuring slowly, with variations in content and affect. They can be identified, however, by the listener's "free-floating" attention. Free-floating attention seldom suffices in reading; indeed, if attempted, it usually constitutes bad reading. In dealing with well-organized written material, we are presented with a thinking process that has distinct linear qualities, with few repetitions of ideas and images. In order to keep pace with the author, the reader must invest considerable effort. Sometimes such an investment is needed in order to integrate a novelty contained in just a few lines of written material.

Logical reasoning and disciplined imagination are the two main mental functions exercised by readers in their efforts to master the input derived from reading. Both functions can be stimulated easily, but they can also be interfered with by intense stimulation and the strength of the elements transferred to the reading material from the reader's psyche. In order to maintain a harmonious balance between logic and imagination, the reader has to regulate both the external and internal input.

The first reading of a book that challenges the reader's self-perception and disturbs his notions about the universe is likely to arouse resistances that press him to bypass conscious awareness of the novelty that he is unprepared to deal with. Under such circumstances, imagination provides temporary connections that enable the reader to maintain his attention and achieve some sense of continuity and gratification at the expense of better understanding. The psychologically sophisticated reader, however, will surrender to the author's imagination and not to his own. Only in this way can empathic communication between author and reader allow the reader to read not only the lines but between the lines as well. Readers who simply surrender to their own imagination always read the same book, no matter what the text.

I believe that very little reading actually takes place during the first reading of a book. Apprehension requires more than one reading; this allows the necessary time and effort for the slower-moving logical reasoning to enter more fully into the process, to provide more structure and discipline to the work of the imagination. Multiple readings more closely resemble a dialogue between author and reader, the extent of which depends directly on the ideas and themes that evolve from the process. This dialogue is the attempt to bring the ideas of the author and the reader into some form of synthesis that will do justice to both.

Authors do not provide us with free associations. On the contrary, they make deliberate and systematic efforts to edit the material and to organize it so as to reflect an image of man and the universe that serves a conscious purpose and goal. Their conscious intent is to report their perceptions of external or internal reality in the most convincing way. In doing so they produce as much evidence as possible and assume a defensive posture vis-à-vis real or imagined criticism and distortions. The unconscious editing by authors goes much farther. It stems ultimately from their efforts to effect changes in others and in the world around them by bringing their own perceptions and those of others into some form of alignment. Authors often fail to realize that their works are not simply reports, but efforts to create a new reality. This is particularly true with authors whose writing skills have enabled them to produce work of great persuasive power.

Biographers have great persuasive power because they introduce controversial theories and ideas in the form of a story of one individual's life. This approach invites the reader to surrender to the imagination of the author and remain at the level of a first reading. I doubt that biographies are often reread the way theoretical publications or fiction are. They are more often reenacted in fantasy or reality, in an effort to reproduce the affects their reading generated.

A complete biographical study can be conceptualized as a psychological entity which has boundaries, structure, and content. Invested with the author's creative imagination, a new figure has emerged that has the capacity to affect the reader profoundly; yet, once the study is published, this figure is invulnerable to the later intentions even of its own creator. The biographer may be compared to a parent giving his "child" its physical existence and molding it by conscious and unconscious design. Once he releases it, however, he no longer controls its effect or use; indeed, with the passing of time, the author tends to become increasingly alienated from his own creation.

A good piece of scholarly work is characterized by its capacity to stand on its own and pass the test of time. Biographical studies that pass this test may exercise enormous persuasive power over a period of many generations. Whether accurate or not, they become relatively stable perceptual structures that can be utilized as points of reference in our continual efforts to master the universe and the inner depths of our own psyches.

The stability of these perceptual references is related not only to content but also to form. An author's persuasive power depends as much on the power of his ideas as it does on the form and rhetoric he uses. Biographical studies represent a form of language that is likely to invite a response in the same or comparable form. Biographies generate more biographies. In our times we express affects and define perceptions by referring to the lives of particular people. Biography can be viewed as a language that the contemporary intellectual cannot escape because it reflects the intellectual climate of our times.

I have made several references to the biographer's identification with his subject and more generally to transference phenomena in biographical studies. Such terms and concepts have by and large been borrowed from the clinical theory of psychoanalysis. When applied to the field of scholarly writing and creativity in general, they need clarification.

Reading commonly arouses transference reactions, which occur as the reader makes connections between the content of the text and experiences in his past with which it resonates. This process is close to consciousness and triggers pleasurable affects, even when the reading gives rise to sadness and tears. In this way transference reactions to written material are comparable to experiences in everyday life.

The transference reactions of the biographer to materials he reads are substantially different. The biographer's systematic, long-term effort to place himself in another's world produces not only reverberations with old memories and experiences, but challenges to the investigator's values and sense of self. The defensive maneuvers that result from this intrusion aim to reduce the sense of novelty that the input creates. The biographer's identification with his subject is a powerful barrier against the realization of the novelty involved. By accentuating the similarities between what he knows about his subject and what he knows about himself, the biographer may experience the situation as if it were familiar and overlook important differences. In the case of negative identification, the opposite takes place. Similarities are ignored while differences are defensively accentuated. These transference reactions aim to maintain the stability of the biographer's perceptual world, and to limit or slow down the registration of new perceptions.

Transference reactions facilitate adaptation by reinforcing well-established perceptual schemata whose presence maintains the sense of continuity, familiarity, and predictability. Even painful transference phenomena may have a soothing effect and reinforce the feeling of protection from the unknown. While under the influence of transference, the biographer experiences a distinct sense of knowing his subject—a knowing that he cannot fully substantiate. Such perceptions could be understood as intuitions or identifications based on a deeper, preverbal level of communication.

It is important to keep in mind, however, that identification does not necessarily lead to knowledge or discovery. More often it obstructs it. Nor can the biographer be sure about the validity of these transference intuitions until he has succeeded in conveying his insights to his readers by reproducing comparable emotional responses in them. The biographer's subject is not usually a living person with whom the scholar has come in contact. More accurately, the biographer's subject can be described as a construct that can easily be molded into different forms. If the biography were to be written exclusively under the influence of the biographer's personal psychological needs, the product would have a fictional character that fit the fantasy world of the author. Opposing these needs, however, are the biographer's professional motives and intellectual values that pertain to his urge to know and to discover. This second set of motives demands that he look beyond the familiar schemata and set aside, temporarily at least, his urge to maintain continuity and familiarity. Furthermore, the biographer's professional motives are reinforced by his awareness of his prospective readers, whom he must persuade of the validity of his perceptions.

In order to conceptualize the distinction between transference and nontransference elements in biographical studies, we must distinguish between professional and adaptive motives within the structure of an individual's personality. True scholarly activity is, by and large, in the service of the individual's professional motives. The scholar's primary aim is not personal adaptation but intellectual discovery, and this can be achieved only through strict adherence to his professional ethics and values. The scholar must grant his professional motives a certain level of autonomy from the rest of his personality. Such autonomy protects him from experiencing new ideas and input as an immediate danger to his sense of self and capacity to adapt. Furthermore, it provides him with the opportunity to work through these ideas gradually and systematically, in the absence of a massive intrusion of affects and urges from the rest of his personality.

Inevitably, transference reactions will arise from the new input, but not before the biographer has given himself the opportunity to be persuaded, at first unconsciously and later consciously, by aspects of his subject's communication. Internal harmony is seldom, if ever, experienced by the biographer who attempts to grasp the complexities of an individual's psyche. His struggle is creative when, with the help of his professional value system, he allows new input to register and gives his subject the opportunity to persuade him. The biographer must first reach a certain level of awareness of his subject before he can utilize any self-awareness through the recognition of transference phenomena.

In the collaborative situation I have described, the biographer identifies the psycholoanalyst as his special reader, who becomes the trusted recipient of his still-untested insights. Such transference reactions will enable the biographer to receive much-needed feedback from his collaborator about the nature and origin of his perceptions. Only through interaction with a living person can the biographer test the relative validity of his conceptual construct of his subject and develop a clearer anticipation of the reactions of his prospective readers.

The psychoanalytic collaborator will, of course, be aware that his role in this situation is substantially different from his role in a therapeutic psychoanalysis. His comments and interpretations do not aim to bring into consciousness the overall system of perceptual schemata of the biographer and the fantasies associated with it. Instead, he attempts to help the biographer regulate the input of self-awareness and the affects generated in his scholarly work. In so doing he keeps in mind that the biographer must balance his awareness of his subject with self-awareness in such a way that neither obstructs the view of the other. The biographer's anger at, idealization of, or identification with his subject indicates an excessive input of self-perception into his biographical work, which requires corrective action by reinforcing the awareness of his subject. On the other side, excessive theorizing and psychologizing in an effort to be "objective" and "clinical" could indicate the biographer's reluctance to use his self-perceptions and valuable intuitions. In such a case, the psychoanalytic collaborator would do whatever possible to facilitate the biographer's introspection in order to increase the role of his self-awareness in his biographical work.

It has become fashionable in biographical studies to adopt a multiplicity of possible explanatory propositions and attempt to do justice to them all. Without entering into a debate about the advantages and disadvantages of such an approach, the psychoanalytic collaborator should keep in mind that this may be another way to provide a "dispassionate" account of an individual's life—an account in essence as unpsychological as an exclusive emphasis on "objective" facts.

No biography can possibly succeed in reproducing the past, and it is of little value if it simply reflects the present. A successful biographical study provides the reader with a new sense of reality that involves some degree of integration of past and present, personal and nonpersonal, as well as anticipated relevance in the future. The psychoanalytic collaborator who helps a biographer in arriving at such a product should refrain from any attempt to become a co-author. He should restrict himself to the role of special reader.

Interdisciplinary studies in psychoanalysis are as old as the science of psychoanalysis itself. Freud often turned to the social sciences and the humanities in search of evidence that could validate the universality of his theories. He raised issues and posed questions that aroused powerful reactions from professionals in other disciplines, and some of these questions are still debated today.

Interdisciplinary exchanges between psychoanalysts and scholars in the humanities and the social sciences have often led to an impasse or premature closure. Those who have applied the results of psychoanalysis in these other fields have often been accused of "reducing" scholarly work to relatively few predictable propositions and conclusions. By and large, psychoanalysts have been generous enough in providing other scholars with ideas and questions derived from their clinical theories and experience, but they have done very little to develop an instrument or method with which to test these ideas and assess their validity. The term "applied psychoanalysis," widely used to describe these enterprises, suggests that the interdisciplinary activity moves in one direction only, with psychoanalysis lending its acquired knowledge to other disciplines, while receiving nothing in return.

Some time ago, John Gedo and Ernest Wolf pointed out that "it has been fashionable among psychoanalysts to look upon Freud's discipline as something *sui generis,* created from the void."[3] The myth can probably be traced to Freud's reluctance to acknowledge that his humanistic and philosophical studies (along with clinical data and the physical sciences) helped shape his psychoanalytic theories. The belief in creation from the void may simply represent a romantic perception of the history of psychoanalysis, motivated by the psychoanalyst's need to see this new science as an autonomous and independent entity. Such views inevitably affect not only the analyst's perception of the history of psychoanalysis, but also perceptions of the future position and development of psychoanalysis in the intellectual community and culture at large.

Freud's emphasis on the uniqueness of psychoanalysis is by no means surprising. The autonomy of a discipline can be maintained only by establishing clear boundaries, ones that are, at least to some extent, acceptable to all disciplines operating in a given scientific and scholarly community. Freud drew these boundaries by defining (1) the territory within which psychoanalysis operates and (2) the observational post the psychoanalyst must maintain in exploring this territory. He named his territory "the unconscious" and established the clinical method of psychoanalysis—more specifically, the analyst's stance—as the observational post of the new science.

The physical sciences have not attempted to invade Freud's territory, the unconscious. They have, however, questioned its existence and shown little interest in taking into account the psychoanalytic observational post and the data accumulated from its use. Despite Freud's vigorous efforts to establish psychoanalysis as an autonomous science, the community of scientists has treated it at best with benign neglect and, at times, with contempt.

As opposed to the physical sciences, the social sciences and the humanities not only acknowledge the existence of the unconscious but have entered the field in a somewhat competitive way. Or to phrase it differently, humanists and social scientists tend to perceive psychoanalysis as a guest, and all too often an unwelcome guest, in a territory they have always considered their own. "Know thyself" was not introduced to poetry and philosophy by psychoanalysis. The art of introspection is at least as old as ancient Greek culture, and has been cultivated in modern Western civilization since Montaigne in the sixteenth century. During the last several decades, scholars have directed their attention inward with renewed enthusiasm. They have come to recognize the degree to which their observations are shaped by their own minds. In this contemporary, post-positivistic period of intellectual history, the concept of interpretation and the search for meaning have been advocated as an alternative to the pursuit of knowledge, as a result of which "to doubt" and "to wonder" are more respectable than "to know." To blur is more acceptable than to define. Ambiguity has become a more reliable indicator, and often an acceptable point of arrival. Psychoanalysis has contributed significantly to this intellectual climate, but it is not the only source.

In all scholarly activities there is evidence of an increased sense of awareness of the existence of the internal world and a decreased sense of confidence in the accuracy of man's perceptions of external reality. Our reliance on our own sense organs has been dramatically reduced, and we can no longer afford to use them alone as evidence of knowledge. The intricate nature of the relationship between external and internal that all disciplines have come to recognize seems to indicate that any knowledge of the external world includes some elements of self-knowledge, and that any self-knowledge must derive from perceptions of external reality.

As the boundary between internal and external has blurred, so have the territorial boundaries of psychoanalysis. Psychoanalysis can no longer maintain an illusionary monopoly on the exploration of the unconscious, which has become a field of endeavor for many disciplines.

It can be argued that the autonomy of psychoanalysis as a science and as an intellectual discipline can still be defended as long as its observational post, the psychoanalytic method, is kept intact. The method and pride of the psychoanalyst that Heinz Kohut identified years ago is the outcome of such convictions.[4] Excessive reliance on the method, however, is a defensive position that may result in rigidity and isolation, and interfere with the growth and development of psychoanalysis. If a method is confused with procedures and rituals, its essence will be compromised.

I believe the time has come to redefine both the territorial boundaries of psychoanalysis and its observational post, the psychoanalytic method. This is a critical period in the development of psychoanalysis, one that demands the abandonment of old myths and the acknowledgment of certain realities, Psychoanalysis was not created from the void, nor can it survive in isolation. No science can establish territorial boundaries and observational posts without negotiations with other sciences and scholarly disciplines. Psychoanalysis cannot "export" knowledge without accepting input from other intellectual disciplines in return. To survive in the intellectual community, the professional psychoanalyst must become an active participant, prepared to influence and be influenced, to give and take.

My collaborative work with biographers and historians has convinced me that interdisciplinary research cannot be effectively carried out without the proper methodology. Even more important, it must take into account the humanity of the thinker and the uniqueness of his thinking. Psychoanalysts may have very little difficulty in accepting the notion that ideas are not created from the void but are deeply rooted in the thinker's personality. It seems, however, that the reverse is also true. Ideas have a powerful influence on personality and, to a significant extent, determine its development.

In its essence, the clinical psychoanalytic method is a form of dialogue. Some practitioners may acknowledge this more readily than other, but by and large analysts no longer see themselves as a blank screen. The analyst's experience of the dialogue in the clinical situation must be utilized in his dialogue with professionals in other disciplines. Of course the psychoanalytic method cannot be simply transplanted from the clinical situation to the interdisciplinary field. Modifications are needed to meet the demands of the new situation. They must be carefully thought through. In this volume I have described in some detail the approach I have utilized. Although I am sure there are other possible approaches, it seems to me that for the psychoanalyst the essence of such a collaboration lies in his capacity to acknowledge, tolerate, and—it is hoped—utilize the input these dialogues produce to the science of psychoanalysis.

Psychoanalysis may not be universally accepted among social scientists and humanists. Sometimes their objections are loud and their hostility evident. It seems to me, however, that much of this is rhetorical and should not be taken at face value. In my dealings with professionals in these disciplines, I detect a strong desire for a meaningful exchange with psychoanalysts, when it is offered under circumstances that are not demeaning. The situation is very different as far as the physical and applied sciences are concerned. Despite more than eighty years of intensive effort, we have not yet proved our case to them. From the time of its discovery, psychoanalysis has strongly claimed and defended its scientific status. The physical sciences, however, remain oblivious to our claim and disinterested in our findings.

Psychoanalysis has often been described as the bridge between the sciences and the humanities. By placing his discipline between the two ends of the intellectual spectrum, the psychoanalyst has attempted to maintain a precarious and, to an extent, unattainable balance. Caught between the competition and antagonism of the humanistic community and the "benign neglect" of the scientific one, the psychoanalyst imagines having two homes when in actuality he has none.

Psychoanalysts cannot establish a home for their science by submitting credentials to epistemology. It is not sufficient to "prove" our case through a series of intellectual syllogisms. We must demonstrate our usefulness, so that other scholars and scientists will feel motivated to enter into a dialogue with us. In the clinical situation we never demand from our patients recognition for what we have done for them. After a successful analysis, however, the patient "knows" the analyst's contribution and is grateful for it. Interdisciplinary exchanges should produce a similar sense of satisfaction and discovery on both sides. It is this sense of discovery that constitutes the ground of the psychoanalytic "home" in both the clinical and interdisciplinary fields. In order to achieve this, the psychoanalyst must address the vital issues of the intellectual community and demonstrate the usefulness of his discipline on the frontiers of scholarly and scientific activities.

## NOTES

[1]George Moraitis, "A Psychoanalyst's Journey into a Historian's World: An Experiment in Collaboration," *The Annual of Psychoanalysis* 7 (1979): 287–320. Reprinted here as Chap. 3.

[2]See, for example, Marc Pachter, ed., *Telling Lives* (Washington, D.C.: National Portrait Gallery/New Republic Books, 1979), which contains autobiographical reflections by a number of prominent biographers.

[3]John E. Gedo and Ernest S. Wolf, "From the History of Introspective Psychology: The Humanist Strain," in *Freud: The Fusion of Science and Humanism,* ed. John E. Gedo and George H. Pollock (New York: International Universities Press, 1975), p. 12.

[4]Heinz Kohut, "The Future of Psychoanalysis," *The Annual of Psychoanalysis* 3 (1975): 325–340.

# 17

# *Subjectivity and Biography*

## Carl Pletsch

---

I HAVE BEEN INVOLVED with this project of collaboration between biographers and psychoanalysts ever since 1976, when George Moraitis and I first began to work together. I found the collaboration very useful myself, so I readily introduced my friend Mark Schwehn to Moraitis and recommended the collaborative method to Richard Wortman, too, although he and Moraitis were already acquainted. That was in Chicago, where George Moraitis and I also presented our findings at the Institute for Psychoanalysis. Then we led a workshop on psychoanalysis and biography at a seminar of psychoanalysts organized by Joseph Lichtenberg in Washington, D.C. Once in North Carolina, I discovered that my colleague Samuel Baron was thinking autobiographically about his biography of G. V. Plekhanov, so I recommended the collaborative method to him, too. Baron and I procured a grant from the National Endowment for the Humanities and organized the conference whose papers compose the present volume. Reviewing this history and my memories of it, a somewhat different perspective comes to my mind than the one George Moraitis presents in his conclusion to this book.

I am not a psychoanalyst and, as Moraitis has noted, I do not seem to feel the need of further collaboration. I have different interests in the history and the prospects of our collaboration than he does. Of course, my first interest is in my own further work on Friedrich Nietzsche and other subjects. But with respect to the collaboration, I am primarily interested in its practical and theoretical utility to other historians and biographers. Upon reading this volume, they may ask themselves whether they would play the role that I seem to have played in that first collaboration. And how they answer that question will largely determine whether they will seek to enrich their scholarly work with the aid of such a method as we describe here.

It will not have escaped the reader's attention that the reports of our collaboration involve a certain asymmetry: I reveal a good deal about myself and the role of my personality in my work; Moraitis comments on this, points out how he was able to help me increase my awareness of the role of my personality in my work, but does not reveal much about himself or the personal side of his reaction to our collaboration. One of the early readers of our two papers told me confidentially that he would find this situation quite embarrassing and praised what he took to be my courage in permitting these materials to be made public. When we presented our reports on the collaboration in psychoanalytic forums, I observed a similar reaction: the psychoanalysts seemed unable to think about our work except as a species of therapy, and they praised my courageous willingness to permit them to question me about it. But they directed all their theoretical questions to Moraitis. Their questions to me were all aimed at eliciting more information about my subjective responses. They had categorized Moraitis as the expert and me as the subject of the investigation, not to say the patient. These reactions made me sensitive to a possibility of embarrassment that I did not feel while Moraitis and I were actually engaged in our collaboration. The question is: How significant is this sensitivity?

Future collaborations will probably not yield publications of this sort—even the others described in this volume are somewhat less extensive. Scholars who do take advantage of this method of enriching their scholarship may publish the results, and not the revelations of self that we present here. So it would be inappropriate to resist this opportunity simply for fear of public embarrassment. However, there are other anxieties beneath the surface of this fear: anxiety about psychological regression that might occur in the course of such a collaboration (the regression that is an essential part of psychoanalytic therapy) and anxiety about becoming intellectually dependent on another person. These anxieties seem to inhere in the same asymmetry, and both present risks that a scholar would not want to run. No scholar wants to have a major project, on which his or her future professional identity may depend, placed in the hands of another person or interrupted by such a disturbance as psychological regression.

I have had to consider these anxieties myself, but, oddly enough, only after the experiment itself had been completed to the satisfaction and benefit of both Moraitis and myself. This, then, is the subject of my reflection: Why does the fear of embarrassment, dependency, and regression arise at all, and, in my case, even after the completion of a rewarding collaboration? Part of the answer arises from my own particular experience. My lack of anxiety during the experiment was due to the sheer excitement of discovering new dimensions of my involvement in my research and writing about Nietzsche. And much of the anxiety I have felt since completing the collaboration arises from the prospect of publication. But reflection leads me to think there is more to it than that. The reactions of other people suggest that we all have deep reservations about subjectivity. No matter how loudly we praise introspection and the cultivation of self-awareness, subjectivity remains a frightening thing.

There is a good psychological and perhaps even evolutionary reason for this. The unconscious has obvious adaptive functions in concealing certain feelings from view most of the time. Our capacity to act upon the external world seems to depend on the integrity of the boundary between our unconscious and conscious perceptions of reality. Yet we have also learned that it can be very helpful to relax this boundary periodically, to become aware of particular dimensions of our unconscious feelings, precisely in order to enhance our capacities in the external world. We know that controlled introspection can be an invaluable aid in dealing with realistic challenges. That is what our collaborative method intends: to enhance a biographer's capacity to deal with the emotional impact of his research materials. If we know this and still fear subjectivity, it must be for cultural reasons that we are only subliminally aware of.

In our culture subjectivity is associated with a whole range of negatively valorized characteristics. People who cultivate subjectivity are thought to be (relatively) self-centered, reclusive, inactive, and unproductive. Immediately, on writing this, I hear myself and my prospective readers recoil with two objections: first, "not always," and second, "but it's true!" Putting such objections aside for the moment, however, consider that women are supposed to be more in touch with their feelings than men are; a cultural corollary of this is that subjectivity has feminine connotations. Then, as Moraitis points out in his concluding essay, people who lack power to change their environment resort more frequently to introspection than the powerful, so that the cultivation of subjectivity also connotes weakness. Finally, it is intellectuals rather than "men of action" who introspect and, among intellectuals, the less scientific. Their patterns of thought tend to be circular rather than linear and goal-oriented: compare the hermeneutic circle with the image of scientists pushing back frontiers as metaphors of gaining knowledge. Even when we remember that our culture also provides for a limited positive valorization of introspection and the cultivation of subjectivity, this is an impressive list of negative connotations: emotional, feminine, weak, unscientific, circular, self-centered, reclusive, inactive, unproductive. And there are more: we think people who cultivate subjectivity are likely to be lonely, dependent, morose, morbid, and so on.

I suspect we have two difficulties in dealing with these many negative connotations of subjectivity. First, we hesitate to believe that we really associate all of these negative values with it. Aren't we more rational than that? Don't we think that a moderate amount of subjectivity is a good thing, a kind of leaven to the loaf of objective rationality? But upon introspection (!), when we admit that we do make a number of semiconscious associations of this sort, we may nonetheless discover that these reactions seem natural to us, rather than cultural. These are the associations that warn us against cultivating subjectivity. But there are other cultures that put a much higher value on introspection and self-awareness than we do. In the last century, and to some degree still, our civilization has maintained a condescending attitude (and an imperialistic practice) vis-à-vis the Asian cultures in which these qualities are highly valued. Western military and technological superiority seemed to demonstrate the superiority of Western values and knowledge. Now that we have come to doubt the superiority of those scientific and materialistic values, we have turned back to those other cultures in search of techniques for facilitating introspection, like Yoga. I think there can be no doubt that we do fear subjectivity and that our fear of subjectivity is an artifact of our culture.

The role we allow subjectivity in scholarship is naturally affected by these associations. Scholarship and professional activities are public functions in which all the values opposed to subjectivity have traditionally been cultivated. Most scholars have been men, and the very fact that these men have been engaged in intellectual rather than practical activities seems to have reinforced their loyalty to masculine values in scholarship. Scholars have needed to demonstrate their authority over their materials. They are expected to make strong, invulnerable arguments, as linear and scientific as possible. Meditation upon subjects that one does not "control" has been permitted only a very small number of writers, very seldom scholars. Scholars are supposed, furthermore, to add incrementally to the already accumulated body of objective knowledge. All of these suppositions governing scholarship—and not just the feeble injunction to remain emotionally neutral—are components of objectivity in scholarship. The ideal of objectivity is thus not merely an aspect of the ideology of positivism, something that should have waned as positivism has been progressively debunked in the twentieth century. Objectivity implies virility, power, control, action, success, optimism, progress, and so on. And the cultivation of subjectivity threatens to make a scholar seem less of a scholar on all these fronts.

I know this not only from my reflection on my own experience, but from the reactions of the many biographers who declined my invitation to participate in the collaboration and the conference. Not a few of these biographers were women, and several of them explained that it was important for a woman and especially for a feminist biographer not to appear too introspective and subjective. Precisely because, as women, they were already suspect of being too subjective, their appearance in such a self-revelatory posture as this might discredit them and their biographies. Of course it would be difficult to prove that men are any less capable of subjectivity than women are. But the curious situation of women, who are purportedly more subjective, having to avoid publicly cultivating subjectivity illustrates the inferior position that subjectivity has been assigned in our culture.

The many associations attached to the opposition of objective and subjective constitute a cultural inhibition to recapturing subjectivity for theory and knowledge. The connotations of subjectivity may provoke fears of embarrassment, dependency, and regression even when those fears are not appropriate. On the contrary, however, many of the biographers who have contributed to this volume testify to the exhilaration and sense of discovery that accompany drawing aside this veil of anxiety. But the real interest of the collaborative method—and the enterprise of recapturing subjectivity generally—lies in enlarging the scope of knowledge that we have of human lives. It must give rise to more than personal satisfaction; it must enrich the intellectual products. It will not be enough to discover privately the sources of one's subjective involvement in the research and writing of a biography and then to present the results to the public in the guise of the same old objectivity. If subjectivity is truly to be recaptured for public knowledge, it must be integrated into the more acceptable dimensions of our knowledge of lives. The oppositions between the purportedly weak, feminine, covert knowledge of subjectivity and the potent, masculine, and linear knowledge of objectivity must be called into question. And when these oppositions are called into question, subjectivity may reveal itself to be compatible with the knowledge we have accumulated under the banner of objectivity. The two may even come to seem complementary. Thus, the introduction of the biographer's subjectivity into biography could give rise to a new form of biography.

Practically speaking, this means that the collaborative method described here will be useful primarily to biographers deeply engaged in their projects, with intensive experience with their sources and well-developed theses to defend. Ultimately it may call also for a biographer who is willing to appear as an actor in the biography he or she is writing. Any other practice would represent a refusal of the opportunity to recapture subjectivity, an admission of inappropriate anxieties, and a reassertion of the cultural boundaries between objectivity and subjectivity. Nor is this opportunity a negligible one. It is an opportunity for biographers to contribute to the general reshaping of knowledge in a way specific to the genre of biography. Biography has always been a locus of subjectivity, although this attitude has been assigned to the readers rather than the authors of biographies. Biographers have posed as the objective arbiters of the facts of the lives in question, as writers who could stand out of the way and let the psychological forces of identification, admiration, anger, and so on move between the readers and the subjects of their biographies. This has been so because, for cultural reasons, biographers have felt obliged to subscribe to the ideal of objectivity. But biography is the perfect enterprise in which to transcend that ideal and show the value of assimilating subjectivity in a larger conception of knowledge.

# Index